ZOLLIKON SEMINARS

Protocols— Conversations—Letters

Martin Heidegger

Edited by Medard Boss

Translated from the German
and with notes and afterwords
by Franz Mayr and Richard Askay

Northwestern University Press
Evanston, Illinois

Northwestern University Press
Evanston, Illinois 60208-4210

Originally published in German as *Zollikoner Seminare, Protokolle—Gespräche—Briefe Herausgegeben von Medard Boss* (Frankfurt am Main: Vittorio Klostermann GmbH, 1987). Copyright © 1987 by Vittorio Klostermann.

Printed in the United States of America

10   9   8   7   6   5   4   3   2   1

ISBN 0-8101-1832-7 (cloth)
ISBN 0-8101-1833-5 (paper)

Library of Congress Cataloging-in-Publication Data

Heidegger, Martin, 1889–1976.
  [Zollikoner Seminare. English]
  Zollikon seminars : protocols, conversations, letters / Martin Heidegger ; edited by Medard Boss.
     p. cm. — (SPEP studies in historical philosophy)
  Includes bibliographical references and index.
     ISBN 0-8101-1832-7 (alk. paper) — ISBN 0-8101-1833-5 (pbk. : alk. paper)
     1. Ontology.   2. Time.   3. Psychiatry—Philosophy.   4. Heidegger, Martin, 1889–1976—Correspondence.   5. Philosophers—Germany—Correspondence. 6. Boss, Medard, 1903–1990—Correspondence.   7. Psychiatrists—Switzerland— Correspondence.   I. Boss, Medard, 1903–1990   II. Title.   III. Series.
  B3279.H48 Z6513 2001
  193—dc21   2001001060

Contents

Translators' Acknowledgments

First, we wish to express our deepest appreciation to Dr. Medard Boss and Frau Professor Boss for their gracious and conscientious efforts in helping us work through some of our most difficult translation problems. Dr. Boss had hoped to see this project through to fruition, but, regrettably, he died during the Christmas holidays in 1990.

Next, we wish to gratefully acknowledge the University of Portland for providing financial support for our project. Thanks must also go to Ms. Brenda Tharp and Ms. Sharon Rossmiller, who did most of our word processing.

Special thanks go to Professors W. Richardson and W. Kockelmans, who made significant suggestions during the early drafts of our trans-
tion. We are indebted to Professors C. Schrag, M. Zimmermann, and
heehan, who supported us in critical moments of our translation, and
cially to Dr. H. Heidegger for his support of our translation. We also
o thank Professor H. Dreyfus, the director of the National Endow-
or the Humanities seminar (1984) on Heidegger and Foucault at
versity of California, Berkeley, which was attended by one of the
rs, Dr. R. Askay. We are especially grateful to the former director
estern University Press, Mr. N. Weir-Williams, for his extensive
ur behalf. Furthermore, we especially appreciate the support
ies.

nd most important, we wish to acknowledge a special debt
ayr, M.A., who edited and reworked the final draft of the
tion.

Preface to the American Translation of Martin Heidegger's *Zollikon Seminars*

This translation was initiated by Dr. Franz Mayr and Dr. Richard Askay, both of whom are philosophy professors at the University of Portland. In September 1989 I was invited to the first Applied Heidegger Conference at Berkeley by its organizers, Dr. Hubert Dreyfus of the University of California, Berkeley, and Dr. Michael Zimmerman of Tulane University. They asked me to deliver the keynote address at this conference concerning my cooperation and work with Martin Heidegger. My discussion of Heidegger's new and alternative way of thinking about the human being and his world was received with great enthusiasm. This also happened in response to my lecture on the new "phenomenological" understanding of human dreaming that was delivered at the University of Portland, immediately after the Heidegger conference at Berkeley.

I simply did not anticipate that American philosophers like those mentioned above would master the profound insight of *Da-sein-analytical* or phenomenological thinking.

Some thirty years earlier, in the summer of 1963, during my first encounter with my American colleagues as a visiting faculty member at Harvard University, I delivered lectures on Heidegger's alternative way of thinking. Many more obstacles had to be surmounted at that time.

It soon became clear to me that the participants at the Applied Heidegger Conference at Berkeley continue to be great exceptions among American philosophers. Most of my American colleagues in philosophy and psychology encountered greater obstacles during all other discussions of *Da-seinanalysis* themes than I had to overcome in discussions with European, Indian, and South American colleagues.

The Americans experienced problems primarily in accomplishing the "leap of thought"—which is indispensable, though not always successful—in changing from traditional, causal-genetic, explanatory, and calculative modes of thinking to the entirely different *Da-sein-analytical* approach of Heidegger's phenomenological thinking.

Martin Heidegger and Medard Boss in the Zollikon Seminar Room, 1965

In this new and alternative view, human existence in its unique way, like everything else in our world, no longer appears as something present as an object within a pregiven world space. Rather, human existence can be viewed as *being*, which cannot be objectified and which consists of an openness to the world and of the capacity to perceive what it encounters in that world. Through this openness, human existence itself, as well as any other given facts of our world, can come to their presence and unfolding. The proper task of human *Da-sein* is the event of letting-be what emerges into the openness of being. Human existence is necessary for this event, which constitutes its proper and most profound meaning. Thus, it also becomes clear that this meditative, alternative, and new way of thinking may also disclose meaning and purpose to the art of healing.

Many people who are initially touched by this new and different way of thinking are stricken with great panic. They fear that if they let themselves really be touched by this thinking they will have to abandon the time-honored definition of the human being as an Ego, as a center of personality, and as a separate bodily organism. They believe they will completely lose themselves thereby. As a result, many of them quickly take refuge in the seemingly secure Freudian view of a "psychic apparatus." Yet in doing so they forget that it was Freud himself who called his notion of a "psychic apparatus" a mere "fiction" which only pretends to give human thinking a solid foundation.

Heidegger would not have devoted as much time and energy to instructing medical doctors as he did in the *Zollikon Seminars* had he not thought his new and alternative thinking—meditative thinking—was of essential benefit to all medical therapies. Indeed, if the therapists let themselves be imbued in body and soul with this "new and alternative" way of thinking, they themselves would experience its benefits, primarily in the form of self-transformation. From then on, they would understand themselves as individuals who are called upon to serve all beings including patients, who in their openness to the world encounter the therapist as a place for self-disclosure.

When they are "together with" the therapist in *Da-seinanalysis* situations, the patients are allowed to assume and to perform all their pregiven possibilities of behavior in a reflective and responsible way. This is the essential meaning and the inherent goal of all medical therapies, whether they are physical or psychotherapeutic in nature.

The *Zollikon Seminars* presented here are unique. Nowhere else has this philosopher so directly addressed students who had a purely scientific educational background. This required the teacher to proceed with special care and caution.

Medard Boss
Spring 1990

At this point in the preface, in December 1990, illness took the pen from Medard Boss's hand. Therefore, it may be meaningful to quote a few sentences from the preface to the second German edition for the American reader (Frankfurt am Main, 1994):

Today the reader can take this newly reprinted volume in his hand, although both the author and the editor have gone through the door of eternity—Martin Heidegger in 1976 and Medard Boss in 1990.

Unlike the doctor, Medard Boss, the reader does not have to courageously question the foundation of his science and to ask the philosopher for advice regarding a more sustainable platform for his medical thought and practice.

This publication also addresses a broader circle of readers than just those who are professionally interested in philosophy. The reader gets acquainted with the background of developments which began with Medard Boss's first letter to Martin Heidegger in 1947—from the packet of chocolate to the subtle struggle for an adequate understanding of Being and of the nature of *Da-seinanalysis*. Woven into this fabric of manifold questions and answers—talk and countertalk—is the call for carefulness regarding the originary and proper meaning of phenomena.

The *Zollikon Seminars* were borne by friendship and were written by two hands, like a spiritual child who found its own life and went abroad by being translated into foreign languages.

Martin Heidegger's name appears prominently on the cover. But whenever one associates Medard Boss with that Chinese customs office and its customs collector one is reminded of the thirteenth stanza of the "Legend" ["Legend of the Origin of the Book *Tao-te-Ching* by Lao Tzu on His Way to Emigration"] by Bertolt Brecht, which schoolchildren in Medard Boss's hometown of Zurich can still read in their reading book:

> But let us praise not only the sage
> Whose name shines on the book,
> For first of all one has to tear the wisdom from the sage.
> That is why the customs collector should also be thanked.
> He was the one who asked it of him.

Only a few weeks ago the writer became aware of how much Martin Heidegger loved this poem (see Heinrich Wiegand Petzet, *Encounters and Dialogues with Martin Heidegger, 1929–1976,* trans. P. Emad and K. Maly, with an introduction by P. Emad [Chicago: University of Chicago Press, 1993], p. 217, as well as Hannah Arendt and Martin Heidegger, *Briefe* [Frankfurt am Main, 1998], p. 345).

It was not granted to Medard Boss to participate in the progress of this translation and to review the finished text. Fortunately, Professor William J. Richardson (Boston College) undertook this task. To him and to both translators, I express my cordial gratitude.

In memory of Medard Boss and Martin Heidegger, this book is sent on its way in a further foreign language.

Marianne Boss-Linsmayer
Zollikon, Christmas 1998

ZOLLIKON SEMINARS

Preface to the First German Edition
of Martin Heidegger's *Zollikon Seminars*

This book owes its origin to the wonder that Martin Heidegger, who p. vii received hundreds of letters from all over the world every year and answered only a few of them, found the first lines I addressed to him worthy of an extremely gracious response. That was shortly after the end of the war in 1947. This event had a history of many years.

Like all Swiss men who were not psychologically or physically impaired, I had to do active military duty throughout the whole war. During these years, I was repeatedly torn away from my civilian work as a university *Dozent* and psychotherapist for months at a time and transferred to a Swiss Army mountain troop as the battalion doctor. As prescribed by Swiss Army military ordinance, no fewer than three assistant doctors were assigned to me. The troops I had to care for were composed of strong mountain countryfolk who were accustomed to doing work. As a result I was nearly unemployed throughout the whole long duration of my military service. For the first time in my life, I was occasionally gripped by boredom. In the midst of it, what we call "time" became problematic for me. I began to think specifically about this "thing." I sought help in all the pertinent literature available to me. By chance, I came across a newspaper item about Heidegger's book *Being and Time*. p. viii I plunged into it, but I discovered that I understood almost none of its content. The book opened up question after question which I had never encountered before in my entire scientifically oriented education. For the most part, these questions were answered in reference to new questions. Disappointed, I laid the book aside only half-read, but strangely it gave me no rest. I would pick it up again and again and begin studying it anew. This first "conversation" with Heidegger outlasted the war. Next it extended to research on the [personal historical background] of the author. At first, the information I got was devastating in nature. Serious philosophers I talked with almost always dissuaded me from any further occupation with Heidegger and his work. The recurring argument in these warnings was the characterization of Heidegger as a typical Nazi.

However, this vituperation did not at all fit with what I found in reading *Being and Time*. At first I had more of a hunch than a well-thought-out idea that this work articulated fundamentally new, unheard of insights into the human being's way of existing in his world. Being fully packed with psychiatric knowledge, my mind of course told me that a human being's social and political behavior need not impair the creativity of his genius. Nonetheless, I did not have the heart to have anything to do with a man who could be proved to have committed specific acts of baseness against other human beings. Therefore, immediately after the end of the war, within the framework of the possibilities available to me at the time, I began to make inquiries about Heidegger through the French occupation authorities and through the highest administrative officials of the University of Freiburg i. Br. [in Breisgau]. Both inquiries finally gave me the certainty that for a short time Heidegger had indeed made some initial "worldly innocent" misjudgments and mistakes.

p. ix In all earnestness, he had initially believed that Hitler and the masses behind him would be able to build a wall against political Communism's encroaching waves of spiritual darkness. In spite of that, nothing came to light regarding any concrete, voluntary act of baseness toward Heidegger's fellow human beings. When I tried to be absolutely honest with myself, I had to admit that had I been forced to live in environmental conditions such as Heidegger had at the time, I could not swear to avoid falling victim to similar errors. In spite of the fact that I had definite anti-Hitler convictions at that time because of my Swiss perspective, this could have been the case. Furthermore, I never had a moment's doubt about being prepared to stand my ground to the very end as a soldier against the German invaders.

On the other hand, in all these inquiries Heidegger very clearly seemed to be the most slandered man I had ever encountered. He had become entangled in a network of lies by his colleagues. Most of the people, who were unable to do serious harm to the substance of Heidegger's thinking, tried to get at Heidegger the man with personal attacks. The only remaining puzzle was why Heidegger did not defend himself against these slanders publicly. The astonishing fact of his defenselessness gave me the incentive to stand up for him to the best of my ability.

In any case, from 1947 on, there was no longer any compelling reason which could have kept me from trying to approach Heidegger for the first time on a personal basis. As a doctor, I wrote a letter to the philosopher and asked for help in [reflective] thinking. I was very surprised when an answer arrived by return mail. In it Martin Heidegger agreed in a friendly way to give me any help he could. At first, there was an exchange of letters, which grew to a collection of 256 letters by the time of the thinker's death. In addition, there were over fifty greeting cards from his trips abroad.

p. x

As soon as the border between our countries was somewhat passable, we began to make regular personal visits and return visits to each other's homes. During our first meeting at Martin Heidegger's mountain hut in Todtnauberg in the summer of 1949, a mutual human sympathy developed between us. It gradually grew into a cordial friendship. Only much later did I discover the most important motive for Heidegger's prompt answer to my first letter. From the very beginning, as he himself once admitted, Heidegger had set great hope on an association with a doctor and had a seemingly extensive understanding of his thought. He saw the possibility that his philosophical insights would not be confined merely to the philosopher's quarters but also might benefit many more people, especially people in need of help.

From the time that the seminars were incorporated into Heidegger's private visits to my home, certainly no one thought to take verbatim protocols or to print up protocols afterward. To begin with, I did not think it proper to be the only person to benefit from frequent meetings with the great thinker. Therefore, each year, beginning in 1959, I invited from fifty to seventy colleagues and psychiatry students to seminars at my home on the occasion of Heidegger's usual two-week visits. His visits to my home in Zollikon took place two to three times each semester. Only occasionally did my stays abroad make longer intervals unavoidable.

Heidegger sacrificed three hours, two evenings a week, to be with the guests. He spent the whole day beforehand preparing carefully for these seminars. In spite of his contempt for the psychological and psychopathological theories which filled our heads, Heidegger deserves great credit for taking on the almost Sisyphean task of giving my friends, colleagues, and students a sound philosophical foundation for their medical practice. He continued this task for a full decade within the framework of the Zollikon Seminars, which in the meantime had gained widespread fame. His untiring, unwavering patience and forbearance in carrying out and completing this undertaking to the limits of his physical abilities provide unshakable proof of the greatness of Heidegger's concern for his fellow human beings. By displaying this attitude toward our Zollikon circle, he proved that he could not only talk and write about the highest level of human fellowship, but that he was also prepared to live it in an exemplary way. He exemplified selfless, loving *solicitude,* which *leaps ahead* of the other [human being], returning to him his own freedom.

p. xi

The series of seminars began on September 8, 1959, with Heidegger's lecture in the large auditorium of the University of Zurich psychiatric clinic known as the "Burghölzli." The choice of this location proved rather inauspicious. The recently renovated auditorium had such a hypermodern, technological appearance that its atmosphere was simply not conducive to Heidegger's thinking. Therefore, the impending second seminar was moved to my house in Zollikon. All subsequent seminars continued there for the entire next decade.

From 1970, my conscience as a doctor no longer allowed me to expect that Heidegger could continue to endure the great strain of the Zollikon Seminars. By then Martin Heidegger's physical powers were quickly declining because of his age. From then on, I asked for his intellectual help only by mail or during my visits to his home in Freiburg.

p. xii   It was a full four years after the seminars began that I started to see the light and to become aware that it was possible to gain insights directly from Heidegger's words in the seminars, which were impossible to hear delivered elsewhere. The seminar protocols recorded by the students were unsuccessful, so I took over the recording. Beginning with the next seminar, I recorded Heidegger's every word. I dictated the short protocol into a tape recorder immediately after the seminar. Then my secretary transcribed it into typewritten form. Next the protocol drafts were immediately sent to Martin Heidegger in Freiburg. He corrected them very carefully, made some minor additions here and there, and occasionally added major additions in his German handwriting. He returned the corrected and supplemented protocols to me. Finally, these fully authorized protocols, corrected by Heidegger himself, were mimeographed in typewritten form so that every seminar participant had a record of them and had a chance to prepare for the next seminar.

Some of the seminars were recorded in a way that must make it obvious to the reader, from the written record, just how exceedingly difficult the seminars were at the beginning. This is clearly evidenced by the fact that the discussions and responses were separated by long silences and pauses and by the fact that these scientifically educated doctors had never encountered most of Heidegger's questions as questions. Many participants seemed to be shocked, even outraged, that such questions would be permitted in the first place. At the start of the seminars in the late 1950s, even I was able to assimilate Heidegger's thinking only as a beginner would. I could provide very little help in overcoming the pauses in the conversations. Quite often the situations in the seminars grew reminiscent of some imaginary scene: It was as if a man from Mars were visiting a group of earth-dwellers in an attempt to communicate with them.

p. xiii   Today, more than twenty years after the first Zollikon Seminars, this analogy seems grossly exaggerated. Certainly, some of Heidegger's characteristic neologisms, such as *Being-in-the-world* or *Care,* have become more familiar. One or the other of these terms has found its way into everyday, readable illustrated magazines. Of course, it remains to be seen whether this is the product of a genuine familiarity—in the sense of a deep understanding of its meaning—or whether it is a rather superficial habituation of the ear. In any case, the same question the seminar participants in those days occasionally dared to ask Heidegger directly can frequently still be heard today. The proverbial question used to be why Heidegger did not try to talk about his subject matter in plain understandable German. The thinker's answer was regularly the same: After all, we can only speak as we think and think as we speak. If the essential ground of a subject matter emerges from thinking anew and from seeing different, significant features—even if the subject matter is the human being's being itself— then this demands an appropriate, new discourse. For instance, if we were to define and to speak about the human being as a subject or as an "I," then what remains totally concealed is the understanding of the essential ground of the human being's being, which endures in a domain of receptive openness to the world.

Considering the enormous difficulties in communication then, the strangest thing about the Zollikon Seminars was that neither Heidegger nor the seminar participants grew tired of them. From the beginning and over the years, the teacher and students worked persistently toward achieving a common ground.

Heidegger and I had many hours to ourselves and plenty of time for conversation on the days between seminars. It finally occurred to me to take down Heidegger's remarks in shorthand on these occasions as well. Understandably, I was able to record only a fraction of what was said during the discussions. This collection of shorthand notes forms part 2 of this book. p. xiv

In a few cases the handwritten texts which Heidegger jotted down while preparing for the seminars and for the conversations are included here instead of protocols and shorthand notes. These texts are identified in the table of contents and in the text itself. In quoting philosophical and literary texts, Heidegger usually referred to editions that were easily available at the time with a view toward the compositions of the seminar participants. With a few exceptions, these respective editions were *not* recorded in the protocols. In view of this circumstance, and in consideration of the fact that the *Zollikon Seminars* are addressed to a wide circle of readers and not just to an exclusive or to a "specific" philosophically oriented [audience], the philosophical and literary texts are [now] quoted in reference to editions easily available today. This corresponds to Martin Heidegger's method at the time. When Martin Heidegger rendered texts from the writings of Aristotle, he always provided his own translations. Reference to particular translations of Aristotle was therefore unnecessary.

Part 3 of this book includes excerpts from 256 letters which Martin Heidegger had written to me since 1947. Almost half of them can be read in their entirety or in part.

Most of the abbreviations in the letters have been spelled out, and dates have been written in complete form. Punctuation has been adjusted to current practice. A few apparent mistakes in spelling have been corrected, but unique Heideggerian spelling has been retained. Explanatory remarks by the editor, not placed in the footnotes, have been put in brackets.

Numerous proper names were not printed in this book whenever such anonymity did not detract from the content of the particular passage. Nevertheless, some proper names could not be eliminated without making the whole context incomprehensible. In making each of these decisions, I obtained Martin Heidegger's approval during his lifetime.

Of course, this publication does not fully fathom the reach of Heidegger's spiritual radiance. This thinker's new insights into what is—and how it is—have already started to encompass the world. In any case, there is surely no place on earth that remains entirely unaffected by them. Of course, for the most part these insights are kept alive by only a few people. Basically, they are much too simple to be painlessly understood by masses of people so accustomed to the complicated formulas of the technical age. The philosopher himself often spoke about there being a particular blindness to his insights and about how those [people] who were not struck by them could not be helped.

We also cannot disregard the fact that Heidegger's fundamental thinking further dethrones the human being and causes many people to close their minds in desperation. Sigmund Freud had already called his discovery a second Copernican revolution. It was not enough that Copernicus had displaced our earth from the center of the universe, but Freud had been able to show that autocratic human consciousness is driven back and forth by "Id-forces," as he called them, the origin and nature of which are unknown. Heidegger went even further and recognized that even the human subject could be of little value as a measure and as the starting point for [the knowledge] of all things. Human consciousness is "merely" something which *is*. It is a being among thousands of other beings. In its being-ness as such, it depends on and is sustained by the disclosive appropriating Event [*Ereignis*] of being, unconcealment. Nonetheless, the human being has the great honor and distinction of being able to exist as this openness and "clearing" [*Lichtung*], which, as such, must serve as the unconditional place for the appearance and emergence of everything that is.

Therefore, it can be hoped that Heidegger's fundamental insights—even in any diluted form—may contribute to the humanization of our world in the most positive sense of the word. In no way does this mean a further "subjectivization" of the human mind as the absolute maker of all [*Alles-Macher*]. Rather, it means yielding oneself [*Sich-fügen*] to a love that is granted to the human being's being in all that discloses itself in its being and in all that addresses the human being from the openness of his world.

The editor is deeply grateful to Dr. Hermann Heidegger, whose father granted him the imprimatur for printing all posthumous works. He has taken extraordinary care with this present book as well. I am no less indebted to Professor F. W. von Herrmann, Dr. Hermann Heidegger's expert collaborator. The editor is especially indebted to him for the preparation of the very detailed table of contents. He was also the one who gave me, Dr. Heidegger, and the publisher, Mr. Michael Klostermann, the idea of publishing the *Zollikon Seminars* ahead of schedule, although this volume had been planned to come out at a much later time as part of the *Collected Works*. It is highly improbable that the present editor will be alive in the next decade. At the same time, it is difficult to imagine how someone could arrange and prepare for publication the shorthand seminar notes, the dialogues, and the letter excerpts. In addition, the editor is indebted to Dr. Hartmut Tietjen for his supervision of the bibliographical data. Thanks are also due my wife, Marianne Boss-Linsmayer. Without her expert cooperation in organizing, and selecting from, Heidegger's papers, this book could not have been published. Last but not least, I must thank my student Karin Schoeller von Haslinger for her sacrifice in helping me read the proofs.

Medard Boss
Spring 1987

Synopsis of Contents

self-experience—acceptance (accepting as receiving-perceiving) in the supposition of natural science: space, motion, time, causality—what is closest for perception and closest in itself—the ontological difference p. xx between being and beings—the question concerning space itself—the measuring of time by a clock and the question of time itself—"now," "at the time," and "then"—simultaneity and succession—"just now" and "at once"—"now" and the extendedness of time—counting time and Aristotle's definition of time—the question of the being of time and the determination of being (of presence) from time

The question of what time is: the difficulty in answering the question (Simplicius, Augustine) and the greater difficulty of explicating the question—the hermeneutical circle in the relationship between question and answer—the belonging-together of the human being's unfolding essence and time (Aristotle, Augustine, Bergson, and Husserl)—the meaning of time in psychiatry—of being in the dark concerning the unfolding essence of the human being and the unfolding essence of time—the comportment toward time as mediated by the clock—the saying of "now," "just now," and "at once" and the primordiality of the "now" in naming time—the today, yesterday, and tomorrow and the three different ways of speaking about time—the difference between the determinations of time and the determining of time itself—ascertaining how much time by the clock and the more primordial comportment toward time—the question of the whence of the now, of the at-the-time, and of the then—the always already holding sway of time—the givenness of time as what enables the indication of time—the having time for something: the temporal character of significance [*Deutsamkeit*]— the temporal character of datability [*Datiertheit*]—a psychologically ill person's disturbed comportment toward time—the being-in-time of the utensil and of the ek-sisting human being—the worthwhileness of asking the question of the essence of time—illness as a phenomenon of privation: negation as privation—the temporal character of extendedness [*Weite*]—the temporal character of publicness [*Öffentlichkeit*]—the at-the-time and the past, the then and the future, the now and the present—the nonuniform but equiprimordial openness of the three dimensions of time—daily, established time—the leveling of time's characters in the physical-technical measuring of time—the mere succession of nows—the question of priority—the question of how to interpret a text from the case history of a young schizophrenic—the being-in-time of a thing of use and the having of time by the human being

The question concerning time: Einstein's theory of relativity as a problem
of how time as the sequence of a succession of nows can be measured—   p. xxi
modern natural science's lack of self-criticism—information as the insufficient seeing of the *forma*—the question of the relationship between the
human being and time as substantive and methodological: the natural
scientific concept of time as an obstacle to the appropriate questioning
about what is peculiar to time—time itself as being an exclusive theme
for philosophy—the two aspects of the questioning of time—the medical profession and medical education in natural science—the perma-
nently holding sway of the comportment toward time and the reading
of time by the clock—the *having* of time—the basic rule of phenomenological interpretation—the having of time in the threefold manner in
which the human being exists: expecting [*Gewärtigen*], making present
[*Gegenwärtigen*], retaining [*Behalten*]—the threefold temporalization of
the human being's sojourn in the world—On the phenomenological
interpretation of making-present [*Vergegenwärtigung*]: what is made—
present as being itself is not a "picture" or "representation"—the self-
manifestation of beings as made-present in their various aspects and the
ambiguity of the talk about seeing—the characteristics of making-present
as the being-with-beings themselves—the different possibilities for being
open for beings—the privation of the being-open in schizophrenia

The phenomenological insight into the phenomenon of making-present
as a presupposition of the physiological-psychological explanation—the
sciences' blindness to phenomena; the absence of the desire to see the
phenomena as a result of the claim of the modern idea of science—
the problem of the body and psychosomatics: phenomenological critique
of psychosomatics—the distinction between *psyche* and *soma*—the determination of the domains of *psyche* and *soma* by the respective manner
of access to them and the determination of the manner of access to
them by the subject matter: the hermeneutical circle—the question
concerning the psychosomatic as the question of method—the being-
inherently-spatial of Da-sein as making room [*Einräumen*] and the spa-
tializing of Dasein in its bodiliness—tears, blushing, pain are neither
somatic, nor psychical—the difference between the eye and the hand as
organs of the body, seeing and grasping with the hand—making-present
and bodiliness—the comportment of the body toward space, the phe-   p. xxii
nomenological relationship of the here to my body—the acceptance

of phenomena without possibilities for reducing them (to something else)—the qualitative difference between the limit of the [human] body and of the [material] body—the mineness of my body—the co-determination of bodying forth [*Leiben*] by the human being's ecstatic sojourn in the midst of beings in the clearing—the difference between the human being and the animal through speaking as saying—the motion of the hand as gesture, as distinct from the change of place of a thing of use—standing in the openness of being as ground for the essential necessity to speak—the unified comportment (gesture) of the human being as being-in-the-world that is determined by the bodying forth of the body—blushing as gesture—the ecstatic meaning of bodiliness—the cybernetic representation of language as something measurable

July 6 and 8, 1965, at Boss's Home 92

How the problem of the body and the problem of the method in science belong together—on how theoretical-scientific knowledge is founded in the bodily having of a world—the willingness to reflect upon what occurs in the sciences with their absolute claim: the self-destruction of the human being—the researchable being as object for the measuring "subject" and the transformation of truth into certainty—brain research cannot be understood as a basic research into the knowledge about the human being—the distinctive character of modern science, phenomenology's manner of questioning, seeing, and saying and the relationship between science and phenomenology—hearing and speaking as ways of bodying forth—the bodying forth co-determining being-in-the-world—the difference between speaking and saying—the distinction between what is somatic and what is psychical is not established by natural science—the question of measurability: the representation of a thing as an object in its objectivity, which is the possibility for measuring it—objectivity as modification of presence [*Anwesenheit*]—mere estimation—the foundation of quantitative measuring in the manner in which the human being measures himself with things—the loss of the object in nuclear physics—the distinction between *soma* and *psyche* regarding the modes of access and the problem of method—the connection of the question of measurability and method with the problem of the body—the need for thoughtful physicians—measurability as the manner in which nature can be dominated—the method of modern science, first anticipated by Descartes, as securing the calculability of nature—Descartes's fourth, second, and third methodical rule—science as a method: the a priori positing of nature as a realm of objects, which can be calculated—the

p. xxiii

"I-think" of subjectivity as authoritatively positing truth in the sense of certainty—the act of measuring itself as something essentially not measurable—engaging in the mode of being in which I always already am involved—the position of Descartes, which is in total opposition to the Greek conception—the method of engaging in our relationship toward what we encounter as a turning away from the method of modern science—the relationship to the other human being as a being-in-the-world-with-each-other

Discussion of the objections to Daseinanalysis and the analytic of Dasein and their supposed hostility to science, objectivity and conceptualization: The meaning of analysis and analytic, Freud's understanding of "analysis"—Kant's use of the expression "analytic" and the borrowing of this term in the title "analytic of Da-sein"—L. Binswanger's psychiatric Daseinanalysis—the question of being itself and the question of the being of beings in Parmenides and Aristotle—the change in the human being's position toward beings: ὑποκειμενον and οὐσια, *subjectum* and *objectum*, subject and object—the I as the only subject (Descartes)—three stages in the history of the determination of being—Descartes, Kant, Husserl—*Being and Time* as the question of being as such and the analytic of Dasein—the meaning of "Da-sein" in the tradition and in *Being and Time*—categories and existentials—existential analytic of Da-sein as fundamental ontology—each individual science is grounded in a tacit ontology of its object-domain—critique of the absolutization of natural science—the relation between the analytic of Da-sein and Daseinanalysis—the meaning of science, objectivity and conceptualization in the three aforementioned objections to the method of natural science—the rigor of science as appropriateness to the subject matter

The prevailing characteristic of classical and nuclear physics: method as the precalculability of natural events—the question of the scientific character of psychiatry as a science of the human being, and of the theoretical foundation of the psychotherapeutic praxis—the experience p. xxiv of being human in today's science of man—the familiar and the Daseinanalytic determination of the phenomenon of "stress": being-in-the-world as the basic character of the being of the human being—finding oneself and ontological disposition [*Befindlichkeit*]—"stress" as belonging to the constitution of human existence, characterized by [existential] thrownness, understanding, and language—the ambiguity of language in a science of the human being, the univocity of concepts in the science of nature—stress as a strain caused by being addressed by someone and the response to it—perception as a relationship to the environment—the phenomena of unburdening [*Entlastung*] and burdening [*Belastung*] as a modification of being laid claim on

The spatiality of Da-sein and the utensil's being in space—consciousness and Da-sein—Husserl's phenomenology as description of consciousness

II. CONVERSATIONS WITH MEDARD BOSS, 1961–1972

The variety of the modes of presence and the hallucinating person's mode of presence

The neglect of the question of how the human being as human being exists in traditional psychology, anthropology, and psychopathology—the concept of nature in Galileo and Newton—theory in the modern sense—*humanitas*—physiology as a necessary but insufficient condition for human beings' relationship with one another—making-present and recollection—discussion of the phenomena of the body is possible only on the basis of a sufficient explication of the basic characteristics of existential being-in-the-world—phenomenology of the body as description rather than explanation—possibilities of the historical being-able to-be-in-the-world, what comes toward me, what has been, and the [authentic] present—my Dasein as self-sustaining comportment—the concept of representation—the perception of the other human being—introjection—projection—transference—projective tests—affects—therapy—forgetting—remembering—willing, wishing, propensity, urge—the psychical instances of Ego, Id, and Superego—essence and the concept of essence; being and Da-sein

p. xxv

burdening and unburdening—concerning the hermeneutical circle—motive and cause—the relationship toward the world as setting things up [*enframing*]—concerning the physician's mode of comportment—concerning mood—the ontologically disposed [*befindlich*] understanding as saying and showing—the dependence of nuclear physics on the body

p. xxviii

itself as the possibility for bodiliness—the insight into the immediate and indeterminate belonging of all bodiliness to existence as the basic philosophy of all psychosomatic medicine

PART   I

ZOLLIKON SEMINARS, 1959–1969

September 8, 1959, in the Burghölzli Auditorium of the University of Zurich Psychiatric Clinic[1]

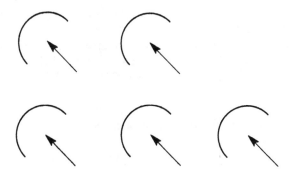

This drawing should only illustrate that human existing* in its essential ground† is never just an object which is present-at-hand; it is certainly not a self-contained object. Instead, this way of existing consists of "pure,"

---

*For Heidegger, existence does not refer to the traditional, metaphysically understood *existentia* (present-at-handness of something). It refers exclusively to the human being's existence as *Ek-sistence* (the human being's "standing out" into the truth of being, i.e., as the "lighting" or "clearing" of being [*Lichtung des Seins*]). In contrast to any misunderstanding of the human being as a self-contained "subject" vis-à-vis "objects," *Ek-sistence* literally means standing outside oneself into the open region of being in which beings can come to presence (the human being as "being-in-the-world," "Da-sein"). See *ZS* 272, 286, 292, etc. Unless otherwise indicated, citations of page numbers are to the in-text marginal page numbers (hereafter *ZS* [*Zollikoner Seminare*]), which refer to the page numbers of the first German edition.—TRANSLATORS

†For Heidegger, "essence" (*Wesen*) must not be understood in the traditional, metaphysical sense of a timeless *essentia*, i.e., *quidditas*, but in the verbal sense of the old Germanic word *wesan* (to dwell), as the temporal way of unfolding, of a coming to presence, and as an enduring of the being of something. The essential ground of human existing is not a first cause, nor any other cause, but rather the revealing-concealing mystery of being, which grants the human being his Da-sein. See M. Heidegger, *Introduction to Metaphysics*, trans. R. Manheim (New York: Doubleday, 1961), p. 59. In the following, we translate "human-ecstatic essence" as "unfolding essence."—TRANSLATORS

invisible, intangible capacities for receiving-perceiving [*Vernehmen*]* what it encounters and what addresses it. In the perspective of the Analytic of Da-sein, all conventional, objectifying representations of a capsule-like psyche, subject, person, ego, or consciousness in psychology and psychopathology must be abandoned in favor of an entirely different understanding. This new view of the basic constitution of human ex-istence may be called *Da-sein,* or being-in-the-world. Of course, in this context the *Da* of this *Da-sein* certainly does not mean what it does in the ordinary sense—a location near an observer. Rather, to exist as Da-sein means to hold open a domain through its capacity to receive-perceive the significance of the things that are given to it [Da-sein] and that address it [Da-sein] by virtue of its own "clearing" [*Gelichtetheit*]. Human Da-sein as a domain with the capacity for receiving-perceiving *is* never merely an object present-at-hand. On the contrary, it is not something which can be objectified at all under any circumstances.

p. 4

p. 5 January 24 and 28, 1964, at Boss's Home

Kant writes: "Being is obviously not a real predicate, that is, it is not a concept of something, which could be added to the concept of a thing. It is merely the positing of a thing or of certain properties themselves."[1]

According to Kant, *real* has nothing to do with what is *actual* or *nonactual,* but because of its origin from *res,* it means accordingly: *relating to the nature of a thing;* something which can be found in a thing. For instance, the real predicates of a table are: round, hard, heavy, etc., whether the table actually exists or is merely imagined.

In contrast, *being* is not something that can be found in the nature of a table, even if the table were to be broken down into its smallest parts.

If one elucidates and explicates the term "obvious," which is not the same as merely using different words for the same thing, it means the same as *manifest,* or *evident,* which is derived from *evideri*—to let oneself

---

*We translate the German *vernehmen* with the hyphenated expression "to receive-perceive." In its existential-ontological meaning *vernehmen* implies receptivity (Greek νοεῖν: to perceive, to understand, to listen in). In a more active, juridical sense, it means that which the judge comes to perceive through the interrogation of witnesses. *Vernehmen* refers to a phenomenologically immediate, nontheoretical, receptive perceiving. This contrasts with *vor-stellen,* "to represent," literally, "setting-before" that which objectifies and reifies.—TRANSLATORS

be seen (ἐναργής, luminously shining; *argentum,* silver), showing itself from itself.

Therefore, according to Kant, it is *obvious* that *being* is not a real predicate. This means that this "not-being-a-real-predicate" simply has to be taken for granted, that is, accepted.

On the whole, "acceptance" has three different meanings.

1. To assume: to expect, to guess, to think of something
2. To be supposed: suppose that . . . , if . . . , then . . . ; to suppose something as a condition, that is, as something which actually is not and cannot be given in itself; acceptance as hypothesis, as *suppositio,* literally, something to be "put under" an object
3. Acceptance: accepting something that has been given; to keep oneself open for a thing, *acceptio*

In our context, the second and third meanings of "acceptance" are of special importance. p. 6

a. "Acceptance" can be taken to mean *suppositio,* hypothesis, "placing under." For example, in Freud's treatise on the parapraxes,* *drives* and *forces* are such suppositions. These supposed drives and forces *cause* and *produce* the phenomena. The parapraxes can be explained in such and such a way, that is, their origin can be *proved.*
b. Acceptance can be taken as accepting something, as a pure and simple receiving-perceiving [*Vernehmen*] of what shows itself from itself, as the *manifest,* for instance, the existence of the table in front of us, accepted as that which cannot be proved by suppositions. Or, can you "prove" your own existence as such? That which is accepted by simple receiving-perceiving does not need to be proved. It shows itself. That which is received-perceived is itself the *base* and the *ground* [*Grund*], which founds and supports any assertion about it. Here we are dealing with a plain and simple showing of what is asserted. We get there by simply pointing it out. There is no further need for arguments here.

A strict distinction has to be made between those cases where we must demand and seek proofs and those cases where no proof is needed but where, nevertheless, the highest kind of grounding [*Begründung*] can be

---

*Heidegger refers to Freud's *Psychopathology of Everyday Life,* vol. 6, *The Standard Edition of the Complete Psychological Works of Freud* (London: Hogarth Press, 1960).—TRANSLATORS

found. Not every grounding must nor can be a proof, whereas every proof is a kind of grounding.

Aristotle had already said: "For not to know of what things one may demand proof, and of what one may not, argues simply want of education."[2] If we have gained insight into this distinction, it is a sign that we are trained and educated for thinking. Whoever lacks this insight is not trained, nor educated for science.

p. 7   The two ways of acceptance, supposition and accepting, are not on the same level in rank so that one or the other could be chosen arbitrarily. Rather, each supposition is always already grounded in a certain kind of *acceptio*. Only when the presence* of something is accepted, can one have suppositions about it.†

That which shows itself, the phenomenon, is what is accepted. There are two kinds of phenomena.

a. Perceptible, existing phenomena are *ontic* phenomena, for example, the table.
b. Nonsensory, imperceptible phenomena, for example, the existence of something, are *ontological* phenomena.

The imperceptible, ontological phenomena always already and necessarily show themselves *prior to* all perceptible phenomena. Before we can perceive a table as this or that table, we must receive-perceive that there is something presencing [*Anwesen*]. Ontological phenomena, therefore, are primary [in the order of being], but secondary in [the order of] being thought and seen.

With regard to the contrast between the *psychodynamic* and the *Dasein-analytic* view of the human being: What is being discussed and decided upon there? The determination of the being of that being,‡

---

*We translate *Anwesenheit* as "presence," *Anwesen* as "presencing," and *das Anwesende* as "that which comes to presence."—TRANSLATORS

†*Acceptio* [*Annahme*], as the pure acceptance of phenomena, is the ground for scientific supposition, i.e., a hypothesis and theory. According to Heidegger, *acceptio* is rooted in the projecting [*Entwurf*] of Da-sein's existential possibilities. By means of this existential projecting, a domain of things is always already opened up in advance, as for instance in the projecting of Galileo's scientific worldview. See M. Heidegger, *Being and Time*, trans. J. Macquarrie and E. Robinson (New York: Harper and Row, 1962), p. 145 ff.; originally published as *Sein und Zeit* (Tübingen: Max Niemeyer, 1927). All subsequent citations are to the Macquarrie and Robinson translation.—TRANSLATORS

‡In order to ensure the nonsubstantial, yet verbal meaning of this term, Professor Boss suggested "to-be-ness" for *Sein*. Since this is now commonly known, the translators have elected to stay with the term "being" for *Sein*.—TRANSLATORS

which we ourselves are. What kind of being [*Sein*] do we see in advance? According to Freud, in what respect must phenomena take a back seat to [scientific] suppositions? With respect to what we consider to be real and actual: acccording to Freud, only that which can be explained in terms of psychological, unbroken, causal connections between forces is actual and genuinely actual. As the world renowned, contemporary physicist Max Planck said a few years ago: "Only that which can be measured is real." In contrast to this, it can be argued: Why can't there be something real which is not susceptible to exact measurement? Why not sorrow, for example?

Even this kind of supposition, that is, that "real" presupposes unbro-   p. 8
ken, causal connections, is founded upon an *acceptio*. It is accepted as self-evident that being is a precalculable, causal relationship. With this supposition, the human being is also posited as an object which can be explained causally.

Two kinds of evidence must be always kept in view.

1. We "see" the existing table. This is ontic evidence.
2. We also "see" [phenomenologically] that existence is not a quality of the table as a table; nevertheless, existence is predicated of the table when we say it *is*. This is ontological evidence.

We affirm the table's existence, and we simultaneously deny that existence is one of its qualities. Insofar as this occurs, we obviously have existence in view. We "see" it. We "see" it, but not like we "see" the table. Yet, we are also unable to immediately say what "existence" means here. "Seeing" has a double meaning: optical, sensory sight, and "seeing" in the sense of "insight" [*Einsehen*].*

Therefore, we will call on Kant for help. He says: Being is not a real predicate, yet it is still a predicate. What kind [of predicate]? It is "simply the pure positedness of a thing"—therefore, the positedness [existence] of something which is given (Kant, *Kritik der reinen Vernunft* [*Critique of Pure Reason*], A.598, B.626). We posit; we put it. For instance, the table can be procured, encountered; a cabinetmaker produces it.

Positedness: I posit. With the "I," therefore, the human being comes into play here. Whereby? In perceiving; in seeing the table which exists.

---

*Here Heidegger refers not to a vague or arbitrary "intuition" in the subjective-psychological sense but to the primordial, immediate grasping (understanding) and apprehending of being, of what is. This "in-sight" is the ontological supposition for any other categorical or sensory intuition. See *Being and Time,* secs. 7, 31; M. Heidegger, *The Basic Problems of Phenomenology,* trans. A. Hofstadter (Bloomington: Indiana University Press, 1982), pp. 1–29.—TRANSLATORS

Does the table exist because I see it? Or can I see it because it exists? Is the existence of the table only a matter for the table itself? But in production it is released away from the human being's action. Released to where? Into existing in its own way, the table shows itself by being used; by the human being's having [something] to do with it. We see that the table exists as a utensil.

How does Dr. R. comport himself to this table here? The table shows itself to him through space. Space is also pervious for the appearance of the table. It is open, free. A wall can be put between the observer and the table. Then space is no longer pervious to seeing the table but is open for building a wall. Without its openness, a wall could not be built between them.

Therefore, the spatiality of this space consists of its being pervious, its being open, and its being a free [realm]. In contrast, the openness itself is not something spatial. The open, the free, is that which appears and shows itself in its own way. We find and situate ourselves in this open [realm], but in a different way than the table.

The table is in its own place and is not simultaneously there where Dr. R. is seated. The table there is present-at-hand [*vorhanden*], but as a human being Dr. R. is situated in his place on the sofa, and he is also simultaneously at the table. Otherwise, he could not even see the table at all. He is not only at his place and then also at the table, but he is always already situated here *and* here. He is ontologically *situated* in this space [the room]. We are all in this space. We reach out into the space by relating to this or that. In contrast, the table is *not* "situated" in space.

The open, the free [realm]—that which is translucent [*das Durch-scheinende*] is not grounded on what is in space. It is the other way around: What is in space is grounded on the open and on the free.*

p. 9

p. 10 July 6 and 9, 1964, at Boss's Home

I. July 6, 1964

MARTIN HEIDEGGER: For once we must disregard all science in view of what

---

*With the terms "the open" and "the free," the later Heidegger referred to the very presence of being [*Anwesenheit*], which grants the "spatiality" of Da-sein and the derivative, homogeneous "space" which Galileo and Newton determined as nature. See M. Heidegger, *Basic Writings*, ed. D. Farrell Krell (New York: Harper and Row, 1970), pp. 384–85, who provided an overall, general introduction and an introduction to each section, and *Parmenides*, trans. A. Schrawer and R. Rojcewicz (Bloomington: Indiana University Press, 1992), pp. 148–49. Also see Heidegger, *Being and Time*, secs. 23, 24, 70.—TRANSLATORS

we will now discuss, that is, no use should be made of it now. It must be asked then in a positive sense: How then should we proceed? We must learn a new way of thinking—a thinking which was already known to the ancient Greeks. Returning to the theme of our last meeting, we ask: Is this the same table which stands before me today?

SEMINAR PARTICIPANT: I remember it differently. It's really not the same! It's been exchanged.

MH: Suppose it is the same [*derselbe*]. Is it also alike [*der gleiche*]?*

SP: No, I remember it differently.

MH: In the aide-mémoire [seminar protocol] which lies in front of you, the expression "pure and simple" is used. How about it?

SP: It has something to do with something simple and plain.

MH: Yes, but is this "acceptance" [*hinnehmen*] actually so simple? Obviously not. Direct acceptance is not an absolute certainty. Does it have the character of certainty at all?

SP: It has a momentary certainty: It is here and now, not absolute.

MH: What characteristic of certainty does direct receiving-perceiving have?

SP: Empirical existence. p. 11

MH: It is an actual, but unnecessary existence. This is called assertoric certainty. This is in contrast to what is called apodictic certainty, for example, $2 \times 2 = 4$. Apodictic certainty is not absolute either, but it is necessary. Why isn't it absolute? . . .

In $2 \times 2 = 4$ "the same as" [=, equals] is presupposed. It is also presupposed that two always remains identical to itself; therefore, it is a conditional certainty.

Now, we first described this table, but that is not what interests us. Only "the table which exists" is of interest to us. We took this existence for granted in the sense of what is called *acceptance*. Now, what does it mean to exist? Being is not a real predicate according to Kant, but we speak about the table's existence. What is meant by this "real"? It indicates *relating to the nature of a thing* [*Sachhaltigkeit*]. In this sense, existence is not real. Nevertheless, we attribute existence

---

*In contrast to the formal-abstract identity or equality (*das Gleiche*) of something (object) with itself, the later Heidegger's term "sameness" (*das Selbe*) refers to the ontological relationship of reciprocal *belonging-together* [*Zusammengehören*] of being and beings in their difference. It points to the self-differentiating, self-giving of being, called *Ereignis* (the disclosive appropriating Event of being). See M. Heidegger, *Identity and Difference*, trans. J. Stambaugh (New York: Harper and Row, 1969). See *Poetry, Language, Thought*, trans. A. Hofstadter (New York: Harper and Row, 1971), p. 218.—TRANSLATORS

to the table. Existence belongs to it. How does it belong to it? What does existence mean?

SP: The table is in space.

MH: Does this belong to the nature of the thing?

SP: Extension is a property of space.

MH: How?

SP: It has extendedness [*Ausgedehntheit*]: how high it is; how wide, and so forth. These are its dimensions.

MH: Are extension and dimension different? What is the difference?

SP: Dimension is an arbitrarily selected extension.

MH: How do particular spaces relate to "space"?

SP: Space contains them.

MH: Space is not "the universal" in relation to [particular] spaces, as with trees, for example, as the tree is [the universal] to particular trees. Now, what characterizes this space?

p. 12

SP: It is space, which is demarcated.

MH: It is a space for living; it contains useful things. There is an orientation to things in space. Things have a special meaning for the people who live there. They are familiar to some [of the people], but strange to others. This space has characteristics other than "space." How is the table in space now?

SP: It belongs to space; it takes up space.

MH: But how?

SP: It has a shape which limits it according to its space.

MH: Yes. Now you can see how it is with this aide-mémoire, as they call it. What meaningless sentences! That's why we're so helpless with this scribbling on paper!

Now, we are asking whether this table would still be here if Dr. R. were no longer here to see it.

SP: Both of them are located in the space, which separates the observer from the table, as well as connects him to it.

MH: Separates? Are you sure? If something is separated, it must have first been connected.

SP: Better to say distant from, removed from.

MH: Distance [in the originary, ontological sense]* has nothing to do with separating and connecting. Now, last time we asked: If we put a wall between the table and Dr. R., [then] is the table still there?

---

*Heidegger distinguishes the ontological meanings of "de-distancing," "re-moting," and "de-severing" [*Ent-fernen*] as an existential characteristic of Da-sein's "being-in-

SP: Then the table is no longer visible to the observer.

MH: But is the table still there?

SP: It's behind the wall. It's hidden.

MH: No, not even hidden. p. 13

SP: We don't have an immediate perception [of it], but we can remember and imagine it.

MH: Do you see? It's not so easy.

SP: For a child or for a primitive man, it wouldn't be there anymore. Existence not only consists in its being seen.

MH: Close your eyes. Where is the table now?

SP: Concerning perception, the table is gone—but with [your] eyes closed you can still trip over it.

MH: Yes, that would be a particularly stark perception. Then, is the table only represented in my head?

SP: The table remains in its place, but that's not absolutely certain. Someone could have taken it away. . . . When I close my eyes, I still have a particular relationship to it. It doesn't make any difference whether the table is still there.

MH: Let's assume you close your eyes. When you open them again, is the table gone? What then?

SP: Amazement, disappointment.

MH: What does disappointment mean?

SP: An unfulfilled expectation.

MH: Yes, exactly. Even when your eyes were closed, you were by the table. Dr. R. then perceives the table here from over there. How does this happen? Then where is R.?

SP: Here and there.

MH: R. is here and there at the same time, but the table cannot be here and there at the same time. Only the human being can be here and p. 14

---

the-world" in the privative sense of *abolishing* a distance or a farness (i.e., bringing something closer as "ready-to-hand" or "present-at-hand") from the ontic category of "distance" [*Abstand*]. The latter is understood as a measurable continuum which connects and which separates things within the world (e.g., tables) from each other. In contrast to the "distance between things in space," Da-sein's "spatiality," in the active, transitive sense, refers to existential "de-severing" and "de-distancing." See Heidegger, *Being and Time,* p. 138.—TRANSLATORS

there at the same time.* The table is in space in a different way than the human being.

SP: R. has a relationship to the table, but the table does not have a relationship to him.

MH: But what about space?

SP: I move in space.

MH: How?

SP: I move myself. The table is moved.

MH: Then, how about this clock? Doesn't it move by itself as well?

SP: No, its hand is moved by people.

MH: It runs by itself.

SP: No, a spring moves it. The spring is made by people.

MH: The spring belongs to the clock. The clock runs. That is part of it.

SP: No, the clock does not move itself, only the hand.

MH: Then the hand. . . . What part of the human being is in space?

SP: The body.

MH: Where are you yourself? I change my position like this. Then, do I only move my body? . . . The table does that too!

SP: Last time we reached the point where we characterized space as the open and as pervious. How does the human being relate to the open now?

MH: Yes, that's the question.

SP: I am not only in space. I orient myself in space.

p. 15   MH: What does that mean?

SP: I am in space, as far as I comprehend it.

MH: In what way?

SP: Space is open for me, but not for the table.

MH: Space is open through you. And how is it for the table in this case?

SP: Space is not open for the table.

MH: Is space anything at all for the table?

SP: The human being has space present to him. . . . The table was made. The human being has space and has [also] made the table.†

---

*See M. Heidegger, "Building Dwelling Thinking," in *Basic Writings*, pp. 343–64, 335.—TRANSLATORS

†See Heidegger, *Being and Time*, p. 146.—TRANSLATORS

MH: Can't the table, which has been made, be in space the same way as the human being? Here "to make" [produce] means "to stand here." The table has been released away from its relationship to production. The meaning of handicraft and art is that something has been made and can stand on its own. So what does it mean [when I say]: I orient myself in space, but the table does not?

SP: We suppose that the table doesn't do it.

MH: Doesn't the table have anything to do with orientation?

SP: The human being can orient himself or herself to it. For example, the table itself is oriented in relation to the four cardinal points of the heavens (N, S, E, W). It has a definite location and has been placed there for Professor H.

MH: It has been arranged in the room. It is oriented according to a way of living. Orientation has something to do with the rising of the sun. Why then not *occidentalization?*

SP: "Orient" means the rising of the sun and of the light.

MH: With the rising of the sun, it gets light and everything becomes visible. Things shine. In certain burial rites, the face is turned toward the east. Churches are oriented in the same way as well. By the way, when the light is turned off, how is it then with the clearing [*Lichtung*]? . . . "Clearing" means "to be open." There is also clearing in darkness. Clearing has nothing to do with light but is derived from "lighten" [unburden].* Light involves perception. One can still bump into something in the dark. This does not require light, but a clearing. Light—bright. "Light" comes from "lighten," "to make free." A clearing in the forest is still there, even when it's dark. Light presupposes clearing. There can only be brightness where something has been cleared or where something is free for the light. Darkening, taking away the light, does not encroach upon the clearing. The clearing is the presupposition for getting light and dark. It is the free, the open. p. 16

SP: What is that—the free, the open?

SP: The free and the open is space. Is it only the free space or the space occupied by the table?

---

*With the term "lighten," Heidegger is referring to lightening a load in the sense of clearing away the forest's thicket. The later Heidegger uses this metaphor to describe Da-sein's "clearing" [*Lichtung*]. See Heidegger, *Being and Time,* p. 135, and "The End of Philosophy and the Task of Thinking," in *Basic Writings,* pp. 373–92.—TRANSLATORS

MH: If space were not free, the table couldn't be there. Space frees the table. Space is then "occupied," but that doesn't mean it's no longer free.

SP: Then is it the same space as the space of this room?

MH: The room belongs to it. Once more, you see that language is wiser than we think. "Space" comes from "making space" [for]. What does this mean?

SP: "To free" . . . but also "to make space for," that is, to arrange, to put in place, or on the other hand, to make a place for.

MH: Space has places. To clear away [*aufräumen*], to make order among things that are not in place. That is something different from simply being present-at-hand [*Vorhandensein*].

SP: We also speak about "being cleared up" [*aufgeräumt*] if someone is in a good mood.

p. 17　MH: Yes, then one is serene [cleared up], free. Are space and clearing identical, or does one presuppose the other? . . . Now, that cannot be decided yet. There can be something else in the clearing: time. We haven't talked about that yet. Let's occupy ourselves some more with the difference between *free* and *open,* on the one hand, and with something *empty,* on the other.

SP: Something "empty" means "containing nothing."

MH: Therefore, not occupied. "Free" also means "not occupied," but in a different way.

SP: "Free" means "free for something."

MH: It is able to be occupied. "Empty," however, means "not occupied." Space can also remain *free,* even when it is occupied. Something is empty only because there is the free.

SP: Is it possible then that *unoccupied* is different from *not able to be occupied?*

MH: The empty [a void, a vacuum] is the unoccupied free [realm].*

SP: The free has a ground [*Boden*]. Under certain circumstances, the empty does not. You can have a groundless void.

MH: Outer space, for example. Isn't it able to be occupied? It's very much occupied indeed. There is no void without the free [realm]. The void is grounded in the free.

---

*Here the "free" does not refer to psychological "freedom of choice," but rather to Da-sein's being exposed into the open region, i.e., being in which beings (and space) can come to presence. See Heidegger, *Basic Writings,* pp. 129–32, and *Being and Time,* pp. 145–48, 183.—TRANSLATORS

SP: What is meant here by "ground"? The *ground for* what?

MH: It is a relation concerning the nature of a thing, not a logical ground [between concepts].

SP: That's difficult for the students because *ground* is always understood in the sense of logical conclusions alone. You say: having *the nature of a thing* [*sachhaltig*]. But what kind of a thing [*Sache*] is this?

MH: Thing [as a subject matter] is that with which we are dealing.

SP: I cannot understand the open or the free as a "thing."   p. 18

MH: Is "subject matter" only a "thing"?* Indeed, there are nonperceptible subject matters. Space, or $2 \times 2 = 4$, for example. These are subject matters. Here "subject matter" means "something with which we are dealing."

SP: Then what does being a "subject matter" mean?

MH: A ground for a subject matter means that one subject matter cannot exist without another subject matter. There cannot be a void without the "free." "Free," that is, "capable of being occupied," is more original than "void."

SP: We feel that it could also be stated inversely: There is the "free" only because there is the void [empty].

MH: The difference between *ratio essendi* and *ratio cognoscendi* comes into play here. Something empty is the ground for knowing [*Erkenntnisgrund*] the free, but the free is the *ratio essendi* [*Seinsgrund*] for something empty. It is a ground for being, not a [physical] cause.

Then how is the human being in space? Does the human being only occupy space, or am I in space in a different way?

SP: I use my place. I sit.

MH: Does the table sit? What does "it sits" mean?

SP: I can take different positions [*verschiedene Haltung*] in space. . . . The human being fills up space.

MH: So does the table. . . . When I refer to the human being, I am already referring to space too.

SP: The human being and space belong to each other.

MH: How? Space also belongs to the table.

SP: The human being is able to comport [*verhalten*] himself toward space.

MH: He is always comporting himself [toward something].

---

*Here Heidegger shifts the meaning of *Sache* [thing] to *Sachverhalt* [subject matter].
—TRANSLATORS

SP: Space belongs to the human being's essential characteristics. I comport myself toward things in space, therefore, also toward space.
Space is open to the human being.

p. 19

MH: For the table too.

SP: I'm already in this space in which I move.

MH: I walk by occupying space. The table does not occupy space in the
same way. The human being makes space for himself. He allows space
to be. An example: When I move, the horizon recedes. The human
being moves within a horizon. This does not only mean to transport
one's body.

SP: Then how is it with an animal?

MH: Again, it is a different relationship toward space. The animal does
not speak. The human being is a ζῷον λογον εχον. The animal does
not experience space *as space*.

SP: What does this "as" mean?[*]

MH: The animal is acquainted with the ditch it jumps over as a simple
matter of fact [*Sachverhalt*], but not as a concept.

SP: The animal cannot reflect.

MH: Is language so essential? Surely there is also a way of communicating
without language.

SP: Language and verbal articulation are confused with each other here.

MH: The human being cannot comport himself in any way without language. Language is not only verbal articulation. *Communicatio* is only
one possibility. "To say" [*sagen*] originally meant "to show" [*zeigen*].[†]

SP: When we talk about "occupying space," the usual understanding is
that we are there, where our body is.

MH: I sit here. I talk with you. I sit opposite the wall. I am related to things
in space. The table as a table is not related to other things! To comport
oneself to something *as* something means to speak and to say: I am

p. 20

---

[*]See Heidegger, *Being and Time*, secs. 31–34. See also Heidegger, *The Fundamental Concepts of Metaphysics*, trans. W. McNeil and N. Walker (Bloomington: Indiana University Press, 1995), secs. 45–63.—TRANSLATORS

[†]Compare the foundational relations among "understanding," "interpretation," and "assertion" [*Aussage*], which in turn encompass the three phenomena of "pointing out" [*Aufzeigen*] as prior to mere "representation" [*Vorstellung*], "predication" [*Prädikation*], and "communication" [*Mitteilung*]. See Heidegger, *Being and Time*, pp. 195–203.—TRANSLATORS

open to space. I can move. I know where something belongs, but I don't need to view space *as* space. Without paying attention to it thematically, without being occupied with it, I let space be as the open.

Conclusion. All this should only indicate to you that this subject matter is by no means easy. Aristotle said: "For as the eyes of night birds are to the blaze of day, so is the reason in our soul to the things which are by nature most evident of all" (*Metaphysics* II.1.993b9 ff.). That is just how it is with *being*. It's the most difficult for us to see. As Plato said: When man tries to look into the light, he will be blinded.

You should learn not to be afraid when Aristotle is quoted to you. Aristotle and the ancient Greeks are not "finished" or "outdated." On the contrary, we have not yet begun to understand them. Science does not really move ahead. It's walking in place. It's not easy at all to walk in place!

II. July 9, 1964

MARTIN HEIDEGGER: The last seminar was rather a failure. However, the difficulty lies in the subject matter itself. As Kant says: The point is to catch a glimpse of being. We tried to do this with the example of the table. Nevertheless, the difficulty lies in the subject matter, which is *being* itself. For science the domain of objects is already pregiven. Research goes forward in the same direction in which the respective areas have already been talked about prescientifically. These areas belong to the everyday world. However, it is not the same with being. Of course, being is also illuminated in advance, but it is not explicitly noticed or reflected upon. Since being is not the same as beings, *the difference between beings and being** is the most *fundamental and difficult* [problem]. It is all the more difficult if thinking is determined

---

*For Heidegger the "ontological difference" between being and beings is prior to Western metaphysic's distinction between *existentia* (that a thing is) and *essentia* (what a thing is). In its unique, temporal-ecstatic ek-sistence, human Da-sein transcends all beings by its understanding of being. According to Heidegger, Western metaphysics has forgotten being in favor of beings because of the epochal (historical) withdrawal of being itself. Even the metaphysical concept of God as the "supreme being" has been substituted for the question of being, which is never asked. See M. Heidegger, "What Is Metaphysics?" in *Basic Writings*, pp. 95–112, 190–242; *Identity and Difference*, pp. 61 f., 128 ff.; Heidegger, *Contributions to Philosophy (From Enowning)*, trans. P. Emad and K. Maly (Bloomington: Indiana University Press, 1999), pp. 145–55, 176–87.—TRANSLATORS

by science, which deals only with beings. The prevailing opinion nowadays is [that it is] as if science alone could provide objective truth. Science *is* the new religion. Compared to it, any attempt to think of *being* appears arbitrary and "mystical." Being cannot be glimpsed by science. Being demands a unique demonstration, which does not lie in the human being's discretion and which cannot be undertaken by science. As human beings, we can only exist on the basis of this difference [between being and beings]. The only thing that helps us catch a glimpse of being is a unique readiness for receiving-perceiving. To let oneself into this receiving-perceiving is a distinctive act of the human being. It means a transformation of existence. There is no abandonment of science, but on the contrary, it means arriving at a thoughtful, knowing relationship to science and truly thinking through its limitations.

p. 21

Today we will make a new attempt to arrive at the *difference between being and beings* by starting with the question of what *nature* means. We will contrast *causality* with *motivation*. In doing this we encounter the phenomenon of ground and grounding. However, *grounding* [*Fundierung*] is not the same as causality or motivation. What is causality? How is it understood in natural science? Let's take an example: "When the sun shines, the rock gets warm." This is grounded on an observation and on a state of affairs that is immediately perceived. We are dealing with a *sequence*. However, if we say: "Because the sun is shining . . . ," we are dealing with an *empirical proposition*. "Whenever the sun is shining . . ." designates only a temporal sequence. The "because" does not just mean one after another but rather a necessary condition of "one after another." This is causality, as it is understood in the natural sciences. It has dominated modern thought since Newton and Galileo. Then Kant undertook the critique of pure reason. In Aristotle one finds a *causa efficiens*—that which produces an effect. Is this the same as the modern concept? The necessary "one after another" leads to the interpretation of an "effect determined by a cause." Kant said cautiously: "Everything that happens, that is, begins to be, presupposes something *upon which it follows according to a rule*" (Kant, *Kritik der reinen Vernunft* [*Critique of Pure Reason*], A.189). (Of course, in modern language one would say: from *which* it follows!) *Upon which* means temporal, but according to a rule, it is necessary. It is impossible to know *from which*, that is, how something develops from something else!

p. 22

SEMINAR PARTICIPANT: Recent scientific formulations are more cautious. They state: Up to now, it has always been the case. Supposing that nothing changes, everything will happen the same way in the future.

MH: Nevertheless, this means on the condition that no other events intervene. When new factors intervene, the law must be reformulated because of new observations and new conditions. Aristotle's *causa efficiens* still belongs to the natural, prescientific worldview. It is an αἰτια. Cause is a legal term—a thing with which we are dealing. Cause is where something first comes from—what has to be dealt with first. *Causa* has the same meaning. The Greeks distinguished four causes: material, formal, final, and efficient. Let's take the example of a silversmith who is going to make a bowl. Four causes must be distinguished in making it: the order [to make the bowl] is the determining factor, "what ought to be done," something final, the "for the sake of which," the οὐ ἕνεκα. The second cause is the shape of the bowl which the silversmith must have in mind as its form. This is the ειδος. *Forma* is already a reinterpretation of ειδος, which means [visible] shape. The final and the formal cause are interrelated. Together, they determine the third cause, the material, the ἐξ οὐ, here, the silver. The fourth cause: this is *causa efficiens,* the production, ποιησις or ἀρχη της κινησεως; this is the craftsman. The modern *causa efficiens* is no longer the same! ποιησις and πραξις are not the same: making and doing. πραξις has a motivation!

In the modern sense, causality presupposes a process of nature, not a ποιησις. The Greeks viewed and interpreted the κινησις [motion] of nature as they understood it from the perspective of ποιησις [production].[*] Galileo argued this. In today's science we find the desire to have nature at one's disposal, to make it useful, to be able to calculate it in advance, to predetermine how the process of nature occurs so that I can relate to it safely. Safety and certainty are important. There is a claim for certainty in having nature at one's disposal. That which can be calculated in advance and that which is measurable—only that is real. How far can we get with a sick person [with this approach]? We fail totally! In physics, the law of causality has reality [*Wirklichkeit*], but even there only in a very limited way. What Aristotle said is true according to the worldview of those days: the Aristotelian concept of motion, for instance. What is motion?

p. 23

SP: A change of location in time.

MH: Aristotle called it φορα. This means that a body is transported from one place to another, to *its* place. Galileo abandoned notions of above and below, right and left. Physical space is homogeneous. No

---

[*]Concerning the understanding of "being" from the perspective of "productive" comportment [*herstellen*] in ancient ontology, which in turn was imposed upon the interpretation of the Hebrew-Christian notion of "creation" in medieval theology, see Heidegger, *The Basic Problems of Phenomenology,* pp. 112–19; *Basic Writings,* p. 290 f.—TRANSLATORS

point is more distinctive than any other. Only this conception of space makes it possible to determine locomotion. Space must be homogeneous because the laws of motion must be the same everywhere. Only then can every process be calculated and measured. Nature is viewed in a very specific way to satisfy the condition of measurability. Beings acquire the character of being mere objects and of being objectified. No such "objectivity" can be found in Greek thought. Being "an object" only makes its appearance in modern natural science. The human being then becomes a "subject" in the sense of Descartes. Without all these presuppositions, the expression "objective" is meaningless.

p. 24 SP: Does "objective" mean just what is ascertained "scientifically"? Is everything else subjective?

MH: Is our totally different conception of space indeed merely subjective? . . . This is already a glimpse of being! A genuine insight! It's a different kind of truth than in physics, perhaps a higher one! If one sees that, then one has a free stance toward science.

PS: There is also calculability in psychology, which is correct, necessary, and applicable in many cases. Professor Boss says that this concept of causality should *not* be applied. How about that?

MH: The question is: What is the domain of science? What can its domain be? For the most part, science today is understood exclusively as natural science (English: *science* vs. *arts*). In psychology, where is the scientific way of questioning meaningful now? Is this questioning applicable to the psychical? What is "psychical"? Have you considered this question?

SP: Freud wanted to transfer scientific causality to the psychical. He came to the idea of an apparatus, a mechanistic conception.

MH: And the remarkable thing is that something comes out of it! But does something significant really come out of it? Does it correspond to reality? Have the physicists ever seen reality? This talk about a correspondence to reality does not make sense at all. Electrons and so forth are hypothetical. They permit us to operate in a certain way, but no one has seen them. In cybernetics nowadays there is even the opinion that nature conforms itself to the "apparatus." People who operate with this apparatus will be changed as well. What is psychical? One asks about *processes* and about *changes in the psychical*, but *not* about what *psychical is*. How does one look at human beings thereby? p. 25 The uncanny thing is that one can view human beings in this way, but should one? Or should one *also* consider them this way?

SP: If one does, one conceals the possibility for a different understanding.

SP: One should *also* [take the mechanistic view into account], but on a lower level.

MH: Nowadays it appears that cybernetics is increasingly becoming the universal science and that consciousness is already considered a *disruptive factor.* Now we still want to see how it is with *motivation.* Give me some examples.

SP: We talk about motive most of all when discussing criminals, as, for example, the burgher-prince [and] the motive for the [criminal] act. It could have happened because of [emotional] excitement. The act comes from some agitation.

MH: Is [emotional] excitement a motive?

SP: No, on the contrary, a motive is a *causa finalis.*

SP: Suppose a girl is stealing milk because in childhood she did not get enough milk from her mother. We say then that hunger was the motive for eating.

MH: Really?

SP: No, it is a cause of motion.

MH: Cause and purpose are getting mixed up.

SP: [Emotional] excitement can be a motive if one attempts to attain it.

MH: What is a cause of motion? What kind of motion do you mean?

SP: Motion toward something—acting.

MH: What is action [*Handlung*]?

SP: It requires an actor, a human being, for this.

MH: Can an animal act? For example, by taking a piece of bread [in its paws]? By closing the window because it's noisy outside? What kind of motion is that? p. 26

SP: The motive is: I would like to have quiet.

MH: Is this a sequence as in causality?

SP: No, it's not a necessary sequence. There's freedom in it.

MH: Where's the freedom?

SP: It can be a decision between two motives, for example, pleasure and lack of pleasure. We follow the stronger stimulus.

MH: What is motive now? That which determines me to close the window. Motive calls forth free will. It does not restrict it. Motive is not coercive. One is unconstrained—free. Motive addresses me for something. Motive is a ground I think about and experience as something which determines me. In this case the motive is that I want to have quiet. Now the whole event: Is the closed window an effect of the noise? Is there a causal relationship?

SP: No.

MH: That which determines [the human being's free will] (*das Bestimmende*), hearing a voice* and responding to it, is characteristic of a motive. It is characterized by a particular relationship to the world and by a particular situation. Noise is not the cause of getting up.

SP: However, a machine could be built to close windows when it's noisy outside!

MH: Yes, then the noise would be the cause. Does the machine hear the noise as noise? The machine has no possibilities for decision making. Another example: You see smoke.

SP: Then you suspect fire.

p. 27   MH: What role does the smoke that you see play in relation to the fire?

SP: It's an experimental fact that where there's smoke, there's fire. The smoke I saw is the observed "reason" [*Grund*] for my assumption that something is burning.

MH: What's the consequence?

SP: I alert the fire department.

MH: That means that the fire is not simply perceived, but also seen as a threat. The threat is the motive for alerting [the fire department]. Where does the motive belong?

SP: It's an anticipation.

MH: No, it belongs to the experience of life. It is not an anticipation. The disturbance already lies within the noise. Nothing at all is anticipated here.

---

*The German *bestimmen*, derived from *Stimme* [voice], has the connotation of "hearing a voice" (e.g., "the voice of a friend—a friend every Da-sein carries with it" [Heidegger, *Being and Time*, p. 206]), which gives "motive" an existential meaning. *Stimmen* in the active sense means to let one's voice be heard or "to tune" (e.g., an instrument). Da-sein as "being-in-the-world" is *gestimmt* [tuned, in a mood]. Yet "moods" [*Stimmungen*] are not ontic, psychical states or feelings but the all-encompassing *ontological* characteristics of man's "being-in-the-world" (e.g., anxiety, boredom, etc.). The English word "determine," from the Latin *de-terminare* [to limit, to fix, to decide], is not quite able to express the same ontological meaning. See *ZS 29.*—TRANSLATORS

SP: I let myself be moved by expecting that something will happen if I let myself be moved. The closed window is the cause that the noise doesn't come in.

MH: What kind of ground is a motive? The familiar world is needed for that—the context of the world in which I live. A cause follows according to a rule. In contrast, nothing like this is required for determining a motive. The motive's characteristic is that it moves me and that it addresses the human being. There is obviously something in a motive that addresses me. There is an understanding, a being open for a specific context of significance in the world.

SP: Therefore, a motive would not be understood in a purely psychological sense. How can we understand that?

MH: From what is experienced. From what is seen. Not only from the psychical realm. What does motivation mean in psychiatry?

SP: For instance, market research can be conducted to determine what people respond to.

MH: There's no psychology involved. p. 28

SP: Yes, there is, a psychology of marketing.

MH: What is psyche? Is the market something psychical?

SP: It's a stimulus.

MH: How can we compare causality with motivation at all?

SP: It's possible because both are grounds.

MH: Motive is a ground for human action. Causality is the ground for sequences within the process of nature. But what is ground? One could say, that upon which one stands. Or one could say that there is nothing without ground. This is *the principle of ground* [*the principle of sufficient reason*]. All that is has a ground. (This was first formulated as a principle in the seventeenth century by Leibniz.) On what ground do we know this? The principle of causality is based on the principle of ground. It is valid in the domain of natural science. The principle of ground: "Ground is that which cannot be further reduced." Aρχη is the first. It is whence something is, becomes, or is known as follows: (1) *ratio essendi*, the ground of being; (2) the ground of becoming; or (3) the ground of knowing. (Having seen smoke, one thinks of fire. However, in relation to smoke, fire is the ground of becoming.) Ground of being: ground of what, and how, a thing is. Essential ground of being: Every color as color is extended. Color is grounded in extension (but extension does not produce color). The ground of being is that which grounds [something].

All different grounds are themselves based on the principle of ground. All that is has a ground.

SP: Isn't that arbitrary?

MH: Natural science posits conditions and then observes the result. We have not proceeded in this way. We have only seen the phenomena: θεωρειν means "to see." *Causality* is an idea, an ontological determination. It belongs to the determination of the ontological structure of nature. *Motivation* refers to the human being's existing [ek-sistence] in the world as a being who acts and experiences.

p. 29

There is still the question whether the *principle of ground* is a self-evident principle or whether it can be reduced to the *principle of contradiction*. Is it a *principle of thinking or of being?*

p. 30

November 2 and 5, 1964, at Boss's Home

I. November 2, 1964

By Way of Introduction: An Anecdote about Socrates

A widely traveled sophist asks Socrates: "Are you still here and still saying the same thing? You are making light of the matter." Socrates answers: "No, you sophists are making light of it because you are always saying what's new and the very latest [news]. You always say something different. To say the same thing is what's difficult. To say the same thing about the same thing is the most difficult."[*]

Socrates was the West's greatest thinker insofar as he did not write anything. We will also endeavor to say the same thing about the same thing here. That seems odd to common sense. That's called a tautology.[†]

---

[*] This anecdote is also mentioned in M. Heidegger, *What Is a Thing?* trans. W. B. Barton, Jr., and V. Deutsch, with an analysis by E. T. Gendlin (Chicago: H. Regnery, 1967): "The most difficult learning is to come to know actually and to the very foundation what we already know. Such learning, with which we are here solely concerned, demands dwelling continually on what appears to be nearest to us, for instance, on the question of what a thing is. We steadfastly ask the *same* question—which in terms of utility is obviously useless—of what a thing is, what tools are, what man is, what a work of art is, what the state and the world are."—TRANSLATORS

[†] "Tautological" thinking in Heidegger's sense (as opposed to tautology [identity] in formal logic and in dialectical thinking, which moves between opposite "identities" [as noted by Hegel]), is the meditative-phenomenological thinking toward the hidden abyss and mystery of being in its unfolding and "epochal" withholding in Western

Seen logically, it is a proposition that says nothing. Therefore, we are taking a position counter to logic.

. The pervading difficulty in our endeavor is a *methodological* one. It concerns our access to the phenomena and the manner and way of demonstrating [*ausweisen*] them and being able to demonstrate them. It is understandable that the more one feels at home with the natural sciences' way of thinking, the stranger it is to reflect on the phenomena of space, temporality, the human being, and causality as we practice it.

If you are familiar with the natural scientific mode of thinking, does that also mean that you already have an understanding of your scientific procedure as well? One thing is certain, if you are at home with the way of thinking in the natural sciences, then your thought is always directed toward nature. I ask you: What is the meaning of nature here? The basic characteristic of nature represented by the natural sciences is conformity to law. Calculability is a consequence of this conformity to law. Of all that is, only that which is measurable and quantifiable is p. 31 taken into account. All other characteristics are disregarded. Question: What are the presuppositions for thinking about nature in this way? What is the primary consideration? Projecting a homogeneous space and a homogeneous time. What is measured there are the lawlike movements of mass-points in regard to locomotion and time.

Kant was the first to articulate explicitly the characteristics of nature as represented in the natural sciences. He was therefore also the first to state what a law means in the natural sciences. That a philosopher was the real spokesperson for the natural sciences is an indication that the task of reflecting on what natural science is constantly focused upon belongs

---

philosophy. Such thinking of the selfsame is not a "representation" [*Vorstellung*] of being in a conceptual "identity," but rather a deepening of the sense that being as the abysmal, concealed ground of beings is always more than what can be conceptualized and represented. Being and beings, as well as being and the human being, "belong together" (*zusammengehören*) in a reciprocal, unifying-differentiating [*Unter-Schied*, dif-ference] relation. See Heidegger, *Identity and Difference*, pp. 27 ff., 64 ff., 133 ff.; *The Question concerning Technology and Other Essays*, trans. and with an introduction by Q. W. Lovitt (New York: Harper and Row, 1977), p. 57. Being is in excess of any articulation in terms of formal identity and difference, the inexhaustible non-ground [*Ab-grund*] of both (see *Contributions to Philosophy*, p. 249: "The Overflow in the essential Sway of Be-ing" [*Das Übermass im Wesen des Seins*]). Silence, therefore, is the hidden source of such tautological thinking. In the *Der Spiegel* interview (1966), Heidegger said: "All great thinkers think the same—this same is so essential (deep) and rich that no single thinker accomplishes (exhausts) it; rather every thinker is bound even tighter and more rigorously to it."—TRANSLATORS

not to natural science but to philosophy. Natural scientists themselves, however, are usually not explicitly aware of this.

Kant's definition of law regarding nature states: "*In general, nature*" is "the conformity of phenomena in space and time to the law" (*Kritik der reinen Vernunft* [*Critique of Pure Reason*], B.165 [p. 173]). In addition, he writes: "*Nature* is the existence [Da-sein] of things as far as it [Da-sein] is determined according to universal laws"(see loc. cit. p. 16).[1] As a law of nature, causality is a law according to which phenomena constitute nature for the first time and are able to become objects of experience. Nature *materialiter spectata* is the totality of the *phenomena* insofar as they are necessarily linked to each other according to an inherent principle of causality. This refers to [material] content, nature in the sense of all of nature. Nature *formaliter spectata* is the totality of the rules to which all phenomena must be subsumed. This does not refer to all of nature, to all things, or to their material content, but rather to the [formal] nature of things.

p. 32   Kant distinguished between rule and law. Rule is derived from the Latin *regere* [to lead, to rule, to plumb-line, to regulate]. As he notes: "The representation of a universal condition, according to which a certain manifold can be posited in uniform fashion, is called a *rule,* and when it *must* be so posited, [it is called] a *law*" (Kant, *Kritik der reinen Vernunft* [*Critique of Pure Reason*], A.113 [p. 140]).

That entire domain, determined *materialiter* and *formaliter,* a domain called "nature," where you feel at home thinking in the way of the natural sciences, was first projected by Galileo and Newton. This projection was established or was set up as a supposition regarding the determination of laws, according to which points of mass move in space and time, but not at all regarding that being we call the human being.

The entire gap between natural science and our consideration of the human being is evident from this factual statement.

According to natural science, the human being can be identified only as something present-at-hand in nature. The question arises: Can human nature be found at all in this way? From the projection of the natural sciences, we can see the human being only as an entity of nature, that is, we claim to define the human being's being utilizing a method, never designed to include its special nature.

Questions remain as to what takes precedence: this method of the natural sciences, which grasps and calculates laws of nature, or the claim to determine the human being's being as such from the human being's self-experience? We ask: Where is the natural scientific projection about nature grounded? Where is its truth? Can it be proved? It cannot be proved. One can only look at the results, at the effects, which can be obtained through the natural sciences as a criterion showing that natural scientific thinking does justice to its domain. Effect is never a proof, much less a criterion for the truth of the method leading to the effect. What does effect mean? The capacity to dominate nature. Nietzsche says: "With its formulas, the natural sciences will teach how to *subdue* nature's powers. It will not put a "truer" interpretation in place of the empirical-sensory one (as does metaphysics)."[2]

p. 33

The great decision is: Can we ever claim to determine human *being* according to natural scientific representation, that is, within the limitations of a science projected without regard to the specific being of human *being*? Or must we ask ourselves regarding this projection of nature: How does the human being's being show itself and what kind of approach and consideration does the human being's unique being require?

We repeat: Natural science's entire truth consists in its effect.

What do we usually understand as truth? The proposition's correspondence to what shows itself. *Adaequatio rei et intellectus*. How does natural scientific truth stand in comparison to this?

In physics, a theory is proposed and then tested by experiments to see whether their results agree with the theory. The only thing demonstrated is the correspondence of the experimental results to the theory. It is not demonstrated that the theory is simply the knowledge of nature. The experiment and the result of the experiment do not extend beyond the framework of the theory. They remain within the area delineated by the theory. The experiment is not considered in regard to its correspondence to nature, but to what was posited by the theory. What is posited by the theory is the projection of nature according to scientific representations, for instance, those of Galileo.

Yet today even pioneers in physics are trying to clarify the inherent limitations of physics. It is still questionable whether physics, as a matter of principle, will ever succeed in doing this.

p. 34

This method was derived from the spatiotemporal movement of bodies [in space]. The point is to recognize the strangeness of this method regarding the human being and what constitutes the human being's *being*.

It has been said that the one part which in the human being belongs to nature, let us say the human being's *soma*, can be investigated by natural science. The numerous and quite efficient treatment methods of today's medicine have resulted from such investigations. Nevertheless, most people grant that the central characteristic of being human cannot be approached by natural science.

Of course, the human being *can* be seen as part of nature in the scientific manner. Yet, the question still remains whether something human will result—something, which relates to the human being as a human being.

The human being cannot be subdivided into parts, one that is a part of nature and the other, the more central one, that is not a part of nature. For how could two such heterogeneous things be brought together and be mutually influenced by each other? It must be the scientifically unascertainable reality, the so-called more central part, which constitutes the essence of the so-called peripheral area, such as the human being's soma. This is the case whether or not one still also looks at it scientifically. We have come to an impasse here as long as we have not yet advanced to the basic principles.

II. November 2, 1964

p. 35 The projection of nature in natural science was enacted by human beings. This makes it [a result of] human comportment. Question: What aspect of the human being appears in the projection of things moving through space and time in law-governed fashion? What character does Galileo's projection of nature have? For instance, in the case of the falling apple, Galileo's interest was neither in the apple, nor in the tree from which it fell, but only in the measurable distance of the fall. He, therefore, supposed a homogeneous space in which a point of mass moves and falls in conformity to law.

Here we must refer to what we said in the seminars of January 24 and 28, 1964, about supposition and *acceptio,* in short, about *acceptance.* What then does Galileo accept in his supposition? He accepts without question: space, motion, time, and causality.

What does it mean to say—I accept something like space? I accept that there is something like space and, even more, that I have a relationship to space and time. This *acceptio** is not arbitrary, but contains necessary relationships to space, time, and causality in which I stand. Otherwise I could not reach for a glass on the table. No one can experiment with these [a priori] assumptions. That there is space is not a proposition of physics. What kind of proposition is it? What does it indicate about the human being that such suppositions are possible for him? It indicates that he finds himself comported to space, time, and causality from the beginning. We stand before phenomena, which require us to become aware of them and to receive-perceive them in an appropriate manner.

---

*Acceptance approximates that which contemporary philosophy of science calls a "paradigm." See T. S. Kuhn, *The Structure of Scientific Revolutions* (Chicago: University of Chicago Press, 1962).—TRANSLATORS

It is no longer up to the physicist, but only to the philosopher to say something about what is accepted in this way. These assumptions are out of reach for the natural sciences, but at the same time they are the very foundation for the very possibility of the natural sciences themselves.

To what extent and in what way can something be said about that which immediately shows itself?* The word "immediate" is itself in question. What do we mean by "immediate"? The table, the things, what is in space, and what occurs in time. These things are also what is closest to us. And space, if we want to confine ourselves in it? I certainly cannot see something spatial without space. Space is prior to all things, and yet it is not conceived as such.

p. 36

Here we must recall the distinction already made by Aristotle. He distinguished προτερον προς ημας [prior in knowledge] from προτερον τη φυσει [prior in nature]. In our example, this means the table in space is closest *to our perception*. However, space is closest to the table's being. Space has a priority *in nature*. It is what makes it possible for the glass to be extended in the first instance. The closest in nature [space] is the closest in the proper sense. But the closest *in the proper sense* is the most difficult for our perception. Therefore, there are two kinds of being closest—two kinds in relation to which they are closest to, namely: (a) in relation to the nature of space, and (b) in relation to our perception of it.

And how about time? I see from the clock that it is eleven o'clock. Where is time here? Is it in the clock? It is said that one experiences time through the movement of the hands of the clock. But what happens when the clock stops? Even when the clock has stopped, time does not disappear at all. I am just unable to tell what time it is.

III. November 5, 1964

No conclusions should be drawn here, but each proposition we come up when doing this kind of thinking must be pointed out and rethought. We often succeed and we often fail. Indeed, sometimes one *understands* one's subject matter, but in a darker moment, one no longer *sees* it.

---

*To see how Heidegger departed from Husserl's phenomenology of "consciousness" (intuition of essences) and how he developed his own existential understanding via the analytic of Da-sein and its temporality, see *Being and Time*, p. 187; *History of the Concept of Time*, trans. Th. Kisiel (Bloomington: Indiana University Press, 1985), pp. 90–131; and *Basic Problems of Phenomenology*, pp. 1–23. See ZS 152, 156, 157.—TRANSLATORS

At the beginning of our last seminar our question was: What does "nature" mean to modern natural science? We called upon Kant for its determination. He gave us the definition: Nature is the conformity to the law of phenomena. This is a strange proposition. Why have we bothered to ask about "nature" in the natural sciences at all? Because natural science does not expressly think about this determination of nature. Galileo developed this projection of nature for the first time. In doing so, did he simply make a "presupposition" [*Voraussetzung*]? What kind of presupposition would it be? It is a supposition [*Unterstellung*]. What is the difference between a presupposition made to reach logical conclusions and a supposition? The difference is that we can derive something else from logical presuppositions through inferences—that a logical relationship exists between presupposition and conclusion. In contrast, in a supposition, the scientific approach to a specific domain is grounded in what is supposed. Here we are not dealing with a *logical* relationship, but with an *ontological* relationship.

p. 37

To what does modern natural science make its supposition? As a natural scientific observer, Galileo disregarded the tree, the apple, and the ground in observing the fall of the apple. He saw only a point of mass falling from one location in space to another location in space in law-governed fashion. In the sense of natural science, "nature" is the supposition for the tree, the apple, and the meadow. According to this supposition, nature is understood only as the law-governed movement of points of mass, that is, as changes in location within a homogeneous space and within the sequence of a homogeneous time. This is natural science's *supposition*.

In this supposition, that is, in this assumption of "nature" determined accordingly, there lies simultaneously an *acceptio*. In such a supposition, the existence of space, motion, causality, and time is always already accepted as an unquestionable fact. Here accepting and taking mean immediate *receiving-perceiving*. What is accepted in natural science's supposition is a homogeneous space. [It is] a space where, among other things, a cup can be found. The cup itself is something extended, and therefore, is something spatial. If I lift the cup and take a sip from it, where is the space in which it exists and in which it is moved? It is not perceived thematically. In this situation, the cup is the closest to us. It is προτερον προς ημας [prior in knowledge]. The space is προτερον τη φυσει [prior in nature]. Space is not the closest or the immediately given fact to our perception, but it is the closest according to the nature of things, that is, regarding the cup's potentiality-to-be [*Seinkönnen*]. Newton's law of inertia states: Every body continues in its state of rest or in uniform motion in a straight line,

p. 38

unless it is compelled to change that state by force impressed upon it.*

Consequently, this law begins with: *every* body. Has anyone ever been able to observe *every* body in each instance? Certainly not. Nevertheless, this proposition is pronounced as valid for every natural phenomenon. Therefore, in this case it is really a supposition, an assumption. The law of motion determines the state of a natural body. Therefore, according to Kant nature is the conformity to law of phenomena in their motions, and these motions are changes of a continuously underlying stratum. This should be only a brief indication of all that is supposed here in such a law.

Aristotle described this fundamental subject matter of the double aspects regarding the closest at hand in his *Physics*. The summation of the final section under consideration reads: At first children address all men as father and all women as mother. Only later do they learn to distinguish between man and father, and between woman and mother (see *Physics* I.1.184b12 ff.).

To the child, a man is his father. He does not yet have an idea of the specific nature that makes a man a father and a woman a mother. That comes later. To what extent does the relationship between father and man illustrate the relationship between cup and space?

In the man-father relationship, man is the generic determination of father, for every father is a man, but not vice-versa. Space is not the [generic] concept for the cup. Space is not a concept. A more fundamental relationship exists between space and the cup. We already encountered such a relationship in Kant when he said: Being is not a real predicate; it is merely position. This means: existence is not the [generic] universal with regard to the table. p. 39

When you say that the cup exists, then you are related to the cup, which is present. What about the cup's existence? Nevertheless, this existence is not a property of the cup. Presence [as existence] cannot be discovered in the cup. Existence must be even closer to the nature [of the cup] than space.

Here the *ontological difference*† comes into view, that is, the difference between being and beings. The first [being] is accessible in a different way than beings.

When you consider that space is always already given to us implicitly in

---

*M. Heidegger, "Modern Science, Metaphysics, and Mathematics," in *Basic Writings*, pp. 247–82.—TRANSLATORS

†See T. Kisiel, *The Genesis of Heidegger's* Being and Time (Berkeley and Los Angeles: University of California Press, 1995), pp. 365 f., 372 f., 503, concerning the origin of the concept of "ontological difference."—TRANSLATORS

each experience, then what really is space? If we want to receive-perceive space, then how must we comport ourselves regarding the cup? We let it become nonthematic, and we make space our theme. Thereby, does this mean that we make an abstraction? Not at all. Certainly, we have already emphasized that space is in no way the universal with regard to the cup, as, for example, the concept "tree" regarding an actual birch. We merely make something thematic that was concomitantly given [*mit-gegeben*] as unthematic and necessary. What happens to the cup when we look away from it and turn toward space as the theme? The process of thematization is reversed. Nevertheless, if I make space the theme, I cannot leave the cup out of consideration. Space as a theme is where the cup exists. Therefore, if I were to leave the cup out of consideration completely, I would not be able to apprehend [*erfassen*] the character of space as that where the cup exists. I must merely let the cup become nonthematic.

In book 4 of Aristotle's *Physics,* the determination of space is explicitly formulated and made authoritative for the first time in all of Western thought. Aristotle's original determination is τοπος—"place" (the Greeks did not have a special word for "space"). A body's place is determined by what it delimits as extended. Yet for the Greeks, limit is not where something discontinues, not something negative; rather, limit is where something starts from, where it is determined in its form. Limit—περας— is a positive determination for the Greeks. The other [reality] granting space to an extended corporeal thing, the Greeks called χωρα: space can contain a limited thing such as this [the cup]. Space has the character of containing. It grants a thing its place. Space embraces what is delimited by the corporeal thing, granted by space itself.

p. 40

For the Greeks, all bodies had their proper place according to their specific nature. Heavy bodies are below. Light bodies are above. Various places in space are distinguished qualitatively as above and below, and so forth. Galileo eliminates all these distinctive positions in space. For him there is no longer an above and a below.

When we observe the cup, we receive-perceive that space, spaceness [*Raumhaftes*] surrounds the cup and grants it place, but we *never* perceive what space itself is. In Western thought up to the present, space has only been seen in relation to bodies and objects, but never in relation to space as space for itself and as such.

At the end of our last seminar, we spoke about time. I look at the clock and see that it is 9:25 in the evening. Tomorrow, when Dr. Boss comes and sees the slip of paper where I wrote the current time, he will find out that in the meantime this written assertion has become false.

When we looked at the clock, we asked: Where is time? Can "where" even be asked at all? "Where" can only be asked in relation to something in space. Therefore, it is a confusing question. Then how can we ask about time appropriately? We ask: When? Can I ask: When is time? This does not work either. I would be asking about a time in which time is. "When is time?" is as incorrect as is the question: "Where is space?" How should one ask what time is? If I ask about clock time, I am asking how many hours, p. 41 minutes, and so forth. I am asking how many as well as the measurement. For any measurement of time, time must already be pregiven. Now we ask: As what is time pregiven while one is looking at the clock?

To repeat: We ascertain that it is now 9:37 according to the clock. Am I speaking about time now? What are you doing when you read the clock? Basically, you are saying: It is 9:37 *now.* Whenever you look at the clock, you say "*now,*" whether out loud or not. I am writing on the slip of paper: It is 9:37 *now.* When Dr. Boss reads this tomorrow, the slip of paper will not be correct. Dr. Boss will have to say: It was 9:37 at *that time.*

IV. November 5, 1964

During the break, some of you seemed to be quite surprised that we insisted so much on certain words. It would be a big mistake to see this as a personal whim of ours. A specific word says just what it says and only what it says: This is the mystery of language. It is the reason one cannot simply talk around the issue and use so-called synonyms arbitrarily for the same matters [*Sachen*].

Let us return to the proposition: It is 9:37 *now.* Tomorrow morning we must correct the false sentence as follows: It was 9:37 *at that time.* Has this indication of time definitely passed now? No. It returns again. When does it return again? Namely, *then,* when it becomes evening once again.

I could not read the clock without saying: It is such and such a time *now,* whether I articulate the "now" or leave it unsaid. That this "now" usually remains unsaid shows that the "now," of course, is pregiven. Is it always only "now" when you read the clock? No, even if I do not look at the clock, but look out the window, for instance, it is "now." Therefore, is it always "now"? Is there always another "now"? Why is the "now"? Is p. 42 there another "now" in each case? It is earlier or later. If an earlier "now" were again to become "now," just as the present "now" is a "now," then time would be running backward. Time doesn't do that. How does time go then? Time *passes away* [*ver-geht*]. Remarkable; time passes and stands [still] at the same time. We also talk about the flow of time.

How do "at that time" and "then" relate to now? Time always passes away between "at that time" and "now" and between "now" and "then."

I determine every "now" as *related to something*. Suppose I fall asleep, still saying "now," and wake up later, again saying "now." How do I recognize the other "now" in waking up from the "now" of falling asleep? When I fall asleep, I say "now." I say "now" it is evening, and when I wake up, I say "now" it is morning. Evening and morning are related to the sun's orbit, which generally measures time. It is an initial rough measurement compared to the reading of the clock. How do these hours of the day relate to time? A day is a delimited, specific time. How is the specific time of a day related to time in general? Is this analogous to the relationship between the space of a room and the space of the whole house? Each demarcated space is within a larger space in the same way that a definite span of time is within time. How are they within?

Particular small spaces limit only the particular larger space. The particular forms of space, the space in a room and the space in a glass, for instance, limit the larger space of the house. The particular parts of the house, as such, are simultaneously limitations of the whole space. In contrast, the parts of time are not simultaneous, but are necessarily *one after another*. What is in space is beside, above, or behind something, but periods of time are always *one after another*. Time is one-dimensional. In physics, this one-dimensionality is posited as the fourth dimension to the three dimensions of space as . . . that is, as a line whose direction is counted. All "now's" are one after another. Obviously, we still have to look at "now" more precisely. How far is the distance from "now" to "at that time" and to "then"? "Just now" [*soeben*] is next to "at that time" and to "now"; and "at once" [*sogleich*] is next to "then." Each "now" we say is simultaneously also "just now" and "at once," that is, the time we have addressed with the word "now" has a *span*. In itself every "now" is still also a "just now" and an "at once."

p. 43

At the moment we start to count time, we no longer pay any attention to the "just now" and to the "at once," but we only pay attention to the sequence of "now's." Counting time is a specific comportment to time in which the characteristics of being spanned toward "just now" and toward "at once" are no longer noticed. Nevertheless, these characteristics are still present in a certain way. "Just now" becomes the past, the "before," and finally the "no longer." "At once" becomes "after" and finally "not yet."

Aristotle's definition of time already reads: "For time is just this— number of motion in regard to 'before' and 'after' " (*Physics* IV.11.219b1).

This determination of time by means of a moved thing has become standard for the whole West as the determination of space by means of a [moving] body. Thus, time too is always determined only by what moves within it but is not [determined] as time as such.*

Is there time at all? Therefore, if we ask whether time exists, what is the time we are now considering? According to the common understanding of being, it means "presence" [*Anwesenheit*]. What characteristic of time corresponds to the understanding of being as presence? Present means the same thing as being present. Present in time is always only "now." The "just now" is no more, and the "at once" is not yet, in the sense of the present now. Yet, the past and the future have "being" and are not "nothing." If I limit being and existence only to presence as the present time, then the past and the future are only "nothing." Now the question is, if I am tumbling about in nothing with the concept of "is," can I comprehend [*fassen*] the being of time at all according to the common understanding of being as presence? For insofar as the "just now" [*soeben*] and the "at once" [*sogleich*] belong to time, to every "now," I do not apprehend the being of time with this concept of being. Whether and how time is—this is the crucial question. What relationship could there be between being and time?

p. 44

We have said that "now" has the characteristic of making present [*Gegenwärtigen*]. The "just now" has passed, and the "at once" is that which will come. Both the "just now" and the "at once" are two different modes of not-being, that is, a no-longer-being and a not-yet-being, respectively.

Therefore, the concept of being, in the sense of presence regarding time, is insufficient because presence in terms of time is determined as "now." Therefore, the question arises: If being is determined as presence, why not the reverse? Does it receive its determination from time, and is it granted by time? For the next step, space must no longer be determined by the bodies in it, and time no longer be determined by the things moved in it. Instead, the task is to think space as space and time as time.

What counts in all this kind of thinking is that one does not simply pay attention to and to memorize spoken sentences, but that an attempt is made to receive-perceive directly what is [being] said by them. Receiving-perceiving means much more than merely sensory, optical seeing. We receive-perceive exactly what is essential here without seeing it in a sensory fashion with the eyes.

---

*Compare Aristotle's concept of "time" to *Being and Time,* p. 473 ff., and to *Basic Problems of Phenomenology,* p. 232 ff.—TRANSLATORS

January 18 and 21, 1965, at Boss's Home

I. January 18, 1965

We still continue to ask: What is time? This has been asked for two-and-a-half thousand years, and still there is no adequate answer. It is important for contemporary thought to recall tradition and not to fall prey to the notion that one can begin without history. It is unfortunate that today the immediate experience of history is disappearing. Only in dialogue with tradition can questions be clarified and arbitrariness stopped.

There are two authorities who will clarify how the question about time has been asked. Simplicius, a Neoplatonist who lived in Athens circa A.D. 500, wrote an extended commentary on Aristotle's *Physics*. Simplicius is important because many writings of the Pre-Socratics—those of Heraclitus, Parmenides, and Anaximander—were passed down in his text. Simplicius wrote: That time always already holds sway [*waltet*] in advance is not only evident to the wise alone, that is, to thinkers, but to everyone beforehand. If someone were asked what time is itself, even the wisest of men could hardly answer.[1]

On the other hand, in book 11, chapter 14 of his *Confessions*, Augustine wrote: "What then is time? I know what it is if no one asks me what it is; but if I want to explain it to someone who asked me, I find that I do not know."[2] What could Augustine have meant by this sentence? Where does the difficulty lie with the whole question of time? It looks as if time were something ineffable. Nevertheless, in the same book of Augustine we also find the passage: "My soul is on fire to solve this most complicated enigma" (*Confessions* II.22).

We will not reflect further upon these two texts, but in retrospect so much becomes evident from reflecting on tradition that it is not only difficult to find the answer to the question of time, but it is even more difficult to explicate the *question* of time. There is need for explicit reflection upon how one can, and how one may, ask the question about time.

If I am looking for the right way to pose a question about time, then how must I ask it? If I want to ask it in a proper way, I must already be familiar with the subject matter. Therefore, I always already know the subject matter I am asking about. But, if I already know the subject matter, then surely I do not have to ask about it any longer. Does this mean that an appropriate formulation of the question cannot be developed at all?

The whole relationship between question and answer inevitably and continuously moves in a circle, only this is not a *circulus vitiosus*—not a circle that ought to be avoided as supposedly fallacious. Rather, this circle belongs to the nature of all questioning and answering.* It is quite possible that I have some knowledge of what I am asking about, but this does not mean that I already know explicitly what I am asking about, that is, in the sense [that I] have made a thematic apprehension and determination.

Thus, time is already known to us in some way, that is, we have a relationship to time beforehand without expressly paying attention to it as such or to the relationship to it as such. In view of this matter, we begin with a relationship that is most familiar and realizable [*vollziehbar*] at any time, namely, the relationship to time as mediated for us by the clock.

In the previous seminar we already touched on this question, but we have not yet developed it sufficiently. We have only given a preview of it. Its protocol is very good but is misleading just because of this. It could give the impression that the subject matter has already been dealt with sufficiently and that we should move on. We are not going on, but rather we are going back. You will see then how crudely we have spoken about time up to now.

It is important to attend to the fact that the belonging-together of the human being and time, of "soul" and time, or of mind and time is repeatedly mentioned in all discourse on time. For example, Aristotle has said: "It is also worth considering how time can be related to the soul."[3] If the soul were not capable of receiving-perceiving time, of counting (in the broadest meaning of "to say something about it"), then it would be impossible for there to be time if there were no soul.[4] In short, this means: If there were no soul, there would be no time. *Soul* is to be understood here as the distinctive and enduring being (entelechy) of the human being's unfolding essence [*Menschenwesen*], and not, let us say, in the modern sense as an ego-subject and an ego-consciousness. On the contrary, for Greek thought, the human being's distinctive character is receiving-perceiving and saying. Its main feature is always unconcealing [*entbergen*] something, which must not be represented as an event "immanent in the subject." In Augustine we read: "It is in you, my mind [anim*us*, not *anima*], that I measure time" (*Confessions* XI.27).

Meanwhile, we can gather from both authorities that the relationship to time consists in counting and measuring, that is, in a *reckoning with* [*rechnen mit*] time. This matter of the belonging together of time and the human being's unfolding essence is expressed in modern thought in the way and the manner in which the problem of time is approached, that is, with the expressions: *sense of time, experience of time, and consciousness of time.*

p. 47

p. 48

---

*See Heidegger, *Being and Time*, p. 194 f.—TRANSLATORS

For instance, in 1889 Bergson published *Essai sur les données immédiates de la conscience,* in which he dealt with such a datum of consciousness: time. In 1928 Husserl published *On the Phenomenology of the Internal-Time Consciousness.* In modern psychiatry one speaks of "a sense of time." What does this mean? There seems to be an analogy to all the senses of perception: The sense of seeing, hearing, tasting, and touching.* If this were the case, then [the sense of] time would be an organ, for example, as is hearing for the sense of hearing. What we really mean is that we have a sense of time. This talk about a sense of time is only a confusing expression for the human being's relationship to time. In the phrase "sense of time," time is not a subject, grammatically speaking, like hearing. Rather, it is an object, the reason for which we have a sense. In using the phrase "sense of time," we are expressing the experience that time concerns us in a special "sense."

With this theoretical attribution of time to a *sense of time,* to a *consciousness of time,* and to an *experience of time,* a great deal has already been uncritically prejudged, regarding how time and the human being's unfolding essence† belong together. We must come back to it later. For the time being, we will disregard this problem, and we will pay attention only to the fact that there is obviously something necessary about the belonging together of time and of the human being's unfolding essence. Yet for now, everything about it is still in the dark, including the nature of the human being, as well as the existence of time, and, above all, the belonging together of the human being and time. In terms of priority, this belonging together is the first and not, as it might appear, the third element which results from putting the human being and time together.

In order to open a viable path into the realm of these difficult questions, we adhere to the previously mentioned relationship to time, that is, to time mediated for us by the clock. First of all, regarding that relationship to time, let us make a parenthetical, methodological remark: We would do well to disregard entirely and immediately what we believe we already know about time. We must also disregard the manner and the way in which we are accustomed to treat the theme of "time," for example, the distinctions between subjective and objective time, between cosmic and personal time, between measured and lived time, and between quantitative and qualitative time. We will eliminate all these distinctions, not because we maintain that they are totally false

p. 49

---

*Heidegger omits the olfactory sense.—TRANSLATORS

†"Essence" must be understood in the ecstatic, temporal sense of abidingly coming-to-presence, i.e., unfolding essence.—TRANSLATORS

or unfounded, but because they remain questionable. For instance, if we speak of "objective time," we are holding onto a representation of objectivity about which the question remains whether such objectivity can be determined only after reflecting sufficiently on time. The same holds true for subjective time.

You certainly do not expect us to solve the puzzle of time. Much would already be gained if we could bring ourselves to face the puzzle of time. Now, reflecting upon the clock, we begin the inquiry about time[*] and its relationship to the human being's unfolding essence. We tell time from the clock. We are turned toward time by using the clock. The clock, therefore, is a utensil. As such, it is accessible, present-at-hand, ready-to-hand, and always available. It is around us continuously, an ever-abiding [verweilend] and enduring utensil that has a remarkable characteristic. It runs. Remarkable: An abiding, present-at-hand thing that runs, and in running, completes a regularly recurring motion, that is, a periodic motion. The periodic character of the clock's motion derives from the fact that it relates to the course of the sun. Yet the clock's relationship to the sun can vary. Accordingly, there are different kinds of clocks. The question is whether each clock has to relate to the sun. How is it with the sundial? There the shadow moves regularly, periodically, if not in a circle, then like a pendulum, to and fro. What character does this running of the clock have? With this question, we remain in the area of our contemporary use of clocks (watch, wristwatch). The hand of the clock moves and slides over certain numerals. Suppose we go to the jungle and show a watch to a tribesman who has never seen one. Because it moves, he will think the thing is alive. The thing is not a watch for him, and so it is not an indicator of time. Of course, this does not mean that the relationship to time is foreign to this human being. Presumably, he lives in a more original relationship to time than we modern Europeans, who recommend our strange products to him. A watch [or clock] is out of the question for him.

p. 50

When does this technical thing, which we conversationally call a "machine," become a "clock"? When "the clock" is set so that it runs synchronically with other clocks or in conformity to a radio signal? The radio announcer speaks very precisely, but not entirely precisely. Why not? He says: "At the tone, it will be exactly such and such a time." When he says this, the tone does not yet exist at all. It is still coming. When he says, "at the tone," we must ask: From what kind of relationship to

---

[*]See Heidegger, *Being and Time,* p. 370 ff., 456–80, and *Basic Problems of Phenomenology,* p. 229 ff.—TRANSLATORS

the tone is the radio announcer speaking and is the hearer listening? This happens by *waiting for* the sixth tone. Strictly speaking, the radio announcer should say: "At the sixth tone, it will be such and such a time." At first, this correction seems like an entirely harmless piece of hairsplitting. Nevertheless, it is very important.

If we set the clock by the sixth tone, then it is ready to use, but not before. Of course, our clock is running, but it is not running accurately. How does this happen, if we tell or ascertain the time by the clock? In doing so, we say: "Now it is exactly nine o'clock." I say "now." From where do I get this "now"? The "now" as such does not have the slightest thing in common with the clock as a thing. The "now" is not a thing. Nevertheless, there is no telling time by the clock without saying "now," whether or not it is said out loud, or whether or not we pay attention to what is said. There is always a "now" for us [even] without a clock. For example, I say: "Dr. H. is smoking now." Is the "now" merely a supplement, if I look at the clock? Can we tell time by the clock without saying "now"? Indicating the place where the hand of the clock rests at the moment is in itself not yet a telling of time [*ablesen*]. What kind of relationship exists between determining the position of the hand and saying "now"? Saying "now" provides the foundation for indicating the hand's position on a point of time. In saying "now," we are speaking about the matter that time is somehow already given to us in advance. Nevertheless, this speaking about time does not only happen in saying "now." Even when I say: "It was such and such a time just now," I am speaking of time. To what direction am I referring with the words "just now"? I am speaking back into the past. If I say, "In twenty minutes, it will be half past nine," I am speaking about something that is coming. I am speaking ahead into the future. We say this as if it were self-evident. By using a clock, we not only say "now," but we also say "just now" and "at once" (immediately) in accordance with the different "directions" of time. Don't we say "now" when we state, "In five minutes (immediately) it will be 8:10" (i.e., "now" in five minutes)? Doesn't "now" seem to have special *priority* in the telling of time?

Besides the clock-timed and numerically determined *now, at that time,* and *then,* I can also say *today, yesterday,* and *tomorrow.* "Now" and "today" have to do with making present. The "just now" and the "at that time" have to do with letting-go into the past and with the retaining of what has been. The "at once" and the "then" have to do with a letting-arrive, with an expecting. Thus, there are three distinctive modes for how I speak of time and for how I designate time. Here the question asserts itself: Do we also already relate to time itself by how we determine time from the clock and by how we comport ourselves to time? Is time also already given *as* time in our ways of ascertaining time? Thereby, what characteristic of

p. 51

time is being addressed? Now, just now, at once, today, yesterday, and p. 52
tomorrow are determinations of time. Thereby, in what respect is time
[being] determined? It is not a determination of time as time. What is
given is not time as such. Rather, the only thing indicated is *how much*
time the clock shows. In using the clock, we measure time. Thereby, we
never measure what time itself is, nor do we determine it as time itself.
Such talk about the *determination of time* is ambiguous. To ascertain time
by using clocks always means to ascertain how much time there is—to
ascertain what time it is. By looking at the clock, I am certainly dealing
with time, but always in terms of how *much* time.

How does ascertaining "how much" time by using the clock relate to
the indication of time when I say "today," "tomorrow," and "yesterday"?
By "today," "yesterday," and "tomorrow" I mean the sequence of days,
the times of which *can* but which *do not have to be* determined more
specifically by indicating the number of hours with the aid of the clock.
Saying "today," "yesterday," and "tomorrow" is, therefore, a more original
comportment toward time than ascertaining "how much" time by the
clock. Ascertaining time by the clock is merely a calculative determination
of the particular today, yesterday, or tomorrow. We can always use a clock
because there is a today, a tomorrow, and a yesterday for us in advance,
but even these remain indications of time, which cannot give us time itself
as such any better than can the indications of clock time.

In ascertaining the time by the clock, as in any indication of time
generally, we talk about time, but we do not yet catch a glimpse of
time itself. If we want to know what time itself is, the relationship to time
expressed in the different indications of time cannot give us any further
help. Rather, we must ask: From where do I take the "now," the "just now,"
and the "at once"? This question, as well as its eventual answer, are only
possible because we already have time. More specifically, they are possible
because time is already holding sway over us from the present, the past,
and the future. For I can only take something if it can be given to me, and
that which can be given is that which is always already *holding sway* [*walten*]. p. 53
The term "holding sway" should only provisionally and cautiously point
to the fact that we are confronted and affected by time everywhere and
always. Regarding the relationship to time, we should, on one hand, first
see the difference between the *indication* [*Zeit-Angabe*] of time by the
clock, as well as the *indication* of today, yesterday, and tomorrow without
the clock, and on the other hand, the givenness of time [*Zeit-Gabe*]. There
is no indication of time without a prior *givenness* of time. Nevertheless,
a question still remains whether time in our everyday comportment, be
it scientific, prescientific-practical, nonscientific-artistic or religious, can
be given to us at all, other than by some sort of indication of time.

Addendum. The acceptance of the *givenness* of time, which underlies all our indications of time, that is, catching a glimpse of this phenomenon and of time as such thereby given, obviously requires a way of thinking which is fundamentally different from our everyday relationship to time. Nevertheless, this means that this different relationship to time must start with a prior elucidation of our everyday relationship to time. Indeed, from the start, everything depends on this elucidation. We say "depends" and not "depended" because everything we have said up to now is still not sufficient for this necessary elucidation.

II. January 18, 1965

In all quantitative determinations of time, which are carried out with the aid of reading a clock, it is always only "how much" time is given to us. Yet, this measuring of time is possible only if something like time is already given to us, when we already have the time. Measuring time
p. 54 already presupposes "to have *the* time." What "to have *the* time" means is still in the dark. In our daily relationships to time, we do not pay attention to it, let alone reflect on it explicitly. However, a relationship to time is familiar to us when we use the expression "to have time." What do I mean by "time" when I say "I have time," or "I do not have any time"? It is best to start with the assertion "I do not have any time." Here it is very obvious that in these expressions time is always already understood as "time *for* something."

How is this characteristic, which I designate by "for," to be understood as characteristic of time? Is this "for" added to time, or with "for" do I designate precisely what is essential to time?

Even when I say "tomorrow," I do not say this "tomorrow" simply as an empty "tomorrow," but always as a "tomorrow" in which I will do something "tomorrow" or in which something will happen. Even if the *what-for* is still undetermined. This reference belongs to time . . . or is a pointing to an action or happening, a pointing toward something. Therefore, we call this characteristic of time, that is to say, that it is always time for something, the characteristic of [temporal] *significance* [*Deutsamkeit*].*

---

* "Significance" [*Deutsamkeit*] should be understood in the sense of temporal significance, i.e., appropriate or inappropriate time, a concept which was overlooked by Aristotle and by the whole subsequent tradition. As a characteristic of the human being's

This characteristic of significance is essential to time itself. Therefore, this "for" of time has nothing to do with "intentionality" in the sense of an ego-subject's act, or a human comportment toward something, or even a human directedness toward something, which adds something to time whereby it is subsequently related to something else. Significance belongs to time itself and not to a subject's "I intend something."

Another characteristic of time must be distinguished from this characteristic of "time for," that is, the significance of what we perceive as "having time for." We receive-perceive this other characteristic of time when we say: "Now, *while* we are talking to each other," or "at that time, *when* Kennedy was assassinated," or "then, *when* Mardi Gras will take place." We call this second characteristic the datability [*Datiertheit*] of time. This does not mean simply a date in the sense of a calendar date. Here, we are dealing with a more original dating upon which calendar dating was originally based. Under certain circumstances, the datability of time can be entirely indeterminate; nevertheless, the datability of time belongs necessarily to time.

p. 55

By the way, in Greek discourse on time it was also always tacitly understood as "time for." . . . Yet in all subsequent theories of time it remained concealed because of the Aristotelian doctrine of time as a sequence of successive nows.[*]

Here the question arises regarding the relationship in priority between time, which can be ascertained by calculation, and time with the two characteristics we just received-perceived. The question is whether clock time is first in priority such that the other datable and significant time is derivative; or whether the relationship is reversed, given the supposition that we are dealing generally with two different "times." We are not

---

temporal-ecstatic existence, it must be distinguished from existential [*Bedeutsamkeit*] or statistical significance [*Bedeutung*]. See *Basic Problems of Phenomenology*, pp. 261–64.—TRANSLATORS

[*]Before Aristotle defined time technically as a sequence of now points, the customary Greek term for time was χϛόνος which implied a particular time, season, or period. The interrelated Greek term καιϛός emphatically meant the right time for action, the right season, the critical moment. Although Heidegger's use of Καιρός as the singular and authentic moment [*Augenblick*] (*Being and Time*, p. 387) was derived primarily from his study of early Christian writing and from Kierkegaard, he also occasionally quoted Aristotle's use of the word in the *Nichomachean Ethics:* "For the end of action varies according to the καιϛός" (3.1.1100a14). See Heidegger, *Basic Problems of Phenomenology*, pp. 229–324; Kisiel, *Genesis of Heidegger's* Being and Time, pp. 185, 224, 229, 253, 441, 529, 540 f.—TRANSLATORS

sufficiently prepared to ask and to answer this question of priority in a satisfactory way.

In any case, much can be presumed already. For instance, the disturbed relationship to time accompanying some forms of mental illness can only be understood from the human background of original, significant, and datable time. This relationship cannot be understood in terms of calculated time, which originates with the idea of a sequence of empty, "qualityless" points.

Now that we have elucidated some of the characteristics of "having time," the question can be asked on what ground is the human being's "having time" possible. Dr. B. asked: "Can we just 'have time' because we as humans are in time?" In other words: Is our *being*-in-time then what grounds our "*having* time"? What does it mean to be "in time"? This "being-in-time" is very familiar to us from the way it is represented in natural science. In natural science all processes of nature are calculated as processes which happen "in time." Everyday common sense also finds processes and things enduring "in time," persisting and disappearing "in time." When we talk about "being-in-time," everything depends on the interpretation of this "in." In order to see this more clearly, we ask simply if the glass on the table in front of me is *in* time or not.

p. 56

In any case, the glass is *already* present-at-hand and remains there even when I do not look at it. How long it has been there and how long it will remain are of no importance. If it is already present-at-hand and remains so in the future, then that means that it *continues* through a certain time and thus is "in" it. Any kind of continuation obviously has to do with time. Question: By referring to continuation, have we sufficiently determined already the glass's "being-in-time"? This question leads to another question of no less importance: Is the "being-in-time" of the glass the same as the "being-in-time" of an ek-sisting human being?

III. January 21, 1965

It remains entirely unclear how the time we have seen up to now, that is, the time measured by the clock, and the time already given to us (and its characteristics) mutually belong together. Most of all, we are far from being able to answer the question as to what time is. Whether the question "What is time?" is appropriate must remain open regarding time and whether we *thus* can and may ask about the specific characteristic of time. For the question concerning "what something is" implies that we always want to determine what is interrogated [*befragt*]* *as something,* that is, as something other than itself. For instance, when we ask "what is a table," we cannot simply answer "it is a table." Rather, we say it is something useful. As such, it is generally a thing, [for instance] the thing here, the table, is a being. Like the question about the table, if we ask what time is, we are asking about time insofar as it is such and such. Nevertheless, we must face the possibility that we must not ask the question in this manner. If we have already put it in these terms, the answer to this question must ultimately read: Time is time. Still we are not close to understanding what this tautology legitimately means. Not only is the question "what is time" undecided, but so is the question whether time generally *is.* Insofar as it is not *nothing,* but also not something, the question arises how it should be determined regarding its supposed *being.* We have talked provisionally about time as holding sway over us. Sometimes one speaks of the power of time. This may be mentioned beforehand in order to be prepared for the fact that we advance slowly and that we need continued patience and care to bring anew the phenomena into view. Above all, this means to maintain the direction of seeing [*Blickrichtung*] in a way that is adequate to the phenomena.

p. 57

Finally, two questions have been raised.

a. First, there is the question of priority regarding clock time and the time already given to us. Is clock time, which we characterized a sequence of nows, the more original time, or is it a modification, a derivative of the time already given and about which we learned some characteristics?

b. The other question about being-in-time contains, first of all, a special difficulty in that "in" implies the presupposition of time as something like a container, something spatial. Bergson, for instance, says that the time we count with is a spatialized time, time represented in terms of space. We have yet to see to what extent this is an error.

Presumably, these two questions about priority and "being-in-time" belong together.

The question regarding the difference in priority refers, on one hand, to the relationship between clock time, and on the other hand, to the time already given to us. In referring to the time already given to us, we say: "We have time." We directed our attention to the strange fact that it becomes

p. 58

---

*Concerning the difference between what is asked about [*Gefragtes*], what is interrogated [*Befragtes*], and what is to be found out by the asking [*Erfragtes*], see Heidegger, *Being and Time,* p. 24.—TRANSLATORS

very clear what "having time" means precisely when we reflect upon what we mean by the phrase "having no time." I have no time now or tomorrow morning. What character does the grammatical form of this statement have: I have no time now? It is a negation. Thereby, does one deny time? Has time disappeared? Not at all. It is a negation, of course, but only a negation of having time *for something determinate.* It is, therefore, not a negation in the sense of a denial of time *pure and simple.* I can say: "I don't have time to ski because I have to write an essay." Thus, in "having no time" the character of having time for . . . is especially striking. Since all having time is having time for something, we say: Time is [temporally] significant [*deutsam*] (i.e., not "signifying" [*be-deuten*], because "to signify" can easily suggest something such as a symbolization [by a subject]). The time meant at any given time points as such to a what-for [*Wofür*].

"I have no time" is, therefore, a negation and yet not a negation. I lack time for skiing. Indeed, I have time, but I don't have it "to spare for. . . ." Time for that activity is not at my disposal. In a sense, it is taken from me. If we negate something in the sense that we do not simply deny it, but rather affirm it in the sense that something is lacking, such negation is called a *privation.**

It is a remarkable fact that your whole medical profession moves within a negation in the sense of a privation. You deal with illness. The doctor asks someone who comes to him, "What is wrong with you?" The sick person is *not healthy.* This being-healthy, this being-well, this finding oneself well is not simply absent but is disturbed. Illness is not the pure negation of the psychosomatic state of health. Illness is a phenomenon of privation. Each privation implies the essential belonging to something that is lacking something, which is in need of something. This seems to be trivial, but it is extremely important, especially because your profession moves within this context.† In that you deal with illness, you are actually dealing with health in the sense that health is lacking and has to be restored. The character of this privation is generally misunderstood in science as well, as for instance, when physicists talk about material nature as dead nature. Being dead can only refer to what can die, and only what lives can die. Material nature is not a dead nature but nature without life.

p. 59

---

*See Heidegger, *Being and Time,* pp. 75, 286; *Fundamental Concepts of Metaphysics,* sec. 46; and *Basic Problems of Phenomenology,* p. 309, concerning the concept of "privation" [Greek: *steresis, stereo,* "to rob a person of something," "to deprive"].
—TRANSLATORS

†See Heidegger, "Building Dwelling Thinking," in *Basic Writings,* p. 335, concerning psychiatric depression as privation.—TRANSLATORS

Correspondingly, the state of rest is not a mere negation of motion but its privation, that is, it is a kind of motion. Otherwise, no new motion could ever originate from rest. The number 5, which cannot move, cannot also be something at rest.

It took Greek thinkers two hundred years to discover the idea of privation. Only Plato discovered this negation as privation and discussed it in his dialogue *The Sophist.* This happened in connection with the insight that not every instance of nonbeing simply means not existing but rather that there is nonbeing which, in a certain sense, *is.* The shadow is such a nonbeing in the sense of privation because it is a lack of brightness. Thus, not being healthy, being sick, is also a mode of existing in privation. The nature of being sick cannot be adequately grasped without a sufficient determination of being healthy. You will immediately see that we encounter this remarkable phenomenon of privation even more often in the context of the phenomenon of time. It is an ontological phenomenon, that is, it refers to a possibility of being and not merely to the logic of a propositional negation.

In order to lay the ground for a sufficient discussion on the question of priority, we will once again explain the essential characteristics of time already given to us. First, we said that time is first always a time for. . . . It can be characterized quite generally as time remaining for . . . , as time expendable for . . . , and as time to use for . . . taking-time-for oneself . . . takes time, not to hold on to time, but to use it for . . . something. If it is especially hard to use one's time for something, one speaks of sacrificing time. Someone else again wastes time, or we take our time. All these various phenomena of having time have not yet been sufficiently described in detail. We called this characteristic of time, that is to say, that it is always time *for* something, the *significance* of time. p. 60

Second, in addition to this characteristic of significance, time also has the characteristic of *datability.* For example, we say "now" when we speak to each other. In so doing, the "date" is used in the original sense of the word as "that which is given"; in our discussion the "now" refers to this "givenness." Third, the "now" of time already given to us is not like a point but always has a certain *temporal extendedness* [*zeitliche Weite*].* This refers to a "now," for instance, this evening when we talk with each other. We can even say that now, during this winter, such and such is happening. Then "now" has the completely extended span of a wintertime. In contrast, the

---

*Hofstadter translates this feature of the temporal "now" as "spannedness," a term which includes its primordial extendedness (Heidegger, *Basic Problems of Phenomenology,* p. 269).—TRANSLATORS

"now" is a now-point according to the common concept of time as a mere sequence of nows. One can even speak of a point in time.

Fourth, the datable, significant, and extended "now" is also never initially a "now," merely referring to me. This erroneous opinion could impose itself insofar as at any given time I am the one who says "now." In each instance that very "now" I just said is the "now" *we* say; that is, in each case, without reference to the particular I who says "now," we all jointly understand it immediately. It is a "now" that is immediately commonly accessible to all of us talking here with each other. There is no need to mediate between the individual egos through an [act of] reflection as if they said "now" separately and only subsequently agreed with each other that they were referring to the same now. Therefore, the "now" is neither something first found in the subject, nor is it an object which can be found among other objects, as for instance this table and this glass. Nevertheless, at any given time the spoken "now" is immediately received-perceived jointly by everyone present. We call this accessibility of "now" the *publicness* [*Öffentlichkeit*] of "now."

p. 61

However, these characteristics of datability, significance, extendedness, and publicness do not only belong to the "now," but also to each particular "at that time" and each "then." We are addressing something different from the "now" with the "at that time" and with the "then." We speak into the past by saying "at the time" and into the future by saying "then." However, by saying "now," we speak into the present. Without determining more specifically what "dimension" means here, we call the dimensions of time the past, the future, and the present. One usually speaks of dimensions in regard to three-dimensional space. When we think of time as a sequence of "nows" and as represented as a line, we say it is *one*-dimensional. The present, past, and future are not simultaneous, as with the dimensions of space, but always only sequential. Viewed this way, it is at first strange that we talk about three, if not four, dimensions of time, and that we say they are simultaneous and not consecutive. These dimensions obviously have nothing to do with space. All three dimensions of time are equiprimordial, for one never occurs without the other. All three are open to us equiprimordially [*gleichursprünglich*], but they are not open uniformly [*gleich-förmig*]. First, one dimension is predominant, then the other one in which we are engaged, or in which, perhaps, we are even imprisoned. In this way, each of the other two dimensions have not just disappeared at any given time but have merely been modified. The other dimensions are not subject to mere negation, but to privation.

For now, we leave aside the thoughtful attention [*Besinnung*] to the time that is usually given to us. Once again we turn to clock time. It only seems that we have dealt with it sufficiently. What about clock time?

p. 62

What kind of time is it? Is it also a time we have? We have it by means of the clock. Last time we gave the following as a rough estimate. Clock time does not give us time itself, but only the "how much" of time. What characteristic does this "how much" of time have? For instance, the indication of time. That it is ten o'clock does not exhaust its meaning by designating a number on the dial plate. If I say it is ten o'clock, we are not interested in the number 10, but rather that it is ten o'clock in the morning when such and such is happening or agreed upon [for an appointment]. At six o'clock, it is evening. Thus, routinely observed clock time is not merely concerned with differences in numbers. Even this purely numerical indication of time has a "qualitative" character. It refers to time as significant. Therefore, even regularly observed clock time is not thought of as a mere "how much," as a mere quantity of time. Even at a downhill race measured by a stopwatch where a hundredth of a second counts, the indication of time always refers at any given time to the faster pace of one competitor compared to another. This means a time that was used in regard to a record performance. The fastest skier established the record. In English "record" originally meant a recording, that is, an official entry. It was only later that the meaning of the word "record" was eventually narrowed down as the numerical notation recording performance in sports. The history of language shows everywhere a universal tendency toward a narrowing and leveling down of the meaning of words. For example, take the word "plunder." Originally it meant clothing, laundry, household utensils, dowry. Precisely, it means that which is of value. If such things are robbed, one speaks of plundering, which usually is not "plunder" in its modern [German] meaning at all, namely, the worthless stuff one takes.

Thus, the time routinely measured by a clock is essentially always a time for. . . . Such and such a time for. . . . This becomes especially clear from the word "hour." Until the fifteenth century it meant rest, a while, a break, free time. It was only from then on that its meaning increasingly was narrowed down to a time of exactly sixty minutes. Even now in the verb "to grant [a delay]," time is spoken of and understood as time for. . . . "To grant a delay" means to give an extension of time for. . . . The Latin word for hour, *hora* (Greek ὥρα), means the hours of choral prayer for the monastic life. Think of Rainer Maria Rilke's *Book of Hours* [*Stundenbuch*] and Ingeborg Bachmann's collection of poems, *The Time of Delay* [*Die gestundete Zeit*].

p. 63

Once again we state that in the daily reckoning by clock time as well the characteristic of significance is still retained. But then through a very specific use of the clock (for instance, in the use of the physical-technical measuring of a mere process, of a motion) the characteristics of time are leveled down without disappearing. Leveling down is a kind of privation. Our age of progress itself is one of privation. Where everything is uniformly accessible to everyone indiscriminately, an elimination of difference in rank is at work.

Clock time is always *datable* time. If there were no datatable time, there would be no clock time. Then the use of the clock would not be possible at all. In technical experiments or in psychological experimental research in the laboratory, when one measures only the duration of a process the respective "now" refers solely to a specific place—to the here or to the there of the moving object. Finally, even this fact is still covered up in a certain sense, and the "now" is understood only in reference to itself: "now," "just now," "at once"—only the pure sequence of "nows."

Now the question of the order of priority arises again—a question that could also be reformulated by asking: Which is the "true" time? Let us suppose that time were merely given to us as a sequence in which the aforementioned characteristics—*datability, significance, extendedness,* and *publicness*—were all leveled down to an empty "now" sequence. Affected only by time represented this way, we would become deranged. Worse still: we would not even have the possibility to become deranged. For to become "de-ranged" [*ver-rückt*], we must be able to be moved from one state into another. Because of time, we must have the possibility of being removed from the time usually given to us and of being banished into an empty passage of time. This [empty passage of time] appears as a uniform monotony without a what-for [of time].

p. 64

Then how about the question of priority? If you ask a physicist, he will tell you that the pure now-sequence is the authentic, true time. What we call datability and significance are regarded as subjective vagueness, if not sentimentalism. He says this because time measured physically can be calculated "objectively" at any time. This calculation is "objectively" binding. (Here, "objective" merely means "for anyone," and indeed only for anyone who can submit himself to the physicist's way of representing nature. For an African tribesman, such time would be absolute nonsense.) The presupposition or supposition of such an assertion by a physicist is that physics as a science is the authoritative form of knowledge and that only through the knowledge of physics can one gain a rigorous, scientific knowledge. Hidden behind [this presupposition] is a specific interpretation of science along with the science's claim that a specific form of viewing nature should be authoritative for every kind of knowledge. [The scientist has not asked] what this idea of science itself is founded upon nor what it presupposes. For instance, if we talk about time with a physicist sworn in favor of his science, there is no basis whatsoever to talk about these phenomena in an unbiased way. The physicist refuses to descend from his throne. He is unwilling, a priori, to permit us in any way to question his position. So long as this does not happen, a dialogue with him is impossible. The physicist is spellbound with the way physics represents time as a mere now-sequence. Therefore, he cannot see at all how someone, if exclusively tied to time as a mere now-sequence, might become deranged, or even how someone might become deranged at all. For people who cannot immediately and adequately understand the objectifying thought of physics, this state of affairs, the one-sided relationship to time in physics, is covered up. For example, [it is covered up] by the way the mode of thinking in physics makes it possible to construct internal combustion engines and, therefore, to produce automobiles. The man on the street sees the truth of physics only in its effect, namely, in the form of the car he is driving. Driving a car increasingly becomes a "natural" thing , and it is not seen as deranged at all, that is, not for people who are already deranged in the sense that they have moved uncritically into the technical-scientific way of thinking and view it as the only one that is valid.

p. 65

Yet here we still leave the question of priority undecided. The decision about the question of priority can be made only after first clarifying whether the time that is known to us from our daily, human, historical existence—that is, the time as it is given to us in being with and for each other—can be derived from the idea of the sequence of "nows" or, conversely, whether time as a sequence of "nows" is grounded in a leveling down of "true" time.

A cue word for what we have been talking about so far is the old [German] name for a flower, *Zitelosa* [timeless]. If one had no knowledge of *privation*, nor any correct concept of time, this would be a flower without time. The name [*Zitelosa*] refers to a flower that does not bloom at the right time. Originally, the crocus was known as a *Zitelosa* because it bloomed prematurely, not at the usual time. Later on, the autumn *Zitelosa* [meadow saffron], which blooms later than usual, was spoken of in analogy to the spring *Zitelosa*. Thus, "timeless" [*zeitlos*] means "not at the right time."

IV. January 21, 1965

p. 66

At the beginning of [this] last part of our January seminars, we present a text from an article by Franz Fischer, "Space-Time Structure and Thought Disorder in Schizophrenia" (*Zeitschrift für die gesamte Neurologie und Psychiatrie* 124 [1930], p. 247 ff.).

The author says that the text comes from a case history of a young schizophrenic who had been examined and observed in a subacute stage and whose psychosis did not show any essential peculiarities apart from time and thought disorders. The author continues with the following words:

Experience 3. Looking at the hands of a wall clock, the patient indicated the following:

What should I do with the clock? I always have to look at it. I am compelled to look at the clock. There is so much time. I am different again and again. If the clock on the wall were not there, I would have to die. Am I a clock myself? Everywhere, in all places? But I cannot do anything else. It changes too fast.

Now I am watching the clock again, the hands and the face, and I notice that it is running. It tears itself apart, as if by itself, and I am in on it, but I cannot change anything.

I tell myself over and over that it is a clock, but it does not quite fit together, the hands, the face, and that it is running. It gives a particular impression. It is as if it had disassembled itself, but it is all together. But there is still something else here too. I am very surprised. I have never experienced anything like it before. For the hands are always different. Now it is here, then it jumps away, so to speak, and turns like that. Is it a different hand every time? Maybe there is someone standing behind the wall and always slipping in a new hand, each time into another place. I must say that this clock is not running. It jumps and changes place. One is so absorbed in observing the clock that one loses the thread to himself—since I am a clock myself, through and through, since it always gets mixed up. I am all that myself. It is getting lost for me, when I look at the clock on the wall. It is running away from itself. I am on the run, and I am no longer here. I only know that the clock is jumping about with many hands and cannot quite be brought together.

Now again I am finished with the wall clock, but not of my own free will, and I have to [be] at the other place, in the other way. As I said, I am the living clock. I am a clock, through and through. It comes and goes, always on and on.

If I pull myself out again, because everything is so mixed up, then I look at the clock on the wall again. It can help me, like the tree in front of the window. Noises are not as good.

p. 67

Now, how is this text to be interpreted? First, we notice that the author introduces the patient's report with the following sentence: "Looking at the hands of a wall clock, the patient indicated the following." We must ask whether this report actually expresses the state of affairs indicated. Second, we should notice that the patient is not speaking about time or about the indication of time, but about the clock. He speaks simultaneously and alternately about the "wall clock" and the "clock." First, he speaks about the wall clock, at which he feels *compelled* to look. Second, not of his own free will, [he says] "I am finished with the wall clock again, and I have to [be] at the other place, in the other way," that is, away from looking at the wall clock and looking at and observing a fragmented, disintegrated clock, which is a no longer running, jumping "mere" clock that is no longer opposite him on the wall, but is, as it were, without a place. Here we must look for the decisive discrepancy on which everything depends. In the first case, it is a question of the patient's relationship to the wall clock. In the second case, when he is pulled the other way, it is his relationship to the "mere" clock. "Mere" means without a particular place, without familiar surroundings. The difference between the two things, the wall clock and the mere clock, corresponds to the difference in the relationship the patient has to the wall clock and to the mere clock. His relationship to the wall clock is looking at it (toward it). In this relationship "toward-over against" [*Gegeneinander-über*], the patient relates to himself by means of the familiar wall clock and, thus, is with himself. The relationship to the mere clock is an observing, a looking at, a kind of seeking after, where this looking at is absorbed, as it were, by the thing observed. The observer can find himself only in the thing he observes as such, and, therefore, he can say: I am the clock myself (not the wall clock). This means: I am like a clock myself. Therefore, he can say: I am a clock "through and through." Thereby, he does not project something psychological, something "subjective" or internal onto the clock, but he is so dazed by the object he observes that he no longer has a distance to what he observes. [There is] no over and against anymore, and he therefore "loses the thread to himself." "It is getting lost for me"—this means he is losing [his] being himself.

p. 68

In what way does looking at the wall clock "help" him? In what way does the wall clock as a thing give him a hold? In order to understand this, we must clearly distinguish his relationship to the wall clock from his relationship to the mere clock. Here the decisive point is that the wall clock, precisely because it is opposite *to him*, addresses him, so to speak, whereas the clock, toward which he is pulled, is no longer opposite to him. The mere clock does not permit any relationship to *himself*. He is so dissolved into the mere clock that he can say that he is this clock himself. Then he must again try to free himself over and against [*Gegenüber*] the wall clock. At the very moment in which he can stand over and against

a thing and remain over and against it, he has a "world." When he is
through with the over-and-against, he is then spellbound once more by
the clock he observes, that is, he is pulled out of the world, removed.
Accordingly, "the tree in front of the window" is also an environment for
him, letting him dwell, and able to grant him a familiar, natural abode.
"Noises are not as good." For what are they not as good? As help. This
means that a human being cannot exist amid mere noises, which refer
to nothing, any more than he can exist with time as a mere sequence
of nows.

The author introduces the story with the statement: "Looking at the
hands of a wall clock." In so doing, the matter under discussion is already
misinterpreted beforehand. We can see here that the interpretation of
such reports does not happen automatically. We need a critical, thoughtful attention to the leading ideas and concepts with which the interpreter
is working. The art of interpretation is the art of asking the right questions.
In the case discussed above, the question is neither about time, nor
about the structure of time, but about the different relationships to the
wall clock and to the mere clock, both of which are not understood
as timekeepers at all. Accordingly, even the title of the article "Space-
Time Structure and Thought Disorder" is already misleading. First of
all, an interpretation is concerned not with how to explain something,
but rather with seeing the phenomenological facts of the case. In so
doing, we immediately discovered that the whole text, as read to us, has
nothing whatsoever to do with the problem of time. Nevertheless, the
interpretation of the text was only a rough attempt to show how one
must start with an interpretation. [One must] not start by looking at a
supposed "inner experience," but by asking how the relationship to a
thing is determined—how the genuine thing is a reference to the world.
Nevertheless, from what we have said so far, it is not yet clear in what sense
the problem of time plays a role. For the time being, in interpreting this
text, it is essential to reveal that we are *not* dealing with two different
clocks but with the same clock, even though it is presented to the patient
as a wall clock at one point, while it captivates and consumes him at the
next point as just a mere clock. Only where the same [thing] stands before
the human being can it confront him in a different, "split" way.

Here we interrupt our interpretation of the text and return once
again to the other question—the question of "being-in-time."

For this question, we start with the glass on the table in front of us. At
first, the phrase "in time" suggests, as we have mentioned, the idea that
time is some kind of container with something in it. We went so far as to
say that this glass is in time insofar as it *lasts*. But what does this mean?
Is it a special characteristic of the glass here? No, it is a characteristic of

p. 69

p. 70

all things. They all last in different ways, long or short. Are things doing something by lasting? Then where is the duration on the glass? If we leave afterward, and no one is there anymore, then what is the case with the glass? Does it always last? After we leave, we would have to say from our home that the glass is *there* on the table at Professor Boss's home. If we are not allowed to say "here" any longer, but must say "there," did the glass change places, or does the difference in talking about "here" and "there," due to our change of place, testify to the fact that the glass has simply remained in the same place? Of course, from another place, we can always say that the glass is "there." By such a "there" we mean present somewhere in general. Nevertheless, now we are once more concerned with space and no longer with time. We said that all things last. Duration is quite different here. The glass, for instance, can break while the table is being cleared. Then we just have pieces. When something has been broken, there are pieces. Pieces are the privation of the glass. If the pieces were to arrive at the garbage dump, then what? The fragments are no longer juxtaposed, but have become separate pieces of glass. They last as pieces of glass, but no longer as a drinking glass. Then does the drinking glass p. 71 have its own time as a drinking glass? Each thing has its time. The drinking glass has its fully specified time in which it is used, for instance, at a feast. That is something different than the time for blossoming. Blossoming time is a specific time for the sprouting and arrival of the blossoms. The time of the glass is defined by its characteristic as a utensil. Its time is not mere duration, but "time for." . . .

We still do not know at all what the "in" means in [the phrase] "being-in-time." Why are we unable to define this fact precisely? From where does the drinking glass get its time? Its time is connected with use. Use is connected with the human being, and the human being is distinguished by having time. Roughly speaking, the human being is, therefore, the one who gives time to the glass. Is that so? And what if no human being existed at all? Then would there be no glass at all? No, the glass could not have been produced without the human being. It enters time by being produced. What about the Alps, which were not made by a human being? Are they also in time? They also have their time. They last. Do they last longer than the human being? Were they already in time before the human being? The time of which *one* speaks, when *one* says "before the human being was," is also related to the human being in each case. Then can it really be known at all what there was in the time before the human being existed? Can it be even said: "at the time before the human being existed?" It is not even decidable whether one can say—that is, without a relationship to the human being—that the Alps existed before there was a human being. Strictly speaking, we cannot say what happened before the human being existed. Neither can we say that the Alps existed, nor can we say that they did not.*

Can we abstract from the human being altogether?

Geologists count with atomic clocks. Think, for example, of Teilhard de Chardin [1881–1955, French Jesuit] for whom the human being suddenly appears.† You see we are not making any progress. It is obvious that we are not making any progress because we still do not know how the human being is in time and how the human being relates to time. We are not going to make any progress through pure speculation. We have to proceed step by step. Therefore, in our case, we must ask: How does the human being get his time? Does the human being have his time only in that he is born one day and dies another day? We are dealing with the following questions here: How does the human being exist as a human being, and how does he endure his Da-sein? Thereby, how is he touched by time? How does the relationship to time essentially co-determine his existence? This is to say that we must disengage ourselves from the common linguistic usage of *being-in-time*. The point is to interpret what "in" means in a nonspatial sense, in relation to the human being's comportment to time.

p. 72

March 10 and 12, 1965, at Boss's Home

p. 73

I. March 10, 1965

Today, and in subsequent sessions, it is necessary for us to look at a phenomenon we have already spoken of, but up to now without seeing it expressly *as itself* and, accordingly, without regarding it [for itself]: time. Departing from our previous discussion's style, first I will try to point [out] the way with a comprehensive presentation. Subsequently, we will conduct a step-by-step examination of what was said, clarifying it by situating [*Erörterung*] the questions that arise.

At the end of the previous seminar we inquired into the meaning of the expression "something is in time." Does a thing exist in time the same

---

*See Heidegger, *Being and Time*, pp. 268–69.—TRANSLATORS

†See P. Teilhard de Chardin, *The Phenomenology of Man*, trans. B. Wall (New York: Harper, 1959). Teilhard de Chardin proposed a tripartite conception of evolution: prelife, life, thought. Its goal and destiny is "Point Omega," which is identified theologically with the cosmic Christ.—TRANSLATORS

way as we humans do? We have provisionally taken into consideration the question about "being-in-time." It is easy to see that we cannot deal with it as long as we have not clarified what "time" is and as long as we have not clarified what "being" means, as it relates to a thing, and as it relates to the human being, who exists. Of course, the question of "being-in-time" is exciting, but it was also raised prematurely. The question is exciting specifically with regard to natural science, especially with the advent of Einstein's theory of relativity, which established the opinion that traditional philosophical doctrine concerning time has been shaken to the core through the theory of physics. However, this widely held opinion is fundamentally wrong. The theory of relativity in physics does not deal with what time is but deals only with how time, in the sense of a now-sequence, can be *measured*. [It asks] whether there is an absolute measurement of time, or whether all measurement is necessarily relative, that is, conditioned.* The question of the theory of relativity could not be discussed at all unless the supposition of time as the succession of a sequence of nows were presupposed beforehand. If the doctrine of time, held since Aristotle, were to become untenable, then the very possibility of physics would be ruled out. [The fact that] physics, with its horizon of measuring time, deals not only with irreversible events, but also with reversible ones and that the direction of time is reversible attests specifically to the fact that in physics time is nothing else than the succession of a sequence of nows. This is maintained in such a decisive manner that even the sense of direction in the sequence can become a matter of indifference. In addition to the predominant opinion that physics has caused the downfall of the traditional metaphysical doctrine of time, there is a further opinion frequently held nowadays that philosophy lags behind natural science. Contrary to this, it must be pointed out that contemporary natural scientists, in contrast to scientists working on the level of Galileo and Newton, have abandoned vigorous philosophical reflection and no longer know what the great thinkers thought about time. For example, Hegel is one of them. Supposedly, Hegel did not understand much of natural science. If physicists make judgments about metaphysics, which is quite absurd in itself, then one must demand that physicists first reflect on metaphysical ideas, for instance, this idea about time. Of course, physicists can do this only if they are prepared to go back to the underlying suppositions of physics, and beyond this, to what remains and continues to be standard in this domain as *acceptio*, even when the physicist is unaware of it. It is no accident that in a strict sense

p. 74

---

*See *Basic Problems of Phenomenology,* p. 237.—TRANSLATORS

p. 75   modern science's self-critique is lacking today. It is not due to negligence or laziness on the part of the respective scientists. It is due to blindness determined by the destiny of the present age. This is where we get [the idea] that philosophy itself, insofar as it survives, is not lagging behind the sciences, but that it is lagging behind its own tradition. In inquisitive dialogue, philosophy is no longer able to put the matter of thinking itself into question.

    Why do I say this at this time? I say this in order to see more clearly how difficult it is everywhere to let the phenomena speak for themselves today instead of pursuing information. The characteristic of the latter is precisely to obstruct, from the beginning, our access to the *forma,* the essence, and the proper character of the being of things. Information precludes our ability to see *forma.* Why do I say this? I say this in order for us to see the seminar's intention in raising the question about phenomena more clearly even though these attempts are provisional and the successful steps are minimal. We are trying to see *the phenomenon of time.* The comprehensive protocol of the last two seminars enables us to try once again to clarify our relationship to time. This insight into this relationship to time should clear the way for us to experience something about time itself. Only when we have arrived at that point will we be in a position to settle the issue of how the human being stands and lives in relationship to time.

    As psychotherapists, you are especially interested in this question because the question of what, who, and how the human being *is,* including contemporary human beings, is fundamentally important to you. Together with this *substantive question* about the relationship between the human being and time, we are impelled by a *methodological* question. As scientifically educated physicians, you are influenced today largely by the scientific way of thinking. A particularly distinct idea of time is paradigmatic to this. This fact triggers the question whether the concept of time guiding natural science is appropriate at all when discussing the

p. 76   existing human being's relationship to time, or whether the concept of time, paradigmatic to natural sciences, hinders the way in discussing the relationship between the human being and time, thus blocking proper questions about the peculiar characteristic of time. Therefore, our question about time, which we have attempted in our discussions, is determined in two ways. First, it is determined by your medical profession and domain, that is, by the existing human being and its needs. Second, it is determined by your medical-scientific education, that is, by modern natural science and its technical structure. Now then, time as such is exclusively the theme of philosophy. Nothing can be said about time itself by natural science or by anthropology. Therefore, we are forced to think philosophically in our discussions, but in such a way that we do not approach the philosophical topic immediately, but instead take our clue from the aspects mentioned above—the existence of the human being and natural science. This situation makes our procedure especially difficult. In the course of our discussion, we must learn to disregard the scientific and psychological way of thinking as we go along, as it were, and enter the *phenomenological* way of thinking. The latter demands that we do this while we bear in mind the tradition of philosophical thought on space and time. This is because scientific and psychological concepts of time and space, taken as self-evident in current usage, also have been basically formed by this tradition. Three things must be kept in mind about the tradition of the concept of time. First, time is the succession of sequences of now-points. Second, time is not without psyche, *animus*, consciousness, mind, and subject. Third, time in its being is defined by the understanding of being in the sense of presence. We have intentionally mentioned only in passing these paradigmatic determinations regarding all thinking.* Instead of discussing them thoroughly in the context of their historical changes from Plato to Nietzsche, we have taken another route. We have done so to gain an insight into what time is and into p. 77 [the question of] how there is something like time. We started from the everyday experience of time, according to what we say in phrases like "having time," "having no time," "to take time," "to use time," "to spend time," and "to waste time." In all this, we are dealing in a certain way with a kind of concern for time. Such concern is obviously only possible insofar as we already have time in general and that it is granted to us to use in this or that way. Even then, and especially when we have no time, we are hard-pressed by the time given to us. We are afflicted by time. Time concerns us.

Thereby, we have considered the phenomena of "having time" [and] of "having no time" in order to find out how and with what characteristics time shows itself. Time is time *for* something. In each case, time is time *when* this and that happens. Therefore, time is *significant for* something and is *datable for* something. Thus, simultaneously time is *extended* in

---

*Before writing *Being and Time*, Heidegger developed his new understanding of "time" for the first time in a lecture, which he delivered to the Marburg Theological Society in July 1924; see M. Heidegger, *The Concept of Time*, trans. William McNeill (Oxford: Blackwell, 1925). This is still an excellent and concise introduction to the problem of time. See also M. Heidegger, *History of the Concept of Time: Prolegomena*, trans. T. Kisiel (Bloomington: Indiana University Press, 1985); Th. J. Sheehan, "The 'Original Form' of *Sein und Zeit:* Heidegger's *Der Begiff der Zeit* (1924)," *Journal of the British Society for Phenomenology* 10 (1979): 78–83.—TRANSLATORS

its way and is not an isolated now-point. Furthermore, everyone knows time. [It is] accessible to human beings in their being with and for each other. It is *public*. In these characteristics, time shows itself as time we have. For now, in order to gain an insight into what time is, in itself and as such, we must try to determine more clearly then what shows itself. With this task, we have reached a decisive point in our discussion. Quite decisive, indeed, for at this point, after the previous discussions about time and about "having time," everything depends on how we inquire further about time itself. Regarding "having time," "having spare time," and "having no time," we speak of being involved with time [*Umgang mit der Zeit*].* Regarding the previously mentioned phenomena and their transformations, it is a matter of reckoning with time, insofar as we use our time sparingly or waste it. We calculate and measure time only because we reckon with time. It is said that time is money. Insofar as we reckon with time, time concerns us. Our concern with time also includes reading the clock. In doing so, we are not thinking of time as such. We are only noting the "how-much" of time. This happens whenever we inevitably say "now" each time, expressly or not. The respective "now" is not spoken incidentally, but it is said in advance. This way, the relationship to time is taken over explicitly by reading the clock so that we can determine the "how-much" of it. [The fact] that the relationship to time is accepted does not mean that this relationship is established for the first time, as if it did not exist independently from the reading of time. The relationship to time is accepted by reading the clock, yet this does not mean that we already see time itself and as such. The always-present relationship to time, "the having of time," is merely performed in a special way, namely, in saying "now."

p. 78

From where do we take the so-called "now"? Obviously, from time. But how do we have time, which we address, although unthematically, by saying "now"? What does being involved with time mean? What does "having" mean here in relationship to time? For instance, if we ask, "Do you have time?"—is time here a thing that we have like a watch—something we possess? When we state, "Today we have beautiful weather," does this "having" mean possession? Obviously not. We have beautiful or bad weather in a different way than we possess our watch. Someone says

---

*See T. Kisiel, *Genesis of Heidegger's* Being and Time, s.v. *Umgang,* concerning the meaning of *umgehen* as "getting around, going about, being concerned, moving about, coping with" as a primordial mode of human life as *caring (Sorgen),* which differentiates itself in progressive ways of "seeing" (*aisthesis,* perception; *episteme,* knowledge; *techne,* art; *praxis;* action; see Aristotle, *Metaphysics* Al.980b28 ff.).—TRANSLATORS

of his friend that he has a wonderful Cézanne in his room. This does not mean that the picture belongs to him or is owned by him. He might have a borrowed object hanging in his room.

Someone says: "I have anxiety." Do we have a relationship to anxiety just as we have to weather and to cars? Perhaps we have a relationship to anxiety as we have a relationship to time. What does "to have" mean here and there? The city of Zurich has more than five hundred thousand inhabitants. Does the city exist, having inhabitants in addition to itself, or do the inhabitants constitute the city? Obviously, this is also not the case. The city and its inhabitants are not identical, but different. But these different things, that is, the inhabitants and the city, belong together. We p. 79 have beautiful weather. We humans and weather conditions are different kinds of things. Nevertheless, something like weather belongs to our existence. Therefore, what "having" means is something different from the subject of the sentence. Nevertheless, it is something belonging to it. Thereby, the subject, which has something, is not acting, and what is had does not suffer something by having it. Thus, this verb "to have" indicates a peculiar relationship.* However, the characterization just elaborated is obviously insufficient to determine the unique and supposedly peculiar way of having in having time. It still remains unclear whether and how the time we have is something different from us; nevertheless, it belongs to us in its difference. Our having time is not an action. There is no special performance on our part. Yet, we participate in this kind of "having." Of course, the time that we have certainly does not suffer by our having it. Nevertheless, something happens to the time we do or do not have whenever we divide it this way and that and put it on a calendar.

However, what about the fact that we say "now"? A spontaneous activity lies therein—one originating with us after all. Yet saying this does not affect the "now," but perhaps it does affect the time we name by saying "now." If, because we are too busy, we say spontaneously, and perhaps with ill humor, "I have no time now," the time that I use otherwise and of which I have nothing left—this time is not affected by saying "now." It is neither affected nor changed. The time I no longer have for other things, because

---

*Aristotle listed the category of "state" or "having" as one of his ten categories for classifying things: substance, quantity, quality, relation, place, time, position, state, action, passion. To have (Greek, ἔχειν; Latin, habitus) refers to a predicate which expresses the human being's relationship to "having" something: "having shoes," "having weapons," etc. This category could not express that to which Heidegger refers: the existential and original having of time, i.e., Dasein's "being-in-time," ecstatic temporality. See Heidegger, *Basic Problems of Phenomenology,* pp. 256–74.—TRANSLATORS

it is already used for something else, is addressed by the "now." The fact that we refer to time by saying "now" is an obvious triviality. For time is the sequence of nows. At any given time, one "now" is extracted from the sequence of nows. Does this statement express that state of affairs? Let us see. If I say: "I have no time now," am I thereby related to time as the succession of now-points? Not at all. In saying "now" this way, we take the "now" from the time we have or simply do not have. With "now," we address the time we have or do not have. When said this way, "now" is not extracted from a now-sequence, from a mere succession. It is important to remember this fact in all further considerations. The "now," as it is usually expressed in reading the clock or otherwise in everyday life, is not a moment in a now-sequence, but belongs instead to the relationship with the time we already have and how we have it. We already know the characteristic of this kind of time. It is significant, datable, extended, and public. Therefore, when we say "now," the spoken "now" articulates these characteristics, and only these, without giving special attention to them.

Therefore, in view of this state of affairs, one would like to infer that there are two kinds of time: the time we have with these characteristics, and time as a mere succession of nows. Whatever we note about this, one thing may have become clear during these seminars: We must not draw any conclusions from the discussion and elucidation of phenomena. What the phenomena, that is, that which shows itself, require from us is only to see and accept them as they show themselves. "Only" this. This is not less than a conclusion, but it goes beyond [a conclusion] and is therefore difficult. These recently provided indications may be important in our further reflection on time. We seem to have made no progress concerning the question we are most interested in. Our question is: What does it mean "to have time"? Time thus mentioned is not a thing such as a house. "Having" is not a possession here, as when someone owns a house, even if he does not stay there. The time mentioned is not similar to having anxiety, for time is not an emotion, not a mood, and not a psychological attunement, although such states may have a peculiar relation to time. One may only point at boredom [Langeweile, a long while], a phenomenon indicating a relationship to time in its very name, although we have hardly clarified it yet. Therefore, it could be fruitful to our entire purpose if we were to enter into a phenomenological interpretation of boredom.* An obvious hint might facilitate our attempt to define this "having of time" more clearly. Again and again, it always remains to be considered that the very phrase "I have time" easily misleads

p. 80

p. 81

---

*See Heidegger, *Fundamental Concepts of Metaphysics*, secs. 19–44.—TRANSLATORS us by suggesting the following assumption: On one hand, there is time. On the other hand, there is a "having" which, as such, has nothing to do with time. For we can have a great deal, not only things, but also what affects us immediately insofar as it belongs to us. I have a broken arm. I have a buzzing in my ears. I have a stomachache. I have anxiety. Does "have" here always mean the same neutral relationship to what we have, a relationship which remains the same, so that only the object of "have" is different at any given time? One will answer that we find ourselves in different situations by having a broken arm, a buzzing in our ears, a stomachache, and anxiety. Our "ontological disposition" [*Befindlichkeit*] varies from case to case, according to what we "have." According to this view, "having" is simply different in its emotional quality in each case, but otherwise our having is the same. It is the simple relationship to what one has, a relation of having, which has nothing further to do with what one has in each case. Or is it a completely different matter?

Let us choose a case that immediately brings the real subject matter a bit closer. I am in a state of anxiety. I live in a state of anxiety about something that is threatening, but I am unable to put its nature into words. I am in a state of anxiety, or more specifically we say: I am anxious. It makes me anxious, not because I am making myself anxious, but because anxiety overcomes me. What about "having" in such a case of having anxiety? The having itself, and just that, is full of anxiety. Anxiety is located just in that having. The having is being in a state of anxiety. No, anxiety in itself is this state we find ourselves in. What do we gather from this p. 82 preliminary elucidation in view of the aforementioned state of anxiety? Nothing less than this: that in this case "having" is not an indifferent relationship to what we have, but to what is supposedly "had"—namely, anxiety is not simply what is had, but is really the having itself. There is no anxiety one can have, but there is a having as being in such and such a state, an ontological disposition that is called "anxiety." Here anxiety can only exist in the realm of how one finds oneself. It has the fundamental characteristic of an *ontological disposition* that can be interpreted at any given time as "attunement." Thereby, how we are to think mood and attunement here must also be left open. The question of where "ontological disposition" belongs must also be left open. Whether "ontological disposition" correctly captures the phenomenon must also be left open.

Our *guiding theme* is time and, above all, what "having time" means. We could quickly say with a certain right that what has been noted about anxiety cannot be transferred to what "having time" means because time is not a mood or attunement in the way that anxiety is. To say that someone is in a temporal mood obviously seems senseless. Now we must not think of simply transferring what has been noted provisionally about anxiety to "having time." This is true, quite apart from the fact that such a procedure would violate the fundamental rule of phenomenological interpretation (as we have already mentioned). This rule requires us to let each phenomenon show itself explicitly in its unique features. One is not permitted to infer from the elucidation of one phenomenon [anxiety] the constitution of the other [time]. This must not be done, even if the modes of expression of "having anxiety" and "having time" are similar, and even if both of them affect us as human beings. Within phenomenology, conclusions cannot be drawn, nor are dialectical "mediations"* allowed. It is crucial to keep open a reflective attitude toward the phenomenon. Apart from this basic methodological reflection, one could furthermore maintain that anxiety does not always come upon us as time does continuously and unavoidably. Nevertheless, we have purposefully placed the elucidation of "having anxiety" prior to the reflection on "having time." For what purpose? In order to show how peculiar and strange the familiar relationship of "having" to what is had can be in each case. But now without prejudice, we will attempt to reflect on "having" in the phenomenon of "having time." "To have" generally means that something belongs to us, that we possess it, and that we dispose of it in some way. A friend asks: "Do you have time for a walk tomorrow afternoon?" After a short consideration, I answer, "Yes, I do have time." When we elucidate such a statement along with the phrase "having time," it seems as though we have spoken only about the meaning of words in linguistic usage. Nevertheless, we mean the subject matter, the phenomenon, and not the words, even though each phenomenon shows itself only within the realm of language.

p. 83

To avoid the risk of proceeding arbitrarily in our interpretation of "having time," we shall first try a brief discussion of the entries in the Brothers Grimm's *Great German Dictionary*. In an extensive article on the verb "to have" (vol. 4, sec. 2, col. 68), it states: "The concept of ownership, of belonging, of possessing, entirely disappears in a number

---

*The term "dialectical mediations" refers to the method of "dialectic" reconciliation of opposites (thesis-antithesis) into a higher unity (synthesis) in Hegel's philosophy. According to Heidegger, phenomenological description is prior to any dialectical mode of thinking and to any representational, calculative (inductive, deductive) way of thinking. Phenomenological description is a listening response to and a "saying/showing" of the emergent phenomena. See ZS 254. See also Heidegger, *Hegel's Concept of Experience*, trans J. Glenn Gray (New York: Harper and Row, 1970); Heidegger, *Phenomenology of Spirit*, trans. P. Emad and K. Maly (Bloomington: Indiana University Press, 1988); Heidegger, *Contributions to Philosophy*, pp. 141–42.—TRANSLATORS

of phrases when "having" expresses no more than mere existence and when the object coming to the fore [namely, what we have] has only a slight relationship to the subject: We are having good weather is almost equivalent to "there is good weather." We have rain. We had a Christmas without snow and then we will have a white Easter. This year we have a late Pentecost. In this sense, it is also said that I have time to do something, i.e., the time for it is here. It exists." The passage further states: "We have a quarter of an hour to the next village, [i.e.,] the distance is that far   p. 84 from our location." Grimm's statement, "I have time to do something," surely can be paraphrased as follows: The time for it is here. It exists. In a sense, the content of what "having time" means is correctly rendered. Nevertheless, this is not the point in question. Rather, [the point is] the appropriate interpretation of the phenomenon of "having time," that is, of the relationship to time that holds sway here. Referring to this, Grimm says: "Having" expresses no more than mere existence. When placed entirely into the foreground, the object offers only a faint relationship to the subject. What we have in this case—namely, time—Grimm considers to be an object, and he asserts that it moves into the foreground. Time for something is what we deal with objectively. Accordingly, the relationship to the subject, who has time, remains only a slight one, that is, a negligible one, and is therefore irrelevant.

When we look at the phenomenon of what is referred to here as "having" time, what should be said about it? When I have time for something and I state it, the previously mentioned "having time" is not made into an object and we do not focus on it at all. Rather, we remain directed toward that for which we have time. Nevertheless, there is something in that remark whereby time comes to the fore, but in an entirely different and, as it were, opposite sense. In having time for something, I am directed toward the what-for, toward what has to be done, toward what is forthcoming. I am expectant, but only in such a way that I dwell simultaneously on what is present to me just now—what I make present now. Furthermore, I simultaneously retain—whether directly considered or not—what concerned me just now, prior to this. The time that I have in this case I have in such a way that I am "expecting" [*gewärtigend*], "making present" [*gegenwärtigend*], and "retaining" [*behaltend*] [time]. I am in this threefold mode, which is the "having" time for this and that. This having, namely [in the mode of] expecting, making present, and retaining, is the authentic character of time. The "having" in "having   p. 85 time" is not an indifferent relationship to time as an object.* Rather, it is

*See *ZS* 78.—TRANSLATORS

time insofar as the human being's *sojourn* temporalizes itself in it. This is characterized by the fact that it equiprimordially, but not uniformly, gives what concerns us, what is present [to us], and what has passed us already. This threefold temporalizing [*Zeitigen*]* of sojourn offers us, in each case, time for something. It has to bestow such a time, namely, the then, the now, and the once by which we reckon with time. Of course, I must admit that these simple phenomena are difficult to glimpse, and for one reason only—because for a long time, and today more than ever, we have persisted in the habit of representing time merely as the determinable succession of a sequence of nows. But now you also notice why the short interpretation of having anxiety was discussed earlier. It [was done] with the intention of loosening up the fixed gaze at time as a now-sequence and freeing [us] for the insight that just as anxiety is located in the very act of having anxiety, so time also plays a role in the very act of having time, although not in the same way, but in a certain similar way—in the sense of temporalizing as expecting, making present, and retaining.

Nevertheless, with this now-acquired insight into "having time," in no way have we clarified how what is called "time" must be characterized as the "time we had"—that is, how what is called "time" belongs to the temporalizing of sojourn. Similarly, we have not determined what we call a "sojourn." Nevertheless, one thing should have become clear— that by no means do we capture the phenomenon "I have time for . . ." when we only circumscribe it in the statement "time is here." Time is present-at-hand. As a result, we specifically overlook the phenomenon of "having" [time], and we take time merely as something present-at-hand. It is as though "time for something" were like an object before us as something present-at-hand—something we could pass by as an arbitrary thing in order to tangibly get a hold of it on occasion and in passing as an obvious present-at-hand thing. The relationship we have to time at any

---

*In the unity of its ecstases, Da-sein's irreducible "temporalizing" (Heidegger, *Being and Time*, p. 328 ff.) *is* the original condition for "care" (*Being and Time*, p. 372) and for the contextualizing, "meaning"-giving ground of all its "potentiality-to-be" [*Seinkönnen*], including its "understanding of being." With its openness toward the future and toward one's own impending death, this phenomenological, primordial experience of time is presupposed by any other derived, conceptualized meaning of time, especially in the natural sciences, which most recently includes the big bang theory of the universe, string theory, etc. Similarly, the theological and metaphysical concept of "eternity" is a derivative of Da-sein's temporal being—"the empty state of perpetual being, the *aei*" (Heidegger, *History of the Concept of Time*, p. 1, and *Fundamental Concepts of Metaphysics*, secs. 12–13).—TRANSLATORS

given time is in no way something tacit [or] something negligible, but is   p. 86
precisely what sustains our dwelling in the world. The time we have or
do not have, the time which we sacrifice or waste, is such that we have
it at our disposal. We can plan or arrange it for ourselves in this way or
that, but do take notice: It is as time. Therefore, in this manner, we bring
together past, present, and future events. To join-together [*fügen*] means
to bring together what fits into one another—thus, to build and establish
the [threefold] structure of time in each case, and to temporalize the
sojourn in this manner. We take time, and we let time be by retaining it
in making it present. By this making present, we have it at our disposal
in each case. At any given time, time as disposable and disposed of for
something, emerges as such in expecting, retaining, and making present.
This is the temporalizing of the time we "have" and "do not have" in its
threefold unity. Still, we remain completely in the dark as to how the unity
of this threefold temporalizing must be determined.

II. March 12, 1965

During the previous seminar I learned more from you than you did from
me. That is quite all right too. (Compare *What Is Called Thinking?*)*
    What did I learn? I learned where the primary obstacle lies for
you, which makes it difficult, if not impossible, to see a simple and
basic phenomenon. When brought into view, this basic phenomenon
opens up the realm where my thinking begins. What I learned about
this primary obstacle to an appropriate seeing I owe to the fact that
Dr. H. did not just repeat my words, but instead honestly and openly
explained what makes him hesitant to embrace my thinking. Due to the
importance of the phenomenon in question for all our discussions, I
would like to try to remove this obstacle. It is a question here of clarifying a   p. 87
difference already mentioned repeatedly, namely, the difference between
recalling [*Erinnerung*] and *making-present* [*Vergegenwärtigung*]†—first, by

---

*M. Heidegger, *Was heisst Denken?* (Tübingen: M. Niemeyer, 1954) [*What Is Called
Thinking?* trans. F. D. Wieck and J. Glenn Gray (New York: Harper and Row, 1968)].—
TRANSLATORS

†*Vergegenwärtigung* [making-present], in contrast to the temporal *gegenwärtigen*
[making present] and *gewärtigen* [expecting], is typically translated as "to envisage,"
or "to enpresent." In order to avoid any modern epistemological subject-object
dichotomy, we chose to translate *Vergegenwärtigung* in hyphenated form as "making-
present."—TRANSLATORS

considering a sufficient interpretation of making-present. This is merely a modification of the basic phenomenon. Everything depends on its clarified appropriation [*Nachvollzug*]. We have already made a few attempts to elucidate the phenomenon of making-present with the example of making-present the Cathedral of Freiburg. Now I will select instead a case of making-present which is familiar to all participants in this discussion. We now make-present—that is, each person by himself [makes-present]— the central train station of Zurich. We ask two questions which everyone should also answer by himself. First: What am I directed toward in making-present Zurich's main train station? What is the thing I refer to while making-it-present? Second: What characteristic does making-present itself have, insofar as I perform it? We should deal with these two questions without prejudice, without regard to any knowledge acquired through psychology, physiology, and epistemology. Rather, we should stay within the everyday experience where we live our lives. We should simply name what shows itself as we look at [the phenomenon of] making-present.

Concerning the first question: What am I directed toward by making-present Zurich's central train station? I answer: Toward the train station *itself*. This train station is what I mean in the act of making-present. I do not mean a picture of it, nor do I mean a representation of it, but rather the station itself, which is standing, or in other words, located over there. Of course, each one of you will make-present the aforementioned station in a different way, from different sides, and from different places. Therefore, I now ask Dr. B.: If you are directed toward Zurich's central train station by making-it-present, what shows itself to you? Answer: I saw the front entrance. And you, Dr. W.? Answer: The huge clock over the entrance.

p. 88 And you, Dr. R.? Answer: The interior of the hall with electric signs. And you, Dr. S.? Answer: The wall outside in front of the first platform. And you, Dr. F.? Answer: Quite a lot, a confusing mess, a lot of people, tracks.

What is meant by the act of making-present shows itself from different sides and places. Yet in each case what is meant is the central train station there in Zurich. The fact that what is meant shows itself from different sides, and therefore differently in each case, is necessarily due to reasons which should not be further discussed for the time being. For this fact holds true, not only for what we mean in making-present, but also and already prior to it, for the everyday perception of physically given things. We see things, for instance, this bowl and this book, only from a particular side after all. Yet we "see" and mean this whole bowl, this whole book. In this case I do not have the bottom of this bowl in my visual field. Neither do I have the back cover of this book in my visual field. Nevertheless, I see—that is, I "mean" and perceive as present—this bowl here, this book, and not, let us say, a damaged book, which has no back cover.

Yet let us go back to the Zurich train station! The train station itself there in Zurich is what is meant by making-it-present. It itself is in front of us. It presents itself, and the different sides, which are seen at any given time, belong to it and are of it. By making-present Zurich's central train station, we are not directed toward a picture of it, nor toward a representation which *we* would make of it. We are directed toward the station present over there. If we examine without bias that toward which we are directed in making-present, then we find only this. We are directed toward the train station itself present there. What has been found so far is the initial finding in an attempt to elucidate making-present in relation to what is given in it. This finding, that Zurich's train station itself is what p. 89 is made-present while making-present, cannot be proved. This finding is unproved, not because the necessary proofs are lacking, but because the desire for proofs and the demands for proofs are not appropriate to the subject matter here. Information about what is present for the making-present can only be given by the making-present itself. We must be instructed by *it* where to look in order to find what the content of [the phenomenon of] making-present is. It is not a shortcoming that the finding referred to is not provable. On the contrary, it is precisely to its advantage that the finding does not need any proof. For if a state of affairs and a statement about it have to be proved first, then for this reason we must return at any given time to something else which is different from this state of affairs in order to derive it with regard to its givenness from there. In view of the phenomena and their interpretation, all proofs and all desire for proofs come too late. In the case of making-present, it as such gives the reference to what it makes-present. To follow the instruction given by the reference itself is especially difficult nowadays because the human being, obsessed by science, would like to acknowledge truth as only what has been proved, that is, as what is derived from presuppositions and conclusions. But can a physicist prove, for instance, that he exists? Nevertheless, he practices physics. Fortunately, there are things that need no proof. Concerning these, the desire to prove remains not only a harmless misunderstanding, but also a failure to appreciate the state of affairs on what the existence of the human being depends, including even the whole of beings and truth. States of affairs, propositions, and truths, which first need the crutches of proof, are always such that they belong to the second or third rank. In reference to making-present, the answer to the first question, namely, what is it that it makes-present? is: the Zurich train station, present there itself.

Concerning the second question: What character as such does making-present have as I perform it? This means: How do I relate to what p. 90 making-present offers to me—therefore, to the train station at Zurich itself present there? We answer with what we have said many times before: While making-present we are at Zurich's train station itself. Making-present has the character of being-at . . . [Sein-bei],* more precisely, of our being-at the station. This answer has made you rebel, and it continues to disturb you. You dispute that making-present has, or in any way even could have, something to do with being at the train station in Zurich. And how do you prove your negative assertion? You cannot prove it at all. You can only point to something, obviously clear to everyone, that is, what shows itself to everyone, namely, this: During the performance of this making-present, we are here at Boss's house. Surely, we are not at the train station in Zurich. No reasonable person wants to maintain that while making-present, we are transposing ourselves, as it were, to the station in order to be at and next to the station. Making-present itself shows plainly that we remain seated here leisurely during its performance. In making-present the Zurich train station, we are here in our chairs, gathered around the tables, and not at the station. And yet, our interpretation of making-present says that it is a being-at the station. We are, in a real sense, at the station itself. One replies: No, we are really here and only here. Both statements are correct, for "really" is used in a different sense in each statement. First we take the statement: At best, we are at the station only in thought. Therefore, we admit that we are at the station in some way. What we admit, we cannot also deny, for in making-present, we are directed toward the train station itself. This was the answer to the first question. Thus, what we have to admit is that by making-it-present, we are at the Zurich station in some way. We interpret this state of affairs by saying: "We are at the station only in thought." This interpretation could, perhaps, be understood in the following sense: What does this "in thought" mean? Thoughts exist only in thinking. According to this interpretation, our being at the station is merely something thought of. In making-present the Zurich train station, we merely think we are at the station. If you make-present the Zurich train station, are you thereby thinking that you are standing in front of the station? In the simple making-present of the Zurich train station, do you find yourselves thinking something of being there with the station? No, you just think that you think that. In the phenomenon of simple making-present in this sense, no trace can be found of such a thought. Whoever maintains this cannot appeal to a [phenomenological] finding. Rather, he talks about a mere invention.

p. 91

---

*We do not translate Sein-bei in the usual way as "being-alongside," "being-amidst," or "being together with," but rather as "being-at," in order to point out the directional sense of the word. See Being and Time, p. 80.—TRANSLATORS

Nevertheless, this interpretation gives us the opportunity to point out an important distinction. Suppose that making-present the Zurich train station had the character of "thinking" that we were standing there at the station. Then, in no way would we be directed toward the station in this making-present, but toward the fact that we were standing there. Accordingly, we would make-present that we are present at the station [only in thought] and not [at] the station itself. The making-present would not be the one we used as our example. Still more important, this would not be a making-present of something really present in any way. What we have momentarily called "making-present" in truth is merely a product of imaginary representation [*Sich-einbilden*]. To "think" that we were at the station is a totally different phenomenon than the making-present of the station. But if we interpret it in this way, by saying that our thinking consists of our being at the station—in other words, that we are merely at the station in thought—then we misinterpret the phenomenon of making-present so thoroughly that we substitute an entirely different phenomenon for it. Instead of simply following the indication contained in making-present itself, we replace it with the phenomenon of imaginary representation. Instead of keeping our minds open for what shows itself, we unexpectedly make a supposition: We think we are actually at the station. However, by interpreting making-present with the phrase "merely in thought," you mean something else, perhaps something correct. "Merely in thought" will say: to think of the station, but in such a way that it itself is given in the making-present but not physically present-at-hand itself. The phrase "merely in thought" should mean, furthermore, that we are not at the station bodily but that we are actually here in this house. We get closer to the phenomenon of making-present with the correct understanding of the phrase "merely in thought." If, however, we follow the reference, which lies in making-present itself, then we find nothing like "merely in thought." The peculiarity of making-present consists specifically of the fact that it itself in its way permits us to be at the station. It is a *mode of being** with beings, where being-at . . . in no way needs to be supplemented by "merely in thought."

p. 92

---

*Like "making-present" [*vergegenwärtigen*], "representing" [*vorstellen*] in the modern epistemological or psychological sense is another, although very derivative, *mode of being,* another "comportment" [*verhalten*] toward beings. See *Being and Time,* p. 260. Therefore, all modern theories in the tradition of Descartes and Locke, which reduce human "thinking" [*denken*] to "representational thought" [*Vorstellung*] are inadequate *for grasping the originary phenomenon of Da-sein's comportment toward things.* See ZS 206.—TRANSLATORS

Let us now examine whether and in what sense this being *at the station* truly characterizes making-present itself! Let us suppose something which is neither unusual nor out of place. Suppose you have to pick up someone at the Zurich train station after this seminar. You drive to the station. You would never arrive at the station if you had not made-present the station during the drive, indeed already beforehand. [You would never arrive at the station] if the making-present absolutely necessary for the drive, even if not always actually performed, had not been directed toward the station in Zurich itself. Or are you driving to something we have only in our thoughts, to a mere image, to a mere representation of the station in our head? The answer is superfluous because the very question asks something impossible. For I can never drive by car to a mere image or to such a representation of the station. One will reply that this becomes clear specifically from the example of driving to the station—that we are not at the station by making-it-present. But the point is overzealous and too quick. We have not yet arrived at the station, but this "not yet" is not due to the making-present. For in it, and thanks to it, we are simply already *in the manner of making present* at the station, otherwise we could never arrive there by driving. Therefore, what does this *being-at* mean, which we find characteristic of making-present? In no way does this being-at mean that during making-present we are actually, or even only in thought, standing in front of the station. It does not mean that we are [bodily] present by it and next to it. During the making-present of the station, we are clearly, in fact, here inside this house. Yet, our *being* here offers us various possibilities. We can participate in the discussion, look at the clock, and follow how one of our colleagues answers a question directed to him. We can also make-present the Zurich train station. This making-present is then a possible way for us to be seated here. In this case, according to the previous interpretation of making-present as a being-at the station, we are here inside Boss's home and simultaneously at the Zurich train station. Now for once let someone perform this magic trick: Be here and at the Zurich train station simultaneously. But that is not at all the meaning of our interpretation of making-something-present. In the act of making-present, I am not here and at the Zurich train station in the same sense as I am here. In being here, I perform the making-present. In being here, making-present the train station, I am, of course, at the station in the manner of making-present. As a performance of making-present, my being here is a being-at the station. Our being here happens continuously and necessarily in such a strange and even wondrous way. Our being here is essentially a being with beings which we ourselves are not. This "being-at" is usually characterized by the bodily perception of things physically present. But our being here can also engage [*einlassen*]

p. 93

p. 94

itself in being with things not present physically. If this possibility did not exist and could not be performed, then, for instance, you could never arrive at home this evening. But while making-present the Zurich train station, we are at the station in the manner of making-present, and we remained gathered here around the tables and their utensils. Thus, our being-at the things physically present can be a being-at the station if here inside the house, being with things, we take advantage of our possibility for making-present. We do not then abandon our being-here with things. At any rate, our being-here with things is always already a being-there with distant things not physically present, even if these things are not meant and made-present explicitly. When we speak of "being-at" the meaning of being is unique and fundamentally different from that being which we term "present-at-hand" and "occurent" [*Vor-kommen*]. "Being-at," which among other things characterizes making-present, is fundamentally different from present-at-hand, for instance, the shoes we put in front of our room door. Of course, we can say that the shoes are at the door. Here, this "being-at" means the spatial juxtaposition of two things. In contrast, the "being-at" of our being here with things has the fundamental characteristic of *being-open-for* [*Offenstehen für*] that which comes to presence [*das Anwesende*] where it is. By way of contrast, the shoes at the door are not open for the door. The door is not a door to the shoes; indeed, it is not present to them at all. We cannot, and must not, even say that the door and shoes are closed off from each other. Closedness as privation exists only where openness holds sway. Door and shoes are only there at different places in space. Their distance is a nearness to each other. Being-open to what is present is the fundamental characteristic of being human. But being-open for being contains distinct possibilities.* The pervasive way of all being-open is our immediate being with things that affect us physically. In schizophrenia the loss of [this] contact is a privation of being-open, which was just mentioned. Yet this privation does not mean that being-open disappears, but only that it is modified to a "lack of contact." Now, another mode of being-open as being-at is making-present. This being-at does not merely mean being present, a mere occurrence of the human being that we erroneously

p. 95

---

*In *Being and Time* Heidegger determined the temporal being of the human being as "Da-sein" and "existence" as "potentiality-to-be" [*Seinkönnen*] in the sense of a *being-in-possibilities*. In this way, he attempted to avoid traditional, metaphysical definitions of the human being as a fixed entity—as a "substance," a "subject," a "soul," an "Ego," and a "person." In its existential possibilities, Da-sein *is* and is disclosed to itself as always "ahead-of-itself." See Heidegger, *Being and Time*, pp. 68, 279 ff., 292 f.—TRANSLATORS

imagine as if (in the case of a misinterpretation of making-present) one were there at the train station next to a waiting taxi. Our being-open, that is, being-here in this house with things as this being here, indeed only as such, can be open to a distant being in the manner of making-present, for instance, by being at the station. Recall: Being-open, as *being-at* [*Sein-bei*], is the way of making-present beings which are there. Our being-open as being-here with the things is, as such, a being-open as being-at the station. Here we no longer characterize the phenomenological state of affairs appropriately if we say: We simultaneously can be here among things and at the station. These are not two modes of *being-at* occurring simultaneously, but it is our being-open for things which, in the mode of making-present, is a being-open as being-at the train station in Zurich. Therefore, being-here with things does not disappear. It does not vanish, but is only modified in the way we do not pay any special attention to the things present-at-hand here in making-present the train station. The human being's being-open to being is so fundamental and decisive in being human that, due to its inconspicuousness and plainness, one can continuously overlook it in favor of contrived psychological theories. But even if we notice this phenomenon, this does not mean we are prepared to simply accept this simple fact in its amazing character as what shows itself in this way. Not by a long shot. The phenomenological interpretation of making-present as a way of being-open as being-at [*offenständiges Sein-bei*] the train station in Zurich does not demand that we mentally transfer ourselves away from this room, as if we were dealing with the kind of being-at as with the shoes at the door. Rather, the correct phenomenological interpretation of making-present as a being-open as being-at the station requires that we remain seated here and perceive ourselves as following the indication given within the phenomenon of making-present itself, namely, as following the indication for what is given in making-present, the indication identifying itself as a *mode of being-open*, as being-at things coming to presence. What matters is simply to accept what shows itself in the phenomenon of making-present, and nothing more.

p. 96

We are living in a peculiar, strange, and uncanny age. The more frantically the volume of information increases, the more decisively the misunderstanding and blindness to the phenomena grows. Furthermore, the more excessive the information, the less we have the capacity for the following insight: Modern thought is increasingly blinded and becomes a visionless calculation, providing only the chance to rely on effect and possibly on the sensational. But there are a few [people] left who are able to experience a [kind of] thinking which is not calculating but "*thanking*." These few are able to experience "thanking" as being indebted, that is, remaining receptive to the claim of what manifests itself: Beings are, and are not nothing. In that "is" [i.e., the presence of beings], the tacit language of being addresses the human being, whose distinction and peril consist in his being open in manifold ways to beings as beings.

May 11 and 14, 1965, at Boss's Home

I. May 11, 1965

Last time we tried to clarify the phenomenon of making-present. The point was to become aware of this phenomenon as a simple relationship to the world without reference to philosophical theories, for instance, without regard to viewing the human being as a subject and the world as an object, without regard to physiology and psychology, without regard to the question of how making-present is possible, and without regard to whether the phenomenon might be conditioned somatically and psychologically. If we grant that there are brain processes involved in making-present—namely, somatic processes in the broadest sense—then the question of what relation these processes have to the phenomenon can only be asked when we clarify sufficiently to what these processes are related. Therefore, this question can only be asked if the meaning of the making-present we perform is clear in advance. In the prevailing physiological-psychological approach, such a phenomenon is presupposed as self-evident and known. And indeed, the phenomenon not only remains indeterminate, but even more significantly, a decisive state of affairs goes unnoticed. What goes unnoticed is that an acquaintance with the phenomenon must be presupposed if physico-psychological explanations are not to be totally unfounded. At this point, the precision usually claimed by science suddenly ceases. Science becomes blind to what it must presuppose and to what it wants to explain in its own purely genetic way. This blindness to phenomena dominates not only the sciences, but nonscientific behavior as well. For instance, we walk in a forest and see something moving along the way. We even hear it rustle and receive-perceive it as something living. When we look at it more carefully, it turns out that we were mistaken, for a barely noticeable gust of wind had moved the leaves on the ground. Therefore, it was not any living thing. Yet in order to be able to be mistaken in this assumption that it was something living, we must have seen something like life in advance, something like the nature of living things within the context about which we were mistaken. Only one thing should become clearer through this illustration:

p. 97

p. 98

that it is not a matter of indifference whether we pay attention to the phenomena or not. Even if the insight into the phenomena of making-present and recalling does not make a contribution to the explanation and to the identification of what concerns physiological research, the phenomenological insight, nevertheless, remains a contribution, indeed *the* fundamental contribution. Foremost, it procures what research claims to explain. But now the strange thing is that this contribution is not noticed properly, either in its content or in its necessity. Due to an unusual frugality in what is usually demanding and exact research, one is satisfied, in all these cases, with arbitrarily selected, popular ideas. However, the noteworthy fact that scientific research has no need for this most crucial contribution is not accidental. It is founded in the history of European man during the course of the past three centuries. This kind of frugality is the consequence of the claim of a new idea of science. Even if we paid minimal attention to it, the questions with which we are concerned in all these seminars gain an importance that cannot be exaggerated.

Let us now return to the phenomena of making-present, recalling, and perceiving. Indeed, from your scientific point of view, something unsatisfactory still remains. For it certainly cannot be denied that at any given time making-present and recalling are dependent on a previous perception. But perception includes the functions of our sensory organs by which we are able to see, hear, smell, taste, and touch. These organs belong to the somatic realm. Or should we say furthermore: to the psychosomatic? In each case of clarifying the phenomenological differences between the phenomena of making-present, recalling, and perceiving, we have omitted the *body*. In so doing, we have eliminated the question which upsets you most of all, namely, the determination of the psychosomatic. In order to increase this upset, not eliminate it, this evening I would like to discuss the so-called problem of the body and, at the same time, the question of the psychosomatic. With this, we must first realize where the main problem area of the issue of the body lies. In order to clarify this to some extent, I proceed from a lecture Dr. Hegglin gave at the first meeting of the Swiss Psychosomatic Association.[1] Presumably, you all know it. Even someone outside the profession is immediately impressed by the sovereignty of these presentations. By this I mean that Dr. Hegglin's sovereignty lies in his preparedness, gained from rich experience, for what is worth questioning. If I take a few sentences from the text and use them as an opportunity for explicating what is to be questioned in psychosomatics, then by no means should this be interpreted as a know-it-all critique. Critique is derived from the Greek word κρίνειν. It means "to distinguish," "to set off." Genuine critique is something other than criticizing in the sense of faultfinding, blaming, and complaining.

p. 99

Critique, as "to distinguish," means to allow the different as such to be seen in its difference. What is different is only different in one respect. In this respect, we catch sight of what is the same beforehand regarding what different things belong together. This same[ness] must be brought into view in each distinction. In other words, true critique, as in this letting-be-seen [Sehenlassen], is something eminently positive. Therefore, genuine critique is rare. A rough example of this distinction is the following: Green and red are only distinguishable insofar as something like color is pregiven. It is the same regarding which distinction can be performed in the first place. In order to explicate the psychosomatic as a problem, a genuine, that is, a phenomenological critique is needed. The critical question must be asked [concerning] which *distinction* we are talking about regarding the theme of the psychosomatic. How can this distinction be made? What different things stand in question regarding their difference? In respect to what sameness and unity do the different things [*psyche* and *soma*] show themselves as different? Is it already determined? If not, how is it determinable in the first place? As long as we are not thinking clearly and critically, that is, not *asking* in the preceding manner, it is as if we are groping about in an impenetrable fog with a very brittle stick. The results of scientific research might be ever so correct and useful, but it is not proved that they are also true. They are not proved to be true in the sense of making manifest the being of beings in its peculiarity, [the being] of beings in question at any given time. In psychosomatics the concern is the concrete humanity of the human being. The following attempt at a critique by means of our conversation and mutual reflection is not concerned primarily with medical science. It is a self-critique of philosophy and its entire history up to the present. And now to the text of the lecture: "What does the internist expect from psychosomatics?" I read on page 3, column B, above: "If psychiatrists do not dare to give a definition (of the psyche), we must go back to the origin of the word. Psyche means: *anima,* soul. The physician who is not specialized in the psyche understands this word to mean manifestations of an individual's life, those [manifestations] expressing themselves in *emotions* [*Gefühle*] and *in the process of reasoning* [*Denkprozess*]. Since disorders of mental processes, as we tacitly assume, do not obviously lead to symptoms of illness, we speak of psychosomatic illnesses if disorders of the emotional life cause symptoms of illness. If we comprehend them under the rubric of emotional illnesses, as proposed by some people, then we exclude a large group of illnesses from the concept of psychosomatic illness, namely the *primarily bodily* illnesses, which have secondary repercussions on the psyche. These *somato-psychic illnesses,* as Plügge once called them, if I am not mistaken, play an especially great role in medical practice.

p. 100

p. 101

Therefore, we would like to unite all *mutual* influences between *psyche* and *soma* under the concept of psychosomatics and not to reserve this word exclusively for emotional illnesses. I have been reproached for the fact that we internists have made too sharp a separation between *psyche* and *soma*. The *psyche* does not exist as something separate from the body, but pervades the whole organism. This is quite possible, even probable. But we suspend all philosophical speculations and hold to a simple principle in order to distinguish *soma* and *psyche: Psychic phenomena cannot be weighed and measured,* but only felt intuitively, whereas everything somatic can be somehow grasped by numbers. As soon as numerical values change, they indicate a change in somatic structures, a change, which of course can be conditioned emotionally. Sadness cannot be measured, but tears formed by sadness (due to psychosomatic relationships) can be investigated quantitatively in various directions. It is possible that emotional tension, by itself not measurable in terms of natural-scientific methods, can also result in a contraction of the capillaries, leading to an increase in blood pressure. Both states of tension [*Spannungszustände*] must not be equated, of course, because a person with a high degree of emotional tension does not always have the symptoms of an arterial tension (contraction). An essential problem which we would like to understand better arises right here, namely:

p. 102

a. What kind of *emotional tensions* result in illness for which states of tension of the organs can be diagnosed functionally and objectively? For instance, I think of contractions of soft muscles, of capillaries with high pressure, of the bronchia in asthma, and of the smooth muscles of the gastrointestinal and the urogenital tracts.
b. Does this kind of psychological tension *always* lead to these illnesses, or is a special condition of the affected organ necessary?

Although much has been said and written about possible connections between psychic, that is, emotional, disorders and bodily illness in the last few years, we still lack the foundations, acceptable as proof of these connections to someone educated in the natural sciences.

Thus, the author is after a "simple principle" for the distinction between *psyche* and *soma*. What does "principle" mean? The Greek word for it is ἀρχή, which means the first "where-of" or "from-where" something begins, in its being, its becoming, and its knowability [*Erkennbarkeit*]. This "from-where" [*Von-wo-aus*] dominates, determines, and directs what begins. In the context of the above lecture, the principle of the distinction between *soma* and *psyche* involves a different comprehension of *soma* and *psyche,* which can be stated in the following way: Psychical phenomena cannot be weighed and measured, but only felt intuitively, whereas all that is somatic can somehow be comprehended by means of numbers. Therefore, the two thematic domains of *psyche* and *soma* are determined in their material content relative to accessing them. The way of disclosing a realm of being, the way into it, refers to its intelligibility. But discussing and determining it is the subject matter of philosophy as the "theory of knowledge." The "simple principle" mentioned in the lecture is obviously a philosophical one. Any attempted distinction whatsoever between *soma* and *psyche* depends on a "simple," that is, philosophical principle. Accordingly, it calls for thoughtful attention to the fact of whether the principle itself is understood appropriately and sufficiently and of whether, and of how, it is circumscribed in its scope [*Tragweite*] and applied accordingly. In the present case the question arises as to whether its objective content can be determined in its being-what and being-how from the manner of access [*Zugangsweise*] to a domain. From where is the manner of access itself determined? It is said: Psychical phenomena can only be felt intuitively and cannot be measured. What is the reason that the access to the psychical involves intuition, while [the access] to the somatic involves measurement? The reason is obviously due to the kind of beings *soma* and *psyche* are. Therefore, the "simple" principle applied here states: The thematic domains of *psyche* and *soma* are determined by the manner each case can be accessed, and in turn, the way of access is determined by the subject matter, hence, by *soma* and *psyche*. We move in a circle. However, this circle is not a *circulus vitiosus,* not a "vicious" one.

p. 103

What is called a "circle" here belongs to the essential structure of human knowledge (see *Being and Time,* p. 2, especially p. 193 f.). For instance, a painting by Cézanne of Mont Ste. Victoire cannot be comprehended [*erfassen*] by calculation. Certainly, one could also conduct chemical research on such a picture. But if one would like to comprehend it as a work of art, one does not calculate, but sees it intuitively. Is the painting, therefore, something psychological, since we have just heard that the psychological is what can be comprehended intuitively? No, the painting is not something psychological. Obviously, the above-mentioned "simple principle" for distinguishing *psyche* and *soma* is not simple at all. Accordingly, we are faced with the question of the nature of the distinction between *psyche* and *soma,* how it must be made, and what thoughtful attention is necessary in order to see clearly here. In the first place, the question of the psychosomatic is a question of method. Of course, its meaning requires a special discussion.

p. 104

The last sentence of the cited article states: "We still lack the foundations, which would be acceptable as *proof* of these connections for someone educated in the natural sciences." Here, what do foundations mean for the connection between *soma* and *psyche*? Obviously, [they mean] something for which one can demand a scientific proof. Yet, a scientific proof for the connection between *psyche* and *soma* is completely impossible, since these foundations, according to the demands of science, would have to be somatic due to the fact that in the natural sciences only what can be measured is "provable." Therefore, the proof would be supported by only one of the two related domains, that is, by the somatic. In other words, what satisfies the natural scientist's claim for valid knowledge must be provable and proved by measurement. Therefore, the author demands that the relationship between *soma* and *psyche* be measurable. But this is an unjustified claim, because it has not been derived from the subject matter in question, but from the [following] scientific claim and dogma: Only what is measurable is real.

But are the connections between *psyche* and *soma* something psychological or something somatic, or neither one nor the other? We wind up in a dead end, which shows you better than anything else how essential the question of method is.

p. 105   II. May 11, 1965

Now we will leap to the problem of the body.

To begin, let us consider two statements made by Nietzsche. *The Will to Power*, number 659 (originally written in 1885), reads: "The idea of the body is more astonishing than the idea of the ancient 'soul.'" Number 489 (originally written in 1886) reads: "The phenomenon of the body is the richer, the more distinct, the more comprehensible phenomenon. It should have methodological priority, without our deciding anything about its ultimate significance."

The first statement contains a truth. However, what is asserted in the second statement does not seem to be the case, that is, that the body is more comprehensible and more distinct. Rather, the opposite is the case. Therefore, the following statement concerning "the spatiality of Being-in-the-world" appears in *Being and Time*, section 23: "Da-sein constantly takes these directions [e.g., below, above, right and left, in front, and behind] along with it, just as it does its de-severances. Da-sein's spatialization in its "bodiliness" is similarly marked out in accordance with these directions. (This "bodiliness" hides a whole problematic of its own, though we will not deal with it here.)"*

---

*See *Being and Time*, p. 143.—TRANSLATORS

The *Da-sein of the human being* is *spatial* in itself in the sense of *making room* [in space] [*Einraümen von Raum*]* and in the sense of *the spatialization of Da-sein in its bodily nature.* Da-sein is not spatial because it is embodied. But its bodiliness is possible only because Da-sein is spatial in the sense of making room.†

We will now try to move somewhat closer to the *phenomenon of the body.* In doing so, we are not speaking of a solution to the problem of the body. Much has already been gained merely by starting to see this problem. Once again we refer to the text by Professor Hegglin. Among other things, it notes: "Sadness cannot be measured, but the tears formed by sadness due to psychosomatic relations can be investigated   p. 106 quantitatively in various directions." Yet you can never actually measure tears. If you try to measure them, you measure a fluid and its drops at the most, but not tears. Tears can only be seen directly. Where do tears belong? Are they something somatic or psychical? They are neither the one, nor the other. Take another phenomenon: Someone blushes with shame and embarrassment. Can the blushing be measured? Blushing with shame cannot be measured. Only the redness can be measured, for instance, by measuring the circulation of blood. Then is blushing something somatic or something psychical? It is neither one nor the other. Phenomenologically speaking, we can easily distinguish between a face blushing with shame and, for instance, a face flushed with fever or as a result of going inside of a warm hut after a cold mountain night outside. All three kinds of blushing appear on the face, but they are very different from each other and are immediately distinguished in our everyday being-with and being-for each other. We can "see" from the respective situations whether someone is embarrassed, for instance, or flushed for some other reason.

Take the phenomenon of pain and sadness. For instance, bodily pain and grief for the death of a relative both involve "pain." What about these "pains"? Are they both somatic or are they both psychical? Or is only one of them somatic and the other psychical, or is it neither one nor the other?

---

*See ibid., p. 146: "Da-sein can move things around or out of the way or 'make room' for them only because making room—understood as an *existentiale*—belongs to its Being-in-the-world."—TRANSLATORS

†*Raum-geben* (giving space) and *Einräumen* (making room) are equivalent as constitutive elements of the human being's spatial "being-in-the-world" by which he orients himself in space. See Heidegger, *Being and Time*, p. 146 ff. See also Heidegger, *Basic Writings*, pp. 144–87, 320–39.—TRANSLATORS

How do we measure sadness? Evidently, one cannot measure it at all! Why not? If one approached sadness with a method of measuring, the very approach would already be contrary to the meaning of sadness. Thus, one would preclude sadness as sadness beforehand. Here, even the claim to measure is already a violation of the phenomenon as a phenomenon. But do we not also use quantitative concepts in our speech about sadness? One does not speak of an "intense" sadness, but of a "great" or a "profound" sadness. One can also say, "He is 'a bit sad,' " but that does not mean a small quantity of sadness. The "a bit" refers to a quality of mood. This very depth, however, is by no means measurable. Not even the "depth" of this room as experienced in my being-in-the-world is measurable. That is, when I attend to depth in order to measure it by approaching the window over there, then the depth experience moves with me as I move toward the window, and it goes right through it. I can objectify and measure this depth as little as I can traverse my relationship to this depth. Yet I am able, more or less, to estimate the distance precisely from *me* to the window. Certainly. Yet, in this case, I measure the distance between two bodies, not the depth opened up in each case by my being-in-the-world. Regarding the depth of a feeling of sadness, there is no reason or occasion whatsoever to estimate it quantitatively, let alone to measure it. As far as sadness is concerned, it can only be shown how a person is affected by it and how his relationship to himself and the world is changed.

A further phenomenon of the body may be mentioned in the following example. If I look at the crossbar over there and pick up the glass in front of me, is the crossbar then "in my eye" in the same way as the glass is "in my hand"? Certainly not. But where lies the difference [between these phenomena of distance] we can easily identify without being able to determine it at the same time? Obviously, the hand is an organ of our body and so is the eye. Therefore, we ask the question: How are these organs distinct from each other despite their belonging to the same body? Of course, one could say that the picture of the crossbar is in the retina of my eye. Nevertheless, I cannot see the picture in the retina. The picture in the retina is surely not the crossbar. After all, the question is whether this crossbar is seen through my eye, and not whether the retina's picture is in my eye as the glass is in my hand. Obviously, there is a difference between the way I see "with" my eye and how I grasp "with" my hand. How does the body come into play here? When I grasp the glass, I not only grasp the glass, but can also simultaneously see my hand and the glass. But I cannot see my eye and my seeing, and by no means am I able to grasp them. For in the immediacy of seeing and hearing turned toward the "world," the eye and ear disappear in a peculiar manner. If someone else wants to ascertain how the eye is functioning when seeing, and how it is anatomically constituted, he must see my eye as I see the crossbar.

p. 107

p. 108

We call the eye a sensory organ. And what about the hand? We can hardly call it a sensory organ. But the sense of touch belongs to it. Yet is the hand something more than a moving collection of movable, tactile surfaces—perhaps an organ of grasping? Then, what is seeing in contrast to grasping? For one thing, in seeing, the eye itself is not seen, whereas the hand, when grasping, cannot only be seen, but I can grasp it with my other hand. When I grasp the glass, then I feel the glass and my hand. That is the so-called double sensation [*Doppelempfindung*], namely, the sensation of what is touched and the sensation of my hand. In the act of seeing, I do not sense my eye in this manner. The eye does not touch. On the other hand, there are sensations of pressure in my eye when someone hits it. Yet that is an entirely different phenomenon. But do we not also feel the motion of the eye when, for instance, we look askance? Nevertheless, what is felt cannot be classified as "double sensation" because I do not feel the window I see when I look askance at it. The difference between the seeing of the crossbar and that of my hand consists, among other things, of the fact that the hand is my hand, whereas the crossbar is over there. I perceive the hand in its position, so to speak, "from the inside" as well because it is my hand. Is the body, therefore, something interior? What is the reason I see my hand in grasping and yet that I do not see my eye in seeing?

In grasping, the hand is in immediate contact with what is grasped. p.109 My eye is not in immediate contact with what is seen. What is seen is in my horizon, that is, it is in front of my eyes. I can only see forward, but the glass I grasped is in front of me too. However, sitting at the table, I can grasp the glass only when it is within a definite reach in front of me. Grasping is only possible when something is nearby to be grasped. Therefore, touch is called the sense of proximity. Seeing is a sense of distance.

Is the physicist able to say anything about the phenomenon of seeing? He can state that sources of light come into play, but when one sees the crossbar, nothing concerning these sources is involved.

One says that seeing is "superior" to grasping. One can control grasping through seeing because sight, like hearing, is essentially oriented to distance. Yet in a dark room, I can "control" seeing too, through touching. If seeing has a wider range than grasping, then grasping and seeing obviously have something to do with our relationship to space. Then, how does bodiliness, which is still left undetermined, relate to space?

SEMINAR PARTICIPANT: The body is nearest* [*Nächste*] to us in space.

---

*We use "near" for the ontic-spatial measurable sense and "close" for the ontological-existential sense of the German *nahe*. See Heidegger, *Being and Time*, p. 135: "What

MARTIN HEIDEGGER: I would say it is the most distant. When you have back pains, are they of a spatial nature? What kind of spatiality is peculiar to the pain spreading across your back? Can it be equated with the surface extension of a material thing? The diffusion of pain certainly exhibits the character of extension, but this does not involve a surface. Of course, one can also examine the body as a corporeal thing [*Körper*]. Because you are educated in anatomy and physiology as doctors, that is, with a focus on the examination of bodies, you probably look at the states of the body in a different way than the "layman" does. Yet, a layman's experience is probably closer to the phenomenon of pain as it involves our body lines, even if it can hardly be described with the aid of our usual intuition of space.

p. 110

In connection with these remarks regarding the phenomenon of the body, we will return once again to what we have said about *making-present*. What did we fail to take into account? We merely tried to clarify that by making-present we mean the train station itself, yet we do not see the station physically as we see the glass in front of us on the table. Is the phenomenon of making the station present thoroughly determined thereby? We said: We are not physically present [*körperhaft*] at the station while making-it-present. But [are we] perhaps [there] in a "bodily" manner [*leibhaft*]? Yet, didn't we just say that the station is not present in a physical sense, as is the glass we perceive in front of us on the table? Nevertheless, the body is part of this making-present in some way, [and so] within the making-present relationship toward the train station there.

How does my body come into play in the [act of] making-present? Just as far as I am here. What role does the body play in this being-here? Where is the here? Phenomenologically, how is the here related to my body?

SP: Here is where my body is.

MH: But my body is not identical with the here. Where is my body? How do you determine the here? Where am I? Where are you? What big and difficult questions are we dealing with here? Obviously, we are dealing with the question of how the body relates to space. Obviously, the body relates to space in a totally different way than, for example, a chair is present (ready-to-hand) in space. The body takes up space.

---

is ready-to-hand [*zuhanden*] in our everyday dealing has the character of closeness." English "close" (Latin: *claudere*, to shut, to close) expresses familiarity and intimacy, whereas "near" (akin to Old English *neah* and *nigh* and to Old High German *nah*) refers more to nearness in space and time.—TRANSLATORS

Is it demarcated from space? Where are the limits of the body? Where does the body stop?

SP: It does not stop at any point.

MH: Does that mean it has unlimited extension? If that is not what we mean, what then is the meaning of this assertion? Presumably, we think of its reach [*Reichweite*]. Yet, from where and how does the body have a reach? Is the reach of the body of the same kind as that of a rocket on a launching pad? If someone lives, as we say, "lost in space," what function does his body have then? When the philosopher Thales, lost in thought, walked along a road, fell into a ditch, and was ridiculed by some servant girl, his body was in no way "lost in space." Rather, it was not present. As in the case above, precisely when I am absorbed in something "body and soul," the body is not present. Yet, this "absence" of the body is not nothing, but one of the most mysterious phenomena of privation.

p. 111

III. May 14, 1965

In our previous session we tried to familiarize ourselves a little more with the problem of the body. We did not make much progress. Our first task was, and still is, to enable us to see certain phenomena, such as blushing, grasping, pain, and sadness.

It is crucial to leave these phenomena the way we see them without trying to reduce them to something else. In other words, it is imperative to refrain from any possibility of reductionism. Instead, we must pay attention to the question of to what extent these phenomena are already sufficiently determined on their own terms and to what extent they refer to other phenomena to which they essentially belong. We speak of "phenomena" here, although this concept is, of course, not yet sufficiently clarified.

At the end of the last seminar, we came to the question of the human being's being-here. This is a question in which space, body, and their relationship to one another obviously play a role. One could venture the following proposition: I am "here" at all times. Nevertheless, the proposition is ambiguous. Or is it not completely false from the start? For instance, we certainly are not here in this space at all times. What meaning does this proposition have then? What is the meaning of "here" in this proposition? The particular "here" is not specified. Nevertheless, I am surely present "here" at all times somewhere. Therefore, "I am here at all times" means that I always live in a "here." However, in each case

p. 112

the "here" is *this one.* I am always at some particular "here," but I am not always at this particular place.

In each case the body always participates in the being-here, but how? Does the volume of my body determine the being-here? Do the limits of me as a corporeal thing coincide with myself as a body? One could understand the living body as a corporeal thing. I am seated here at the table, and fill this space enclosed by my epidermis. But then we are not speaking about my being-here, but only about the presence of a corporeal thing in this place. Perhaps one comes closer to the phenomenon of the body by distinguishing between the different limits of a corporeal thing [*Körper*] and those of the body [*Leib*].

The corporeal thing stops with the skin. When we are here, we are always in relationship to something else. Therefore, one might say we are beyond the corporeal limits. Yet, this statement is only apparently correct. It does not really capture the phenomenon. For I cannot determine the phenomenon of the body in relation to its corporeality.

The difference between the limits of the corporeal thing and the body, then, consists in the fact that the *bodily limit* is extended beyond the *corporeal limit.* Thus, the difference between the limits is a quantitative one. But if we look at the matter in this way, we will misunderstand the very phenomenon of the body and of bodily limit. The bodily limit and the corporeal limit are not quantitatively but rather qualitatively different from each other. The corporeal thing, as corporeal, cannot have a limit which is similar to the body at all. Of course, one could assume in an imaginative way that my body qua corporeal thing extends to the perceived window, so that the bodily limit and the corporeal limit coincide. But just then the qualitative difference between the two limits becomes clear. The corporeal limit, by apparently coinciding with the bodily limit, cannot ever become a bodily limit itself. When pointing with my finger toward the crossbar of the window over there, I [as body] do not end at my fingertips. Where then is the limit of the body? "Each body is my body." As such, the proposition is nonsensical. More properly, it should say: "The body is in each case my body." This belongs to the phenomenon of the body. The "my" refers to myself. By "my," I refer to me. Is the body in the "I," or is the "I" in the body? In any case, the body is not a thing, nor is it a corporeal thing, but each body, that is, the body as body, is in each case my body. The *bodying forth** [*Leiben*] *of the body* is determined by the way of my being. The bodying forth of the body, therefore, is a

p. 113

---

*See M. Boss, *Existential Foundations of Medicine and Psychology,* trans. Stephen Conway and Anne Cleaves (New York: J. Aronson, 1979), pp. 102–4.—TRANSLATORS

way of Da-sein's being. But what kind of being? If the body as body is always my body, then this is my own way of being. Thus, bodying forth is co-determined by my being human in the sense of the ecstatic sojourn amidst the beings in the clearing [gelichtet]. The limit of bodying forth (the body is only as it is bodying forth: "body") is the horizon of being within which I sojourn [aufhalten].* Therefore, the limit of my bodying forth changes constantly through the change in the reach of my sojourn. In contrast, the limit of the corporeal thing usually does not change. If it does, it does so at most only by growing bigger or growing thinner. But leanness is not merely a phenomenon of corporeality, but of the body as well. The lean body can, of course, be measured again as a corporeal thing regarding its weight. The volume of the corporeal thing (body has no "volume") has diminished.

Everything that has been stated about the limits of a body and of a corporeal thing is still insufficiently specified, and must be raised explicitly once more.

For the time being, we note only that the "mine" in this talk about "my body" relates to myself. The bodying forth has this peculiar relationship to the self. Kant once said that man distinguishes himself from animals by the fact that he can say "I"![2] This assertion can be formulated still more radically. The human being distinguishes himself from animals because he can "say" anything at all, that is to say, because he has a language. Are saying and language the same? Is every saying a speaking? No. For instance, if you assert: "This watch lies here," what is involved in this assertion? Why doesn't an animal speak? Because it has nothing to say. In what way does it have nothing to say? Human speaking is saying. Not every saying is speaking, yet every speaking is saying, even speaking that "says nothing." Speaking always makes sounds. In contrast, I can say something to myself silently without making a sound. p. 114

Therefore, I can assert that the watch is on the table. Thus, what I say by this assertion refers to a certain state of affairs. Saying makes something visible as a matter of fact. According to its ancient etymological meaning, to "say" is to "show," to let be seen. How is this possible? When I asserted something about the watch, you all agreed with it. You could only do

---

*We translate both Aufenhalt and sich aufhalten as "sojourn" rather than as "dwelling/to dwell," as in the Macquarrie and Robinson translation of Being and Time, since the verb wohnen is usually translated as "to dwell" in Heidegger's later writings. See Heidegger, Basic Writings, p. 320 ff. "Sojourn" means to stay for a short time as a guest and then to reside (Old French: sojuner; from Latin: subdiurnare, diurnum-dies, day; "journey" is a day's march; "journeyman" is a worker by the day; "journal" is a daily record).—TRANSLATORS

this because you saw the watch lying here. That is, it has not been here merely since the time I made the assertion. For those of us who are sitting here, the watch is obviously lying here on the table. How does the body participate in this assertion? The body participates by hearing and seeing. But does the body see? No. I see. But certainly my eyes belong to such a seeing, and thus to my body. Nevertheless, an eye does not see, but my eye sees—I see through *my* eyes. The body never sees a watch, and nevertheless it is present. When I say: "The watch is lying in front of me," this is an assertion about a spatial relationship of the watch to me. The watch is in space, and "I" am in space. But am I beside the watch the same way as the book is beside the watch on the same table? We find ourselves reverting to the question we have already touched on: How is the human being in space insofar as he is bodying forth? I take the watch lying in front of me into my hand. Now I put it away again. What has happened to the watch? And to me? I have placed the watch away from my hand. How did I do this? I performed a movement, and the watch has been moved. By the movement *I* performed, I have moved *the watch and myself.* Are the movements of the watch and of my hand the same, or are they two movements, which are quite different from each other? The watch is moved, and I move myself. But the watch also moves itself insofar as it "runs." Yet now the question is not about the "running" of the watch, but about the movement of the watch, insofar as it is still running when removed from my hand and placed on the table. One calls the movement of a thing from one location to another a transporting. A thing is transported [φορα].* When Dr. Boss drives my suitcases to the train station, they are transported. When he drives me to the station, I am not transported, but I go with him. The movement of the watch from my hand to the table is locomotion of the watch, that is, a movement from here to there in a curve, which can be measured. What is the case with the movement of my hand in contrast to the movement of the watch?

I just saw how Dr. K. was "passing" his hand over his forehead. And yet I did not observe a change of location and position of one of his hands, but I immediately noticed that he was thinking of something difficult. How should we characterize this movement of the hand? As a movement of expression? Admittedly, if it is a movement that expresses

p. 115

---

*This Greek word is related to the Old English *beran*, to carry; to the Latin *ferre*; and to the Greek φέρειν. Also see "bearing," the manner in which one bears or comports oneself. Compare the Greek word *metapherein*, to transfer; hence, *meta-phora*, metaphor (a figure of speech in which a word or phrase with one literal meaning is "transferred" by analogy to another meaning).—TRANSLATORS

something which is internal, then this characterization only states the effect of the movement. But nothing whatsoever is said yet about the kind of movement itself as a hand movement. We specify this hand movement as a "gesture" [*Gebärde*]. Even when I place the watch on the table, I move within a gesture. And the hand? How does it belong to me? The hand belongs to my arm. Putting the watch away is not only a movement of the hand, but also of the arm, the shoulder. It is *my* movement. I moved myself.

IV. May 14, 1965

During the break you were protesting that putting the watch on the table is a gesture, the same way that the movement of Dr. K's hand over his forehead supposedly expressed the fact that he was pondering something difficult. Thus, you see gesture as expression. But what were we asking about? We were asking about the kind of movement to which we were referring. Were we asking about the difference between the change of place of the watch in a spatial path and the movement of my hand? When I say that the movement of the hand is a gesture, this concept characterizes a kind of movement and should not to be taken as an expression of something else. To you, the word "gesture" is perhaps an arbitrary designation. But when you say "gesture" is an expression, are you then answering my question? No. The answer given by the term "expression" is already an interpretation and does not answer the question as to what kind of movement it is. "Expression" refers instead to something that is expressed by the movement of the hand. It refers, therefore, to something supposed to be behind it that causes it. The term "gesture" characterizes the movement as my bodily movement.

p. 116

    Here I would like to make a few isolated remarks. One often hears the objection that there is something wrong with the distinction between a corporeal thing and a body. This is raised, for instance, because the French have no word whatsoever for the body, but only a term for a corporeal thing, namely, *le corps*. But what does this mean? It means that in this area the French are influenced only by the Latin *corpus*. This is to say that for them it is very difficult to see the real problem of the phenomenology of the body. The meaning of the Greek word σῶμα is quite manifold. Homer uses the word merely for the dead body. For the living body, he uses the term δεμας, meaning "figure." Later on, σῶμα refers to both the body and the lifeless, corporeal thing, then also to the serfs, to the slaves. Finally, it refers to the mass of all men. In Greek, σῶμα has a much broader meaning than our present "somatic." In general, it

p. 117

can be said that the Greek meaning of the word has been reinterpreted from the Latin. Our [German] conception of a corporeal thing stems from Latin *corpus*. According to the Scholastics, the body is an ensouled, corporeal thing, a determination that, in a certain sense, goes back to Aristotle, though only in a certain sense of course. (Our German world *Wirklichkeit* [reality], for instance, is connected with the word *wirken*, "to work." *Wirklichkeit* is the translation of the Latin word *actualitas,* which, in turn, stems from *actus,* from *agere.* Cicero translated the Greek word ἐνέργεια with the Latin *actualitas.* Nevertheless, to translate this with the word *Wirklichkeit* is totally contrary to the Greek meaning.[*] Yet if we have the necessary fundamental insight, we can listen once again to the Greek language. If we called for a universal language, one which could be understood uniformly by all, then we would level down language entirely to one that would say nothing at all. The Greek language was even the necessary condition for the origins of Western thought.)[†]

Let us return to the foregoing distinction between the animal and the human being. In contrast to animals, why do we as human beings have something to say if to say means "to let see," "to make manifest"? What is saying founded on? If you perceive something as being such and such—for instance, this thing as glass—it must be manifest to you that something *is.* Thus, the human being has something to say because saying, as letting-see, is a letting-see of something as such and such a being. The human being, therefore, stands in the openness of being, in the unconcealedness [*Unverborgenheit*] of what comes to presence. This is the reason for the possibility, indeed the necessity, the essential necessity, of "saying," that is, the reason that the human being speaks.

And now let us return to our discussion of gesture. What does the word "gesture" [German: *Gebärde*] mean? Etymologically, it comes from *bären* [cf. Latin *ferre:* to carry, to bring]. To bear or to bring forth [*gebären*] comes from the same root. The German prefix *Ge-* always refers to a gathering, to a collection of things, as in *Ge-birge* [mountain range], which is a collection of mountains. From its human origins, "gesture" means one's gathered [*gesammelt*] bearing and comportment. Within philosophy we must not limit the word "gesture" merely to "expression." Instead, we must characterize all comportment of the human being as

p. 118

---

[*]See *ZS* 250.—TRANSLATORS

[†]Here Heidegger emphasizes the *historical* character of all human languages in contrast to artificial languages (e.g., mathematics, mathematical logic, technical languages, Esperanto, etc.). See Heidegger, *History of the Concept of Time,* pp. 216–74. —TRANSLATORS

being-in-the-world, determined by the bodying forth of the body. Each movement of my body as a "gesture" and, therefore, as such and such a comportment does not simply enter into an indifferent space. Rather, comportment is always already in a certain region [*Gegend*]* which is open through the thing to which I am in a relationship, for instance, when I take something into my hand.

Last time we spoke about blushing. We usually take blushing as an expression, that is, we immediately take it as a sign of an internal state of mind. But what lies in the phenomenon of blushing itself? It too is a gesture insofar as the one who blushes is related to his fellow human beings. With this you see how bodiliness has a peculiar "ecstatic" meaning. I emphasize this to such a degree in order to get you away from the misinterpretation of "expression"! French psychologists also misinterpret everything as an expression of something interior instead of seeing the phenomena of the body in the context of which men are in relationship to each other.

In closing, I give you a riddle, and I quote: "The configuration of a mnemonic-information plan, which must be directed by signal groups toward a receiving station." What is this? "Configuration"? I know that it is impossible to guess what it is. But, according to Mr. Zerbe, it is the idea of the human being (see *Zeitschrift für psychosomatische Medizin,* vol. 11, no. 1 [1965]). Zerbe's assertion is based on the fact that the model of the human being must be understood in [terms] of antiaircraft cybernetics.† p. 119 This becomes evident from the following proposition from the founder of cybernetics, Norbert Wiener, which reads: We can construct an anti-aircraft gun, which is designed to observe the statistically determined trajectory of a targeted airplane by itself. It can transfer the determined trajectory to a control system using it to bring the position of the gun rapidly toward the direction of the observed airplane, thereby adjusting itself to the motion of the airplane.

Gegend [region] is the original place of Da-seins's spatiality regarding things ready-to-hand [*zuhanden*]. Only the deprivation of this originary spatiality, by giving up this comportment and focusing on thing as "objects" in pure, homogeneous space, opens up the "space" [*Raum*] of things as just present-at-hand [*vorhanden*], i.e., the world of nature, the world of the Cartesian *res extensa.* See Heidegger, *Being and Time,* p. 146 ff. Also *ZS* 106.—TRANSLATORS

†*Cybernetics* is derived from the Greek *Kybernan* [to steer, to govern] and from the Greek *Kybernetes* [pilot, governor]. It is usually described as the comparative study of the automatic control system formed by the brain and nervous system and by mechanical-electrical communication systems.—TRANSLATORS

Wiener's definition of the human being is as follows: "Man [is] an information [device]."[3] Wiener goes on regarding the human being: "Nevertheless, one characteristic distinguishes man from other animals in a way which leaves no doubt: Man is an animal that speaks. . . . It also will not do to say that man is an ensouled animal. For, unfortunately, the existence of the soul—whatever one may take it to be—is not accessible to scientific methods of inquiry" (p. 14). As an animal who speaks, the human being must be represented in such a way that language can be explained scientifically as something computable, that is, as something that can be controlled.

You see the same thing here, we already encountered in the statement by Professor Hegglin: What the human being is, is determined by the method sanctioned by natural science. In cybernetics, language must be conceived in a manner that can be approached scientifically. In the basic determination of what the human being is, the foundation of cybernetics seemingly agrees with the ancient tradition of the metaphysical definition of man. The Greek determined the human being as ζῷον λόγον ἔχον, that is, as a living being possessing language. Wiener states: Man is that animal that speaks. If man is explained scientifically, then what distinguishes him from the animal—namely, language—must be represented so that it can be explained according to scientific principles. In short, language as language must be represented as something that can be measured. A more thorough interpretation of the nature of cybernetics will have to wait for later discussion. We must also postpone the question posed last time, that is, where does the measurability of something belong, whether to the thing itself, or not. This question is to be posed again within the context of a discussion on cybernetics.

p. 120

p. 121 ## July 6 and 8, 1965, at Boss's Home

I. July 6, 1965

When I arrived, Dr. Boss gave me a bagful of questions concerning our previous seminar. It contains sixteen questions in no apparent order. But one can easily see that we are dealing with two sets of questions [here]. One refers to the characterization and highlighting of the phenomenon of the body; the other contains questions pertaining to the determination of psychosomatics as a science, that is, questions concerning the distinction between *psyche* and *soma*, at the same time concerning the relationship of each to the other. It is evident that both sets of questions belong together. Without a sufficient characterization of the phenomenon of the body, one would not be able to state the nature of psychosomatics, whether and how it could be constructed as a unitary science and how the distinction between *psyche* and *soma* must generally be viewed. We must raise the question as to the way that distinction can be made and how it can be given a foundation. The question of the way is the question of method. Therefore, we read in the protocol of May 11, 1965 [p. 104 above]: "The question of the psychosomatic is in the first place a question of method." At the same time, the statement is added: "What this term (method) means requires, of course, a special discussion."

One set of questions revolves around the question: What is the body? The other set of questions refers to the question: What does method mean? Is the body something somatic or something psychical? Or is it neither of them? If the latter is the case, then what is the nature of the distinction between *soma* and *psyche*? Can this distinction eventually be discarded? Thereby does psychosomatic theory prove to be an insufficient, or even impossible, statement of the problem? But what does "statement of the problem" mean here? What is *method* in modern science, and what role does it play? Does this term simply mean the mode of an inquiry into a domain of objects [*Gegenstandsgebiet*], a procedural technique in research? Or does method in modern science have an entirely different importance [*Gewicht*] and character [*Gesicht*], even though science does not possess the necessary insight into this matter? At the end, or even better, at the outset, do the problem of the body and the problem of method in science (not only in psychosomatics) belong together generally? The answer to this question, one worth asking, can be expressed pointedly in the following statements: The problem of method in science is equivalent to the problem of the body. The problem of the body is primarily a problem of method.

p. 122

In physics, the *theory of relativity* introduced the position of the observer as a theme of science. Yet physics, as such, is unable to say what this "position of the observer" means. It obviously refers to what we touched on by saying: I am here at any time. In this being-here, the bodiliness of the human being always comes into play. In the area of microphysics, the act of measuring and the instrument themselves interfere with comprehending the objects during experimentation. That means that the bodiliness of the human being comes into play within the "objectivity" of natural science. Does this only hold true for scientific research, or is it true here precisely because in general the bodying forth of the human being's body co-determines the human being's being-in-the-world. If this is the case, the phenomenon of the body can be brought into view if and only when being-in-the-world is explicitly experienced, appropriated, and sustained as the basic characteristic of human existence. This can only be done by critically overcoming the hitherto dominant subject-object relation [in human knowledge]. One must see that science as such (i.e., all theoretical-scientific knowledge) is founded as a way of being-in-the-world—founded in the bodily having of a world.[*]

p. 123 It is necessary to indicate the entire realm of what is worthy of questioning so that we may avoid deceiving ourselves about the protracted difficulty of the questions posed in this seminar. But we must come to the insight that the description of particular phenomena and isolated answers to particular questions are insufficient unless a reflection on the method as such is raised and at the same time kept alive. The more the current effect and usefulness of science spread, the more the capacity and readiness for a reflection upon what occurs in science disappears. This is especially true insofar as science carries through its claim to offer, and to administer, *the* truth about genuine reality.

What happens in the course of science when it proceeds in this manner and is left to itself? What occurs is nothing less than the possible self-destruction of the human being. This process is already delineated at the outset of modern science. For among other things, modern science is based on the fact that the human being posits himself as an authoritative subject to whom everything that can be investigated becomes an object. Underlying this state of affairs is a decisive change in the unfolding essence of truth [*Wesen der Wahrheit*]: It changes into certainty, according to which the truly real assumes the character of "objectivity."[†] As long as

---

[*]Concerning Einstein's relativity theory, Heidegger remarks: "Here we shall not go into the problem of the measurement of time as treated in the theory of relativity. If the ontological foundations of such measurement are to be clarified, this presupposes that world-time [*Weltzeit*] and within-time-ness [*Innerzeitigkeit*] have already been clarified in terms of Dasein's temporality [*Zeitlichkeit des Daseins*], and that light has also been cast on the existential-temporal constitution of the discovery of Nature and the temporal meaning of measurement. Any axiomatic for the physical technique of measurement [in physics] must rest upon such investigations, and can never, for its own part, tackle the problem of time as such" (Heidegger, *Being and Time*, p. 499, n. 4). This also holds true for Stephen Hawking, *A Brief History of Time* (New York: Bantam, 1988).—TRANSLATORS

[†]See Heidegger, *The Question concerning Technology*, pp. 115–54, 155–82; "Modern Science, Metaphysics, and Mathematics," *Basic Writings*, pp. 243–82; *Nietzsche*, ed. D. Farrell Krell, trans. F. A. Capuzzi (San Francisco: Harper and Row, 1982), 4:96–118; H. Alderman, "Heidegger's Critique of Science and Technology" in *Heidegger and Modern Philosophy*, ed. M. Murray (New Haven, Conn.: Yale University Press, 1978), pp. 35–50.—TRANSLATORS

we do not explicitly bring into view what was just said and what has been often pointed out, and as long as we do not constantly keep it in view, our efforts in this seminar will succeed only halfway. As long as this is the case, we also will be unable to understand what is already implied, although not thought out, in some extreme positions within modern science.

When, for instance, the assertion is made that brain research is a fundamental science for our knowledge of the human being, this assertion implies that the true and real relationship among human beings is a correlation among brain processes. Indeed, it implies that in brain research itself all that happens is that one brain, as the saying goes, "informs" another brain in a specific way, and nothing more. Then, when one is not engaged in research during semester vacation, the aesthetic appreciation of the statue of a god in the Acropolis museum is nothing more than the encounter of the brain process of the beholder with the product of another brain process, that is, the representation of the statue. Nevertheless, if during the vacation one assures oneself that one does not mean it that way, then one lives by double- or triple-entry bookkeeping. Of course, this does not coincide very well with the claim made elsewhere for the rigorous nature of science. This means that one has become so undemanding regarding thinking and reflecting that such double bookkeeping is no longer considered disturbing, nor is the complete lack of reflection upon this passionately defended science and its necessary limits considered in any way disturbing. It seems to me that we should be allowed to demand from science, which attaches decisive importance to consistency, this same claim to consistency, especially where the meaning of the human being's existence is at stake.

p. 124

Customarily, one labels the reference to this threatening self-destruction of the being of the human being within science (with its absolute claims) as hostility toward science. Yet, it is not a matter of hostility toward science as such, but rather a matter of critique regarding the prevailing lack of reflection on itself by science. But such a reflection includes, above all, an insight into the very *method determining* the character of modern science. We are now trying to clarify the peculiarity of this method and to do this in connection with questions indicating the direction of the method. By doing so, we will touch necessarily upon certain aspects of *the phenomenon of the body,* and we will finally encounter questions on the unfolding essence of truth. From my experience in all of our previous seminars, it has become increasingly clear to me that the discussion of particular problems and the isolated interpretation of selected phenomena have repeatedly come to a standstill. And this is because the guiding perspectives are insufficiently elucidated, and thus, thinking cannot turn explicitly to these guiding perspectives.

p. 125

First, our thoughtful attention is directed toward the unique and distinctive character of *modern science*. Second, it is directed toward the way of questioning, seeing, and saying of *phenomenology* in the broadest sense. Third, it is directed toward the *relationship* between science and phenomenology. With regard to the third problem, I return to the question Dr. H. raised in a previous seminar. The discussion of the three questions mentioned above must also explain how one might be afraid—and properly so—that a phenomenological reflection on science and its theories would deprive one of a hold on one, leaving one groundless. With this, the question cannot be avoided as to how far science, as such, is able to give human existence grounding at all. But we shall try to deal with the three themes mentioned above—namely, science, phenomenology, and their mutual relationship—following the line of questioning posed in relation to our previous seminar. One group refers to the phenomenon of the body and the other to method. Although we will work with the second group first, I will start with a question from the first group.

I will select the following question: When I am involved "body and soul" in the discussion of the theme, is my body not absent, or is it no longer sitting on the chair where it was before I began to pay attention to this theme?

The answer to all questions always presupposes that we ask the *right* questions. In our question, I take the body first as a corporeal thing present-at-hand on the chair. But actually, *I* sit on the chair. This involves something quite different from the presence-at-hand of one corporeal thing above another.

Where is the body when I am involved "body and soul" in the theme of the discussion? On the other hand, how is the content of the discussion related to space? I am listening to the discussion of the theme "I am all ears."* Thus, hearing is a mode of bodying forth—of the bodily participation in the discussion. I am not only hearing but also speaking and participating in the discussion. Hence, I must continue to sit on the chair in a bodily manner in order to be all ears. If I wandered around the room, this would be lessened or not done at all. Hearing refers to the theme uttered in the discussion. Therefore, we also speak of a verbal articulation [*Verlautbarung*]. For something to be uttered means: It is said. Hearing and speaking on the whole belong to language. Hearing

p. 126

---

*See M. Heidegger, "Logos: Heraclitus B50," *Vorträge und Aufsätze* (Pfullingen: G. Neske, 1954), pt. 3 [*Early Greek Thinking*, trans. D. F. Krell and F. A. Capuzzi (New York: Harper and Row, 1975), pp. 59–78]. See also Heidegger, *Being and Time*, sec. 34.—TRANSLATORS

and speaking, and thus language in general, are *also* always phenomena of the body.* Hearing is a being-with-the-theme in a bodily way. To hear something in itself involves the relation of bodying forth to what is heard. Bodying forth [*Leiben*] always belongs to being-in-the-world. It always co-determines being-in-the-world, openness, and the having of a world.

Even when I merely think to myself silently and do not utter anything, such thinking is always a saying. Therefore, Plato is able to call thinking a dialogue of the soul with itself.

Even what has been heard and written about the theme plays a role in such a silent thinking and saying. Silent thinking occurs as an unthematic making-present of sounds and letters. Such making-present is therefore co-determined by bodying forth. For instance, one cannot daydream about a landscape without necessarily saying something to oneself insofar as saying is always a letting-be-shown of something, for instance a [letting-be-shown] of the landscape, which is the subject matter of the daydream. Such a letting-be-shown always occurs through language. Therefore, speaking in the sense of verbal articulation must always be strictly distinguished from saying, since the latter can also occur without verbal articulation. Someone who is mute and cannot speak might under certain circumstances have a great deal to say.

To be involved in something "body and soul" means: My body remains here, but the being-here of my body, my sitting on the chair here, is essentially always already a being-there at something. My being-here, for instance, means: to see and hear you there. p. 127

A second question concerns Professor Hegglins's distinction between the somatic and the psychical regarding the measurability or nonmeasurability of both realms. The question is the following: Is any [other] distinction at all possible for the natural sciences, given the fundamental dogma that nature be understood as determined by its universal measurability?

But then, the distinction between the somatic and the psychical is not an act of stating something within natural science, that is, it does not involve a measuring of both realms. Therefore, when Professor Hegglin draws his distinction, he is necessarily delving into philosophy and taking a step beyond his science. For the natural scientific [way of] thinking there is no other distinction. Not only this, but it cannot make any distinction whatsoever referring to the difference between the two realms of beings [the unmeasurable and the measurable]. Distinctions in natural

---

*By referring explicitly to the "phenomenon of the body" [*Leibphänomen*], Heidegger goes beyond what he said about the different modalities of "hearing" in *Being and Time*, sec. 34. See also Heidegger, *History of the Concept of Time*, pp. 265–68.—TRANSLATORS

science necessarily move only within the realm of the measurable. They concern only and always "how much" of some other previously measured "how much."

A third question is this: Is measurability a property of the thing? Does it belong to the thing, or to the human being, who is measuring? Or to something else?

The measurability of things, of course, is a domain within which you are continuously moving as natural scientists. It is something about which you are always explicitly concerned. Thus, measurability is not a matter of indifference to you.

Is a thing only measurable by the fact that you measure it? No. Therefore, measurability is at least a characteristic of the thing as well. Wherein is measurability [founded]? [It is founded] in the extendedness of the thing. Take our old example once again: This table in front of us. The tabletop is round. You can measure its diameter. You are able to do this only because the table is extended.

p. 128

But is measurability a characteristic of the table the same way as hardness or its brown color? Am I saying something about the table when I assert that it is measurable? I merely say something about the relation of the table to me whereby this relation consists in my measuring it, that is, in my measuring comportment toward the table.

On one hand, measurability is founded in the extendedness of the table. This can be measured. On the other hand, measurability also designates the possibility of the measuring comportment of the human being toward the table. Thus, our speech about measurability refers to something concerning both the table and the human comportment to it.

Is there something that designates *both* of them in their belonging-together-ness? Measurability does not belong to the thing, yet it is also not exclusively an activity of the human being. Measurability belongs to the thing as *object*. Measuring is only possible when the thing is thought of as an object, that is, when it is represented in its objectivity. Measuring is a way I am able to let a thing (present by itself) stand over against me, namely regarding its extension, or still better, regarding the how much of its extension. When a cabinetmaker orders a table of a certain size, it becomes an object [by means] of the measuring of its breadth and height during its production. But these numerical measurements by themselves do not determine the reality of the table as table, that is, [they do not determine it] as a definite thing that is useful. This measurability, of course, is a necessary condition for the possibility of producing the table, but it is never a sufficient condition for the very being of the table.

Yet measurability plays this decisive role in natural science, indeed it must play it, because in natural science the being of a thing is represented mainly as something objective that can be measured.

II. July 6, 1965

Where does the objectivity belong through which natural science views
the being of things? It belongs to the phenomenon by which something
present as present to the human being can manifest itself. Yet something
present can also be experienced in such a way that it is experienced in
itself insofar as it emerges by itself. In the Greek meaning, the name is
φυσις.* In Greek and medieval thought, the concept of an object and of
objectivity did not yet exist. This is a modern concept and is equivalent to
being an object. *Objectivity* is a definite *modification of the presence of things.*
A subject thereby understands the presencing of a thing from itself with
regard to the representedness [*Vorgestelltheit*]. Presence is understood as
representedness. Thereby, presence is no longer taken as what is given by
itself, but only as how it is an object for me as the thinking subject, that
is, how it is made an object over and against me. This kind of experience
of being has existed only since Descartes, which is to say, only since the
time when the emergence of the human being as a subject was put into
effect. From all of this you can see that one cannot understand the whole
phenomenon of measurability unless the history of thought is present.

The fundamental difference lies in the fact that in the former experience, beings were understood as present in and of themselves. For
modern experience, something is a being only insofar as I represent it.
Modern science rests on *the transformation of the experience of the presence of
beings into objectivity.*†

Yet it would be wrong to interpret this change in experience as the
mere contrivance of the human being. At the end of this seminar, we
will discuss measurability once again. What happens when I measure
something? What happens, for instance, when I measure the diameter
of this table?

p. 129

---

*According to Heidegger, in classical Greek philosophy prior to the distinction between
the "physical" realm (nature) and the "metaphysical" realm (beyond nature), the Greek
word *physis* originally meant "being as a whole." In this sense *physis* comprised two
aspects: (1) coming forth, to rise and surge, to emerge and unfold; and (2) remaining,
enduring as standing-in-itself, and decaying. Thus, it refers to the originary unity
of movement and repose. See M. Heidegger, *An Introduction to Metaphysics*, trans.
R. Manheim (New Haven, Conn.: Yale University Press, 1987); "On the Being and
Conception of Physics in Aristotle's *Physics* B, 1," trans. T. Sheehan, *Man and World*
9 (1976): 219–70. See also Heidegger, *Fundamental Concepts of Metaphysics*,
pp. 25–56, and *Contributions to Philosophy*, pp. 133–38.—TRANSLATORS

†Heidegger, "The Age of the World Picture," in *The Question concerning Technology*,
pp. 115–54; "Modern Science, Metaphysic, and Mathematics," in *Basic Writings*,
pp. 243–82.—TRANSLATORS

Measuring always involves some sort of comparison, that is, in the sense that one compares, for instance, the diameter of the tabletop to the selected measure. What one compares is taken regarding "how many times"; thus, one takes the measure.

p. 130   A mere estimate is certainly a comparison, but it is something other than measuring. The estimate [*Schätzen*] becomes measuring when I actually apply the ruler to what is to be measured in such a way that I "pace off" [*abschreiten*] the diameter with the ruler. I lead the ruler along the diameter in such a way that I repeatedly put the ruler end to end and then count how often I can do it.

All measuring is not necessarily quantitative. Whenever I take notice of something as something, then I myself have "measured up to" [*anmessen*] what a thing is. This "measuring up" [*Sich-anmessen*] to what is, is the fundamental structure of human comportment toward things.

In all comprehending of something as something, for instance, of the table as a table, I myself measure up to what I have comprehended. Therefore, one can also say: What we say about the table is a "saying" [*Sagen*] which is "commensurate" [*angemessen*] to the table.

Customarily, the truth about a thing is also defined as *adaequatio intellectus ad rem*. This is an assimilation as well, a continuous measuring-up of the human being to a thing. But here we are dealing with measuring in a completely fundamental sense, [the sense] on which scientific-quantitative measuring is based in the first place.

The relationship of the human being to measure is not entirely comprehended by quantitative measurability. Indeed, it is not even raised as a question. The relationship of the human being to what gives a measure is a fundamental relationship to what is.* It belongs to the understanding of being itself.

These are certainly mere suggestions. I speak about them only in order to show the limitation of discourse on measurability in a quantitative sense. This limitation consists of the reduction of presence [the presencing of being] to the relation of the human being, who represents it in the sense of objectivity. Due to further limitations, objects do not exist at all in the realm of nuclear physics.

p. 131   As his fourth rule of the *Regulae ad Directionem Ingenii*, Descartes wrote: "*Necessaria est methodus ad [rerum] veritatem investigandam*" [There is need of a method for finding out the truth].[1]

You will say that this is trivial. Yet Descartes indicated the necessity for a research method for the very first time. This assertion was directed

---

*See Heidegger, *Being and Time*, p. 141; Heidegger, *Poetry, Language, Thought*, trans. A. Hofstadter (New York: Harper and Row, 1971), pp. 221–28.—TRANSLATORS

against Scholasticism, which, in its assertions, gained support, not from the subject matter itself but rather from what authorities had already said about it.

III. July 8, 1965

You were probably quite astonished that I so obstinately persisted in clarifying what constitutes the proper characteristic of simple, everyday measuring. Nevertheless, this is only the first stage of the kind of measuring meant by the title "measurability," but one that has not been interpreted sufficiently by any means. Regarding this measurability, we talked about the distinction between the somatic as what is measurable and the psychical as what is unmeasurable. In the above-cited text, the latter was said to have been what could be felt intuitively. What is meant here by intuition and feeling remains equally indeterminate. We have taken the distinction here between *soma* and *psyche* regarding measurability and unmeasurability as an opportunity to develop the phenomenon of the body and its phenomenological determination as a problem. Regarding this, we asked the following question: Is the body and its being—that is, the bodying forth as such—something somatic or psychical, or neither of the two? But this way of formulating the question is disastrous because neither the somatic as such has been determined, nor has it been settled what constitutes the peculiarity of the psychical. We merely observed that the distinction between *soma* and *psyche,* supposedly based on the distinction between measurability and unmeasurability, is as it is regarding the way of access to the somatic and the psychical. Of course, the way of access to a realm of being is somehow determined by the respective being's manner of being [*Seinsart*] itself. Yet, this appeal to the way of access still does not guarantee that the regional domain and the objective content of the somatic as such, or of the psychical as such, are sufficiently characterized. The way of access to the somatic—that is, measuring—and the way of access to the psychical—that is, the unmeasuring, intuitive feeling—obviously refer to what is called *method.* This word "method" is a composite from the Greek μετα and ὁδος. ἡ ὁδος means "way," while μετα means "from here to there," "toward something."* Method is the way leading to a subject matter—to a subject field. It is the way we

p. 132

---

*Heidegger frequently quotes Aristotle, *Metaphysics* IV.4.1006a6 f., according to which the method (access to beings) is determined by the subject matter of the investigation.—TRANSLATORS

pursue a subject matter. How the particular subject matter determines the way toward it, and how the way toward it makes the subject matter obtainable, cannot be easily determined in advance for each case. These relations depend upon the manner of being of what should become thematic, and similarly, on the kind of possible ways which should lead to the respective region of beings [*Bereich des Seienden*].* Therefore, there appears an immediate connection between the question of measurability, as such, and the question of *method*. If we want to discuss the problem of the body appropriately, we must develop both questions and their interconnection. But since measurability and measuring are themes of the natural sciences and are their thematization in a distinctive way, we find ourselves compelled to respond in detail to questions of measurability and measuring. For only with the aid of this clarification are we able to see how the phenomenon of the body resists measurability and what entirely different method the determination and interpretation of the

p. 133   body's bodying forth are required in and of themselves. There is no need to show in detail that the task before us is unusually difficult. This is so because matters under discussion, such as measurability, method, and the phenomenon of the body, are basically quite simple. What makes an impression upon our customary [way of] representing things is only what is complicated and what requires expensive equipment to handle it. The simple hardly speaks to us any longer in its simplicity because the traditional scientific way of thinking has ruined our capacity to be astonished about what is supposedly and specifically self-evident. If this astonishment had not been awakened and sustained among Greek thinkers, neither European science nor modern technology would exist. They are now surrounded by an organized idolatry reaching the so-called mass media. By way of comparison, the supposed superstitions of primitive peoples seem as child's play. Whoever tries to preserve some sobriety in the contemporary carnival of idolatry (look at the hustle and bustle of space travel), especially when one is devoted to the profession of aiding

---

*Accordingly, ontological phenomena such as "being," "existence," "temporality," etc., require a unique "phenomenological method" for an immediate apprehension of what shows and manifests itself in its original "givenness," although for the most part this is concealed. This phenomenological method, which Heidegger practices throughout the Zollikon Seminars, is ontologically prior to "method" in the modern, scientific sense, which was first established in Descartes's *Regulae ad Directionem Ingenii* [*Rules for the Direction of the Mind*], ed. H. Springmeyer, L. Gäbe, and H. G. Zekl (Hamburg: F. Meiner, 1973). See Heidegger, *Basic Problems of Phenomenology*, secs. 1–6, and "Science and Reflection," in *The Question concerning Technology*, p. 155. See also *ZS* 143, 144.—TRANSLATORS

the mentally ill, must know what is happening nowadays. One must know one's historical position. One must make clear to oneself daily that the long-approaching fate [*Schicksal*] of European man is at work everywhere here.* One must think historically and give up the unconditional and absolute acceptance of progress under pressure of which the humanity of Western man threatens to perish. The power of [our] world civilization has now become so irresistible that the prophets of the disintegration of human Da-sein use the phrase "Western Man" in an exclusively sarcastic manner, and film festivals are extolled as the highest cultural event. When we continuously and fundamentally reflect on all of this, one of these days we will have to consider whether a reflection on measurability and measuring is merely a tedious matter with which [we] medical professionals are unable to deal. Thure von Uexküll[2] sneers at "philosophizing doctors." In p. 134 opposing them, he appeals to the "critical consciousness of science." He does not see that science is dogmatic to an almost unbelievable degree everywhere, i.e., it operates with preconceptions and prejudices [which have] not been reflected upon. There is the highest need for doctors who *think* and who do not wish to leave the field entirely to scientific technicians.†

Did I stray from the theme with what I have just said? No, we are in the middle of its realm. Of course, the tasks set for us are extremely difficult. They require protracted and careful discussion. This was the idea, when regarding the theme of *measurability* in the previous seminar, I started with simple references to the phenomenon of everyday measuring. Today, I would like to take *another route*, not to expedite the work of reflection, but to show you where the attempt to inquire into the connection between *measurability* and *method* regarding the phenomenon of the body is leading. The following discussion is resigned to giving some hints in broad strokes. For that reason, there is no guarantee that you will be

---

*The later Heidegger called this fateful history of the West *Geschick* ["what is sent": destiny] as the "epochal" unfolding and withholding of being itself. This destiny did not begin with, but was completed by, the scientific, technological revolution in eighteenth-century England. Technology itself is not an accidental happening but a *Geschick der Entbergung* (fate of unconcealing) of being itself. See *ZS* 228, 241.—TRANSLATORS

†M. Boss, *Psychoanalysis and Daseinanalysis,* trans. L. B. Lefebre (New York: Basic Books, 1962). See also M. Boss, "Martin Heidegger's Zollikon Seminars," trans. B. Kenny, *Review of Existential Psychiatry and Psychology* 16 (1978–79): 7–20; W. J. Richardson, "Heidegger among the Doctors," in *Reading Heidegger: Commemorations,* ed. J. Sallis (Bloomington: Indiana University Press, 1993), pp. 49–63; F. Dallmayr, *Between Freiburg and Frankfurt: Toward a Critical Ontology* (Amherst: University of Massachusetts Press, 1991), pp. 210–37.—TRANSLATORS

able to carry out and reenact everything immediately with the necessary thoughtfulness and from the necessary proximity to the phenomena.

We began by measuring the diameter of the top of the table in front of us. We paid attention to the distinction between estimating [*Schätzen*]* and measuring. The former is approximate and is a measuring that is not actually performed. The latter applies to the selected measure. To what? To the diameter of the table we looked at specifically. We "traverse" [*fahren*] (which means, we draw along the diameter with the ruler) in such a way that at any particular time we mark along the diameter at the end of the ruler and set down a new starting point. Therefore, each time we set the ruler in front of the last point marked. Since ancient times, the (foot) step counted as a measure. We set the chosen measure (ruler) step by step. In the ancient manner of speech, this means step by step along the diameter, calculating steps. Therefore, we speak of pacing off [*Abschreiten*]. This manner of speech does not refer to pacing in the sense of the movement of human feet but to steps considered as a measure. The number of measured steps shows the length of the diameter. It is equal to the resulting number of the measurement. Measuring as a comparison aims at an equation of the two. Such a comparison is a calculation. Nowadays, measurement is the subject matter of a special discipline, surveying [*Messtechnik*], which has a decisive function in both technology and natural science. In surveying, a peculiar phenomenon manifests itself: Modern technology is at the point where it gets entangled in itself, and necessarily so. To calculate [*calculus*, pebble used in calculating] originally meant *to depend on something*, that is, to take something into account and thereby at the same time calculate *with* something. Counting something and calculating with something means aiming at something and thereby taking something else into account. Measuring is counting in this sense. The primary focus is not to use numbers in this manner. For instance, when we "count" on the fact that others participate in a certain project, then numbers, as an indication of the how-much, do not play any role in this kind of counting on something and counting on the participation. If scientific research and its theme—nature—is characterized by measurability, then we have an insufficient concept of this measurability if we believe that it is merely a matter of acquiring some definite numerical statement. In fact measurability means calculability, that is, a view of nature guaranteeing knowledge of how we can, and how we must, count on its processes. Measurability means calculability in this characterization. But calculability means *precalculability*. And this

p. 135

---

*See Heidegger, *Being and Time*, p. 140.—TRANSLATORS

is decisive because the point is *control* and *domination* of the processes of nature. But control implies power to have control over nature, a kind of possession. In the sixth and final part of his fundamental work *Discourse on Method,* Descartes writes that in science everything depends on the fact that "[*n*]*ous rendre comme maîtres et possesseurs de la nature*" [we render ourselves the masters and possessors of nature].[3] The method of this new science, that is, modern science, consists of this: To secure* the calculability of nature. The method of science is nothing but the securing of the calculability of nature. Therefore, method plays an eminent role in modern science. After reflecting on this, we can at least now sense that the fourth rule of Descartes's *Regulae,* as cited in the previous hour, means something other than the truism that science as research needs a certain procedural way in its investigation: "*Necessaria est methodus ad* [*rerum*] *veritatem investigandam*" [There is need of a method for finding out the truth]. In order to understand this assertion, here we must pay careful attention to what is expressed by *veritas rerum,* "truth of things." Here the word *res* does not simply refer to "things" in the vague sense of something present-at-hand. The meaning of the word *res* is decisively determined by the following second and third rules.

p. 136

The second rule reads: *Circa illa tantum objecta oportet versari, ad quorum certam et indubitatam cognitionem nostra ingenia videntur sufficere* [Only those objects should engage our attention, to the sure and indubitable knowledge of which our mental powers seem to be adequate]. Perfectly determinate things are proposed by this rule as possible objects of science. A decision has already been made in this rule about the basic character of what alone can be the theme of the science of nature.

Therefore, the subsequent third rule already speaks about *objecta proposita,* about objects placed before science beforehand: "*Circa objecta proposita non quid alii senserint, vel quid ipsi suspicemur, sed quid clare et evidenter possimus intueri vel certo deducere quaerendum est; non aliter enim scientia acquiritur*" [In the subjects we propose to investigate, our in-quiries should be directed, not to what others have thought, nor to what we ourselves conjecture, but to what we can clearly and perspicuously behold and with certainty deduce; for knowledge is not won in any other way].[†]

p. 137

Sicherstellen [securing] has its cognates in *Sicherheit* [certainty, security] and *Gewissheit* [certainty, firmness]. These terms are especially important for Cartesian epistemology, upon which the new scientific "method" was based. See Heidegger, *The Question concerning Technology,* pp. 52–112, esp. p. 88.—TRANSLATORS

[†]Descartes, *Regulae ad Directionem Ingenii,* p. 5.—TRANSLATORS

In this new science this proposition (proposal) of *res* as *objecta*, the approach to things as objects beforehand and the fact that they should be taken into consideration merely as objects, plays the decisive role. This proposal of the theme of science as objectivity (i.e., a true objectivity of a special kind) is the basic characteristic of its method. In modern science, as already mentioned, method does not merely play a special role, but science itself is nothing other than method.*

What does method mean then? Method is the way the character of a domain of experience is disclosed and circumscribed in the first place. This means that nature is projected as object beforehand, and merely as object of a general calculability. The *veritas rerum*, the truth of things, is *veritas objectorum*, the truth in the sense of objectivity of objects, not truth as the very being of things presenting themselves. Therefore, here truth does not mean the self-manifestation of what is immediately present. Truth is characterized as what can be ascertained clearly and evidently, [that is,] indubitably certain for a representing Ego. The criterion of this truth as *certainty* is the evidence we obtain when, after discarding everything doubtful, we hit on that indubitable [thing] that can be acknowledged as the *fundamentum absolutum et inconcussum*, as an absolute and unshakable foundation. When I doubt everything, then this one thing remains indubitable throughout all doubt—that I, who am doubting at any given time, exist. Basic certainty consists in the evidence: *Ego cogitans sum res cogitans.* I am a thinking substance. In elucidating the third rule, Descartes says: "*At vero haec intuitus evidentia et certitudo non ad solas enuntiationes, sed etiam ad quoslibet discursus reguiritur*" [This evidence and certitude, however, which belongs to intuition is required not only in the enunciation of propositions, but also in discursive reasoning of whatever sort (*Regula* III.7)]. He continues: If, for instance, the conclusion that 2 + 2 = 3 + 1 is given, therefore one must not only intuitively perceive that 2 + 2 = 4 and that 3 + 1 also equals 4, but one must also grasp that the equation above follows necessarily from the former two propositions. From this remark it becomes clear that the evidence of mathematical propositions, conclusions, and subject matters comes very close to that fundamental proof and certainty expressed in the proposition: *Ego cogito sum,* I think I am. In the immediate insight into "I think," that I am is also immediately given. In principle, mathematical things possess the same proof and certainty. This is the reason that the projection of nature as a calculable domain of objects at the same time implies that calculability

p. 138

---

*See Heidegger, "Science and Reflection," in *The Question concerning Technology,* pp. 155–82.—TRANSLATORS

is understood as a mathematical determination. In this method—that is, in this manner of the anticipatory projection of nature as a domain of calculable objects—a decision has already been made, immeasurable in its consequences. For this decision means that everything not exhibiting the characteristics of mathematically determinable objectivity is eliminated as being uncertain, that is, untrue and therefore unreal. In other words: The criterion for what truly exists is not being as it manifests itself by itself, but rather exclusively the *ego cogito sum,* and therefore that authoritative kind of truth in the sense of certainty, based upon the subjectivity of the "I think." To put this in yet another way: The science thus projected, that is, this method, is the greatest assault of the human being on nature, guided by the claim to be *maître et possesseur de la nature.* In the claim of modern science thus understood, a dictatorship of the mind expresses itself, reducing the mind to that of a technician of calculations. Therefore, thinking gets passed off as nothing more than a manipulation of operational concepts, representational models, and models of thinking. And not only this. This dictatorship of the mind even dares to claim that consciousness, dominant in the sciences, is "critical" consciousness.

    If in this historical era of science's domination it is a question of opening up the way to very different domains of beings (one to which the human being's existence belongs), then above all it is necessary to gain an insight into the peculiar character of modern science and to keep this insight continuously in mind. The purpose of all this is to weigh, in a genuinely critical sense (i.e., discriminatingly), the scientific objectification of the world against the self-manifestation of quite different phenomena, ones resisting scientific objectification. Descartes shows how the method of modern science, first thought out by Descartes himself, demolishes, that is, destroys, the world of everyday, familiar things (not to mention works of art) approaching us in its immediacy. Descartes himself shows this by an example that he discusses in his main work, *Meditationes de Prima Philosophia,* published in 1641. He does this in the second meditation. Its title states a great deal, indeed. It says everything: *"De Natura Mentis Humanae: Quod Ipsa Sit Notior quam Corpus"* (Of the nature of the human mind; and that it is more easily known than the body).[4] According to what has been said up to now, this means that the absolute self-certainty of the human being as the subject asserting itself contains and projects standards for the possible determination of the objectivity of objects. Truth, that is, truth and certainty regarding the body, can only be what is calculable in it, in the sense of mathematical proof, that is, the *extensio.* The objectivity of nature is determined in reference to the kind of knowledge the knowing subject possesses regarding himself.

p. 139

p. 140

Objectivity is a determination on the part of the subject. Kant formulates this situation in the proposition he called the supreme principle of all synthetic judgment, which reads: "The conditions of the possibility of experience in general are likewise conditions of the possibility of the objects of experience and that for this reason they have objective validity in a synthetic a priori judgment."[5]

Now I refer to what Descartes has to say about the being of an immediately familiar thing, namely, a wax candle on the table. The Latin text has been published in a relatively good translation in *Meditationes de Prima Philosophia* (ed. M. Schröder [(Hamburg: Philosophische Biblio-thek F. Meiner, 1956), p. 51 ff.]).

Now I remind you once again about what has already been said, that is, that the problem of the body is a problem of method. By discussing this proposition, we would like to stick with the following three examples: (1) One of your questions was: Where is the body while we are contemplating something with "body and soul"? (2) The question about the being-here of the body. Thereby we assert: "I am constantly here or in this place," which is a proposition entirely untrue in one respect, yet very true in another. (3) How far does the body or bodying forth play a role in simple measuring in the everyday sense?

p. 141 From the vantage point of the last question, and returning to what we have already said about measurability, one could formulate the thesis: If measuring is co-determined by bodying forth, then it is something that cannot be measured itself and as such. Measuring as measuring is essentially something unmeasurable. Furthermore, we took a look at the phenomenon of the body or its function. We did so when we tried to reflect upon the fact that I do not have to leave the place where I am sitting, when I am occupied with something "body and soul." Indeed, I must remain seated especially in order to be participating bodily, for instance, in hearing the theme of discussion or in viewing a sunset.

Being-here as an existing human being [the human being] is always one and the same as being-there with you. For instance, take [being] there at the burning candle on the table, [a being-]at with which bodying forth participates as seeing with the eyes. If you were a pure, bodiless spirit, you could not see the candle as a shining, yellowish light. Even when I receive-perceive the meaning of a lamp, even if I merely make-it-present without seeing it in front of me bodily, bodying forth is a participating, insofar as shining belongs to the lamp as a lamp.

In this example, with what method has the function of bodying forth been disclosed to you (if it happens at all)? In what manner have you become aware of the phenomenon of the above-mentioned being-here as being-at?

You became aware that you have always already been at what encountered [*das Begegnende*] you in this way. You had to free yourselves
from the common notion of a merely subjective representation of things
inside your head, and you had to engage in the way of existing [*Weise
des Existierens*] in which you already exist. It was necessary to perform
specifically this "engagement" [*Sicheinlassen*]* in the mode of being in
which you already exist. Nevertheless, what is specifically performed and
engaged in is by no means synonymous with a [reflective] understanding
of this mode of being, as long as by understanding you mean "to think
of something," to be able to grasp [*begreifen*] something, or to believe,
[therefore] a mere understanding of something as something. One can
even understand *being at* . . . in such a way that one "reflects on" it without
having expressly engaged in it at all or having experienced it as the human
being's fundamental relationship to what encounters him.

p. 142

How could such a bright and intelligent man like Descartes come
up with such a strange theory in which the human being, in the first
instance, exists alone by himself in relationship to things? My venerable
teacher, Husserl, generally went along with this theory too (although
he also certainly sensed something beyond). Otherwise, his *Cartesian
Meditations*† would not be his most foundational book.

For Descartes, the *ingenium* of the human being is his natural talent.
It is what the human being can do on his own. He should place confidence
only in what he demonstrates as evident. What is the motivation for such
an attitude?

Descartes's position results from the essential need of a human being
who has abandoned faith—the position that the meaning of his existence
is determined by the authority of the Bible and the church. Rather, he
is someone entirely on his own, and therefore, someone who sought to
hold on to some other form of reliability and trust, who needed another
fundamentum absolutum inconcussum.

In his quest for something indubitable, Descartes received help at
just the right moment from an entirely different conception of nature
which Galileo had employed in his experiment, that is, the dawning of

---

*We translate Heidegger's *Sicheinlassen* [letting oneself into], which has an ontological-
existential meaning here, with the English "engage" (French: en-gager, to gage, to
pledge), which has broader connotations than the German *lassen* (to let; from Old
Saxon, *lactan:* to allow, to permit), namely, to bind oneself to do something [cf.
engaged], to pledge oneself, to promise, to commit oneself.—TRANSLATORS

†See E. Husserl, *Cartesian Meditations. An Introduction to Phenomenology,* trans.
D. Cairns (The Hague: Martinus Nijhoff, 1973).—TRANSLATORS

the possibility of mathematical certainty and proof. Therefore, Descartes arrived at the certitude of the *cogito sum:* I-thinking-am. This proposition is not to be understood as a conclusion, therefore not as *cogito ergo sum,* but as an immediate *intuition,* that is, in the Cartesian sense of the term and not in the usual psychological sense.

p. 143

Descartes gains his position from his will to provide something absolutely certain and secure, therefore something not from an immediate, fundamental relationship to what is or from the question of being. On the contrary, that something is, and may be, is determined conversely by the rule of mathematical proof.

We may refer to Descartes's second meditation as proof once again: *"De natura mentis humanae: Quod ipsa sit notior quam corpus."* In the example given here—that of the wax candle—it is not its qualities that are its simple and, therefore, indubitable characteristics, but only the extension of the wax remains indubitable. (Later Leibniz proved that Descartes did not yet see "force" as a necessary determination in the process of nature.)

The Cartesian position contrasts sharply with the Greek view. The corresponding, basic characteristic of the Greek method is preservation and "saving" the phenomena (leaving them untouched and intact), phenomena which show themselves as pure letting-be-present [*Anwesend-sein-lassen*] of what manifests itself. Surely, Descartes was also influenced by Augustine's meditations and self-reflection, but the object of self-reflection was different for each one of them.

By no means should our discussions be understood as hostile toward science. In no way is science as such rejected. Merely its claim to absoluteness—that is, as the standard measure for all true propositions—is warded off as an arrogant presumption.

In contrast to this inadmissible claim, it seems necessary to characterize our entirely different method as *specifically engaging in our relationship to what we encounter* in which we always sojourn. In a sense, what is characteristic of phenomenology is the act of will not to resist this engaging-oneself. This engaging-oneself does not, by a long shot, mean a mere making myself conscious of my mode of being. I can only speak of "making oneself [reflexively] conscious" when I try to determine how this one originary being-at . . . is connected with other determinations of Da-sein.

p. 144

Engaging-oneself is an entirely different way. It is a completely different method from scientific methods if we understand the use of the word "method" in its original, genuine sense: μετα-όδος, the way toward. . . . You must keep the usual meaning of mere research technique separate from our concept of method.

Therefore, we must proceed on the "path toward" ourselves. But this is no longer the path toward a merely isolated, principally singular I.

IV. July 8, 1965

We recall another bodily phenomenon mentioned above: *blushing*. We said that the one who is blushing is, as a human being, constantly related to other humans. But here what does it mean to be related to other human beings? First, we must clarify our relationship to other human beings [*Bezug zum Mitmenschen*] if we want to perceive the difference involved in the special relationship of the one who blushes and the one who does not.

Therefore, we must ask beforehand: How are other human beings present? Are they related to other humans as you are related to a glass on the table in front of you?

This talk about being-related—about a relationship with, or even among, human beings—is misleading because it seduces us with the idea of two polar [merely] present-at-hand subjects, who subsequently must establish a relationship between their respective ideas, in their respective consciousness to one another. Thereby, this concept of "relationship" obstructs the engagement of our true relationship to others. Yet how are we with one another? Is it the case that one of us is here, another one is there, and still another one is somewhere else in this space and that we count how many we are? The often quoted psychological theory of empathy rests on this obviously incorrect concept. This theory starts by p. 145 imagining an Ego in a purely Cartesian sense—an Ego given by itself in the first instance who then feels his way into the other—thus discovering that the other is a human being as well in the sense of an *alter Ego*. Nevertheless, this is a pure fabrication.

Therefore, we ask once again: How am I in relationship to others? How are they comporting themselves toward me? What character does our being-with-one-another [*Miteinandersein*] have? Is it that we are present in this space as bodies side by side [*nebeneinander*]? Our being with each another is not the same as, for instance, when in my being-here, I am there with Dr. W. For if this were the case, I would see him as an object, as something merely present-at-hand.

If one speaks about the often quoted I-Thou and We relationships, then one says something very incomplete. These phrases still have their origin in a primarily isolated Ego.* We must ask: With whom, and where

---

*This holds true for the "second-person" view (M. Buber), for the "first-person" view (the Cartesian "subjective" reality of consciousness), and for the "third-person" perspective (the problem of "other minds") as discussed in contemporary, analytic philosophy.—TRANSLATORS

am I, when I am *with* you? It is a *being-with* that means a way of existing with you in the manner of being-in-the-world, especially a *being-with* [*Mitsein*] one another in our relatedness [*Bezogensein*] to the things encountering us.

Insofar as each of us is one's own Da-sein as being-in-the-world, being-with one another cannot mean anything else than a being-with-each-other-in-the-world. This means I am not specifically related to one of you thematically as an individual present-at-hand, [i.e. psychologically], but I sojourn with you in the same being-here. Being-with one another is [phenomenologically] not a relationship of a subject to another subject.

As an example, imagine that we are in a restaurant, and each of us is sitting alone at a separate table. Then, are we not with one another? Of course, but in an entirely different way of being-with one another from what occurs in our present group discussion. The way we sit by ourselves in the restaurant is a privation of being-with one another. The ones who exist [this way] are not interested in one another, and therefore are with one another *this way* in the same space. Now, even if I get up and accompany you to the door, it is [still] not the same as in the case when two bodies are merely moving side by side to the door.

For the next seminar, I must think of a method leading you along the path where you can specifically engage yourselves in this "being-with" by being along with what is encountering you.

p. 146

p. 147 ## November 23 and 26, 1965, at Boss's Home

I. November 23, 1965

Almost five full months have passed since we last saw each other. Therefore, let us first reflect on what we talked about in our previous seminar sessions. From this reflection, we can then make a transition to the problem of method.

You may have noticed that I do not want to make philosophers out of you, but I would like to enable you to be attentive to what concerns the human being unavoidably and yet is not easily accessible to him.[*]

---

[*] For the most part, originary "phenomena," such as being, Da-sein, etc., are "covered up" [*verdeckt*] or disguised and therefore need special phenomenological explication. See Heidegger, "The Preliminary Conception of Phenomenology," *Being and Time*, pp. 58–63. —TRANSLATORS

In order to enable you to be more attentive, a special methodological attitude will be required from all of us. We have not spoken about this [explicitly] until now, because I wanted to try working through the matter first, and then speak explicitly about the method.

I would like to introduce this theme with a discussion of the objections and critiques *raised against Daseinanalysis** as Dr. Boss communicated them to me some time ago. Therefore, the question must first be raised whether these objections are directed against Daseinanalysis or the analytic of Dasein or both. The use of these two titles obviously causes a great deal of fuss.

First, the following three objections must be discussed:

1. Daseinanalysis is antiscientific.
2. Daseinanalysis is against objectivity.
3. Daseinanalysis is anticonceptual.

In order to be able to explain these objections appropriately, we must first clarify for ourselves what might be properly meant by such titles as "analysis," "analytic," and "to analyze." Better still, perhaps we should even go back a bit further and ask: What did Freud understand by analysis when he spoke of it? I expect this clarification from you. p. 148

SEMINAR PARTICIPANT: Freud meant the reduction of the symptoms to their origin.

MARTIN HEIDEGGER: Then why did he call this reduction "analysis"?

SP: In analogy to chemical analysis, which also intends to go back to the elements.

MH: It was therefore a matter of a reduction to its elements in the sense that the given, the symptoms, are dissolved into elements, with the intention of explaining the symptoms by the elements obtained in that manner. Therefore, analysis in the Freudian sense is a reduction in the sense of a dissolution [*Auflösung*] so that we might develop a causal explanation.

But then not every reduction to "from where" [*Woher*] something exists and subsists is necessarily an analysis in the sense just stated. Neither in the writings of Freud, nor in the biography of Freud by

---

*Here Heidegger refers to his existential analysis [Analytic of Da-sein] in *Being and Time,* which is different from the actual performance in "Daseinanalysis," from Freud's psychoanalysis, and from L. Binswanger's "psychiatric Daseinanalysis." See *ZS* 150–51.—TRANSLATORS

Jones, is there a passage which shows why Freud selected the word "analysis" alone as the title for his theoretical endeavor.

The most ancient usage of the world "analysis" can be found in Homer, the second book of the *Odyssey*. It is used there for what Penelope did night by night, namely, unravel the fabric she had woven during the day. Here αναλυειν means the unraveling of a woven fabric into its component parts. In Greek, it also means to loosen, for instance, to release a chained person from his chains, to liberate someone from captivity. Αναλυειν can also mean to disassemble building materials belonging together, for instance, to dismantle tents.

Much later, the philosopher Kant used the term "analytic" in his *Critique of Pure Reason*. It was from this text that I took the word "analytic" in the phrase "analytic of Da-sein." Yet, this does not mean that the analytic of Da-sein in *Being and Time* is merely a continuation of the Kantian position (see Heidegger, *Kant and the Problem of Metaphysics*, 1929).

p. 149

The first part of the "Transcendental Doctrine of Elements" in Kant's *Critique of Pure Reason* is subdivided into the "Transcendental Aesthetic" and the "Transcendental Logic." In Kant the term "aesthetic" does not mean the doctrine of the beautiful in today's customary sense, but refers to the ancient meaning of αἴσθησις, and therefore to *sensory perception* [*Anschauung*]. The transcendental aesthetic is the doctrine of the a priori conditions for the possibility of the sensory perception of an object. These conditions are *space* and *time*, through which anything sensorially perceived is determined as such. But then all knowledge in the sense of scientific experience is not only sensory perception, but is also always perception or observation determined by *thought* [*Denken*], or more specifically— experience. Kant comprehended this experience scientifically, that is, as a mathematically founded knowledge of nature. Science is equivalent to mathematical natural science according to the model of Galileo and Newton. The question concerning conditions of the possibility for the other component of knowledge, i.e., *understanding* [*Verstand*], is answered by the transcendental logic. In its first part, the transcendental logic is analytic in the sense that Kant traces the conditions for the possibility of scientific experience back to a unified whole, that is, the faculty of understanding. (The system of categories and one of the transcendental principles, i.e., causality, was discussed in an earlier seminar.) [See Kant, *Critique of Pure Reason*, "The Analytic of Concepts" (A.65 f., B.90 f.): "By Analytic of Concepts I do not understand their analysis or the procedure usual in philosophical investigations, that of dissecting the content of such concepts as may present themselves, and so of rendering them more distinct; but the

hitherto rarely attempted *dissection of the faculty of the understanding*   p. 150
itself, in order to investigate the possibility of concepts a priori by
looking for them in the understanding alone, as their birthplace,
and by analyzing the pure use of this faculty. This is the proper task
of a transcendental philosophy." ("Transcendental," for Kant, means
the same as "ontological," which is different from "ontic.")]

From this Kantian concept of analytic, it follows that it is a dissection [*Zergliederung*] of the faculty of understanding. The fundamental
character of a dissection is not its reduction into elements, but the
tracing back to a unity (synthesis) of the ontological possibility of
the being of beings, or in the sense of Kant: [Back to synthesis] of
the objectivity of objects of experience. Therefore, there can be no
talk about causality here either because it always refers merely to an
ontic relation between cause and effect. Therefore, the goal of "the
analytic" is to expound the original unity of the function of the faculty
of understanding. "The analytic" is concerned with the return to a
"context within a system." In the ontological sense, "the analytic" is
not a reduction into elements, but the articulation of the [a priori]
unity of a composite structure [*Strukturgefüge*].[*] This is also essential
in my concept of the "analytic of Da-sein." In the course of the analytic
of Da-sein in *Being and Time,* I also speak about an analysis of Da-sein
where I always mean the actual performance of the analytic.

But now what is the difference between the analytic of Da-sein
and Daseinanalysis?

SP: If one understands by Daseinanalysis Ludwig Binswanger's "psychiatric Daseinanalysis," then one could say that Binswanger also spoke
about moments [*Glieder*] [of a unity] and that he possesses the idea
of Da-sein as a whole.

MH: Then would Binswanger's "psychiatric Daseinanalysis" form a section
of Heidegger's analytic of Dasein? But as Binswanger himself had   p. 151
to admit a few years ago, he misunderstood the analytic of Dasein,
albeit by a "productive misunderstanding," as he calls it. You can
see this from the fact that there is a "supplement" to Heidegger's
"gloomy care" [*düstere Sorge*] in Binswanger's lengthy book on the
fundamental forms of Dasein.[†] It is essentially a treatise on love, a
topic that Heidegger has supposedly neglected.

---

[*]See Heidegger, *What Is a Thing?* trans. W. B. Barton and V. Dentsch with an analysis by
E. T. Gendlin (Chicago: H. Regnery, 1967), and *Kant and the Problem of Metaphysics,*
trans. J. S. Churchill (Bloomington: Indiana University Press, 1962).—TRANSLATORS

[†]See L. Binswanger, *Grundformen und Erkenntnis menschlichen Daseins* (Zurich:
Niehans, 1942). See *ZS* 236.—TRANSLATORS

What was Binswanger expressing in his endeavor to develop a supplement? What is lacking in reference to the thinking in *Being and Time*, when Binswanger attempts to make such a supplement? In *Being and Time* it is said that Da-sein is essentially an issue for itself. At the same time, this Da-sein is defined as originary being-with-one-another. Therefore, Da-sein is also always concerned with others. Thus, the analytic of Da-sein has nothing whatsoever to do with solipsism or subjectivism. But Binswanger's misunderstanding consists not so much of the fact that he wants to supplement "care" with love, but that he does not see that *care* has an existential, that is, *ontological* sense. Therefore, the analytic of Da-sein asks for Da-sein's basic *ontological* (*existential*) constitution [*Verfassung*] and does not wish to give a mere description of the ontic phenomena of Da-sein. The all-determining projection of *being* human as ecstatic Da-sein is already ontological so that the idea of the human being as "subjectivity of consciousness" is overcome. This projection renders manifest the *understanding of being* as the basic constitution of Da-sein. It is necessary to look at it in order even to discuss the question of the relationship of the human being as existing to the *being* of beings (of the non-human being and of existing Da-sein itself). But this question is a result of the question of *the meaning of being in general*.

Therefore, when Binswanger describes *Being and Time* as an extremely consequential development from the teaching of Kant and Husserl, he could not be further from the truth. For the question raised in *Being and Time* is not raised by either Husserl or Kant. Generally speaking, it has never been raised in philosophy.

p. 152

But philosophy asks about being and has already asked about being for a long time. Indeed, in Parmenides we can already read the proposition: "For, there is being." In his *Metaphysics*, Aristotle also asked the question of being.* Thus, the question of being has been asked since ancient times. Yet in the very phrase "the question of being," used so often nowadays, a hidden ambiguity lies.

But in what sense does Aristotle ask about being? In such a way that the question is only about beings and *their* being. If I ask the question about being as being, then I do not consider being as to whether it exists as a chair, a table, or a tree. Rather, I consider "being as being." Therefore, I pay attention to it regarding its being. This is the basic question of all metaphysics. Therefore, is it not true that philosophy asked the question of being? Therefore, the question of being is asked in philosophy. Why should the question still have to be raised in *Being and Time*?

---

*See Aristotle, *Metaphysics* VII.I.1028b4.—TRANSLATORS

When I ask about the being of things as objects, I ask about objectivity. For the Greeks, there were no "objects" (in the modern sense). "Objects" were only possible after Descartes. The Greeks called being what is present-at-hand, what lies in front, and what I always already encounter. The Greeks used the term ουσια for that kind of being of beings. It is the noun derived from the participle ον [being]. Ουσια is usually translated as substance. But in the first instance the Greek ουσια is not a philosophical concept at all. It simply means what is present, exactly in the sense we can still use the term *Anwesen* (what is present) in German today for a farmhouse. The reinterpretation of ουσια as substance by medieval scholasticism* has nothing to do with Greek thought, but this does not mean that scholasticism lacks its own rightful place.

For the Greeks, what comes to presence [*das Anwesende*] is what lies there beforehand. In Greek "to lie" means κεισθαι. Therefore, what lies-in front [*das Vorliegende*] is called υποκειμενον [underlying, substrate]. The Romans translated υποκειμενον literally as *subjectum*, but in the first instance this *subjectum* has nothing to do with the subject in the sense of an "I" (Ego). Still, in the Middle Ages, the term *subjectum* was used for everything that lies-in front [*Vorliegende*]. Conversely, in the Middle Ages, an *objectum* was "something thrown over against" [*Entgegengeworfenes*], but over against whom? Over against my representation [*Vorstellen*], my *repraesentatio*. In the medieval sense, an object is what is merely represented, for instance, an imagined golden mountain that does not actually exist as does the real book here in front of me, called a *subjectum* in the Middle Ages. Finally, at the end of the Middle Ages, all this was turned upside down. Nowadays, a subject is usually understood as an "I," whereas the term "object" is reserved for naming "objects"—things without an Ego. What was "objective" in the medieval sense, that is, what is "thrown against" me by my representation, and only by it, is the "subjective," the merely represented, and therefore the un-real according to present linguistic usage.

p. 153

Here, are we dealing merely with a change in linguistic usage? No. Here, something very different is at play—nothing less than a radical transformation [*Wandel*] of the human being's [historical] position toward being.

This transformation, occurring in the understanding of being, is the presupposition for the fact that nowadays we live in a scientific, technological world. Nietzsche once said: "Thoughts, which come

---

*See Heidegger, *Basic Problems of Phenomenology,* pp. 77–121, concerning the importance Heidegger attributed to the understanding of medieval ontology (Thomas Aquinas, Duns Scotus, and Suarez) within Western metaphysics; also see Heidegger, *The Fundamental Concepts of Metaphysics,* pp. 37–57.—TRANSLATORS

on the feet of doves, guide the world."[1] People of today have largely given up listening to what Nietzsche is talking about here. Just as one only listens to what makes noise, so one only counts as being what works and leads to a practical, useful result.

p. 154 But in what consists the transformation of thinking just mentioned? In other words, how did the Ego (I) get the distinction that it is the only subject, therefore, the only "underlying" reality? This distinction of the Ego (I) appeared with Descartes because he was searching for certitude. Hegel says that it was with Descartes that philosophy gained a secure foundation for the first time. Descartes was looking for a *fundamentum absolutum inconcussum*. But this can only be one's own I. For only I myself am present everywhere, whether I think, whether I doubt, whether I wish, or whether I take a position toward something. Therefore, when searching for an absolutely secure foundation in thinking, the I becomes what "lies-in front" [*Vorliegendes*] in an outstanding sense because it is something indubitable. From then on, "subject" progressively became the term for I. Object now became all that stands over against the I and its thinking, by being able to be determined through the principles and categories of this thinking. As long as you do not understand this connection, you do not understand what is occurring in modern science at all.[*]

If someone speaks about an antiscientific attitude, one must first ask him whether he knows what science is.

But then how was the "being of beings" understood in the Middle Ages in contrast to Greek antiquity? In medieval times, philosophy was understood as *ancilla theologiae*, that is, philosophy was determined by theology in which the being of beings was interpreted as *creatio*, creatureliness. Therefore, we find the following three stages in the history of the determination of being:

1. The being of being as υποκειμενον, which consists of the φυσει οντα, things arising on their own, and the θεσει οντα, things produced by the human being.
2. The being of beings as creatureliness.
3. The object determined by the I-subject.

p. 155 What is ascertained by scientific objectivity is considered to be the true being. This sounds wonderful. Yet with this one forgets all to easily and all too often that this "objectivity" is possible only insofar as the human being has entered into, and interpreted himself according

---

[*]See Heidegger, *The Question concerning Technology,* pp. 3–35.—TRANSLATORS

to, subjectivity, which is not self-evident at all. In his *Critique of Pure Reason,* Kant subsequently undertook for the first time a systematic analysis of Descartes's starting point regarding the determination of the objectivity of the object. With his phenomenology, Husserl defined, unfolded, and gave a foundation to Kant's position on this [matter].

As distinct from the traditional thought of metaphysics, a totally different question is asked in *Being and Time*. Until now, beings *have* been questioned [*befragt*] in reference to their being. In *Being and Time* the issue is no longer *beings as such,* but *the meaning of being in general,* of the possible *manifestness of being* [*Offenbarkeit des Seins*].

The impetus for my whole way of thinking goes back to an Aristotelian proposition which states that being is said in many ways.* This proposition was originally the lightning bolt that triggered the question, What then is the unity of these various meanings of being? What does being mean at all?

If I ask this question, the next methodological step is, How can I generally explicate this question? Where is a guideline allowing me to inquire about being itself? The next step was to look to the Greeks, not only to find out what they said about the being of beings, but especially to consider how the Greeks had understood *being* [*Sein*] beforehand, without specifically reflecting on it. Reflecting on the meaning of being, it seemed to me that the Greeks had comprehended "being as such" in the sense of presence, of the present. Time evidently played a role in this determination of being because "presence" is a temporal term. But here we must first ask how *time* is to be considered, as the traditional idea of time is not p. 156 sufficient for discussing the question of being, even as a question.

This insight led me to the next question, How does the human being relate himself to time? How does time determine the human being so that he can be addressed by being? This way, we are prepared to discuss the question of being by interpreting human existence in its peculiar temporality. Therefore, in *Being and Time* the question of who, what, and how the human being is (which has become necessary) is discussed exclusively and continuously in relation to

---

*See Aristotle, *Metaphysics* VII.I.1028a10. See M. Heidegger, "My Way to Phenomenology," in *On Time and Being,* trans. Joan Stambaugh (New York: Harper and Row, 1972), p. 74 f. Regarding Heidegger's response to the Aristotelian doctrine of the Analogy of Being (*analogia entis*), see H. G. Gadamer, *Heidegger's Ways,* trans. J. W. Stanley (Albany: State University of New York, 1994) pp. 87, 165, 168, 184. See also J. D. Caputo, *The Mystical Element in Heidegger's Thought* (Athens: Ohio University Press, 1978).—TRANSLATORS

the question of the meaning of being. Thereby, it has already been decided that the question of the human being in *Being and Time* was not formulated in the way anthropology would. What is the human being in and for himself? The question of the human being led to the analytic of Da-sein as found *in Being and Time*.

Then, what is the *decisive point* of this *analytic of Da-sein*?

Symptoms are not reduced to elements in the manner of Freud. Rather, the quest is after those traits characterizing the being of Da-sein regarding its relation to being in general. In contrast to Husserl and his phenomenology, the difference in a specific sense does not consist just of the fact that only Da-sein's ontological structures are elaborated, but rather that, generally speaking, being human is fundamentally stated as Da-sein. This is done explicitly, as opposed to the characterizations of the human being as subjectivity and as transcendental Ego-consciousness.

In the philosophical tradition, the term "Dasein" means presence-at-hand, existence. In this sense, one speaks, for instance, of proofs of God's existence. However, Da-sein is understood differently in *Being and Time*. To begin with, French existentialists also failed to pay attention to it. That is why they translated Da-sein in *Being and Time* as *être-là*, which means being here and not there. The *Da* in *Being and Time* does not mean a statement of place for a being, but rather it should designate the openness where beings can be present for the human being, and the human being also for himself. The *Da* of [Dasein's] *being* distinguishes the humanness of the human being.*

p. 157

The talk about human Da-sein is *accordingly* a pleonasm, avoidable in all contexts, including *Being and Time*. The appropriate French translation of Da-sein should be: Etre le là, and the meaningful accentuation should be Da-*sein* in German instead of Dasein.

At the end of this first hour, we must return to the difference between the analytic of Da-sein and Daseinanalysis. Thereby, we will disregard Binswanger's "psychiatric Daseinanalysis." The phenomenology of Husserl, which continued to have an impact on Binswanger and remains one of consciousness, blocks clear insight into the phenomenological *hermeneutics* [*Hermeneutik*] *of Da-sein.*[†] The relationship between Da-sein and consciousness requires special

---

*See Heidegger, "Letter on Humanism," *Basic Writings*, pp. 189–242.—TRANSLATORS

[†]See M. Heidegger, *Unterwegs zur Sprache* (Pfullingen: Neske, 1959) [*On the Way to Language*, trans. P. D. Hertz and J. Stambaugh (New York: Harper and Row, 1966)], concerning the origins of Heidegger's "hermeneutic of facticity" [*Hermeneutik der Faktizität*] in the early 1920s. See also Heidegger, *Being and Time*, pp. 61–63; Kisiel, *Genesis of Heidegger's* Being and Time, pp. 259–61, 373.—TRANSLATORS

discussion. It is outlined in the question of the foundational relationship between being-in-the-world as Da-sein and the intentionality of consciousness. But this question would lead us too far away from our proper theme.

II. November 23, 1965

MARTIN HEIDEGGER: We stopped at the elucidation of Da-sein, or better yet, at the question of why the discussion in *Being and Time* is about Da-sein and not simply about being human. The reason for this is that in *Being and Time* the question of being determines everything, i.e., the question as to what extent being (as presence) manifests itself in time.

But since the human being can only be human by understanding being—that is, insofar as he is standing in the openness of being—being human, as such, is distinguished by the fact that to be, in its own unique way, is to be this openness. In view of the question of being, the time to be determined cannot be understood by the traditional concept of time, which Aristotle explicated authoritatively in the fourth book of his *Physics*. Ever since Aristotle, time has been understood philosophically from the understanding of being in the sense of presence, as "now." Being is not understood through an understanding of time. p. 158

Therefore, the question is also raised, What is the ground for the possibility that the human being is addressed by being as being—that is, what is the reason that being itself can become manifest for the human being in the sense of presence? But manifestness [*Offenbarkeit*] of being to the human being does not mean, by any means, that being as such, or indeed its manifestness, is apprehended explicitly and thematically by the human being and by philosophical thought.

Now the question arises, How must the being of the human being be understood initially in order for the determination of the human being to correspond to the basic phenomenon of the manifestness of being? From where does the insight come that the human being himself is standing in this clearing [*Lichtung*] of being, meaning that the being of Da is ecstatic—that the human being exists [stands out into being] as Da-sein?

The interpretation of the primary structures constituting the being of Da understood as such—namely, its mode of existing—is the existential analytic of Da-sein. "Existential" is used as opposed to "categorical." In contemporary usage, category means a class or group in which certain things belong. For instance, one says: He belongs to this or that category. "Category" is derived from the Greek verb ἀγορεύειν, meaning "to speak publicly in the market" (ἀγορα), especially in a judicial trial. The preposition κατα means "from above down toward something." It is equivalent to our "about"—to say something *about* something. In the special case of a public, judicial trial, it means to tell the accused "to his face." Accordingly, κατηγορια really means "predication." In Aristotle, κατηγορια takes on the meaning referring to all those determinations belonging to predication, as such.* Predication belongs to something that I say something about, the subject of the proposition, *what* is predicated on the κατηγορια is the predicate. For instance, in a predication, I can say something is such and such a kind. Kind is in the category of quality. Something is this high and this wide. The how much, as such, means the category of quantity. In Aristotle, the indication of the number of categories varies. In any case, these categories are not mere determinations of the faculty of understanding as with Kant, but characteristics of the being of beings as such. The same is also true [in a certain way] of Kant, except that for Kant the presence [*Anwesenheit*] of what is present has assumed the meaning of the objectivity of the object.

p. 159

In *Being and Time,* I attempted to exhibit the specific characteristics of the being of Da-sein qua Da-sein as opposed to the characteristics of the being of what is not Da-sein, for instance, nature. Therefore, I called them *existentialia.* The analytic of Da-sein as existential is a kind of ontology in an entirely formal sense. Insofar as ontology prepares the fundamental question of being as being, it is a *fundamental ontology.* Here it becomes clear once again how such a misinterpretation occurs if one understands *Being and Time* as a kind of anthropology.

Given this clarification of what the analytic of Da-sein means and from where it is determined—that is, from the question of being [*Seinsfrage*]—we can now deal with the aforementioned objections and critiques directed against the analytic of Da-sein and Dasein-analysis.

Therefore, it is necessary to show that any science is grounded in a tacit ontology of its object domain. For instance, physics deals with the motion of bodies as something measurable. Therefore, the thinking of physics is calculative thinking. But what is measurable is the motion of a body regarding its change of place. Thus, this physical-calculative thinking takes motion beforehand as a mere change of place.

p. 160

We have explained that, from its inception, philosophy asked the question of being as being. The question "what is being as being"

---

* See *ZS* 78.—TRANSLATORS

is the question of ontology—the question of the structure of being regarding beings.

Since every science is occupied with a domain of beings, it is already necessarily included in, and related to, the manifestness of this being as being, that is, to the fundamental determinations of its being. For instance, physics is related to cause, effect, matter, force, and law. Think of Newton's law of inertia: Each body remains in a state of rest or in uniform, rectilinear motion if no forces are acting on it. Yet no one has ever seen uniform, rectilinear motion (not even once). Therefore, the supposition of such motion is a [theoretical] fiction. Yet, it belongs to the *a priori projection of modern physics*. Insofar as this supposition delineates the object domain of mathematical physics, it becomes obvious that physics is grounded in a tacit ontology.

The precision of the exact sciences cannot be determined precisely, that is, in terms of calculations, but only ontologically. The same is true of the kind of truth belonging to "science" in the sense of the exact natural sciences. Its truth is "verified" by the efficiency of its results. If this scientific way of thinking determines the concept of the human being, and if he is "researched" according to the feedback model, as is now happening in cybernetics, the destruction of the human being is complete. Therefore, I have reservations about science—not science as science—but only about the absolute claims of natural science.[*]

SEMINAR PARTICIPANT: For us, the difficulty lies in the fact that Professor Boss wants to banish the thinking of the natural sciences from psychology, whereas we want to remain natural scientists nevertheless. p. 161

MH: You must first tell me what psychology is. When I speak to you now, two people speak to each other, understand each other. If we now determine being human as *Da-sein*, we must say: You exist and I exist. We are here in the world with one another. If we now speak about what is questionable or necessary in psychology, or if we discuss whether it is already time to ski in the mountains, then I address you as existing Dasein. But how? Is this the analytic of Da-sein? We are now at the decisive point. How do you see me, and how do I see you, and in what regard? These are very simple questions. If we both speak, we are both related to each other existentially. How are you present to me as a

---

[*]See John D. Caputo, "Language, Logic, and Time," *Research in Phenomenology* 3 (1973): 147–55, concerning the young Heidegger's interest in mathematics, logic, and natural science. In his general introduction to Heidegger, *Basic Writings* (p. 12), Krell remarks: "Heidegger never really abandoned his interest in mathematics and the sciences and remained capable enough in the former to serve on doctoral committees for the mathematics faculty."—TRANSLATORS

human being from the point of view of the analytic of Da-sein? *Being and Time* states: Da-sein is that being whose being itself is at issue. You are concerned with me, and I with you. Thereby, are you doing the analytic of Da-sein? No. But you see me, and I am present to you, within the horizon of the determinations of Da-sein as given by the analytic of Da-sein. We stated that the analytic of Da-sein interprets the being of this being. And if you now speak to me without doing the analytic of Da-sein, then this is not speaking in an ontological sense. But you are directed toward me as the one who exists in an ontic sense. Daseinanalysis is *ontic*. The analytic of Dasein is *ontological*.

In the same way that it is possible for the physicist Heisenberg to inquire into the basic structures of the objectivity of nature, not as a physicist, but in the way of a philosopher, it is therefore possible that the relationship between the one who does the Daseinanalysis [the analyst] and the one who is analyzed [the analysand] can be experienced as a relationship between one Da-sein and another. This relationship can be questioned regarding how this specific being-with-one-another is characterized in a way appropriate to Da-sein. For instance, this way, in relation to this concrete existing human being, not only does the interpretation of the analysand's dreams come into play, but also the reflection on what constitutes a dream in general. With this question, the reflection reaches [back] to the realm of an ontology of Da-sein. It is no less the task of the one who does Dasein-analyis to explicate this thematically as it is the task of Heisenberg to discuss the essence of causality or the subject-object relationship.

The decisive point is that the particular phenomena, arising in the relationship between the analysand and the analyst, and belonging to the respective, concrete patient, be broached in their own phenomenological content and not simply be classified globally under *existentialia*.

p. 162

III. November 26, 1965

MARTIN HEIDEGGER: In last Tuesday's seminar we proposed as the theme of the discussion the three reproaches raised against the analytic of Da-sein and Daseinanalysis: First, it is antiscientific. Second, it is against objectivity. Third, it is anticonceptual.

Then we tried to clarify what these reproaches are directed toward. With this, it became necessary to clarify the relationship between the analytic of Da-sein and Daseinanalysis. As the name should indicate, the analytic of Da-sein is a definite ontological interpretation of being human as Da-sein, and, as such, it serves to prepare us for the question of being. If we ascertain something like this, then an assertion of this kind is correct. And we are able to know it. But this statement does not necessarily mean (as yet) that we are   p. 163 also able to appropriate the objective relations between the question of being and the analytic of Da-sein. Yet we shall leave this aside for the moment.

The result was that in *Being and Time* there was often talk about "Daseinanalysis." In this context, Daseinanalysis does not mean anything more than the actual exhibition of the determination of Da-sein as thematized in the analytic of Da-sein. Insofar as the latter is defined as existence, these determinations of Da-sein are called *existentialia*. Therefore, the concept of "Daseinanalysis" [in contrast to psychological "Dasein-analysis"] still belongs to the analytic of Da-sein and, therefore, to ontology.

From this "Daseinanalysis" we must distinguish what demonstrates and describes the actual phenomena showing up in each case in a specific existing Da-sein. In each case this analysis is directed toward existence and is necessarily oriented by the basic determinations of the being of this being, i.e., by what the analytic of Da-sein highlights as existentialia. Thereby, it must be kept in mind that what is exhibited in the analytic of Da-sein regarding Da-sein and its existential structure is limited, i.e., limited by the fundamental task of the question of being. This limitation is given by the fact that regarding the temporal character of being qua presence, the point is to interpret Da-sein as temporality [*Zeitlichkeit*]. Therefore, it is not an analytic of Da-sein that can satisfy the completeness required for laying the foundation for a philosophical anthropology (see *Being and Time*, p. 38).

Here the necessary circle of all *hermeneutics* appears. The analytic of Da-sein as an existential-ontological analytic already *presupposes* certain determinations of being, the complete determination of which should be prepared precisely by the analytic.

A fourth determination of Daseinanalysis can be established along with this third one. This means that there would have to be an entire future discipline with the task of delineating the demonstrable existentiell [*existenziellen*] phenomena of the sociohistorical and indi-   p. 164 vidual Da-sein in the sense of *ontic* anthropology bearing the stamp of the analytic of Da-sein. The third determination is the actualization of the fourth, just as the second determination is that of the first. One can still differentiate this anthropological Daseinanalysis into two parts—a normal anthropology and a Daseinanalytic pathology related to the former. Since we are dealing with an anthropological analysis of Da-sein, a mere classification of the exhibited phenomena is not sufficient. On the contrary, it must be oriented toward the concrete historical existence of the contemporary human being, that is, toward the existing human being in today's industrial society.

Therefore, to a certain extent, we have clarified what it is that the aforementioned reproaches are *directed against*. Now we must discuss the reproaches themselves.

There are three. Those who raise these objections and reproaches must be acquainted with what *science* is, with the meaning of *objectivity*, and therefore with the meaning of *concept*. Above all, they must know how these three determinations relate to one another. How else could the analytic of Da-sein and Daseinanalysis be antiscientific? Unfortunately, there has not been an opportunity to examine this by direct discussion with its critics. Nevertheless, the fact that these three reproaches have already been raised separately reveals just how much the necessary clarity is lacking regarding what this hasty criticism asserts.

Fundamentally, we are not dealing with three reproaches here at all but with only *one* because there is no science without objects and concepts.

p. 165 But what does "science" mean in all these reproaches? We mean the natural sciences. What about natural science? What is the distinctive character of natural science? Were the Greeks also in possession of scientific concepts? No. What characterizes this modern concept of science? Husserl once defined science as the foundational connection between true propositions (*Logical Investigations,* 1900–1901).[2] For instance, the law of free fall. Is this law "objective" in the sense of being independent from the human being? The science's relationship to the human being consists not only in the fact that it is performed by the human being. Rather, the human being is necessarily a participant in the sense that he must form a supposition, a fiction. What does such a supposition render? In classical physics, it characterizes the object domain (called nature) as the connection of points of mass in uniform, rectilinear motion. Thereby, what happens to nature? It is represented regarding its conformity to a law. Only then can it become an object from the outset, that is, an object for the calculability and predictability of all processes. The supposition thus made is nothing other than the basic act of objectifying nature. Linguistically speaking, the term "object" is translated from the Latin word *objectum.* Yet at the very moment I say "object," its relationship to a subject is already added, as well. "Object" is what is set over and against the experience of a subject. This is a very specific idea of object.

In contrast to this, there is a quite natural concept of object as when one says "object of use" [*Gebrauchsgegenstand*]. In philosophy there is yet another concept of "object" referring to something entirely general, here insofar as "object" designates any possible something [*mögliches Etwas*] for a possible thought. This theory of object [*Gegenstandstheorie*] developed along with *phenomenology* at the turn of the century.* Both come from the school of Brentano. Here, object meant nothing more than a mere "something." Here, each something that can become the subject of an assertion is an object, for instance, "identity," "equality," "relation," but also a thing, a machine, an event, a number. [It includes anything possible, which is not nothing.] Basically, even "nothing" is an object here, insofar as I am able to speak about it.

p. 166

Therefore, there are three concepts of an object. In the first case, object is equivalent to the object of natural science. In the second case, object refers to independently existing things, which can be used and thought about. In the third case, object is something as the subject of a possible predication about something.

In the discussion of the object-concept [*Gegenstandsbegriff*] in the first case, that is, in the sense of an object of natural science's experience, we must ask the question, What happens to this object domain? It is an object of research. What does this mean?

SEMINAR PARTICIPANT: Experiments are conducted with objects.

MH: Does experimentation occur only in physics? And what is an experiment? Through the experiment, the object is questioned [*befragt*] in a certain respect. In what respect? How is this respect determined? By a theory determining beforehand what nature is? Where is this theory established? In theoretical physics. Therefore, research in physics consists not only of experiments but equally and necessarily it includes theoretical physics. There is a mutual relationship between the two, insofar as the theory is modified according to the results of the experiments, or respectively, the experiment has the task of proving the theoretical assertions empirically. In turn, this means that the actual result of the experiment verifies the accuracy of the theoretical assertion. This "accuracy" means the validity of the supposition that is made regarding a lawful process.

The theoretical assertion is tested by the so-called facts with the aid of the experiment. Yet, the experiment is not a manipulation of nature. Only a tool can be manipulated this way. In contrast to this, one *services* a machine. One does not handle it. One *maintains* the latest machine (automata).

p. 167

Therefore, the experiment and the theoretical construction are procedures [*Verfahrensweisen*] in the study of nature, which belong together mutually. One calls these two ways of investigation "method."

---

*Here Heidegger is referring to A. Meinong (1853–1921) and his *Gegenstandstheorie* [theory of object], which, in combination with Husserl's phenomenology, was inspired by the logician and psychologist F. Brentano (1838–1917).—TRANSLATORS

In research, method is the way of proceeding, the manner research proceeds in the investigation of its object domain. As a procedure, we call this idea of method *the instrumental conception of method*. What is the proper meaning of method? Is method merely an instrument of research in natural science, or is it more here? Is method merely a means of research, serving science in its performance, or is method something more?

In Nietzsche we find the statement: "What is distinctive of our 19th century is not the victory of *science*, but the victory of the scientific *method* over science" (*Will to Power*, no. 466, written the year before Nietzsche's breakdown in 1888).

What does this statement mean? That method is not merely in the service of science but in a certain way is above it. Science is dominated by method. What does this mean? Nothing more than the fact that first and foremost method determines what the object of science should be and in what way it alone is accessible, that is, determined in its objectivity. In his statement, Nietzsche expressed, without further interpretation, what is actually happening in modern natural science. The primary thing is not nature on its own addressing the human being, but what is decisive is how the human being, in light of the domination of nature, must represent [*vorstellen*] nature.

p. 168 In order to elucidate the concept of object as used by natural science, as well as by Kant, a passage from Goethe may be mentioned here. In his *Maxims and Reflections* (maxims 1025 and 1027), Goethe remarks: "When concepts disappear from the world, the objects themselves often get lost. Indeed, one can say in a higher sense that the conception is the object. . . . Since the objects are only brought forth from nothingness through the human being's conceptions about them, they return again into nothing when these conceptions get lost."[3]

Thereby, nothing more is said than the fact that the objectivity of the object is determined by the means of the representation (views) by the subject (the transcendental making-possible [condition of possibility] of the object through subjectivity).

To the physicist, nature presents itself merely in the sense of objects to be investigated by his method whereby the ontological character of nature is determined beforehand as objectivity. But this means that there is no scientific investigation of an object domain without an explicit or implicit ontology. Kant already taught us this. Yet we must recall that to Kant "transcendental" was merely another term for "ontological." Here, of course, ontological is meant in the sense of an ontology for which what is present [being] has been changed into an "object." Not only the method as procedure but at the same time the determination of the objectivity of its object belongs to the scientific character of science. In the modern sense, method not only has the meaning of a procedure of treating objects, but of a *transcendental* [*pre*]*supposition* of the objectivity of objects. This is the meaning of method in Nietzsche's phrase: "the victory of scientific method over science."

p. 169

Then what about the three reproaches [that Daseinanalysis is] antiscientific, antiobjective, and anticonceptual? We still need to discuss the third one, [that Daseinanalysis is] anticonceptual. What then does "concept" mean? The Latin term for concept is *conceptus*. This is derived from the verb *capere* [to seize, to grasp]. The Greeks, who obviously were not entirely incapable of thinking, did not yet know of "concept" [in its purely logical sense].* Therefore, if one were anticonceptual, it would by no means be something to be ashamed of. How about the Greeks? How is a concept determined as a concept? By definition. What is definition? For instance, the table is defined as a usable thing. Then a usable thing is a general determination. A glass and a pencil are also usable things. Therefore, a definition first gives me the higher and more general determination, the *genus*. In order to determine the table as a usable object, we must state what use it will serve. The statement of this particular use, as opposed to that of a pencil and a glass, is called the "specific difference." *Definitio fit per genus proximum* (usable thing) *et differentiam specificam* (table). In the definition, something general and something specific is predicated of a being, that is, an object. This predication is a way an object and a being are delimited and demarcated in contrast to other beings, for instance, the table in contrast to the glass and the pencil.

In Greek, "definition" means ὁρισμός. It is the same word as "horizon," that is, the limit of the visual field, therefore a delimitation and a demarcation pure and simple. In Greek, what was subsequently called a "concept" was simply λογος, that is, what must be predicated of a particular being as appearing this or that way, as its ειδος, its "look" [form]. This predication is a letting-be-seen [ἀποφαινεσθαι], not a conceptual-representational seizing [*Zugreifen*] or a comprehending [*Umgreifen*].

p. 170

In contrast to λογος, the Latin term *conceptus* always implies a proceeding by the human being against beings.

Now, logic distinguishes among different kinds of concepts. It knows about concepts we gain from experience, for instance, the concept of table. This is an empirical concept. In the Kantian sense,

---

*Stoic logic introduced the forerunner of the modern term "concept" with the terms *lekton* and *prolepsis.* —TRANSLATORS

causality is not an a posteriori, empirical concept but an a priori concept. This means that it is not derived from experience but extracted from [the] subjectivity [of the knower]. To show in greater detail how Kant obtains his table of categories and how he justifies the validity of the categories would be too difficult at this level of our reflection.*
In *Maxims and Reflections* (1106) Goethe says that cause and effect are the "most innate concepts."[4] Every formation of a concept is a kind of representation, a making-something present to oneself.

When I say "tree," something becomes present to me, something is re-presented to me. By tree, I do not mean an oak, a beech, or a fir, but "tree." What does this show? It is said that formation of concepts occurs through abstraction. Does one really obtain the distinctive character of a concept through abstraction? After all, abstraction means a drawing away. What is drawn away? The specific characteristics making an oak an oak and a fir a fir are abstracted. But how does one arrive at a concept by merely drawing something away [abstraction]?

SP: The common feature [*Gemeinsame*] is apprehended and the *particulars* [*Einzelne*] are left out.

p. 171 MH: Yes, but how do you obtain the general characteristics [*Allgemeines*]? Obviously, it cannot be gained through mere abstraction. After all, I can only draw something away from something when that from which something is abstracted and drawn away is already given to me and is already there.

SP: First of all, one must compare all trees with one another.

MH: Yet, comparing is also insufficient by itself—apart from the fact that no one has been able to perceive *all* trees. For when I compare something to something, for instance, a linden tree to an oak tree, I always compare them regarding the fact that they are *trees*. Yet I do not gain the characteristic of "tree" by comparing, but by grasping [*Erfassthaben*] the general meaning of "tree." The fact that one has already grasped what "tree" is, is always already presupposed in comparing particular trees to each other. It is presupposed as that in light of which I can compare a linden and an oak tree with each other in the first place, that is, as trees. As boys you already knew what a tree was. You already had a preunderstanding [*Vorverständnis*] of it. The general characteristic "tree" is identical to what is represented beforehand regarding each tree, that representation by which I can

---

*See Heidegger, *What Is a Thing?* and *Kant and the Problem of Metaphysics.*
—TRANSLATORS

recognize a tree in the first place. According to logic, this sameness [*Selbe*] is apprehended through reflection, that is, in the sense what is identical is made explicit. In truth, I learn to apprehend something identically the same by way of language—at first not reflected on explicitly. Viewing what is identically the same makes possible the perception of different trees as trees in the first place. In naming things, in addressing beings as this and that—that is, in language—all formulation of concepts is already delineated.

Nevertheless, after this merely sketchy discussion of the conceptual character [*Begrifflichkeit*] of the concept, the question arises whether everything can be apprehended conceptually in general or whether there is a limit to conceptual apprehension. During the elucidation of the formulation of concepts, we said that the comparison of diverse instances and examples comes into play. Therefore, abstraction from particulars—for instance, particular trees—belongs to the formulation of concepts. Yet regarding the formulation of concepts, the decisive point is adherence to what is identically the same. p. 172

Now what about this identity? Something is identical when it is the same with itself. There are such strange matters that one merely apprehends when one allows them to *be given as such* to oneself. I can only make negative assertions about identity. For instance, concerning it, I can say that it is not equality [*Gleichheit*]. In a positive way, I can say only: Identity is identity. In a genuine sense this is a tautology. Consequently, there are matters concerning thought [*Sachen im Denken*] not only where a concept fails but where it does not belong at all. Therefore, when made by a critic, the reproach of being anticonceptual is dangerous to him himself. It might be that just then I was thinking precisely in the proper way when I engaged in [*einlassen*] matters not admitting conceptual determination—when I dealt with matters resisting any conceptual apprehension and any grasping, indeed, [all matters] resisting any ruthless attempt to comprehend them. I can only point to these matters. In a "metaphorical" sense, one can only "see" or "not see" such matters. We can only indicate them—point at them. This "only" does not imply a defect. Rather, this kind of apprehension has *priority* and preference *over* all formulation of concepts insofar as the latter always rests in the end on such an [originary] apprehension. Therefore, it is an entirely superficial alternative to assert that there is only either conceptual thought or a vague emotional, subjective experience [*Erleben*]. There is still something else prior to all conceptualization and experience. Phenomenology deals with what is prior to all conceptualization and subjective, emotional experiencing. Of course, we must understand the special character of phenomenology properly and be careful not to misinterpret it as one movement among other "movements" and schools of philosophy.*

Now we can go back only briefly to the question: Is Daseinanalysis antiscientific or not? Even after the elucidation just attempted, we are still unable to give an adequate answer because we have not yet attended to a decisive point. The decisive character of a science is always the fact that its way of inquiry [*Untersuchung*] corresponds to its subject matter [*Sache*]. There are also matters I do not apprehend at all if I make them objects of conceptual representation. Anxiety or fear are not objects. At most, I can make them a *theme*. Therefore, it belongs to the rigorous nature of science that it is commensurate with its subject matter in its projections and in its method. Yet not every rigorous science is necessarily an exact science. Precision is merely a specific form of the science's rigor, for precision exists only where the object is posited as something that can be calculated beforehand. But if there are matters that resist calculability due to their nature, then any attempt to measure them according to the method of an exact science is inappropriate.

March 1 and 3, 1966, at Boss's Home

I. March 1, 1966

MARTIN HEIDEGGER: At the beginning of the seminar, Professor Boss likened these seminar evenings to a kind of group therapy, which

---

*Heidegger took the method of "phenomenological seeing" and "categorical intuition" from his teacher Husserl. Through his study of Aristotle, Heidegger gave it an ontological interpretation. See Heidegger, *Being and Time*, sec. 7; Husserl, *Logical Investigations*, vol. 7; Heidegger, *Being and Time*, pp. 56, 261 ff. Heidegger rejected Husserl's Cartesian and idealist aspiration to a "scientific philosophy" (as a "school of philosophy") in which "phenomena" are the only possible objects [*noemata*] of an intending subjective consciousness [*noesis*], which has "bracketed" [epoche, reductions] the natural world and its own existence. In contrast to Husserl's eidetic, i.e., objectifying, phenomenology of "consciousness," Heidegger saw the primary task of phenomenology as "ontology," which uncovers the hidden "meaning of being" by an interpretation (Greek: *hermeneuein*, interpret) of Dasein's *understanding* of being. See Heidegger, *Being and Time*, pp. 58 f., 62. As a consequence of this "hermeneutical-ontological" phenomenology, Heidegger used the German word *vernehmen* [to receive-perceive; Greek: *noein*] in a double sense: (1) *Hinnehmen* [receive, accept, perceive, take-in], (2) *Vernehmen* [as in interrogating witnesses], which actively uncovers that which is hidden—for the most part, the primordial phenomenon of *being*.—TRANSLATORS

should make possible a freer view, a more adequate letting-be-seen of the constitution of human beings. As in Freudian analysis, much resistance will develop during the course of such group therapy and will be directed against becoming free through the cure. Resistance against the Heideggerian cure can be summarized essentially by two points.

First, it is said that the essential characterization of the natural sciences as developed in the previous seminars is valid only for classical physics but not for nuclear physics.

Second, it is argued that psychotherapy is not a procedural approach like classical or nuclear physics.

I would like to recommend a book by Friedrich Wagner on this theme: *Die Wissenschaft und die gefährdete Welt* [Science and the endangered world] (Munich: Beck, 1964). On the basis of numerous quotations from leading nuclear physicists, it shows very clearly that the essential character of physics, as determined in our previous seminars, is not only valid for nuclear physics, but is even more valid.

Heidegger now asks whether the seminars are a cure and puts forth the following: The Latin *semen* means "seed." During these evenings, perhaps we will succeed in planting a seed for [further] reflection, which eventually might grow here and there. A philosophical seminar still finds itself in the situation of Socrates, who said that the most difficult thing is always to say the same thing about the same thing. p. 175

It was said that the definition given for physics is antiquated, and then [that it is] irrelevant for psychotherapy. What character do these two assertions have? The aforementioned critique says that what has been said is no longer valid and that it is inessential.

What does "critique" mean? The word comes from the Greek κρίνειν, which means "to separate," that is, to set something off from something—in most cases something lower from something higher. In logic, this procedure refers to judgment—to a critical examination. Both of the above assertions contain a negative critique. A positive critique aims at furthering the matter at hand. It is always an indication of new and real possibilities. A negative critique says that something about the theme is wrong.

In order to understand correctly what was said about physics in the previous seminar, we must recall what the theme of the seminar was. We were dealing with method, more specifically, with what characterizes the method of modern natural science. Here, method does not simply and vaguely mean "procedure." Method is the way and manner of how being, in this case "nature," has been thematized. This occurs because nature is represented as something standing-over-against, as an object. Neither the ancients nor the medievals represented being as an ob-ject [*Gegen-stand*]. The modern concept of nature, that is, its objectification, is motivated by the idea of representing the processes of nature in such a way that they can be predicted and, therefore, controlled.

Consequently, this specifically defined objectification of nature is the projection of nature as a realm of things which can be controlled. The decisive steps toward the unfolding of this projection of nature as capable of being completely controlled were taken by Galileo and Newton. What becomes decisive is *how* nature is represented, and not *what* nature is. In this sense, the development of science leads to the point that the method of proceeding against nature determines science in an increasingly direct way. Thus, Nietzsche could say: "It is not the victory of science that distinguishes our nineteenth century, but the victory of *scientific method* over science" (*The Will to Power,* no. 466 [1888]). But this "victory of method" is preceded by a long struggle where the method thus characterized pushes for its complete predominance in science.

When we spoke about classical physics in the previous seminar, our intention was not to stress it as *classical* but rather as *physics,* that is, with regard to what is also valid in modern, nuclear *physics* as physics.

Only when the universal and basic characteristic of classical and nuclear physics are sufficiently clarified beforehand can we ask how both are distinct from each other despite their underlying identity. But if such an important difference should appear between them, [this difference] once again can lie only in the fact that it is distinctive for both in the same way. That is the method—that is, the predictability—of the events and processes of nature.

The objectified representation of these processes is guided by the principle of causality, which Kant determined in his *Critique of Pure Reason* (A.189) with the statement: "Everything that happens, that is, begins to be, presupposes something upon which it follows *according to a rule.*" With regard to the method of predictability, this means that from the state of a system at a definite time (present), its future state can be clearly determined.

Heisenberg formulated this principle (*Zeitschrift für Physik* [Journal for physics] 43 [1927]: 197) in the following way: "If we know the present with precision, we can calculate the future." Yet Heisenberg then says: "Not the final clause, but the presupposition [is] false. In principle, we *cannot* know the present in all of its determinations." This ignorance is due to quantum physic's principle of indeterminacy [*Unbestimmtheitsrelation*], which states that we can accurately measure only either the location or the velocity of a particle but not both simultaneously. At that time, Heisenberg drew the conclusion from this fact that then "the invalidity of the law of causality is definitely

p. 176

p. 177

stated."[1] Even today, talk about "a-causality" partially depends on this thesis.

But the *principle of causality*—and thus, predictability—is not invalidated by the indeterminacy principle. If this were the case, then the construction of the atomic bomb, indeed any atomic technology, would have been impossible. It is not the principle of causality, upon which the validity of physics as such stands and falls, which becomes invalid. It is only an unequivocal [*eindeutig*] and completely precise predictability that becomes impossible. Therefore, regarding the explosion of an atom bomb, only an upper and a lower limit of the magnitude of such an explosion is predictable. But its general predictability remains in principle, since without it, any technical construction would be impossible. Later on, Heisenberg abandoned this confusing talk about a-causality. There is no such thing as an "a-causal worldview." As evidence to support this, one could refer to present research on the technique of genetic mutation in humans (see Wagner, *Die Wissenschaft und die gefährdete Welt,* pp. 225 ff. and 462 ff.).

That which is preserved in nuclear physics is what characterizes it as *physics*—something it accordingly has in common with classical physics as physics. The point of discussing classical physics in the previous seminar was only to [provide] a general characterization of "science" as such. This discussion occurred in response to the thesis that psychiatric Daseinanalysis is "antiscientific." A response to this thesis presupposes that the meaning of "science" has been clarified—that is, [that it has also been clarified] in what way the scientific relationship to the thematic object is distinctive. p. 178

The theme of physics is inanimate nature. The theme of psychiatry and psychotherapy is the human being. How should we determine the scientific character of psychiatry and of the theoretical foundation of psychotherapeutic praxis?

If Daseinanalysis is accused of being antiscientific, then this accusation presupposes that "science" means science such as physics. Therefore, if the science of the human being should meet basic requirements of modern science, then it would have to satisfy the principle of priority of method with the same meaning as the projection of predictability. The unavoidable result of such a science of the human being would be the technical construction of the human being as machine. There are already many signs that scientific research and production of such a human being is already under way. All this occurs under the pressure of the aforementioned "victory of *method* over science" and with the fanaticism of the absolute will to progress for the sake of progress.

Supposing though that the scientific character of a science need not be dogmatically and exclusively measured against modern physics, then the question emerges in what sense, and how, the unfolding essence [*Wesen*] of science can be determined at all. Then one would have to ask how a science of the human being, serving as a foundation for psychiatry and as a theory of psychotherapeutic praxis, could be founded and constructed.

At the same time, if we recollect that science as such is an activity and a work of the human being, then a peculiar interdependence appears between the question of science and the question of the human being (through whom science is possible in the first place).

p. 179

Finally, it should have become clear from the present attempts at clarification that those who argue that "Daseinanalysis" is antiscientific are not sufficiently informed about the distinctive character of modern science in the sense of physics. Neither are they able to determine the scientific character of a science of the human being—especially in psychiatry—in such a way that a clear demarcation from the scientific method of physics can clearly come to light.

Nevertheless, the discussion of physics as science should not merely and initially serve the purpose of refuting the reproaches against "Daseinanalysis." Instead, the point is to bring today's authoritative science into view so that by contrast we can see the possibility opening for another kind of science—that of the human being.

Therefore, during the transition in determining a science of the human being, the question was raised as to what the basic character of science is as such, that is, what basic character remains after we abstract that which distinguishes physics as physics.

We postponed an immediate answer to this question. Beforehand, we must examine how contemporary science of the human being experiences the being of the human being and how it describes and determines its possibilities. For this purpose, we select a review of characteristic answers to an inquiry on stress (Von Dührssen, Jores, and Schwidder, *Zeitschrift für Psychosomatische Medizin* [Journal for psychosomatic medicine], vol. 11, no. 4 [1965]). What is your opinion about this "inquiry"?

SEMINAR PARTICIPANT: The whole inquiry is poorly formulated. The phrase "stress stimulus" [*Stressreiz*] is unclear. The concept of stress is fuzzy, poorly defined, and ambiguous.

p. 180

MH: Certainly, what you say is correct, although it remains merely a negative critique. What would a positive critique sound like? First, it would have to inquire into what is meant by stress. It is not a matter of hastily obtaining a concept. Rather, it is necessary to bring the subject matter into view. Then perhaps it could be conceptualized and defined. Thereby, we aim at "a clear understanding." Nevertheless, this does not mean that the subject matter about which we must reach an understanding must itself be clearly determined. It can be ambiguous in itself. Accordingly, the ambiguity [*Vieldeutigkeit*] of the concept thus obtained is not a flaw. Science, oriented toward calculability, aims at univocity [*Eindeutigkeit*] because calculability would not be possible otherwise. Natural science does not ask whether the "univocal"* concept still corresponds to the subject matter.

How must one proceed in order to make the manifold meaning of "stress" accessible? Stress means to have a claim made on oneself [*Beanspruchung*] and to be burdened [*Belastung*]. Unburdening [*Entlastung*] can be a form of stress as well. Why does a certain amount of stress result in the preservation of life? This is grounded in the [temporal] ecstatic relationship [to the world]. It is a basic structure of being human. What is founded in it is that openness according to which the human being is always already addressed by beings other than himself. The human being could not live without this being addressed. "Stress" is something that preserves "life" in the sense of this necessity of being addressed. As long as we think of the human being as a world-less Ego, the necessity of stress for life cannot be made intelligible. Thus understood, this being burdened—the stress—belongs to the essential constitution of the existing human being. According to *Being and Time*'s terminology (sec. 38), it is an existentiale and belongs in the context of the phenomenon interpreted there by the term "falling" [*Verfallen*].†

In the text of the inquiry, there is talk about "stress stimulation" [*Stressreiz*]. If one understands this stimulation in the sense of "being

p. 181

---

*Based on Aristotle (*Metaphysics* IV.2.1003a33–4; V.7.1017b23–5), medieval Scholastics (see Aquinas, *Summa Theologica* I, q.13, a.5, *Ouaest. disp. De ver.* 2.a11) and modern philosophers distinguish three ways in which concepts can be used: (1) *univocally* (with exactly the same meaning), (2) *equivocally* (with completely different, unrelated meanings), and (3) *analogically* (similarity within difference and difference within similarity of meaning). Specific (e.g., a house), generic (e.g., a building), and categorical (e.g., a substance) concepts are "univocal," while other concepts (e.g., love, a "being") are "analogical." "Equivocation" as a fallacy arising from the total ambiguity of a term is ultimately destructive to discourse and communication. As used above by Heidegger, "ambiguity" implies an "analogical" rather than an "equivocal" use of scientific concepts.—TRANSLATORS

†Prior to any psychological, moral, or religious conception, i.e., the fallen state of "sin" or the state of "grace," *falling* is an existential structure of Da-sein's everyday flight from itself, which does not express a "negative" moral evaluation but points phenomenologically to the ontological constitution of the "inauthentic" mode of Da-sein's being-in-the-world as always already "falling away" from its authentic *Sein-können* [potentiality-to-be]. Thus, Da-sein "drifts along toward an alienation [*Entfremdung*] in which its ownmost potentiality-for-being is hidden

affected" wherein the human being is concerned with and claimed by something, then it becomes clear that the phrase "stress stimulation" is redundant. Certainly, what stimulates can be understood in different ways depending on the realm where it occurs. In the abstract dimension of isolated sensation, stimulation (e.g., an isolated, sound stimulus) means something other than what is in the domain of the human being's everyday sojourning [*sich aufhalten*] in his world, for instance, where a charming landscape appeals to him—invites him to stay. A stimulus [as irritation] can also be found in the domain of being-with-one-another, where someone challenges the other and tries to infuriate him.

The diverse ways of a claim made on one (i.e., "stress") show up in these ways of stimulation. Stress is always oriented toward a particular situation, that is, toward the particular, factical [*faktisch*]* being-in-the-world where the human being, as existing, does not step into occasionally from time to time but, on the contrary, where he essentially and constantly and *always already is.*

We experience being-in-the-world as a basic characteristic of being human. It is not merely assumed hypothetically for the interpretation of being human. Rather, what must be interpreted is just by itself alone always already capable of being received-perceived as being-in-the-world.

If one could understand this situation as such as if it were determined by the three component parts of "Ego," "body," and "world," then the question would have to be asked in what *unity* of being human these *com*ponents could figure. This unity is precisely being-in-the-world itself which is not composed of components, although in its unity it can be brought into one's interpretive view according to its different aspects.

In the text of the inquiry (p. 237b), if it is noted that the human being cannot be "separated from his world," then even this assertion implies the idea of a "composition" of the human being and world, missing the phenomenological-existential state of affairs. Not only can the human being not be separated from his world, but here the idea of separability and inseparability does not have any foundation in the condition of being-in-the-world.

p. 182

"Critical" comments, interspersed here and in what follows, serve merely as an opportunity to indicate the manifold nature of the phe-

---

from it. Falling being-in-the-world is not only tempting and tranquilizing; it is also *alienating*"(Heidegger, *Being and Time*, p. 222).—TRANSLATORS

*Heidegger's *faktisch* [factical, factual], as distinguished from *tatsächlich* [actual], refers to an existential-ontological characteristic of the human being's "being-in-the-world." See ibid., p. 82.—TRANSLATORS

nomena illustrated through the term "stress." Here, a sufficient, critical answer to the research performed by authors of the selected text cannot be claimed. Nevertheless, the texts offer fruitful approaches to a clarifying, phenomenological reflection. For instance, this already holds true for the title of the book by H. Plügge, *Wohlbefinden und Missbefinden* [Well-being and discontent] (Tübingen, 1962).

The book deals with the condition [*Befinden*] which we allude to when we ask someone, "How are you?"—that is, "How is it going with you?" The question need not refer necessarily to one's "bodily condition" [*körperliches Befinden*]. The question can be meant as an inquiry into the very factical [*faktisch*] situation of the other. However, such a condition is to be distinguished from what is interpreted as ontological disposition [*Befindlichkeit*] in *Being and Time*. It is the attunement determining Da-sein in its particular relationship to the world, to the Da-sein-with [*Mitdasein*] other humans, and to itself. Ontological disposition founds the particular feelings of well-being and discontent yet is itself founded again in the human being's being exposed [*Ausgesetzheit*] toward beings as a whole [*das Seiende im Ganzen*]. Thereby, it is already said that the understanding of being as being belongs to this being exposed (thrownness), but in the same way, there cannot be an understanding that is not already a "thrown" understanding.

Thrownness [*Geworfenheit*] and understanding [*Verstehen*] mutually belong together in a correlation whose unity is determined through language.* Here, language is to be understood as a [primordial] "saying" [*Sage*] in which beings as beings, that is, in view of their being, show themselves. Only on the basis of the belonging together of thrownness and understanding through language as saying is the human being able to be addressed by beings (see p. 185 below). But to be able to be addressed is the condition for the possibility of being claimed by something, whether this claim is burdening [*Belastung*] or unburdening [*Entlastung*].

p. 183

Thus, the domain is indicated (even if merely in broad outline) where something like stress and all of its modifications belong. Stress has the basic character of being claimed [*Beanspruchung*] by something as a being addressed [*Angesprochenwerden*]. Such a thing is only

---

*In *Being and Time* Heidegger used the word *Rede* [discourse] for language as an existentiale. The later Heidegger employed a broader understanding of language and used *Sprache* as *Sage* [poetical saying as founding discourse]. See M. Heidegger, *Unterwegs zur Sprache* (Pfullingen: Gunther Neske, 1959), trans., *On the Way to Language*. See also M. Heidegger, *Poetry, Language, Thought*, trans. A. Hofstadter (New York: Harper and Row, 1971), pp. 3–14, 91–142; *Contributions to Philosophy*, pp. 350–54, 358.—TRANSLATORS

possible on the basis of language. Here language is not understood as a capacity for communication but as the original manifestness of what is, [and] which is preserved by the human being in different ways. Insofar as the human being is being-with [*Mitsein*], as he remains essentially related to another human, language as such is conversation [*Gespräch*]. Johann Christian Friedrich Hölderlin says: "Since we are a conversation" (*Friedensfeier*). This must be said more clearly: Insofar as we are conversation, being-with belongs to being human.

As we said earlier, stress belongs to the essential connection of address and response, that is, to the dimension of conversation in the broad sense, including a "speaking" with things as well. Once again, conversation forms the fundamental domain within which an interpretation becomes possible. Thus, the "hermeneutical circle" is not a *circulus vitiosus,* but an essential constitution of being human. It characterizes the finitude of the human being. The human being, in his highest being, is limited precisely by his openness to being.* Yet certainly this statement cannot be understood from what has been discussed so far.

II. March 3, 1966

p. 184

We have spoken about science in view of the question of the standing of Daseinanalytical psychiatry. Our reflection on science was oriented toward the question of the way and the sense in which one can speak of a science of the human being. If nature is assessed regarding the calculability of spatiotemporal processes, then nature is understood within a projection which does not permit one to see it as what comes to presence by abiding in itself [*in sich ruhendes Anwesendes*]. On the contrary, nature is represented as an object upon which the questions of research intrude in the manner of precalculation and control. To represent what is as an object is a thoroughly modern conception. This idea of setting something up against oneself [*Sich-Entgegensetzen*], of making it an object—

---

*The "hermeneutical circle" (see Heidegger, *Being and Time,* pp. 194–95) as the unavoidable circle between implicit "preunderstanding" [*Vorverständnis*] and explicit "understanding" [*Verstehen*], between the reciprocal (ontological) relation of the interpreter to that which is interpreted (e.g., a foreign text, a work of art, a form of culture, etc.), between understanding the "whole" and the "part," belongs to the very structure of our finite, temporal "being-in-the-world." It underlies understanding and interpretation, including "explanation" in the natural sciences. The later Heidegger puts "hermeneutics" (rarely mentioned after *Being and Time*) within the new context of language and being. See M. Inwood, *A Heidegger Dictionary* (Oxford: Blackwell, 1999), pp. 87–90.—TRANSLATORS

this objectification—lies in the nature of natural science's projection. The representation of something regarding what is valid [*gilt*]* in it for many things and is therefore a "universal" we call a "concept." Therefore, concepts are necessary representations for comportment directed toward the calculability of beings.

If something is represented in universal terms regarding what is—for instance, if I represent the table in view of what is valid for it universally—then I say it is a use-thing. The representation of something as this particular thing is called a perception or a sensory intuition [*sinnliche Anschauung*].

The guiding question of the preceding seminar's second hour was: In what context does stress belong? We answered: Stress belongs to the constitution of human existence which is determined by thrownness, understanding, and language. The many meanings of the term "stress" indicate the diverse nature of the subject matter, so that we have to attend to the necessarily many meanings of the assertions and not to consider this as a lack if we want to remain properly attuned to the subject matter. Words and concepts have a different character in this domain. We must now reflect upon these meanings rather than those used in science.

It would be abhorrent to a physicist if the language of the science of the human being, for instance—as with the language of poetry—were by its nature to be without univocal meaning. He [the physicist] believes that conceptual precision is a requirement which must be fulfilled by every science. But this belief is justified only if one believes in the dogma that [everything in] the world is completely calculable and that the calculable world is the [only] true reality. This conception is pushing us toward uncanny developments—already looming now—in which one no longer asks who and how the human being is. Instead, he [the human being] is conceived of beforehand from the background of the technical manipulatability of the world.

p. 185

Stress means a *claim on one* [*Beanspruchung*], and that [claim] initially in an excessive manner. In general, a claim on one requires some kind of response at any given time to which privations also belong, such as the fact of not responding and of not being able to respond. If we speak of a claim on one instead of stress, then this is not merely another term, but the phrase "claim on one" immediately carries the subject matter to the domain of the ecstatic way of being human [*ekstatisches Menschsein*] This is the domain where something can be said about what addresses us, that it

---

*See Heidegger, *Being and Time*, p. 198, n. 1, regarding the broader meaning of the German *gelten* [to be valid] as distinguished from the narrower English meaning of "validity" as a property of logical arguments.—TRANSLATORS

is so and so. To say something as this or that (so and so) is ἀποφαινεσθαι, a showing of the subject matter by itself.* The proper nature of language consists of such saying or showing.

Here above all, we must pay greater attention to, and reflect upon, that by which the existing human being is addressed in the first place—that is, by the world in which he sojourns every day.

But if the human being is understood in the Cartesian sense as *ego cogito,* as consciousness, and if one asks for the primary datum of consciousness according to this approach, then according to the doctrine of British empiricism (which was still dominant in the nineteenth century and influencing Husserl for a long time as well), the answer is: sensation. Husserl determined this fact in greater detail as hyletic data [*hyletische Daten*] (see Husserl, *Ideen zu einer reinen Phänomenologie und phänomenologischen Philosophie* [Ideas: General introduction to a pure phenomenology and to a phenomenological philosophy] [1913], chap. 10, no. 97). In Greek ὕλη [hyle] means stuff, matter, originally wood. H. Plügge (*Wohlbefinden und Missbefinden,* p. 238, col. 2) speaks of "objective states of affairs." These can exist only where something is objectified—only where I am able to measure the acoustic stimulus as a phone [*Phon*]. This is achieved by an apparatus measuring sound waves. Yet such an apparatus is unable to hear the noise of an air drill as air drill noise. Is the perception of a noisy motorcycle initially heard as phones [*Phonen*], and then is the meaning of a motorcycle subsequently added to it? Isn't it just the other way around? In everyday life I always hear the motorcycle, the call of the bird, and the church bell first. It requires a very artificial approach to be able to distill a pure sensory datum [*Empfindungsdatum*] from what was heard. Plügge's conception is derived from Husserl's position. For the latter, things as objects are constituted on the ground of the hyletic data whereby they receive their meaning from the noetic acts of consciousness. On the contrary, the intensity of phones [*Phonstärke*] is not perceived immediately, but rather it is measured as a physical object by a machine.

What is the structure of sensory *perception* [*Wahrnehmung*]? This question can only be unfolded and answered if we search for perception where it belongs—in our everyday preoccupation with things. It has to do with my relationship to the surrounding world [*Umwelt*]. What am I related to in perception? To an [isolated] sensation with a superimposed meaning, or to the children and to the cement mixer (an example from Plügge). Plügge hears the noisy children, but they do not disturb him

p. 186

---

*See Heidegger, *Being and Time,* pp. 51 f., 195 ff., 256 f.; *The Fundamental Concepts of Metaphysics,* pp. 304–43.—TRANSLATORS

because he lets them be *his* children, because he is with them as his own children in his domestic world. On the contrary, the neighbor's "girls" [*Gören*] disturb him because he does not put up with their noisy playing. If he would let the girls play like children as well, it would be impossible for them to disturb and annoy him. Because he does not respond to their being children, they make a claim on him. It becomes clear from this that the claim (as appropriately understood "stress') must be measured by entirely different standards, that is, by the way and manner in which we respond (and in which we are able to respond) to a p. 187 claim in advance—the way in which our existing relationship to the world, to other human beings, and to ourselves is determined. The physical-psychological reduction of stress to sensory stimulation is apparently concrete scientific research on stress. Yet in truth it is an arbitrary and forced abstraction, entirely losing sight of the existing human being. By the way, after the publication of *Being and Time*, Husserl gave up his Cartesian position to a certain extent. Since 1930 the phrase "life-world" [*Lebenswelt*] has appeared in the manuscripts.

Let us now consider the phenomenon of *unburdening* [*Entlastung*]. We know that unburdening can be, or can become, a form of stress (e.g., for a person who returns home after a successful exam, etc.). We are always claimed—addressed in some way. Relief is not merely a negation of the way of being-claimed in the sense that any claim is dropped. Rather, it is another (and even distinctive) way of being addressed. Unburdening is possible within and on the ground of always being-*claimed* [*Immer-in-Anspruch-genommen-seins*]. Unburdening and burdening are possible only because of the human being's ecstatic [temporal] extendedness [*Ausgespanntsein*]. For instance, someone who has retired, of course, is no longer claimed by his occupation. Yet as the one who continues to exist, he is dependent upon a claim still addressing him. If this fails to occur after the end of his occupation, then the dependency on being-claimed does not drop off, but it simply remains as unfulfilled, as empty. In this way it becomes an unusual, and thus excessive, claim ("Depression from un-burdening") [*Entlastungsdepression*].

The phenomena of boredom [*Langeweile*]* and of being-with-one-another with regard to their connection to stress have been merely mentioned briefly at the conclusion of this seminar. They will be discussed more thoroughly in the next seminar in light of the text on inquiry [*Umfrage*].

---

*In his lecture course in the winter semester of 1929–30, Heidegger elucidated the originary phenomenon of "deep boredom" [*Langeweile*] in human, temporal existence. See *The Fundamental Concepts of Metaphysics*, pp. 78–164.—TRANSLATORS

March 18 and 21, 1969, at Boss's Home

I. March 18, 1969

p. 188

For example, the book is lying here next to the glass. But how are two people standing next to each other related to one another? Why can't the glass relate itself to the table on which it is located? Because it cannot receive-perceive [*vernehmen*] the table as a table.

Of course, one could say that the glass is open at the top, or one would not be able to pour a drink. Yet this is an entirely different openness than the openness [*Offenheit*] which is proper to the human being. The way and manner in which the glass is open suggests nothing more than the fact that it is open to being grasped by my hand in space.

Is the human being in space the same way as the glass? In *Being and Time*, being-there [Da-sein] means: Being-there [*da-sein*]. How is the "there" [*da*] then determined as "the open"? This openness has the character of space as well. Spatiality [*Räumlichkeit*] belongs to the *clearing* [*Lichtung*]—to the open in which we, as existing beings, [naturally] sojourn in such a way that we are not expressly related to space *as* space in any way.

The being-in-space of a utensil cannot be reduced to the spatiality of "being-there" (Da-sein). Yet, the reverse is impossible as well. Both spatiality and temporality belong to the clearing. Space and time belong together, but one does not know how. Now how about *consciousness*? To stand in the clearing does not mean that the human being stands in the light like a pole does. Rather, human Da-sein (being-there) is *sojourning* [*sich aufhalten*] *in the clearing* and "concerns itself with" [*beschäftigt mit*] things.

II. March 18, 1969

We are still pondering the question of the difference between the being-in-space of a glass and the being-open of the human being "to" the glass. What does it mean "to be open to"? Does the being-open to the glass occur in the way in which I perceive it, or conversely, is my being-open to the glass a presupposition for being able to perceive it?

p. 189

Glass *as* glass. The word "as" is a basic word in metaphysics.[*] One can think of "as" merely in the manner of something as something. The

---

[*] In *Being and Time*, sec. 33, esp. p. 201, Heidegger points out how the "apophantical" "as" of the assertion [*Aussage, Urteil*] is founded in the "existential-hermeneutical

"some" in something is not nothing. What about "nothing"? When we say the word "as," we are always dealing with a predication of something about something. Being open is only possible when the clearing has already happened to us so that something can be present or absent. The being open "to" lies in the manifestness of presence [*Anwesenheit*]. There would be no relationship without it.

The following question is decisive: What is the relationship between the [existential] *being-sojourning-in-the-clearing* [*Sich-aufhaltend-in-der-Lichtung-sein*]—without noticing it in a thematic way—and what we understand as *consciousness?*

From a purely linguistic point of view, consciousness necessarily refers to knowledge. Knowledge means: to have seen something, to have something as something manifest; to be "wise" about something [*Bewissen*], and someone who is knowledgeable [*bewisst*]. To know means: Someone finds his way. This term is as old as the word "Da-sein" and appears only from the eighteenth century on. The difficulty in experiencing consciousness lies in the meaning the word received at the time of its origin. When does consciousness begin in philosophy? It originated [historically] with Descartes. Every consciousness of something is simultaneously a self-consciousness in which the self, as a consciousness of an object, does not necessarily include an [explicit] self-consciousness of itself. The question is whether this finding one's way amidst things that are present-at-hand [or ready-to-hand] is a presupposition of Da-sein, or whether Da-sein, which is the sojourning in the open, provides the possibility for a relationship to finding one's way in the first place?

The ancient Greek word τοπος is erroneously translated by our word "place" [*Ort*]. Yet it designates that which we are used to calling space [*Raum*].

III. March 21, 1969 p. 190

In his *Physics,* Aristotle develops the nature of τοπος* [place; *Platz*]. He writes: It [space] seems to be enormous and hard to grasp [*Physics* IV.4].

"as" of Da-sein's circumspective concern and interpretation of its involvement with its "being-in-the-world."—TRANSLATORS

*By [qualitative] "space" Aristotle always meant a "natural [proper] place" of a thing, which is its outer surface coinciding with the outer surface of some other body. Thus, the "space," i.e., the place of a thing, is that which embraces it but not something which penetrates it or (in our sense) the space which a thing "occupies." There is no empty place—"abstract space"—with nothing in it, in the sense of Democritus's "void"

Elsewhere we read: The τοπος is like a container [*Gefäss*]. Since it is a space—that is, a variable space—so, conversely, space, so to speak, is an invariable container [vessel] [Physics IV.2]. Thus, the basic character of the Greek experience of space is that of something encompassing—of a container. τοπος is container, a free, encompassing container [vessel]. There is also *Spatium*: σταδιον, and the making of a place [*Räumen*].

What is the relationship between these three conceptions of space? The first two are grounded in what can be experienced in space and in the sense of making space. These two conceptions presuppose something free, something open. The idea of *spatium* covers up the free, open [region] with geometrical space.

"To be knowledgeable" [*Bewisst*] means to find one's way. But where? In the environment [*Umwelt*], among things. At the same time, this means that the finding of one's way is a relatedness to what is given as "objects." Then in the eighteenth century the words "conscious" and "consciousness" assumed the theoretical meaning of a relationship to experienceable objects. For Kant, [it meant a relationship] to nature as the domain of the possibility for sensory experience. Then, a further step was taken. The natural sciences understood this so-called empirical consciousness, this finding one's way, as the possibility for calculating physical processes.

One speaks of "pure" consciousness as well. This is the knowledge, not only relating to what is perceivable in a sensory way, but also relating to what makes possible the experience of objects, namely their objectivity, possible as well. The objectivity of the objects, that is, the being of beings [*Sein des Seinden*] is oriented toward consciousness. Up to and including Husserl, this was called modern Idealism.

p. 191

IV. March 21, 1968

Thus, the term "consciousness" has become a fundamental conception [*Grundvorstellung*] of modern philosophy. Husserl's phenomenology belongs to it as well. It is the description of consciousness. Husserl merely added intentionality as something new. In a certain way, Husserl's teacher Brentano had already noticed intentionality.*

(with which Aristotle deals in *Physics* IV.6–9). See H. L. Dreyfus, *Being-in-the-World. A Commentary on Heidegger's* Being and Time, *Division I* (Cambridge, Mass.: MIT Press, 1995), pp. 128–40.—TRANSLATORS

*Under the influence of Scholasticism, F. Brentano (*Psychology from an Empirical Standpoint* [New York: Humanities Press, 1973]) emphasized the intentional character

Intentionality means that all consciousness is consciousness of something and is directed toward [*gerichtet auf*] something. One does not have a representation; rather, one represents. To represent [*Repräsentieren*] is "to make present." "Re" is "back toward me." *Repraesentatio* is to make present by returning to myself, whereby I myself am not expressly co-represented [*mitvorstellen*].

This is how it is possible that this "re" (to present it back to myself) can expressly become a theme. Through this relationship to myself, I am determined as someone who represents. This is a consciousness of oneself, whereby the self must not expressly become thematic. This is the most general basic structure of representation—in Husserl's sense—consciousness of something.

---

of all psychical experiences: directing oneself (*intentio*) toward something (*intentum*). In his *Logical Investigations* (New York: Humanities Press, 1970) and in the *Ideas: General Introduction to Pure Phenomenology* (New York: Collier-MacMillan, 1962), Husserl elucidated the phenomenon of the "intentionality" of the conscious acts of a knowing subject. For Heidegger intentionality is grounded ontologically in the basic constitution of Da-sein. It is an ontological comportment [*Verhalten*] toward. It is not the cognitive relation between a noetic "subject" and a noematic "object" but rather the way of Da-sein as always already existing with other beings in its "transcendence" toward a world. See Heidegger, *Basic Problems of Phenomenology,* p. 58 ff.; Kisiel, *Genesis of Heidegger's* Being and Time, pp. 407–8.—TRANSLATORS

PART   I I

CONVERSATIONS WITH
MEDARD BOSS,
1961 – 1972

Statements recorded in shorthand that were made by   p. 193
Heidegger about his conversations with Boss during his
visits at Boss's home in Zollikon and during their vacations
together

November 29, 1961, on the Day after the Seminar on Hallucinations

MEDARD BOSS: At the beginning of yesterday's seminar, Dr. F. presented one of his schizophrenic patients. This case involved a simple factory worker. The man had never experienced himself in any other way than as a homosexual. But recently his friend of many years had deserted him. Shortly thereafter, this patient fell acutely ill. Once during the night he woke up and—having awakened fully—he saw the sun rising on the opposite wall of the room. A sleeping man was lying beneath the sun. The question was: How is this hallucination to be understood phenomenologically?

MARTIN HEIDEGGER: Above all, it is important for you as a psychiatrist to see that there are many modes of the presence [*Anwesenheitsmodi*] of what addresses Da-sein from the openness of its world. In addition to the mode of something being present in a physically perceptible and present manner, there is, for instance, also the mode of making-things-present [*Vergegenwärtigungen*] in a physically imperceptible manner. In addition, there is the mode of having remembered something which happened at such and such a time. Furthermore, as in our case, there is the mode of the presence of something which is hallucinated and cannot be altered. There is the mode of the presence of something illusory which can be controlled. Then there is what is imagined and also the mode of the presence of what is absent. A deceased person, who is no longer present, for instance, might have more presence for the survivors in his absence than he ever did during his lifetime.

The one who is hallucinating can only see his world as the physically perceptible, immediate being-present [*Anwesend-sein*] of all there is. This is because he cannot realize the distinction between being present and being absent and because he cannot move in his world freely.

Presence [can be] intensified unto visibility. According to Aristotle, the visible [*das Sichtbare*] is more present than the audible.*

---

*See Aristotle, *Metaphysics* I.1.980.a21–24; VII.1.1028b8 f. *sens.* 1.437.a.3f. The sense of hearing is more important for learning language (*de sensu*, 1.437a4–17). Regarding Heidegger's phenomenological interpretation of Aristotle, see T. Sheehan, "On the Way

What is visible is the highest form of presence. What is striking is the obtrusive character of the patient's hallucination of the sun.

p. 196 The sick person can experience his friend's departure only as the presence of something obtrusive. He does not allow the absence. Being can only be experienced in and by the presence of a [definite] being.*

MB: Why doesn't the friend himself actually appear in this erotically obtrusive hallucination, but a sun?†

MH: The treating physician must be asked further:

a. How is the patient relating to the hallucinated sun and to the sun-man today?

b. How did the sun-man—the man sleeping beneath the hallucinated sun—appear during the night? Actually sleeping and yet obtrusive? Was this sun-man somehow recognizable as the sleeping friend, or did the sun-man have to represent the friend's banishment [*Bannung*], his defense against him?

c. How is the relationship faring now to the friend who left him?

The fact that only "elementary sensations" occur during the surgical stimulation of the brain demonstrates precisely how little the brain really has to do with seeing.

In understanding hallucinations, one must not start with the distinction between "real" and "unreal," but rather with an inquiry into the character of the relationship to the world in which the patient is involved at any given time. What bestows the sensory-perceptible character on the hallucination and allows it to appear as such? Is it its "intensity"? Is it being spellbound by it? Is it the lack of freedom in the patient?

---

to *Ereignis:* Heidegger's Interpretation of *Physis,*" *Continental Philosophy in America,* ed. H. J. Silverman, J. Sallis, and T. M. Seebohm (Pittsburgh: Duquesne University Press, 1983), pp. 131–64.—TRANSLATORS

*Concerning the "ontological difference" *between* being and beings, see Heidegger, *Being and Time,* pp. 3, 33, 86, 193, 211, and *Basic Problems of Phenomenology,* pp. 18, 319, 120, 176. See *ZS* 20.—TRANSLATORS

†See M. Boss, *Grundriss der Medizin und Psychologie: Ansätze zu einer phänomen-ologischen Physiologie, Psychologie, Pathologie, Therapie und zu einer daseins-gemässen Präventiv-Medizin in der modernen Industrie-Gesellschaft,* 2d ed. (Bern: H. Huber, 1975), pp. 483–511 [*Existential Foundations of Medicine and Psychology,* trans. S. Conway and A. Cleaves, with an introduction by P. J. Stern (New York: J. Aronson, 1979), p. 23 f.]. See also C. E. Scott, "Heidegger, Madness and Well-Being," *Martin Heidegger. Critical Assessments,* ed. C. Macann (London and New York: Routledge, 1992), 4:279–98, esp. p. 292 (discussion of the "sun-man" patient).—TRANSLATORS

April 24–May 4, 1963, during Their Vacation Together in Taormina, Sicily

p. 197

Until now, psychology, anthropology, and psychopathology have considered the human being as an object in a broad sense, as something present-at-hand, as a domain of beings, and as the sum total of what can be stated about human beings experientially.

The question of what and how the human being exists as a human being has been omitted thereby; namely, that in accordance with his unfolding essence, he basically comports himself to other beings and to himself and that this is only possible on his part because he understands being. (In this context "to comport oneself" suggests a relationship founded on an understanding of being.)

When they assert that a human being is determined as a being [who stands] in a relationship to other humans, the American [psychologist] Harry Stack Sullivan and his similarly oriented colleagues make an essential assertion [*Wesensaussage*] about the human being, the foundations of which are not even questioned. (Essential means a projection, an a priori determination made in advance.) They take human comportment toward other human beings as a statement [*Feststellung*] of something *about* the human being and not as an essential assertion determining the human being as a human being in the first place.

Relationship to . . . , the being-in-relation-to . . . characterizes the unfolding essence of the human being. ("Characterize" [*kennzeichnen*] is the correct word here and not "constitute" [*ausmachen*] because this would imply that being-in-relation-to . . . is already a complete determination of the human being, while the relationship to the understanding of being refers to a yet "deeper" determination of the human being's unfolding essence.)

A "statement" basically leaves open the possibility that what has been stated might once not be stated about other human beings. [The term] "always" is a consequence of the [unfolding] essence, but the [unfolding] essence does not follow from the "always" because what is meant by "always" cannot be stated at all due to the fact that one cannot make an inquiry about all human beings.

Galileo's and Newton's Concept of Nature

p. 198

Nature is conceived as a spatiotemporal nexus of the movement of points of mass. It is only by virtue of Galileo's essential assertion that an experiment can be initiated. This projection [*Entwurf*] is already determined from calculability. The most fundamental question of all was: How must I view nature in order to be able always to determine it in advance [as calculable]? Galileo saw something no one had seen up to that time. But this forced him to abstract from everything else, that is, from qualities—for instance, from the fact that an apple is an apple, this is a tree, and that is a meadow.

A fact [*Tatsache*] is something real, but it is not reality. Reality is not a fact, otherwise it would be something ascertainable like a mouse beside something else.

Experimental physics is not the foundation of theoretical physics, but the other way around.

Contemporary psychology, sociology, and the "behavioral sciences," which manipulate man as if by remote control [*ferngesteuert*], belong to the Galilean-Newtonian conception of nature. The human being is also[understood as] a spatiotemporal point of mass in motion.

Galileo's conception and projection of nature emerged from a confrontation with the Aristotelian ontology of nature, that is, guided by the claim for nature's calculability.*

Since there was no possibility for calculating nature in Aristotelian ontology, there could be no natural science in the modern sense. For the Greeks, science in the proper sense was philosophy. Ontology was the question of the essence of man and his world.

In the modern sense, *theory* is a constructive assumption for the purpose of integrating a fact into a larger context without contradiction, that is, into the already given context of nature in the Newtonian sense.

p. 199 *Theory* in the ancient sense as an essential determination of nature is already hidden behind this [theory in the modern sense]. But modern science does not deal with this.

Humanitas: The human being's free relationship to what encounters him; that he appropriates these relationships; and that he lets himself be claimed by them.

How to start the Harvard lectures: (Refers to the summer semester in which Medard Boss was invited to Harvard University as a visiting faculty member.)

We do psychology, sociology, and psychotherapy in order to help the human being reach the goal of adjustment and freedom in the broadest sense. This is the joint concern of physicians and sociologists because all social and pathological disturbances of the individual human being are disturbances in adjustment and freedom.

---

*See Heidegger, *Basic Writings*, pp. 247–82.—TRANSLATORS

The concrete case of Ms. [Regula] Zürcher and the encounter with her fiancé, as well as her previous hysterical paralysis and her organic-neurotic stomach and intestinal troubles, ought to be discussed here. (The reference to Ms. Zürcher is from Medard Boss's book *Existential Foundations of Medicine and Psychology*).[1]

Discussion of Physiological Explanations

The physiological dimension is a necessary condition for the possibility of a relationship between one human being and another. Yet the fact alone that the female patient genuinely views the other human being as a "thou" is by no means a sensory perception. Indeed, no sense organ exists for what is called "the other" [human being]. In the literal sense, the physiological dimension is not a sufficient [*hinreichend*] condition for reaching out [*hin-zu-reichen*] to the other human being. The physiological dimension does not reach out to the other human being and is not able to establish a relationship.

The physiological dimension is an objectification of something belonging to the human being, which has resulted from a special [scientific] approach. Such an objectification cannot be reclaimed [*zurückgenommen werden*] as something characteristically human.   p. 200

What is interpreted in physiological terms as a chemical-physical process appears as a completely different phenomenon in an immediate relationship to another human being.

From the fact that human bodily being [*Leibliche*] is interpreted as something chemical and as something which can be affected by chemical interventions it is concluded that the chemistry of the physiological is the ground and cause for the psychical in humans. This is a fallacious conclusion because something which is a [necessary] condition, that is, something without which the existential relationship cannot be actualized, is not the cause, not the efficient cause, and, therefore, also not the ground. The existential relationship does not consist of molecules, and they do not produce it, but it is not without that which can be given a new interpretation as a physiological-molecular process.

If the physiological dimension were the ground of the human, then, for example, there would be "farewell molecules" [*Abschiedsmoleküle*].

Chemical-physical science is not something chemical [in itself]. Therefore, people [scientists] claim something for their theories, which is not chemical. In order to ascertain and to assert that the psychical is something chemical, they need something nonchemical, that is, a definite relationship to the world, a definite comportment to the world in the sense of objectification leading to calculability.

The deception in Professor Prader's inaugural lecture on molecular biology lies in the fact that the concepts of the "individual" and of "individuality" are simply transferred from the human self to molecules.

We must say the following against Professor Frau Fritz-Niggli's article on "memory":[2] From where does she know that worms have memory? One can certainly not speak of memory here. This can be done only where there is consciousness.

p. 201

Addendum

Aristotle knew of four kinds of motion.

1. γενεσις, φθορα: to come into being, to emerge [*aufgehen*] and to pass away [*vergehen*], to disappear.
2. αυξησις, φθισις: increase [*Vermehrung*], growth, and decay [*Verfall*].
3. αλλοιωσις: change [*Veränderung*], for instance, the green leaf's turning to brown.
4. φορα: a carrying, transport from one location to another.

Galileo accepted motion only as φορα. He eliminated all other kinds of motion in the Aristotelian sense. Motion is understood as nothing more than a change of place in time.

For Greek thought, the ground of all motion is μεταβολη, that is, change from something into something else. This is the most "formal" characterization of motion.

In the case of our patient's encounter with her bridegroom, when one speaks of "recalling" [*Wiedererinnern*], the misunderstanding lies in the fact that everything is reduced to perception and that it is then imagined that her bridegroom has disappeared because she no longer sees him. This is a mistake. He has not disappeared at all, but is simply no longer present in a bodily manner [*leibhaftig*], yet he is still there. Thereby, he does not need to be noticed explicitly. (However, what if the question is raised, When he is no longer seen in his bodily presence, where is he? The answer is: wherever he is, even when the bride does not exactly know his precise location and how he looks. He surely did not jump into her brain.) Therefore, she can make-him-present [*vergegenwärtigen*] in some manner.

If one makes-present something which happened at that time [*damals*] and which was experienced by me, then it is a remembrance [*Erinnerung*].

In psychology the presence of what is encountered [the significant situation] is not taken up into perception at all, but the perception is understood as an inner-psychic event. When the perception ceases, then the one who was present is also believed to be gone.

p. 202

If Jean-Paul Sartre reproaches Heidegger for having dealt poorly with the problem of the body, then this "poor treatment" has two reasons:

1. The phenomena of the body cannot be dealt with without a sufficient elaboration of the fundamentals of existential being-in-the-world.
2. So far a sufficiently useful description of the phenomenon of the body has not emerged, that is, one viewed from the perspective of the being-in-the-world.

Such a "phenomenology of the body"* can *only* proceed as a description. Any attempt at "explanation," that is, of derivation from something else, is meaningless. For with explanations and derivations, one does not arrive at this matter's essential feature. Therefore, it is fundamentally inappropriate to the matter at hand.

Any adjustment [by the patient] is only possible and meaningful on the ground of existential being-with [*Mitsein*].†

As to the physician's will-to-help [the patient]: One must pay attention to the fact that it always involves a way of existing and not the functioning of something. If one only aims at the latter, then one does not add to [the understanding] of Da-sein. But this is the goal.

The human being is essentially in need of help because he is always in danger of losing himself and of not coming to grips with himself. This danger is connected with the human being's freedom. The entire question of the human being's capacity for being ill is connected with the imperfection of his unfolding essence. Each illness is a loss of freedom, a constriction of the possibility for living.

---

*Among French phenomenologists only J.-P. Satre and M. Merleau-Ponty came close to a phenomenology of the body. (See *L'Ecircumflextre et le Néant* [Paris: Gallimard, 1943] [*Being and Nothingness,* trans. H. Barnes (New York: Philosophical Library, 1956)]; *Phénoménologie de la Perception* [Paris: Gallimard, 1945] [*Phenomenology of Perception,* trans. C. Smith (London: Routledge, 1962)].) In Heidegger's and Boss's view, the French phenomenologists, still influenced by Descartes, got only halfway to a phenomenology of the body. "It still remains difficult for them to escape the dominating influence of Descartes, and this is why they have managed to get only halfway toward an existential understanding of the bodyhood of human Da-sein" (Boss, *Existential Foundations,* pp. 127, 130).—TRANSLATORS

†See Heidegger, *Being and Time,* esp. secs. 26, 27.—TRANSLATORS

The "psychoanalytic case history" [*Lebensgeschichte*] is by no means a history, but [an explanation by means of] a naturalistic chain of causes, a chain of cause and effect, and even more, a construct. Compare *Being and Time* (pp. 426, 428; "historicity").

p. 203

Possibilities, the possibilities of Dasein, are not a subject's tendencies or capacities. They always result, so to say, only from "outside," that is, from the particular historical situation of being-able-to-comport-oneself and of choosing, from the comportment toward what is encountered.[*]

See *Being and Time* (p. 460) regarding "clearing" and "temporality."

Temporalizing[†] as letting [Da-sein's] temporality come forth is an unfolding and emerging and, thus, an appearing.

Natura (Latin) derives from *nasci,* "to be born." φυσις → φυειν (Greek) means to emerge in a sense of coming from concealment [*Verborgenheit*] to unconcealment. Neither the word *natura* nor φυσις has a connection with *time.*

Knowledge [German: *Wissen;* English: *wise*] is related to "wit"→videa (Sanskrit: *vydia*). Thereby, in the Greek word ιδεα the *v* has disappeared. It always means to put something into the light. To find one's way is only a consequence of seeing, of "being aware," of *Bewissens* (which is similar in form to *beschreiben*), "to surround with light" [*mit einem Licht umgeben*] (see E. Bleuler's essay about disorders of consciousness).[‡] Consciousness presupposes "clearing" and Dasein, and not conversely.

Rather than speaking about possibilities as constituents of Dasein, it is always better to speak about potentiality-to-be [*Seinkönnen*] in the sense of the potentiality for being-in-the-world. The particular potentiality-to-be is glimpsed from the particular, historical Da-sein in the world, determined this or that way. Historical is the way and manner with which I comport myself toward what comes toward me, to what is present, and to what has been. Every potentiality-to-be for something is a determined

---

[*]See Heidegger, *Being and Time,* p. 183, concerning the difference between logical (modal) possibility of things present-at-hand and Da-sein's existential potentiality-to-be. See also Heidegger, *Basic Writings,* p. 196; *Contributions to Philosophy,* pp. 196–98. See ZS 95.—TRANSLATORS

[†]*Zeitigung* [temporalizing, literally: ripening, bringing to fruition] is Da-sein's temporality [*Zeitlichkeit*] appearing in the unity of the "ecstases" of the future, the having been, and the present. It appears in the mode of authentic temporality or of inauthentic temporality, i.e., leveled down to the common "time" as a pure succession of nows. See *Being and Time,* p. 376 f.; *The Basic Problems of Phenomenology,* p. 265 f.—TRANSLATORS

[‡]E. Bleuer, *Dementia Praecox oder Gruppe der Schizophrenien* (Leipzig, 1911); *Dementia Praecox or the Group of Schizophrenias* (New York, 1950).—TRANSLATORS

confrontation [*Auseinandersetzung*] with what has been [*Gewesenes*], in view of something coming toward me [*Zukommendes*], and to which I am resolved.

"Possibilities" in the sense of modalities in metaphysics, that is, as distinct from the other two modalities of being—being "necessary" and being "actual"—always refer to a production by the human being or by the Creator-God.* In the existential sense possibilities are always historical potentialities for being-in-the-world. In the way that I address what comes toward me, I see what is present and what has been. The present world is arranged and organized around the possible threat of a future atomic bomb explosion. Accordingly, what has been [the past] is seen as being "incapable" of confronting this fact, as the world that is still incapable of this confrontation [the present], or as the world in which all this is being prepared [the future]. For example, only from the future threat of the atomic bomb can one also see the significance of the step taken by Galileo. *Everything begins with the future!*

p. 204

MEDARD BOSS: What does the central proposition in *Being and Time* really mean when it is repeated several times, even in a slightly modified form? *Dasein is that being for which, in its being, that being is an issue.*†

MARTIN HEIDEGGER: Da-sein must always be seen as being-in-the-world, as concern for things, and as caring for other [Da-seins], as the being-with the human beings it encounters, and never as a self-contained subject. Furthermore, Dasein must always be understood as standing-within [*Inne-stehen*] the clearing, as sojourn with what it encounters, that is, as disclosure for what concerns it and what is encountered. At the same time *sojourn* is always comportment toward [*Verhalten zu*]. . . . The "oneself" in *comporting oneself* and the "my" in "my Dasein" must never be understood as a relationship to a subject or to a substance. Rather, the "oneself" must be seen in a purely phenomenological sense, that is, in the way I comport myself now. In each case the *Who*‡ exhausts itself precisely in the comportments in which I am [it is] involved just now.

The most useful is the useless. But to experience the useless is the most difficult undertaking for contemporary man. Thereby, what is "useful" is understood as what can be applied practically, as what

---

*See Heidegger, *Being and Time,* pp. 46 and 125, concerning production as the horizon for ancient ontology's interpretation of beings. See also Heidegger, *Basic Problems of Phenomenology,* p. 116 f.—TRANSLATORS

†See Heidegger, *Being and Time,* p. 236.—TRANSLATORS

‡See ibid., sec. 25.—TRANSLATORS

serves an immediate technical purpose, as what produces some effect, and as that with which I can operate economically and productively. Yet one must look upon the useful as "what makes someone whole" [*das Heilsame*], that is, what makes the human being at home with himself [*zu ihm selbst bringt*].

p. 205   In Greek θεωρια is *pure repose* [*reine Ruhe*], the highest form of ἐνεργεια, the highest manner of putting-oneself-into-work without regard for all machinations [*Machenschaften*]. [It is] the letting come to presence of presencing itself.

MB: Our patients force us to see the human being in his essential ground* because the modern "neuroses of boredom and meaninglessness" can no longer be drowned out by glossing over or covering up particular symptoms of illness. If one treats those symptoms only, then another symptom will emerge again and again. Nowadays, people go to psychotherapists with increasing frequency without any "symptoms" whatsoever in the sense of localized, functional disorders of a psychical or physical nature but simply because they no longer see meaning in their life and because they have become intolerably bored.

MH: "Comportment" [*Verhalten*], the "comportments," refer to the interconnected ways of relating to beings as a whole, wherein most of them [beings] are not noticed expressly in each case. *Sojourning with* is the same . . . and at the same time as the letting come to presence of beings. This constitutes my Da-sein in the present situation, at any given time. Nothing more can be said about it. One cannot ask about this comportment's "porter," rather the comportment carries itself. This is precisely what is wonderful about it. "Who" I am now can be said only throughout this sojourn, and always at the same time in the sojourn lies that with which and with whom I sojourn, and how I comport myself toward [them]. "To be absorbed" by something . . . does not mean "to be dissolved" like sugar in water, but rather "to be totally preoccupied by something," as for instance, when one says: He is entirely engrossed in his subject matter. Then he exists authentically as who he is, that is, in his task.

p. 206   Socrates used to ask the shoemakers what they were doing until they realized that they could not be shoemakers at all unless they had already seen the ειδος beforehand, the οὐσια, the essence of

---

*In contrast to classical metaphysics' static concept of "essence" (*essentia* and "essential"), Heidegger's "essential" must always be understood in terms of "emerging, enduring, and unfolding" and in terms of the characteristic, temporal movement of the human being's "essence" (*Wesen*). See ZS 3, 48.—TRANSLATORS

the shoe, that is, what is essentially present [*Anwesende*] prior to the particular thing, prior to the particular shoe. They gave him a cup of poison for that. It is obviously intolerable for most people to see the essence [*Wesenssicht*] and to have a glimpse [*Wesensblick*] of it.

Da-sein means being absorbed in that toward which I comport myself, being absorbed in the relationship to what is present, and being absorbed in what concerns me just now. [It is] a letting oneself be engaged with [*sich-einlassen*] what concerns me.

This relationship of being absorbed in the same world-with-one-another . . . makes *communication* possible in the first place. When I say: Da-sein whose being is an issue for its own being, the phrase "its being" must not be misunderstood as subjectivity; instead, its being-in-the-world is an *issue* for its very being-in-the-world.

The expression "to correspond" means to answer the claim, to comport oneself in response to it. *Re*-spond [*Ent*-sprechen]→ to answer to [*Ant*-worten].

To be absorbed in beholding [*Anschauen*] the palm tree in front of our window is letting the palm tree come to presence. This letting the palm tree come to presence, its swaying in the wind, is the absorption of my being-in-the-world and of my comportment *in the* palm tree.

Concept of Representation

One can only ask people when they see a blackboard whether they really have and perceive a "mental" *representation*.* When they bring up the theory of sensory stimuli, then it must be asked, When does the blackboard, which is over there and on which I write, emerge as a blackboard? The

---

*Here Heidegger is referring to Descartes's, Locke's, and Hume's erroneous "representational" theories of the mind, which, Heidegger argued, ultimately led to modern, epistemological skepticism. According to it the mind is understood to have access only to its own representations ("ideas") and does not have an immediate encounter with the world. With the phenomenological description of Da-sein's original "being-in-the-world" (with its actions, social relationships, etc.), Heidegger opposed the whole "representational" tradition as a construct which falsifies the original phenomenon of Dasein's being-in-the-world (ZS 87–97). See R. Rorty, *Philosophy and the Mirror of Nature* (Princeton, N.J.: Princeton University Press, 1980); C. Taylor, *Human Agency and Language: Philosophical Papers I* (Cambridge: Cambridge University Press, 1985).—TRANSLATORS

theory about the genesis of a "representation" from sensory stimuli is a pure mystification. [This is so] because one is talking about matters not demonstrated [*ausgewiesen*] at all, pure inventions—constructs from a calculative, causal-theoretical, and explanatory comportment toward beings. It is a misinterpretation of the world.

p. 207
When one begins to explain the perception of the blackboard from sensory stimuli, one has indeed seen the blackboard. In this theory of sensory stimuli, where is [there a place for] what is meant by "is" [being]? Even the greatest possible accumulation and intensity of stimuli will never bring forth the "is." [What is meant by it] is already presupposed in every [act of] *being* stimulated.

Even imagining can only be seen as directed into a world [*in eine Welt hinein*] and can only happen into a world. To imagine a golden mountain can always really only happen in such a way that even this [mountain] is somehow situated in a world. Even in such imagining there is more there than just the isolated golden mountain. I do not imagine a golden mountain within my consciousness or within my brain, but rather I relate it to a world, to a landscape, which in turn is again related to the world in which I exist bodily. The golden mountain is present *as* something imagined which is a specific mode of presence and which has the character of a world. It is related to men, earth, sky, and the gods.*

The whole starting point within the psychic and the point of departure from a consciousness is an *abstraction* and a *nondemonstrable construct* [*eine nicht ausweisbare Konstruktion*]. The relationships of a thing to the surrounding world [*Umwelt*] do not require explanation; they must simply be seen [in a phenomenological sense].

Perception of Other Human Beings

The traditional, psychological theory that one perceives another human being through "empathy" and through "projection" of oneself into the other does not mean anything because the ideas of empathy and projection always already presuppose being-with the other and the being of the other with me. Both already presuppose that one has already [existentially] understood the other as another human being; otherwise, I would be projecting something into the void.

---

*See Heidegger, *Basic Writings*, pp. 323–39, concerning the contextual significance of the fourfold [*das Geviert*] of earth, sky, mortals, and divinities for the later Heidegger.—TRANSLATORS

Introjection

p. 208

By imitating the mother, the child orients himself *toward* his mother. He takes part in the mother's being-in-the-world. He can do this only insofar as he himself is a being-in-the-world. The child is absorbed in the mother's comportment. It is exactly the opposite of having-introjected the mother. Even [when the child is] "out there," he is still tied to the ways of another human being's being-in-the-world—his mother's.*

Projection

In psychology it is said that one projects the evil part of one's own unfolding, essential being [*Wesensseite*] onto the enemy. Then one hates him as the evil one, and, thus, one avoids seeing the evil in oneself and having to perceive it in oneself. It is correct that one ascribes the evil which must already be known from the world to the other and that one interprets the other as an evil one. This is far from being a projection. Indeed, it cannot be a projection. For by ascribing the evil to the other, one simply refuses to acknowledge that I too belong to the evil, as do all human beings. If we were really dealing with a projection here, then after the projection, after having expelled my evil and having projected it onto the other, I would suddenly be a good human being. Yet when I ascribe evil only to the other, that is exactly what I am not. For then the evil is still in me even more, that is, my comportment still has the character of evil, except I do not acknowledge it. My unwillingness to acknowledge it means precisely that I am still stuck in my evil comportment.

In such a theory of projection one again overlooks being-with [*Mit-sein*], which is an original, essential characteristic of Da-sein. Each Da-sein is standing in the potentiality to comport itself in an evil manner. As a characteristic of its unfolding essence, each Da-sein always already p. 209 has the potentiality-to-be-evil [*Böse-sein-können*] in relationship to what it encounters, whether or not it is always and expressly enacted.

The enactment of a potentiality-to-be is something completely different from an actualization in the sense of a realization [*Verwirklichung*] of something possible metaphysically.† The difference is that enactment in the existential sense is not producing [*Herstellung*] something evil. Evil is

---

*Boss, *Existential Foundations*, p. 243.—TRANSLATORS
†See Heidegger, *Being and Time*, p. 183 f.—TRANSLATORS

not what lies before one as an abstract possibility, which is then somehow "actualized" by being produced. Rather, the potentiality-to-be evil belongs to my potentiality-to-be, that is, it already belongs to my Da-sein in a wholly original way.* This means that I am always already, and from the very beginning, my potentiality-to-be-evil among [my] other ways of potentiality-to-be. It is always already present, concrete, and belongs to my Da-sein's potentiality-to-be, which under certain circumstances can then also be enacted in a bodily or mental comportment toward what encounters me.

This potentiality-to-be is precisely the *unfolding essence* of Da-sein. I am always my potentiality-to-be as *potentiality* [*Können*]. My potentiality-to-be is not a possibility in the sense of something present-at-hand [*Vorhandenes*], which could then be transformed into something else, for instance, into an action.

For instance, in the domain of the present-at-hand, the corresponding feature is the "possibility" that the trunk of a tree becomes a beam [for a ceiling]. As something present-at-hand, this possibility for being a beam belongs essentially to the trunk of the tree. Yet when I have made the trunk of the tree into a beam, then it is no longer a tree trunk. Thereby, it has been used up as a tree trunk. In contrast to the actualization of the possibility present-at-hand for being a beam from the tree trunk, the enactment of Da-sein's potentiality-to-be is totally different.

Ecstatic being-in-the-world always has the character of the potentiality-to-be. When I sit here now, I can get up at any time and go out through the door. I myself am this potentiality for going out through the door, even if I do not enact it. But when I enact it and actually go through the door, then, nevertheless. this potentiality-to-be this way is still present, exerting its presence, and co-constituting [*mitkonstituierend*] my Da-sein. It is not something that has been used up like the former tree trunk, whose possibility for becoming a beam has been actualized and has disappeared as a tree trunk and remains that way. On the contrary, Da-sein's ecstatic potentiality-to-be is intensified as potentiality-to-be in its enactment and in its being enacted. The more often I repeat and exercise a potentiality-to-be, the easier and richer it becomes. Potentiality-to-be is the authentic [*eigentlich*] phenomenon by which my Da-sein shows itself.

p. 210

---

*This potentiality-to-be-evil is the "existential" condition for the secondary [actualized] "existentiell" possibility for the "morally good" and for the "morally evil." See Heidegger, *Being and Time*, p. 332. See also Boss, *Existential Foundations*, p. 242: "Malice toward fellow men is a potentiality inherent in every human *Da-sein*. It is, then, yet another of the Existentials."—TRANSLATORS

This so-called projection is only a diversionary maneuver by which one diverts and averts the acknowledgment of one's own potentiality-to-be-evil. In the customary, psychological representation of a projection, everything is "objectified" [*verdinglicht*].

Transference

It is essential that the human being, engaging in "transference"* in the psychological sense, be retained as being in a specific attunement [*Gestimmtheit*]. Because of this, he cannot do anything else than to let the man with whom he has to do and whom he meets be encountered as someone hated. This inability to do anything else is also a potentiality-to-be. Thus, [it is] a constituent of my Da-sein.

This ontological disposition [*Befindlichkeit*] or attunement [*Gestimmtheit*] is a basic character of Da-sein and belongs to every comportment. Every comportment is always already in a certain attunement beforehand. Therefore, to talk about "transference" has no meaning at all. Nothing needs to be "transferred" because the respective attunement, from which and according to which alone everything is able to show itself, is always already present. [If one is] within a particular attunement, a human being whom one encounters also shows himself according to this disclosedness (attunement) [*Entschlossenheit*].†

The Term "Projective Test"   p. 211

What really happens when someone says, for instance, [in response] to a Rorschach plate: I see a [female] dancer there? He sees a dancer there because a dancer already determined his world beforehand. From where does this or that come to mind? Certainly, not from the blot on the Rorschach plate. The things coming to mind [*Einfälle*] always come

---

*See the extended discussion of "transference" as the therapeutic interaction between physician and patient in Freudian psychotherapy in Boss, *Existential Foundations*, pp. 257–72.—TRANSLATORS

†The German word *Entschlossenheit* [resoluteness] is obviously a misprint for *Erschlossenheit* [disclosedness]. "Resoluteness is a distinctive mode of Dasein's disclosedness" (Heidegger, *Being and Time*, p. 343).—TRANSLATORS

from a definite world, from such and such an attuned relationship to the world in which one is sojourning at the moment. Therefore, nothing really "comes to mind." Rather, something comes out from, that is, out from a definite, particularly attuned relationship toward the world.[*]

Affects

The example of the young woman's *joyful* encounter with her bride-groom:[†] The joy, the so-called joyous affect, is not triggered by the encounter. When she sees him, she can only be joyful because she already was, and is, prepared for the joyful mode of Da-sein's attunement. The man she encounters does not cause this joyful attunement as little as he might have triggered her anxiety earlier during times of illness. He, the man, surely did not change, but she, the woman, did. In fact, her whole relationship to the world changed in that she encounters people differently, especially this man, that is, according to this new "disclosed-ness" [*Erschlossenheit*]. She has become free for the potentiality-to-be in a joyful attunement. The man does not bring about the joyful attunement, but he fulfills it. The potentiality for the joyful attunement can be, and is, realized through his (the man's) presence.

Even the term "affect" is already disastrous. *Af-ficere* means "to do something to someone." Joy is not brought upon me from the outside, but this attunement belongs to my ecstatic relationship, to my being-in-the-world.[‡]

During the time of this patient's lack of freedom due to hysteria, her basic attunement was indeed anxiety, which dominated her whole

---

[*]See Boss, *Existential Foundations*, p. 242: "The phenomena that occur to a person taking such a test come not from his head but are phenomena in the open realm of perception currently available to his Da-sein. What actually happens when such an idea [of a dancer] occurs to the test subject is that one or more of these phenomena are recalled from an unthematic mode of presence to one of a thematic visualization."—TRANSLATORS

[†]Refers to Boss's discussion of the case history of Ms. Zürcher in *Existential Foundations*, pp. 81–84, 109.—TRANSLATORS

[‡]See Heidegger, *Being and Time*, p. 176 f., concerning the relationship between being affected [*Betroffenwerden*] and the ontologically prior disclosedness of being-in-the-world and its attunement. See also Boss, *Existential Foundations*, pp. 110–14.—TRANSLATORS

Da-sein, even though she could still be joyful in relation to her young, p. 212
female friends. For these friends did not play much of a central role in
her being a woman. The human relationships to her female friends were
not her authentic and essential relationship toward the world as a woman.
They were not the relationships that determined and characterized her
authentic unfolding essence as a woman. This was always already her
relationship to the man.

Therapy

MEDARD BOSS: What does my question mean therapeutically: "How is it
that you always only encounter the masculine essence as something
dangerous?"

MARTIN HEIDEGGER: Through such a question, I open the patient's eyes for
masculinity, for the unfolding essence of being a man as a whole. I let
her be reattuned* [*umstimmen*] to the man's unfolding essence. One
opens a full view for her into the unfolding essence of being a man,
into masculinity. Through this she can become freer for a man, for
the unfolding essence of a man, which fulfills her unfolding essence
as a woman. The being-free for something is a serene and joyful mood
[*Stimmung*] in itself.

MB: Why has it been so impossible for all psychologists, including Freud,
to determine the essence of masculinity and femininity?

MH: This is due to man's innate blindness for the unfolding [historical]
essence.

Forgetting

[To understand forgetting] it is necessary to have a view of being-in-
the-world. If one is tied to subject-object representations, forgetting is
conceived of as a residue in the brain which can no longer be grasped,
and precisely not as something which conceals itself.

In *Dawn* (no. 126) Nietzsche says: "It has not yet been proved that
there is any such thing as forgetting; all we know is that the act of p. 213

---

*See Boss, *Existential Foundations,* p. 110, concerning existential reattunement.—
TRANSLATORS

recollection does not lie within our power. We have provisionally set into this gap in our power that word "forgetting," as if it were one more addition to our faculties. But, after all, what lies within our power!"[3]

The different ways of forgetting:

1. The different ways of "forgetting" are the ways and manners of how something withdraws from oneself, how it conceals itself. When I forget the umbrella at the hairdresser, what is that? I did forget *taking* the umbrella *with me*, but not the umbrella. I omitted it. I did not think of it. I was just concerned with something else. Therefore, here forgetting is a privation of having thought of something. Here, memory [is understood as] recalling something [*Andenken*].[*]

2. I have forgotten the name of someone I know. I cannot retrieve his name. It no longer comes to mind. It slipped my memory. The name slipped my memory. What slipped my memory is a privation. From where did it slip? From retaining it, from memory. Therefore, this forgetting is the privation of retaining something. In turn, to retain something is a specific form of the relationship toward which I comport myself. It is not a mode of thinking about something because I do not need to think continuously about a name, which I retain. Here memory is [understood] as retaining [*Behalten*].[†]

MEDARD BOSS: But according to psychoanalytic theory, the act of leaving something behind, for instance, a purse, in leaving an acquaintance's room, expresses the unconscious wish to return there. How is such a "leaving behind" to be described phenomenologically?

MARTIN HEIDEGGER: There is no unconscious intention when the purse is left behind. On the contrary, in this case leaving [the room] is entirely different from leaving the hairdresser. Precisely because the man she visited was not indifferent to her, her leaving is such that in leaving she is still present, more present, and ever the more present. While leaving, she is still with the man so much so that the purse is not there at all. In this kind of leaving, the purse was left behind

p. 214

---

[*] See ibid., p. 116: "In actual fact, I have forgotten neither the umbrella itself nor the possibility of taking it along. Forgetting [not recalling], as it is used here, simply refers to the fact that something is no longer considered thematically in its presence, though it remains unthematically present. The mode of being present to me has changed."—TRANSLATORS

[†] See ibid., p. 118, concerning the connection between existential retaining (memory) and the openness of human existence to what has been.—TRANSLATORS

because even while being in the room, she was with her friend so much that the purse was not there at all. At that time there was no leaving-for-somewhere.

If the same woman were to leave someone to whom she was indifferent in order to go shopping in the city, then she would not forget the purse. Rather, she would take it with her because the purse belongs to shopping, to the relationship in which the woman would actually be involved. Here, the leaving is a leaving for the city. Only leaving for the city matters here. This having been with the acquaintance to whom she is indifferent is finished.

The matter [attributed to] unconscious intention is an explanation as opposed to a phenomenological interpretation.[*] This explanation is a pure hypothesis that in no way advances the understanding of the phenomenon itself and, as such, of leaving [the purse] behind.

In the Freudian hypothesis leaving [the purse] behind is stressed as a fact which must then be explained. We ascertain this fact of leaving [the purse] behind from the outside. The woman herself does not leave the purse behind unconsciously because the purse is not there [for her] at all, and one can only leave something behind when it is there.

MB: How about forgetting something painful, which according to Freud's theory has been *repressed* into the unconscious?

MH: When I leave the umbrella behind at the hairdresser's, I do not think of taking it with me. When I forget something painful, I do not want to think about it. Here, *it* does not slip away from me, but *I* let it slip away from me. This letting something slip away from me happens in such a way that I occupy myself more and more with something else so that what is uncomfortable may slip away. The painfulness itself is already an indication of the fact that she was, and still is, afflicted by the painful event in her youth. But she does not deal with it, with this painful event. She also knows about this painful event, otherwise it could not be a painful event for her. It is an avoidance of herself as the self continuously afflicted by the painful event. In this

p. 215

---

[*]See ibid., p. 245: "There is little doubt that Freud discovered a facet of human existence whose significance can hardly be exaggerated. Yet Freud's theoretical bias toward the philosophy of the natural sciences blinded him to an understanding of repression as a phenomenon of *existence*. Instead, he tried to force this event into the confines of a dynamic, mechanistic theory. In doing this, however, he distorted the phenomenon itself beyond recognition and produced a purely fictive mental construct. In this mutilated form the Freudian theory of repression has been uncritically adopted by most current practitioners of psychotherapy and psychosomatic medicine." —TRANSLATORS

avoidance of herself, she is present to herself in an unthematic way, and the more she engages in this avoidance, the less she knows about the avoidance. Rather, she is entirely absorbed in this avoidance in a nonreflective way.

The scientific-theoretical representation that forgetting and repressing require a physical or psychical *container,* into which what is forgotten can be thrown, has meaning only from [the perspective of existential] retaining.* The representation of a container can only be motivated from a potentiality-to-retain. Conversely, one cannot derive retaining from a container. An "engram" is never a retaining of something as something. An engram is a physiological change, but retaining is a relationship to something to which an understanding of being belongs. In contrast, an engram is a purely thinglike change. Retaining itself as such is not something physiological.

The human being's bodily being can never, fundamentally never, be considered merely as something present-at-hand if one wants to consider it in an appropriate way. If I postulate human bodily being as something present-at-hand, I have already beforehand destroyed the body as body.

Remembering

To remember [*Erinnern*] is the making-present of something which has been as something which I experienced at that time, at a particular time. If a name which has slipped away comes to mind, this is not a remembering. It would only be a remembering if the name came to mind as something I had heard or learned at that time. But if a name merely comes to mind again as just a name in and of itself, then this is only a making-present again [*Wieder-Vergegenwärtigen*] [as recalling].

p. 216   If one sees forgetting as grounded in a concealment [*Verbergen*], in a veiling, then this making-present is a coming forth from concealment. When I now think of the Cathedral of Freiburg, then this is a bringing-out from the veiling.

The customary correlation between remembering and forgetting is incorrect.

1. In the Greek [understanding] all forgetting occurs when something in my relationship to something remains concealed to me.

---

*Concerning the metaphor of *container* [*Behältnis*] as contrasted to existential retaining [*behalten*], see Heidegger, *Being and Time,* p. 388 f.—TRANSLATORS

2. In the Latin [understanding], it is *oblivisci*—to wipe out, as something written on a tablet can be erased.

3. In German, forgetting [*das Vergessen*] is related to the English *to get* [to keep together], namely, so that it is turned into something negative by [the prefix] *ver,* thus, "not keeping."

In the Greek, forgetting refers to something that withdraws into concealment, whereas Latin *oblivisci* and German *vergessen* [English, *forgetting*] already originate from an ego and, thus, are understood subjectively. The Greek term αληθεια means "unconcealment, truth" [λαθω, I remain hidden].

Simply recalling something is *not* a remembering [memory]. A making-present is a remembering only when I make something present as something I experienced at that time.

Retaining belongs to concealment. The mystery [of being] is concealment, which is [at the same time] unconcealing itself as such.* Being absorbed [*Sog*] by forgetting refers to unconcealment, which withdraws itself. Thus, one can say: The human being as the potentiality-for-retaining [*Behalten-können*] is needed [by being] for sheltering the unconcealment [of being] and, thus, as safeguarding [*Wahrnis*] against being absorbed into concealment.

Answer from Jean Beaufret regarding the question of the French translation of *zeitigen* [temporalize] and *Zeitigung* [temporalizing] in *Being and Time: Being and Time* oppose *ce "saisonnement" dans lequel une présence ne cesse d'affluer, au temps qui, au contraire, ne cesse de s'écouler* (a not-yet-now becomes a now—the "nows" pass away). *Dans* Being and Time *le*

---

*According to Heidegger, logical, propositional truth as *adaequatio intellectus ad rem* is ontologically grounded in Da-sein's primordial standing-out into the truth, i.e., into the openness of being (*a-letheia,* unconcealment). Yet, throughout man's finite, historical Da-sein, truth as ontological unconcealment is permeated simultaneously by "un-truth" in its double form: (1) mystery [*Geheimnis*] as the [forgotten] concealment of being, and (2) errancy [*Irre*] as Da-sein's flight from, and oppression of, the mystery. Thus, Da-sein is always already equally in un-truth. "Open to being and to its own being possible, Dasein nevertheless relinquishes this openness in exchange for the security of whatever 'they' [*man*] say is true. It lets truth slip into the same oblivion as Being and finds its 'truth' as so many scintillating beings there before it, polished yet manipulable. The most dazzlingly finished become 'eternal truths.' Presupposed in such truths of faith or science . . . , however, is a kind of opening or openness by virtue of which something can and does show itself and let itself be seen" (Krell, cited in Heidegger, *Basic Writings,* p. 115). See Heidegger, *Basic Writings,* pp. 114–39; *Contributions to Philosophy,* pp. 247–49.—TRANSLATORS

p. 217 *temps est "saisonnant," sans saisonner* (the difference between arriving and passing away).

The question remains whether *une presence* is misleadingly represented in Beaufret's statement as something present-at-hand.

Willing, Wishing, Propensity, and Urge

In opposition to traditional psychology, one must see to it that willing [*Wollen*] and so forth are not isolated as psychical acts. Psychology customarily construes willing, wishing [*Wünschen*], propensity [*Hängen*], and urge [*Drang*] as forms of psychical activity, as psychical acts and drives, whereby the "psyche" is conceived as an independently existing inner realm. However, one never arrives at the "structure of care" [*Sorge-Struktur*], at *being-in-the-world,* as a result of such psychical acts.* Of course, one can say that willing is an emotional act of consciousness, but such a statement remains without reference to being-in-the-world. Conversely, phenomena such as "I wish something for myself" are founded on the structure of care.

Therefore, a more adequate statement would be: Willing, wishing, propensity, and urge are ways of enacting [*Vollzugsweisen*] being-in-the-world.

If one desires to reduce willing, wishing, propensity, and urge to "drives," one must always first ask the contrary question: Is the human being present within the total construct of Freudian libido theory at all?

Drive [*Trieb*] is always an attempt to explain. Yet above all the issue is never an attempt to explain. Rather, first one must pay attention to what the phenomenon to be explained is and to how it is. With "drives," one is always attempting to explain something one did not "see" in the first place at all. Attempts to explain human phenomena on the basis of instincts have the characteristic method of a science whose object field is not the human being at all but rather mechanics. Therefore, it is fundamentally questionable whether such a method, determined by nonhuman objectivity, is able to assert anything about the human being as a human being.

p. 218 Exemplification of what has just been said in our present conversation:

---

* See Heidegger, *Being and Time,* p. 238.—TRANSLATORS

1. First of all, one must ask, What is this conversation as an encounter with other human beings?
2. The answer to this question basically cannot be reached by asking and stating *what* caused this conversation. For when I say that this conversation is caused by . . . , then I am already indeed presupposing the conversation as such.

MEDARD BOSS: But Professor Heidegger, you yourself have felt urged and driven to our conversation. Thus, there is a "drive" [*Trieb*] which drove you. Therefore, our conversation basically has the character of being driven. Otherwise, one could not and would not say, I feel urged to [*es drängt mich*], I am driven to engage in this conversation. Isn't that true?

MARTIN HEIDEGGER: The desire for this conversation is determined by the task I have before me. This is the motive, the "for the sake of which" [*Weswegen*]. The determining factor is not an urge or a drive, driving and urging me from behind, but something standing before me, a task I am involved in, something I am charged with. This, in turn—this relation to something I am charged with—is possible only if I am "ahead" [*vorweg*] of myself, as you are in the case of the Harvard lectures you have been invited to deliver. Your future potentiality-to-be at Harvard University in America is now a continuous concern for you and is coming toward you. If one says, "I feel urged," then this is already a reinterpretation and an objectification into a process, that is, an improper interpretation. We are not dealing with an undetermined, psychical process here, nor with a "mythical drive" (Freud) impelling me. Rather, our conversation is dealing with something very determined in our Da-sein, namely, a determinate potentiality for being-in-the-world, for which we have *resolved ourselves* [*entschlossen*],* in the sense of having-opened ourselves for it. We have consented to this being-open. We have accepted it. p. 219

One cannot construct being-in-the-world from willing, wishing, urge, and propensity as psychical acts. Rather, this [being-in-the-world] is already presupposed. In this context the threefold, basic structure of being-in-the-world must be taken into consideration: "The being of Da-sein means *ahead*-of-itself-being-already-in-(the world) as being alongside (entities encountered-within-the-world)" (*Being and Time*, p. 237). This threefoldedness is "equiprimordial" [*gleich-ursprünglich*] in itself. Therefore, this so-called wishing, willing,

---

*See ibid., p. 314, concerning the existential structure of "resoluteness."—TRANSLATORS

propensity, and urge also always refer to modifications of all three structural moments of care [*Sorge*], that is, of the being-ahead-of-oneself [*sich-vorweg-sein*], of always-already-being [*Immer-schon-sein*], and of being-alongside [*Sein-bei*]. . . . In this way, none of the three structural elements is lost. They are also present in the modes of unconcern, of indifference, or even of resistance.

Propensity [*Hang*]: A being drawn, as it were, letting oneself be drawn by what propensity is after.

Urge [*Drang*]: What urges is Da-sein. What urges is being-in-the-world itself. The manic human being, urged to ramble erratically from one subject to another, wants to gobble up everything. Here, Da-sein exists only in this seizing upon [*An-sich-reissen*] [everything]. It is not a letting oneself be drawn, but rather a snatching of [*An-sich-raffen*] and a seizing on [everything]. The manic human being even outruns [his own] being-ahead-of by not reflecting on what he can be authentically. Therefore, being-ahead-of-itself is inauthentic [here]. The inauthentic always has the appearance of the authentic. Therefore, the manic human being believes that he is authentically himself or that he is [really] himself.[*]

Psychoanalysis glimpses from Dasein only the mode of fallenness[†] and its urge. It posits this constitution as authentically human and objectifies [the human being] with his "drives" [*Triebhaftigkeit*].

The "Psychical Functions": Ego, Id, Superego

p. 220

This classification seems to be another nomenclature for sensibility [*Sinnlichkeit*], understanding [*Verstand*], and reason [*Vernunft*], that is, for the moral law or the categorical imperative [in the Kantian sense].

When a human being says "I," this always designates the self insofar as he pays attention to it at any given time. "You" is always the name for my partner's self insofar as I pay attention to it. The "self" is what constantly

---

[*]See ibid., p. 240; Boss, *Existential Foundations*, p. 218.—TRANSLATORS

[†]See Heidegger, *Being and Time*, p. 220: "Dasein has, in the first instance, fallen away [*abgefallen*] from itself as an authentic potentiality-for-Being its Self, and has fallen into the "world." "Fallenness" into the "world" means an absorption in being-with-one-another, insofar as the latter is guided by idle talk, curiosity, and ambiguity. Through the Interpretation of falling, what we have called the "inauthenticity" of Dasein may now be defined more precisely."—TRANSLATORS

endures as the same in the whole, historical course of my Da-sein. [It is] what exists precisely in the manner of being-in-the-world, as potentiality for being-in-the-world. The self is never present-at-hand as a substance.[*] The constancy [Ständigkeit] of the self is proper to itself in the sense that the self is always able to come back to itself and always finds itself still the same in its sojourn [Aufenthalt].

The constancy of a substance consists only in the fact that it is always present-at-hand within the course of time, but it has nothing to do with time itself [as temporality]. The constancy of the self is temporal in itself, that is, it temporalizes itself. This selfhood of Da-sein is only in the manner of temporalizing [Zeitigung].

"I" is always the calling of the self as mine, that is, of my own self's being in the moment of calling. For the whole self can never be realized in one moment. In calling myself "I," I need not represent my possibilities expressly. If I were to do this, that is, to represent to myself expressly all my ways of the potentiality-to-be, I could not exist at all (see Being and Time, p. 366).

In the customary, psychological representation of the "I," the relationship to the world is absent. Therefore, the representation of the ego cogito is abstract, whereas the "I-am-in-the-world" lets the "I" be conjoined with the world, that is, as something primordially concrete [ur-konkret].[†]

Essence and the Concept of Essence

One must distinguish between essence and the concept of essence. One always sees something as something. Of course, thereby one can see something as something unknown, strange, unfamiliar, and so forth, but even then still as something.

p. 221

Logic says, a concept is acquired by comparing many individual examples, for instance, of trees. Nevertheless, this kind of logic overlooks the fact that the very search for particular trees already presupposes knowledge of the essence of tree. Otherwise, I would have no criterion at all for [identifying] a particular tree for which I searched.

The assertion that the essence "tree" can be inferred logically and in thought from the perception and investigation of particular trees is a

---

[*]See Boss, Existential Foundations, pp. 143–44. See also Heidegger, Being and Time, p. 114 f.—TRANSLATORS

[†]Concrete comes from the Latin concrescere, to grow together.—TRANSLATORS

pure invention.* When I tell a child, "This is a table," it awakens the child to the intuition of essence—to a glimpse of the essence "table." He/she will immediately recognize the next table *as* a table.† The *phenomenon* is the essence of what shows itself. The phenomenon as what shows itself from itself always means the being of beings and not a particular being.

The *worldliness* of the world is constituted from the contexts of reference [*Verweisungszusammenhänge*] of what shows itself. Spatiality, the space "made room for" [*eingeräumte Raum*], also belongs to these contexts of reference.

Being and Dasein

Being, the manifestness of being, is only given through the presence of beings. In order that beings can come to presence and, therefore, that being, the manifestness of being, can be given at all, what is needed is the [ecstatic] standing-in [*Innestehen*] of the human being in the *Da* [there], in the clearing, in the clearedness [*Gelichtetheit*] of being as which the human being exists. Therefore, there cannot be the being of beings at all *without* the human being.

This assertion stands in gross contradiction to the [following] statement of natural science: Due to the absolutely uniform rate of atomic decay in radioactive substances present in the earth's crust, it can be calculated and therefore proved that the earth has already existed for about four billion years, whereas the first man appeared only about two million years ago. At the very least, the being we call earth was already here long *before* human beings appeared. Therefore, beings and the manifestness of being, and therefore being can also exist entirely *independently* of human beings.

p. 222

---

*In contrast to this "invention," Heidegger is referring to the famous "categorical intuition" in Husserl's *Logical Investigations,* vol. 6, which Heidegger reinterpreted in an ontological sense (M. Heidegger, *History of the Concept of Time: Prolegomena,* trans. T. Kisiel [Bloomington: Indiana University Press, 1985], pp. 47–72). See also Jiro Watanabe, "Categorial Intuition and the Understanding of Being in Husserl and Heidegger," in *Reading Heidegger. Commemorations,* pp. 109–117; also see Kisiel, *The Genesis of Heidegger's* Being and Time, pp. 368–72.—TRANSLATORS

†Language is the presupposition for "saying" and "showing" something *as* something. See *ZS* 19–20.—TRANSLATORS

Therefore, according to this [assumed] contradiction, the central statement in *Being and Time* concerning the human being's relationship to being as the all-sustaining relationship [*alles tragenden Bezug*] cannot correspond to reality.

The following objection has to be made against this so-called contradiction. We can only say that the earth existed before man according to the "atomic clock," which describes the radioactive substances enclosed in solid rock and exhibiting atomic decay. We can calculate and infer indirectly what was present then—the earth. We are able to do this only insofar as *we* stand in the clearing of being and insofar as the "having been" and the "being earlier" belongs to being. The atomic clock is a measuring device for calculating the age of the earth. It is simply presupposed that the earth *is* and already *was* earlier.* The customary statement is: The earth already existed at a time when man did not yet exist. But then the "is" of this statement, and thus the being of the earth, being as such, is undetermined. From where does time come then?

One can abstract from time and say: The earth existed without human beings—independently of human beings. Quite apart from the fact whether the earth already existed before human beings or whether it will go on existing after human beings, the decisive point is that at least one can say that the earth can exist for a moment without human beings. This would already be sufficient to recognize as an error the above statement about the human being's all-sustaining [existential] relationship toward being. Nevertheless, in one way or another, the "is," that is, being, remains undetermined. Thus, it will never be clear, and can never become clear, what all these statements about the being of the earth prior to, or without the human being, are supposed to mean. Obviously, p. 223 the statement merely means that the earth can exist independently of the human being, that is, that there is being [as presencing] without and independent from the human being. This means: There is presencing [*Anwesen*] which does not need the human being.

Presencing is [how] the being of beings has been determined since ancient times. Not only in ancient times, but also in modern times, objectivity [*Objektivität*], standing against [*Gegenständigkeit*], present-at-handness [*Vorhandenheit*], and presentness [*Präsenz*] are simply modifications of presencing.

There is no *presencing* without a "where-to" [*Wohin*] of such presencing and tarrying [*Verweilen*]—of tarrying on [*An-weilen*]; that is, it is a tarrying [*Weilen*] which approaches what lets itself be approached [i.e.,

---

*See Heidegger, *Being and Time*, pp. 269, 429–34.—TRANSLATORS

Da-sein]. If there were not such a being [i.e., Da-sein] letting itself be approached, nothing could come to presence.

The human being is the guardian of the clearing, of the *disclosive appropriating Event* [of being].* He is not the clearing himself, not the entire clearing, nor is he identical with the whole of the clearing as such. But as the one ecstatically "standing out" into the clearing, he himself is essentially cleared [*gelichtet*], and thus cleared himself in a distinguished way. Therefore, he is related to, belongs to, and is appropriated by the clearing. Da-sein's being needed as the shepherd of the clearing is a distinguished manner of belonging to the clearing.

MEDARD BOSS: Indian thought does not require a guardian for the clearing. There is clearing in and for itself. Basically and in reality, there is nothing at all but clearedness in and for itself. Human Da-sein is only a domain of the clearedness itself. The human being himself is not fully aware of his own proper unfolding essence, that is, of the absolute clearedness, since [his] vision is somewhat obscured. Accordingly, the whole meaning of human Da-sein lies in regaining the full knowledge of his unfolding essence as clearedness itself. All other beings are essentially the same, but they have lost the insight into their fundamental essence even more than the human being has. All beings have to work their way up to that insight through all their reincarnations.†

p. 224   MARTIN HEIDEGGER: In contrast, it is very important to me that the human being is a *human* being. In Indian thought, the point is "a giving up of being human" [*Entmenschlichung*] in the sense of Da-sein's self-transformation into the pure luminosity [of being].

"Before" the human being, the earth too comes into the presence of the clearedness as such, of which the human being is the guardian.

The earth's having been [*Schon-gewesen-sein*] is a presencing of the earth, the manifestness of which—the clearing of which—does not at all need a human being, who was already [ontically] present *then;* but nevertheless, it [the presencing of the earth] essentially needs the human being, who stands in the clearing of the total presence and thus also in the clearing of what-has-been [ontologically].

---

*Up to the eighteenth century, *Ereignis* was spelled *Eräugnis* (from "to place before the eye," "to be disclosed") and then was associated with *Eigen* (one's own) and *Ereignis* (happening, event). Heidegger combines all of these meanings in *Ereignis*, i.e., Eräugnis (disclosing), *Eigen* (appropriating), and *Ereignis* (event).—TRANSLATORS

†Here Professor Boss obviously extends the idea of reincarnation as it pertains to man to the entire chain of beings and even to pre-human beings.—TRANSLATORS

Among other things, standing in the clearing of being means the admission of the earth's having been before the human being, that is, the admission of *this* [past] mode of presencing. Only in this way can the ordinary man say: The earth [as present-at-hand] already "was" before the human being. Of course, he does not reflect expressly on the meaning of "it was."

All presencing is dependent on the human being, but this dependence on the human being consists precisely in the fact that the human being as Da-sein and as being-in-the-world is able to allow beings [like the earth] to come to presence in their already having been [*Schon-gewesen-sein*].

[*Technological*] *enframing* [*Gestell*]* [as the revealing of being in the age of technology] also sets upon [*stellt*] and challenges [*herausfordern*] the human being himself once again, and this is a veiled form of the human being's being needed [by being in the age of technology].

The human being's finitude consists in [the fact] that he is not able to experience the presence of beings as a whole, as what has already been, and as what is still to come as an immediately given presence. [He is not able to experience] the presence of being in a *nunc stans* [standing now].† In Christianity such a thing is reserved for God. Christian mysticism also wanted nothing else. (All Indian "meditation" also wants nothing else than to obtain this experience of the *nunc stans,* to realize it as the ascent to the *nunc stans,* in which past and future are sublated [*aufgehoben*] into one unchanging present.)

Finitude can be better said to be the other way around: It is the experience of the presence of beings in the three [temporal] modes of having been, present, and future. p. 225

I am no longer speaking of finitude now, but rather say: The human being's richness consists precisely [in the fact] that he is not

---

*See Heidegger, *The Question concerning Technology,* p. 13 ff., concerning the human being's relationship to modern technology as a destiny of being itself to which humans respond. —TRANSLATORS

†Heidegger says the following regarding *nunc stans:* "The fact that the traditional conception of 'eternity' as signifying the 'standing now' (*nunc stans*) has been drawn from the ordinary way of understanding time and has been defined with an orientation towards the idea of 'constant' presence-at-hand, does not need to be discussed in detail. If God's eternity can be 'construed' philosophically, then it may be understood only as a more primordial temporality which is 'infinite.' Whether the way afforded by the *via negationis et eminentiae* is a possible one, remains to be seen" (*Being and Time,* p. 479, author's n. xiii). —TRANSLATORS

dependent upon the mere presence of a sequence of "nows," through which I cannot understand the whole of being and whereby it remains closed [to me] that Da-sein, in its unfolding essence, has emerged into the fullness of these [temporal] modalities.

That the human being must die does not follow from his being needed [*Gebrauchtwerden*] by the disclosive appropriating Event [*Ereignis*]. It is simply a fact that he must die.

MB: Then in what way is Heidegger's conception of the matter of being more adequate than Indian thought, which does not need a guardian of clearedness? Because according to it [Indian thought], the emergence (Brahman) of the clearedness exists in itself. It illuminates itself and everything which may emerge in it. It is independent from any being that would still be needed expressly as guardian and the one who enduringly sustains [*Aussteher*] this clearedness.

MH: My conception is more adequate, insofar as I am proceeding from Da-sein and from [its] understanding of being, and insofar as I limit myself to what *can be experienced immediately*. Thus, I do not need to assert anything about clearedness in itself. I also do not need to interpret the human being as a manifestation [*Erscheinungsform*] of the clearedness, whereby the being-in-the-world and the standing in the clearing of being as *a* distinctive character, as *the* distinctive character of the human being would become *non*essential. Above all, the above quoted Indian insight cannot be assimilated into my thinking.*

MB: Nevertheless, the Indians, who are experienced in meditation, maintain that immediate experience includes the capacity for seeing that the basic unfolding essence of the human being, but also of all other beings, belongs immediately to the clearedness in itself. One must know, not "interpret," that it [man's basic unfolding essence] co-constitutes [*mitausmachen*] the clearedness.

---

*Heidegger had relatively little interest in Indian thought, which for him was apparently too close to Western metaphysics. Heidegger did have a deep and lifelong interest in East Asian (Chinese and Japanese) thinking. See the following essays in *Heidegger and Asian Thought*, ed. G. Parkes (Honolulu: University of Hawaii Press, 1987): O. Pöggeler, "West-East Dialogue: Heidegger and Lao-Tzu"; P. Shih-yi-Hsiao, "Heidegger and Our Translation of the Tao Te Ching"; G. Parkes, "Thought on the Way: Being and Time via Lao-Chuang"; and Y. Yuasa, "The Encounter of Modern Japanese Philosophy with Heidegger." See also R. May, *Heidegger's Hidden Sources: East Asian Influences on His Work* (New York: Routledge, 1996); G. Parkes, "Heidegger and Japanese Thought: How Much Did He Know and When Did He Know It?" in *Martin Heidegger: Critical Assessments*, pp. 377–406. —TRANSLATORS

MH: *Hellen* [to clear], along with *hell* [clear], mean the same as *Hallen* [to   p. 226
resound] in the sense of "resounding." In the sense of the [primor-
dial] event of the self-manifestation of being, *Hellen* [to clear] occurs
originally as *Hallen* [sounding], as tone. All other beings fall short of
this fundamental tone [*Grundton*]. How close this is to Indian insights
into ultimate truths is best shown by my assertion: "Language is the
house of being."*

May 5, 1963, on the Airplane   p. 227
between Rome and Zurich

1. The clock and measuring by the clock can never prove the presence of
   something, but [they] presuppose presence. For instance, measuring
   never proves the "earlier" [existence] of the earth as a "property" of
   the earth.
2. The natural scientist who does the measuring cannot say anything as
   such about the presence [of being]. Therefore [he can say] nothing
   about [ontological] "having been."

One can argue against such statements [and assert]: This "being-
earlier" belongs to the earth after all. Then, against this one can only
ask: How does the "being-earlier" belong to the earth? The "being-
earlier" belongs to the human being; that is, it shows itself in the clearing
into which he stands out. Unless one had not already presupposed the
presence of the earth, that is, the uncertain age of the earth's presence,
it would not occur to anyone to measure the [earth's] age.

It is decisive for understanding what has been said to comprehend the
"having been," not as a mere shadow of the present, but as an [equally]
immediate being present, as a complete mode of presence [with] just
as much presence [*Anwesenheit*] as the present [*Gegenwart*]. Otherwise,

---

*Heidegger commented on this intimate belonging-together of thinking and of listening
to the Logos (language) of being in his "Letter on Humanism" as follows: "For thinking
in its saying merely brings the unspoken word of Being to language. . . . Being comes,
lighting itself, to language. It is perpetually under way to language. . . . Thus language
itself is raised into the lighting of Being" (*Basic Writings*, p. 259). This is far from
"Indian insights into ultimate truths" without human language as "saying" [Logos]
(*ZS* 226).—TRANSLATORS

one remains with an [objectified] understanding of time as a sequence of points of now.

September 7, 1963, Zollikon

As long as one understands being as presence as it was once understood, and is still [understood], one cannot understand technology and surely not the *disclosive appropriating Event* at all.*

The determination of what was designated in metaphysics as what is present [*das Anwesende*], the *res*, is [re]thought in the new interpretation of a thing (as presented in the lecture *What Is a Thing?*)† from [the background of] the disclosive appropriating Event. In this interpretation of a thing, presence as the [metaphysical] determination of being is abandoned.

The origin of the concept of the self is a very recent one. It is rooted in the Pietism of about 1700, when one spoke about the sinful and evil self and when the human being was thereby objectified [*verdinglicht*].

A correction must be made in the section about "forgetting" in the Sicilian colloquia (p. 214) to the following lines: Because she is still totally with the man while departing, the purse as such is not present to her at all. Then the following should be deleted: "And therefore she allows it [the purse] to be left behind," because she cannot leave it behind at all if it is not present.

If I look at the woman's behavior from outside, I look at the woman as an object moving from here to there, and I do not see her in her being-in-the-world. Going-home-to her parents is really not a going home, but a remaining-with the man.

The ecstatic relationship (and that means the human being's whole Da-sein) cannot be represented. As soon as I represent it, I have two objects, and I am outside the ecstatic relationship.

Concealment is not the antithesis of consciousness but rather concealment belongs to the clearing. Freud simply did not see this clearing; otherwise, he would have succeeded in understanding the consciousness of children.[1]

---

*See *ZS* 351. See also Dastur, "Language and *Ereignis*," in *Reading Heidegger. Commemorations*, pp. 355–69.—TRANSLATORS

†M. Heidegger, "The Thing," in *Poetry, Language, Thought*, pp. 165–86; *What Is a Thing?*—TRANSLATORS

There is a relationship to clearing which need not be "conscious"   p. 229
and reflected on in the Freudian sense. Being in the clearing is also
a presupposition of reflection. The word "reflection" already says that
the clearing is presupposed because it means the re-flected light. Concealment is not a hiding as is Freud's "repression" [*Verdrängung*] because
hiding [as repression] is a special way and manner of being in the clearing.

That little children and old people live exclusively in the present does
not mean that the two cases are the same. On the contrary, one must not
cut off the ecstatic [dimension]. In contrast to the small child, the old
person has having-been-ness, but it conceals itself.[*]

In all pathological phenomena too, the three temporal ecstases[†] and
their particular modifications must be taken into consideration.

In Freud's repression we are dealing with hiding [*Verstecken*] a representation [*Vorstellung*]. In withdrawal [*Entzug*] we are dealing with the
phenomenon itself. The phenomenon withdraws itself from the domain
of the clearing and is inaccessible—so inaccessible that this inaccessibility
as such cannot be experienced anymore. What conceals itself remains
what it is, otherwise I could no longer come back to it.

Clearing is never mere clearing, but always the clearing of *concealment*
[*Sich-Verbergen*]. In the proper sense the clearing of *concealment* [*Lichtung
des Sich-Verbergens*] means that the inaccessible shows and manifests itself
as such—as the inaccessible. And again, this can mean simply inaccessible
or momentarily inaccessible to me. What manifests itself as the inaccessible is the mystery [*Geheimnis*]. The inaccessibility is cleared [*gelichtet*];
I am aware of it, else I could not even ask [about it]. The totality of the
modifications of presence [*Anwesenheit*] in itself is not something present
[*Anwesendes*] anymore. It cannot be characterized as something present.

September 8, 1963, Zollikon   p. 230

The term history [*Historie*] is derived from the Greek ἱστορεῖν, "to explore" in the broad sense, for instance, as with the travels of a geographer;
and "to inquire," in the sense of getting a factual statement in court. There
is no relationship here to what has happened and to what has been.

---

[*]See Boss, *Existential Foundations*, p. 214.—TRANSLATORS

[†]See Heidegger, *Being and Time*, p. 377 f.; Boss, *Existential Foundations*, p. 213 f.
("Modes of illness showing severe impairment in the spatiality and temporality of
human being-in-the-world").—TRANSLATORS

In *Being and Time* historicity [*Geschichtlichkeit*] merely refers to Da-sein and not to the destiny of being [*Seinsgeschick*]. This cannot be explained from the historicity of Da-sein. Conversely, human historicity belongs to the destiny of being.[*] Man is *finite* because he has a relationship to being and, therefore, because he is not being itself, but rather because he is merely needed by being. This is not a lack, but precisely the determination of his unfolding essence. Thereby, "finite" must be understood in the Greek sense of πέρας, that is, limit, as what completes a thing as what it is, provides a limit to its essence, and, thus, lets it come forth.

The [ontological] difference between being [*Sein*] and beings [*Seiendes*] belongs to [the human being's] *relationship to being;* and to experience this difference means to experience what is not a being. The basic experience of what is "not-a-being" is the experience of nothing[ness] [*Nichts*], and this experience of this "not-a-being" is manifest in the relationship to death—to mortality—since death is the leave-taking from [*Abschied*] beings.

When Eastern thought ends with the return to the basic nature of all beings in death into "nothingness," Heidegger is just beginning; because for Eastern thinking the basic nature [of all beings] is still always a "veil of Maya"[†] and being as presence is not yet traced back into the *disclosive appropriating Event.*

Closeness [*Nähe*] always means the manner in which [Da-sein's] potentiality-to-be concerns itself, in the sense of being afflicted [*Betroffenheit*], that is, by being claimed by being, by being needed by being. "Closer" is that which leads [potentiality-to-be] into authentic potentiality-to-be. Yet, the comparative [closer] must not be understood quantitatively, but qualitatively. Closer does not mean a degree more of closeness but rather [it means] different ways, different modes, of closeness. It simply means "close in a different way" [*anders nahe*].

p. 231

There is actually no phenomenology of the body because the body is not a corporeal thing [*Körper*]. With such a thematic approach, one has already missed the point of the matter.

---

[*] M. Heidegger, "The Turning," in *The Question concerning Technology*, pp. 36–49; see also Heidegger, *Basic Writings*, p. 215 f.—TRANSLATORS

[†] In Hinduism, "Maya" originally is the name for the goddess representing the principle of deception in the world. Maya finally becomes the principle of deformation, of mere appearance, and of semblance. The German philosopher Arthur Schopenhauer (1788–1860) talked about the "veil of Maya" in order to express the illusionary character of the world. In Heidegger's view, Maya still belongs to the dualistic thinking pervading both Hinduism and Western Metaphysics. See *ZS* 226.—TRANSLATORS

Without things, there is no potentiality-to-be. Absence is a privation of presence. The receiving-perceiving [*Vernehmen*] and the understanding of the significance of things depend upon the emergence of things.

The "anthropological difference" [between "subject" and "object"] is on the wrong track. It belongs to metaphysics.

January 29, 1964, Zollikon

p. 232

I myself am the *relationship* [*Beziehung*] to something or to someone with whom I am involved in each case. However, "relationship" is not to be understood here in the modern logical-mathematical sense of relation [i.e., a R b], as [a relationship] between objects. The existential relationship cannot be objectified. Its basic essence is one's being concerned and letting oneself be concerned. [It is] a responding, a claim, an answering for, a being responsive on grounds of the clearedness of the relationship. "Comportment" is the way I stand in my relationship to what concerns me in each case, the manner one responds to beings.

A *word* is *not* a relationship. A word discloses [*erschliesst*]. It opens up. The decisive moment in language is significance [*Bedeutung*]. Sounds also belong to language, but they are not the fundamental [characteristics]. I can understand the same meaning in different languages. The essential character of language is the "saying," that a word says something, not that it sounds. A word shows something. Saying means showing. Language is the showing [of something].*

"Standing-within being" [*Innestehen im Sein*] means standing-within the clearing of what conceals itself [being]. What conceals itself comes as such into the clearing and conceals itself. Thus, it points into that which

---

*In contrast to *Being and Time*, the later Heidegger understood language as the *Ereignis* of Language, which "needs" [*braucht*] and uses the human being in its service. "In section 7 of *Being and Time*, Heidegger understands the Greek *logos* as discourse in the sense of the manifestation (*offenbar machen*) of what is in question in discourse. After *Being and Time*, Heidegger deepened his analysis of *logos* in order to carry out the phenomenological 'destruction' of traditional logic in reconducting logic to its fundament, which is *logos* in its initial, i.e., Greek sense. In this way, he ceased thinking of language itself as a phonetic process of expression and communication—which is in fact the metaphysical [instrumental] conception of language that in a way still prevails in *Being and Time*—but as a showing in itself, that is to say, as the happening of lighting" (Dastur, "Language and *Ereignis*," p. 362). See M. Heidegger, *Unterwegs zur Sprache* [On the way to language].—TRANSLATORS

is concealed in it. [Being's] concealment of itself emerges into clearing as what points to what is concealed. As standing-open [*offenständig*] [to being], man stands in the clearing [of being]. He is an open standing-within, whereas the table in front of me stands in the clearing in an entirely different way; for it stands in the clearing merely as something present-at-hand. Only as an open standing-within [being] is man able to see.*

Bodily being [*das Leibliche*] is founded upon responding [*Entsprechen*] [to a world]. Bodily being is *not* first something present for itself [as a subject] through which a relationship-current [*Bezugstrom*] is then transmitted, like a current transmitted through the hand. The body is the necessary condition, but not a sufficient condition, for the relationship.

p. 233

The phenomenon of the body as such is especially concealed to physicians because they are concerned merely with body as a corporeal thing [*Leib-Körper*]. They reinterpret [the body] as corporeal function. The phenomenon of the body is wholly unique and irreducible to something else, for instance, irreducible to mechanistic systems. One must be able to accept the phenomenon of the body as such in its intact being.†
I cannot "understand" something merely causal. That means that I can have no insight into how one thing is derived from something else, that is, how it originates *out from* it. Only in a purely temporal sense does one thing follow *after* another.

[The term] *understanding* may be used only regarding to an insight into the [contextual] connection between motives. Insight [describes] how something is connected with something else—when I can see the meaning of something someone is talking about and how something which was said corresponds to the matter intended.

Motive is the ground for acting this way or that, that is, for moving oneself for this or for that. Ground does not mean an efficient cause here, but it means the "for what" [*Weshalb*], the "reason for" [*Weswegen*]. Something unconscious cannot be a "reason for" because such a "reason for" presupposes conscious awareness [*Bewussheit*]. Therefore, the unconscious is unintelligible.

In Greek ἐναργης means evident, i.e., what shines from itself, what shines in itself.

For Freud [unconscious] forces [*Kräfte*] are the *suppositions* for perceived phenomena. Thus, he creates his psychodynamics. Each supposition presupposes an acceptance. *Acceptio* means acceptance in the sense of receiving as, for instance, at the train station's baggage counter.

---

*See Heidegger, *Being and Time*, pp. 85, 215, 402, 409.—TRANSLATORS

†Heidegger, "Letter on Humanism," *Basic Writings*, p. 204.—TRANSLATORS

"To make a slip of the tongue" [*Sich-versprechen*]:* *Sich* is in the accusative or dative case, for example, the car does not show much promise to me. One cannot find out much about the phenomenon of "promise" [or about its negative meaning as "a slip of the tongue"] unless one has reached clarity about the domain of language.

Acceptio: It demonstrates [*ausweisen*] itself from itself. It demonstrates itself. *Suppositio:* It cannot be demonstrated [immediately] but will be proved [*beweisen*].

With his suppositions [regarding unconscious forces], Freud believes that he understands the phenomenon, for instance, of the slip of the tongue.

In an acceptance (*acceptio*), the thing demonstrates itself by what I say about it. In a supposition (*suppositio*), something is proved by reducing it to a causal connection. According to Aristotle (*Metaphysics* IV.4.1006a6 ff.), someone is educated if he is aware of the difference between immediate demonstration [*Ausweisen*] and causal proof [*Beweisen*]. Otherwise, he is uneducated.

p. 234

I see the existing table immediately, but I do not see existing as such. There are two kinds of phenomena: ontic and ontological. The phenomenon of *being* is the condition for the possibility for the appearance of the ontic, for the appearance of beings as beings.

There are phenomena which are not perceptible. Insofar as we are able to perceive the existing table here as this existing table, only when "existing" as such has somehow become evident to us without being apprehended explicitly has the nonperceptible phenomenon of existing dawned upon us. Existence's evident showing itself cannot be perceived like the table. Therefore, existence as such is a nonperceptible phenomenon—and [these nonperceptible] phenomena are the basic phenomena. They are of first importance. Plato discovered, and Aristotle knew, that beings are given first in ordinary experience and that existence is only noticed later.

According to Kant, a concept is a representation of something in general. What belongs to every possible table is thought of in a concept. However, the idea of a concept presupposes a representation by a subject.

Space is the open, the free [region], the permeable [*Durchlässige*], but this open [region] is not something spatial in itself. Space is something setting [things] free.

Of course, we are assuming that a being would be accessible by the fact that the "I" as a subject would represent an object. It is as if an

---

* *Sich-versprechen* has a double meaning in German: "to promise" and "to make a slip of the tongue."—TRANSLATORS

p. 235

open region would not already need to hold sway beforehand. [Only] within its openness can something be accessible *as* an object *for* a subject, and this accessibility itself can still be traversed as something that can be experienced. Because [the subject and the object] belong to this realm (of what is present), a limit is acknowledged at the same time regarding what is not-present [*Nicht-anwesendes*] here. Therefore, here the human being's self is determined as a particular "I" by its being limited to the unconcealed [particular situation] surrounding it.

A human being's limited belonging to the realm of the unconcealed [situation] constitutes his being a self. The human being becomes an ego by this limitation [to a given situation] and not by being unlimited in such a way that, beforehand, the "I," thinking about itself, boasts about being the measure and center of everything that can be represented. For the Greeks, "I" is the name for a human being who adjusts to the limits [of a given situation] and, thus, at home with himself [*bei sich selbst*]* is *Himself.*

p. 236

March 8, 1965, Zollikon[1]

From the fundamental-ontological analytic of Da-sein, "psychiatric Daseinanalysis" (Binswanger) singled out that basic constitution called *being-in-the-world* in *Being and Time* and made it the sole basis of its science.[†] Nevertheless, this [being-in-the-world] is only that structure which should be shown at the very *beginning* of fundamental ontology—but it is not the only one, and above all, not the one which fundamental ontology has *solely* in view because it sustains Da-sein and its unfolding essence. In the introduction to *Being and Time,* it (this sustaining structure) is clearly and often enough named the *understanding of being* [*Seinsverständnis*]. How far this distinguishes Da-sein as such, wherein it itself is grounded, and to which it itself remains related—this is the sole concern of *Being and Time.*

If one pays attention to this basic characteristic of Da-sein in advance, then two things become clear.

---

*We follow Richardson's translation of this passage in "Heidegger among the Doctors," p. 55, in order to avoid any allusion to a "subject": *Bei-sich-sein* [being-for-itself]. See also *ZS* 204.—TRANSLATORS

†See L. Binswanger, "Heidegger's Analytic of Existence and Its Meaning for Psychiatry," in *Being-in-the-World: Selected Papers of Ludwig Binswanger,* trans. J. Needleman (New York: Harper and Row, 1967), pp. 206–21.—TRANSLATORS

Martin Heidegger in the Zollikon Seminar Room, 1965

1. Everything that "the analytic" [of Dasein] contributes to the elucidation of Da-sein serves to determine the understanding of being
   (being-in-the world), care, temporality, and being-toward-death.
2. Since the understanding of being as ecstatic-projecting standing-within
   [*ekstatisch-entwerfendes Innestehen*] the clearing of the Da properly
   constitutes Da-sein, Da-sein, as the being of the Da, shows itself as
   what in itself is the relationship to being.

This relationship to being can so little be omitted from the decisive
and overall guiding determination of Da-sein that the misunderstanding
of just this relationship (as it happened in "psychiatric Daseinanalysis")
prevents us from ever thinking appropriately of Da-sein as Da-sein. The
understanding of being is not a determination which only concerns the
theme of fundamental ontology, but the understanding of being is *the*

fundamental characteristic of Da-sein as such. Thus, an analysis of Da-sein, omitting this relationship to being which occurs essentially in the understanding of being, is not an analysis of Da-sein.

p. 237
Then the consequence of this omission of the proper fundamental-ontological determination of Da-sein from psychiatric "Daseinanalysis" is an *insufficient interpretation* of *being-in-the world* and of *transcendence*. Certainly, one takes these phenomena as basic phenomena, but in the manner of a Da-sein, which one isolates as a *subject* in accordance with an anthropological representation of the human being. Psychiatric "Dasein-analysis" operates with a mutilated Da-sein from which its basic characteristic has been cut out and cut off.

It is then easy to reach the point where one sees only a more extensive and more useful characterization of the subject's subjectivity in the fundamental-ontological interpretation of Da-sein. While the traditional doctrine of the subject is based on a subject-object-*split*, the view of being-in-the-world (in the mutilated sense of psychiatric "Daseinanalysis") allows a removal of this split in the sense of immediately bridging over the split. [When the understanding of being is understood correctly, it never comes to a representational concept of subject and object in the first place; thus, it follows that no split between them has to be bridged at all.]

Because care is merely conceived as a basic constitution of Da-sein, which has been isolated as a subject, and because it is seen as only an anthropological determination of Da-sein, care, with good reason, turns out to be a one-sided, melancholic interpretation of Dasein, which needs to be supplemented with "love."

But correctly understood (i.e., in a fundamental-ontological sense), care is never distinguishable from "love" but is the name for the ecstatic-temporal constitution of the fundamental characteristic of Da-sein, that is, the understanding of being.

Love is founded on the understanding of being just as much as is *care* in the anthropological [psychological] sense. One can even expect that the essential determination of love, which looks for a guideline in the fundamental-ontological determination of Da-sein, will be deeper and more comprehensive than the one seeing love as something higher than care.

p. 238
The elimination of fundamental ontology from psychiatric "Dasein-analysis" which seems justifiable at the first view (as Binswanger undertakes it) is in truth a misunderstanding of the relationship between fundamental ontology and regional ontology, the latter of which is presupposed in each science and in psychiatry as well.

Fundamental ontology is not merely the general ontology for the regional ontologies, a higher sphere, as it were, suspended above (or a kind of basement beneath), against which the regional ontologies are able to shield themselves. *Fundamental ontology* is that thinking which moves within the foundation of each ontology.* None of these regional ontologies can abandon the foundation, least of all, the regional ontology of psychiatry as a research area, moving within the realm of the unfolding essence of the human being.

What is the meaning of the "reception of *Being and Time*" for psychiatry?[2] Here (in *Being and Time)* [Binswanger sees] the real gain: The foundation "for overcoming the problem of subjectivity scientifically." (In opposition, it must be said) *Being and Time* can only mean that there is no longer a problem with subjectivity. Only when this has been seen has one recognized the importance of the analytic of Da-sein.

What does "subjectivity" mean for Binswanger and Wilhelm Szilasi? Historically: the Egohood of the *ego cogito.* In Kantian terms—subjectivity as the whole of the subject-object relationship—instead of a "split," separation of psyche-physis.

But where there is a "subject," [there is] a "subject of consciousness."   p. 239
As Binswanger notes (*Ausgewählte Vorträge und Aufsätze* [Bern: Francke, 1947], 1:26, 27, quotation on p. 28; in the article "Über Phänomenologie," p. 291 [Husserl]): "pure descriptive doctrine of the essence of immanent forms of consciousness." What does "description" mean? Each description is an interpretation! What is the meaning of "essence"? Of "genus"? Of "idea"? What does consciousness mean? *Ego cogito*—Descartes, Kant!

Binswanger does not distinguish clearly among the following:

1. Descriptive psychology, eidetic psychology
2. Pure phenomenology: transcendental phenomenology as philosophy of subjectivity
3. Psychopathological phenomenology—two branches
4. Descriptive, "subjective" psychopathology of research

Just as Husserl's eidetic psychology is applied in isolation, this psychology of consciousness is replaced by an isolated analytic of Da-sein. However, the isolation is much more catastrophic here.

[According to Binswanger] "The thesis" about Da-sein as being-in-the-world [is understood] as "development" and "expansion" of Kant and Husserl (Binswanger, *Über Sprache und Denken* [Basel, 1946], p. 211). No, rather Da-sein as temporality [must be understood] from the meaning of being. [It is] distinguished by the ecstatic standing-within the clearing of

---

*See Heidegger, *Being and Time*, pp. 34, 182 f., 200 f., 486–88. —TRANSLATORS

Da as the opening into which what is present presences [*anwesen*]. This standing-within is the ecstatic understanding of being, *the understanding of being.*

Binswanger overlooks the properly sustaining and determining characteristic, the *understanding* of being, the disclosedness (*Being and Time*, p. 182), the standing-within the clearing of being, and thus "the pure problem of being" (*Being and Time*, p. 126).

"The correct beginning of the analytic" consists in the interpretation of being-in-the-world (*Being and Time*, p. 78; see pp. 383 and 402). [That characteristic is] certainly a necessary constitution of Da-sein, but is not sufficient by far . . . (*Being and Time*, p. 78). Being-in-the-world is not a condition for the possibility of Da-sein (Binswanger, *Über Sprache und Denken*, p. 209); on the contrary, it is the other way around.

"Transcendence" as being-in-the-world is isolated as a basic constitution, and thus isolated, is misplaced into the subject as characteristic of subjectivity. In this way, everything becomes entangled.

p. 240

Transcendence of Da-sein remains determined from the transcendence qua [as] being (difference). In what sense should the "identification" of being-in-the-world and transcendence, "stepping beyond" (as surpassing), be understood? (Binswanger, *Über Sprache und Denken*, p. 211 f.). As standing-within, abiding in transcendence, *in being as the* [*ontological*] *difference.*

In what way should the cancerous evil, namely, "the subject-object split" (Binswanger, *Über Sprache und Denken*, p. 212), be removed? The split [should] be understood not only as an erroneous opinion, but the subject-object relation *as such* [is] not [to be understood] as primary and authoritative! In no way is "the structure of subjectivity" elucidated as transcendence (*Über Sprache und Denken*, p. 212); that is precisely Kant's version and its further development in Husserl.

"Dasein transcends," that is, as the sustaining [*Ausstehen*] of the Da, which is the clearing of being. It lets "world" happen. But, in the first instance, it [Dasein] does not go out *from itself* and toward something else. As the being of the Da, it is the site of everything encountered.

Dasein is not a "subject." There is no longer a question about subjectivity. Transcendence is not the "structure of subjectivity," but its *removal!*

"Dasein transcends" (see *The Essence of Reasons*);* that is, it is shaping a world [*weltbildend*], allowing being-as presence to come into view;

---

* M. Heidegger, *Vom Wesen des Grundes* (1929; reprint, Frankfurt am Main: Klostermann, 1951) [*The Essence of Reasons*, trans. Terrence Malick (Evanston, Ill.: Northwestern University Press, 1969)].—TRANSLATORS

standing in the difference between being and beings, safekeeping it. Transcendence *as Difference,* as "tarrying within it" [*verweilend*], dwelling in it. *The "self"* [as Da-sein] *is the gathering* [*Versammlung*] *of the tarrying.* Not subject-object, Dasein-World, but Dasein as [appropriated by] being.*

What does the "distinctive transcendence" mentioned in *The Essence of Reasons* mean? An answer can be found in the introduction to *What Is Metaphysics?* †

Transcendence—the name for being *qua transcendence,* as seen from beings *toward* being—the *presencing* [*Anwesen*] *of what is present* [*Anwesendes*]. Transcendence as being *in itself* [is] *the difference* from beings! Transcendence [is] not a property of the subject and of its relationship to an object as "world," but the relationship to being, thus, of Da-sein in its relationship to being. *Transcendens:* "beyond" [*hinüber*], μετα, as [transcending and] returning to itself, as issue [*Austrag*].‡ "To get over toward" [*Hin-*] as going beyond [*Überkommen*] [beings] is the wholly other to any being, and yet is not separate at all, but is as *issue.*

p. 241

1. *"Transcendens"* (see *Being and Time,* p. 62) in difference to the ontic character of beings as present [refers] to presencing as holding sway as presencing of that which is present.

2. "Transcendence" in the sense of Kant's idealistic-subjective transcendental [referring to the a priori transcendental conditions of empirical knowledge] in difference to [empirical] "immanence" or of immanent transcendence.

3. "Transcendence" as the suprasensible transcendent, [i.e.] the absolute and infinite being [God] in contrast to finite and temporal [beings].

---

*The later Heidegger characterized the ontological difference as *Unter-Schied* (*difference, diaphora*), which is neither a distinction of our representative thinking nor a relation between objects (world-thing; being-beings) but the unique *Ereignis* (the disclosive appropriating Event) as the mediation of being with beings (through Da-sein) in the history of being. See Heidegger, "Die Sprache," the first essay in *On the Way to Language,* and *Contributions to Philosophy,* pp. 327–30.—TRANSLATORS

†M. Heidegger, *Was ist Metaphysik?* in *Wegmarken* (Frankfurt am Main: Klostermann, 1967), pp. 1–19 ["What Is Metaphysics?" in *Basic Writings,* pp. 105–6].—TRANSLATORS

‡The old German word *Austrag* connotes "carrying to term" and "to give birth." In Heidegger it refers to the disclosive appropriating Event [*Ereignis*], to the difference [*Unter-schied*] by which being unfolds into, and simultaneously withdraws from, beings and by which "humans," "world," and "things" relate to each other. Heidegger, *Poetry, Language, Thought,* p. 202 ff.—TRANSLATORS

4. "Transcendence" [as characteristic of Da-sein], founded in "being-in-the-world"; the ground of the difference (insufficient).

"Transcendence":

1. From *transcendens*—qua [as] presencing of what is present
2. Transcendence as sustaining the Difference; this *transcendens* is as being human Da-sein, ecstatic, that is, being-in-the-world
3. Being-in-the-world can never be determined from metaphysical transcendence or, similarly, from transcendental subjectivity [Kant]. Rather, the transcendence of Dasein as ecstatic is determined from being-in-the-world. Transcendence then means only: to sojourn with, "being-in" [*In-Sein*].

Transcendence (see *Being and Time*, p. 62) in the sense of transcendence pure and simple (*Being and Time*, sec. 69, esp. pp. 401, 417). Transcendence [is] not [understood] in the sense of the transcendental of Kant, Husserl, and idealism, but taken back to the [originary] difference between beings and being: the clearing in difference. Nevertheless, in this context the difference is still understood within the horizon of metaphysical representation: from beings to being.

Transcendence (as mentioned in *Being and Time* and in *The Essence of Reasons*) is merely the basis for the "relationship to being," for being as re-lationship [*Be-zug*], (the disclosive appropriating Event) [*Ereignis*].

p. 242 "World" [is] not over-against [*Gegenüber*] the subject; it [world] is more subjective than "subject," more objective than "object." Subject and object are also not encompassed [by the world], but it is the holding sway of world and Da-sein—holding sway as essential unfolding of "being" [*Wesen des Seins*]. [What is needed is a] transcendental and ontological inquiry, that is, a fundamental ontological inquiry which is reminiscent of Kant, and yet radically different at the same time.

Transcendence is the word for the being of beings. The distinctiveness of Da-sein's transcendence: a being which transcends and which as care *is* that being [Da-sein].

Transcendence (*Being and Time*, p. 62): Its higher universality is the clearing of being. Presencing, unconcealedness of beings [means]: the difference [between being and beings] as clearing, as the *disclosive appropriating Event*.

The "over-beyond" [*Hinaus über*] every being is never something otherworldly, namely a "being," that is, something suprasensible [Spirit, God]. Trans-scendence [is] the wholly other! "Stepping beyond" [*Überstieg*] [does not mean] out from an immanence, not "up to" a suprasensible being, but rather the relationship to being as the bestowal of beings as such. Stepping beyond [transcendence] is stepping beyond Da-sein, which is always a historical being in each case, insofar as the understanding of being belongs to Dasein and through which it alone can be a "self." Da-sein [exists] as ecstatic stepping *beyond itself,* the clearing in and of itself.

"Transcendence" as the realm for distinguishing the unfolding essence [of Da-sein] from the ground. Thus "transcendence" is determined in a more originary way. How did "transcendence" come to be posited? As *ens* [beings]—as *esse* [beingness]—as *ratio* [reason]—as ἀρχη [origin]? [It is a] question of the *essence of truth.*[*]

May 12–17, 1965, Zollikon

p. 243

Theories of knowledge: (a) idealism, (b) realism

According to idealism, reality is only the subject's representation [of a reality] not actually existing. For Hegel, all being is consciousness.[†] For Marx, all consciousness is being, whereby being is equivalent to material [social] nature.[‡]

"Foundations"

"Foundations" would have to be understood as essential origin—as that wherein everything determinable rests. By contrast, in natural science every foundation is understood in an "objectified" sense, that is, as that by which something is caused. It is understood in a causal-genetic sense instead of making an inquiry into the determination of essence [*Wesenbestimmung*]. As an example: Extension belongs to the essence of color, but extension is not the cause for the origin of color.

It would be necessary for medicine to search for the essential potentiality-to-be human. If one looks for foundations in the causal-genetic sense,

---

[*]See Heidegger, "On the Essence of Truth," *Basic Writings,* 1st ed., pp. 114–41. —TRANSLATORS

[†]See M. Heidegger, "Hegels Begriff der Erfahrung," in *Holzwege* (Frankfurt am Main: Klostermann, 1950), pp. 105–92; *Hegel's Concept of Experience,* trans. J. Glenn Gray (New York: Harper and Row, 1970).—TRANSLATORS

[‡]Heidegger, "Letter on Humanism," in *Basic Writings,* pp. 200, 218.—TRANSLATORS

one abandons the human being's essence beforehand, and thus one misses the question of what being human is.

"Foundation" is something fixed, something layered, something present-at-hand, upon which something is built in the sense of causal-genetic origin.

In physics, "basic" [foundational] research is again something different. Here it means the elaboration of the theory, of theoretical presuppositions, with which experimentation can then work. Indeed, these people who are so exact are [actually] inexact. The effect [of a cause] is not an argument for what the subject matter is itself.

There are two kinds of "foundations":

a. the lowest layer, from which everything is derived.
b. the presupposed theory in the horizon of which experimentation is performed and which, in turn, should always only confirm the presupposed theory.

p. 244 When the particular theory is not confirmed by the experiment, one must seek another theory. However, on their part all these theories are likewise always already based upon the presupposition of the general calculability and measurability of reality.

If electrical impulses were really able to cause moods, then a machine alone and by itself should be able to produce moods. It can only be said that when electrical impulses are present this or that mood appears. However, this is still far from meaning that an electrical impulse can produce a mood. Mood can only be *triggered* [*ausgelöst*]. A certain brain state is correlated with a particular mood. Nevertheless, the brain process is never sufficient [*hinreichend*] for understanding a mood; it is not sufficient even in the most literal sense because it can never reach into [*hineinreichen*] the mood itself.

When one is involved in a subject matter "with body and soul," the ab-sence [*Weg-sein*] of the body means that one is not paying attention to the body. It is a phenomenological statement. It does not mean that a corporeal thing, observable by someone externally, has been transported away from its place.

Descartes's *Regulae ad directionem ingenii* ought to be studied here.

Bodying forth [*Leiben*] as such belongs to being-in-the world. But being-in-the-world is not exhausted in bodying forth. For instance, the understanding of being also belongs to being-in-the-world. [This under-standing of being includes] understanding the fact that I am standing in the clearing of being, and [it also includes] the particular understanding of being, that is, of how being is determined in [this] understanding. This limitation [being-in-the-world] is the horizon of the understanding of being. Bodying forth does not occur here [in the understanding of being].

In [my] pointing to the window's crossbar, the horizon of bodying forth extends to what can be perceived and seen. But in bodying forth itself alone, I cannot experience the significance of any window crossbar as such. For me, to be able to say "crossbar" at all already presupposes an *understanding of being*. Thereby, bodying forth is the gesture of pointing to what I perceived, to what can be reached by my seeing. Bodying forth occurs wherever the senses are involved, but here the primordial understanding of being is always already involved too. When Dr. H. says that the limits of my bodying forth are in Africa, when I am imagining my stay in Africa, then the limits of the bodying forth are in Africa. Yet, these limits of bodying forth are then in an entirely different realm than when I see something in a bodily manner. Then they are in the realm of the capacity of imagination. Therefore, the realm "Africa" is not an extension of the realm of the window's crossbar that I have seen in a bodily manner. But even when I imagine being in Africa, a bodying forth occurs because the imagined African mountains or deserts, or their having been made-present, are given in a sensory manner. When we imagine ourselves to be in Africa, we cannot say that it is actually this way or that there, but we can only say that it could be this way or that. However, when I see the window's crossbar in front of me physically, I can say that it is this way or that. p. 245

Bodying forth is also involved in the design of a painting by an artist in his imagination because it is a sensory design.

Simply imagining things is an entirely different form of comportment than physically seeing something given to the senses immediately. If one says that bodying forth is involved in the understanding of being as well, and if this means that physiological processes in the brain are also involved in this understanding, then one puts body [*Leib*] in place of the corporeal thing [*Körper*]. We have no possibility at all for knowing how the brain is bodying forth in thinking. What we see in an electroencephalogram has nothing to do with the bodying forth of the brain but rather [has to do] with the fact that the body can also be thought of as a corporeal thing—and this as a chemical-physical object.

I can only say *that* the brain is also involved in bodying forth but not *how* [it is involved]. In principle, natural science cannot comprehend the *how* of bodying forth. That one cannot say how the brain is involved in thinking is an abyss. The natural sciences confront the same abyss when they derive the perception of a seen object from a nerve stimulus caused by light rays supposedly transformed into "perception" in the cerebral cortex. Here "transformation" already says too much. It is already a theory. Phenomenology is concerned with that which can be "understood" p. 246

[*Verstehbares*]. The natural sciences do not concern themselves with that which can be understood [phenomenologically].*

In view of phenomenology and the analytic of Dasein, one is only entitled to say *that* such chemical-physical processes as, for instance, changes in blood cells come about in such and such a way within a definite relationship to the world. Yet on this basis the *what* of the chemical-physical changes cannot be explained. For example, it can never be said that an increase in the white blood cells means an increase in the blood cells' "desire to devour" [*Fressenwollen*]. Thus, one would use anthropomorphic language for something which is chemical-physical.

Scientifically speaking, only the *after-which* [*Worauf*], not the *from-which* [*Woraus*], is ascertainable. This after-which was once called "causal connection." Nowadays it is called "information." Every scientific inference is hypothetical. It can always also be otherwise.

The existence of each natural scientist, as well as of each human being in general, always argues against their own theory.

Being present-at-hand itself is not an object of natural science. If there were no being present-at-hand as such, one could not even begin to "prove" *that* there is something. Thinking strictly in the terms of natural science, one would first have to prove that there is [such a thing as] being-at-hand. However, one can surely not do this. According to natural science's methodical principle, something exists only when it has been proved. Therefore, being present-at-hand would have to be proved before anything else. Otherwise, one could not at all begin to prove that something determinate and particular is present-at-hand. Comportment (understood in the terms of the analytic of Dasein) means to engage oneself in and with something, to sustain the manifestness

p. 247 of beings, to sustain the standing-open [toward beings]. In Heidegger's sense, under no circumstances should comportment be misunderstood as an [external] relationship of one pole [subject] to another [object], from something to something else.

[What follows is Martin Heidegger's commentary on the World Health Organization's report on psychosomatic disorders as reported by Schwidder in *Zeitschrift für psychosomatische Medizin* (Journal of psychosomatic medicine) 11, no. 2 (1965): 146 ff. The text reads:]

---

*See Heidegger, *Being and Time*, sec. 31; "Science and Reflection," in *The Question concerning Technology,* pp. 155–82. See also J. Richardson, "Heidegger's Critique of Science," *New Scholasticism* 42 (1968): 1511–36. See also J. J. Kockelmans and T. J. Kisiel, eds., *Phenomenology and the Natural Sciences: Essays and Translations* (Evanston, Ill.: Northwestern University Press, 1970).—TRANSLATORS

The individual is to be understood as a complex, dynamic system in an unstable state of equilibrium, acting and reacting to changes in the environment and in its own system. . . .

If psychological and physiological processes are distinguished, one would be speaking about different aspects of *one* phenomenon. . . .

. . . the double meaning of the adjective "psychosomatic," . . . On one hand, it refers to the basic conception in medicine that an interaction of body and soul is fundamental for the study of all diseases. On the other hand, the same adjective describes how the influence of psychological factors is predominant in certain disorders.

"Stress" . . . being burdened [*Belastung*] by events in the environment . . . the decisive point is always *the relationship, which exists between being burdened and the individual's inner capacity to deal with it* [*Verarbeitungsmöglichkeit*].

MARTIN HEIDEGGER: In such a conception being human is not there at all. Everything is switched over to a system of processes, to a state of equilibrium of such processes, determined by the environment and by a so-called inner [subjectivity]. The relationship between the environment and one's own system is not reflected on.

July 8, 1965, Zollikon   p. 248

The natural scientist as such is not only unable to make a distinction between the psychical and the somatic regarding their measurability or unmeasurability. He can make *no* distinctions of this kind *whatsoever.* He can distinguish only among objects, the measurements of which are different in degree [quantity]. For he can only measure, and thereby he always already presupposes measurability.

To be seated on a chair is not the same as when two corporeal things touch each other in space. Originally, the chair is also not a corporeal thing. It is a thing and as such is already in relationship to a table and to the space in which I dwell. On the other hand, my sitting on it is already a standing-open-being-here [*offenständiges Hiersein*]. Sitting is using equipment [*Zeug*].

The title "psychosomatic medicine" endeavors to synthesize two things which simply do not exist.

Being-in-the-world as such is a bodying forth, but not *only* a bodying forth. There is no sensory affection [sensory intuition] which must be supplemented by a concept of the understanding [*Verstand*] as Kant believed. Kant did not see the body at all here, but only that part of it which involves sensibility [*Sinnlichkeit*].

Bodying forth belongs to being-in-the-world, which is primarily the understanding-of-being. Therefore, this [understanding-of-being] is not just something still added to bodying forth.

A bodying forth always co-participates [*mitbeteiligt*] in the experience of what is present. However, presencing itself is not a bodying forth. A bodying forth also co-participates in the receiving-perceiving of what is present, even if it is addressed silently.

The diagnosis "aphasia" uses a false term. For an aphasic person can indeed say what he means, but he cannot utter it out loud. Language means *glossa*, [the Latin] equivalent for tongue.

Language as saying something, as phenomenology uses it, is not an overextension of the concept of language. Rather, the usual meanings given to language are constrictions. With this constricted concept of language in the sense of verbal articulation [*Verlautbarung*] I cannot understand anything at all.

p. 249

The thing addresses me. If one understands language as "saying" in the sense of the letting-be-shown of something, receiving-perceiving is always language and jointly a saying of words.

It must be said regarding Uexküll's book* on the fundamental questions of psychosomatic medicine that the author breaks down an open door. Motive is a reason [ground for action], and this involves the fact that it is known and represented as such in contrast to a cause which merely acts on its own.

Uexküll understands motive as a cause producing everything. In its essence, a motive cannot be severed from understanding [*Verstehen*]. It belongs to the essence of the motive that it is understood as such in order to be followed. It makes no sense to assert that a motive is present first and then an ego is added. This is a "hypostatization" of the motive.

Science is never able to critique philosophy because it is founded upon philosophy itself.

In the case of Viktor von Weisäcker's† work, the subject is introduced into medicine in such a way that the subject is again subsequently interpreted in the sense of natural science.

Every synthesis always occurs only in a such a way that one has a unity in view already beforehand regarding which one [then] joins things

---

*Thure von Uexküll, *Grundfragen der psychosomatischen Medizin* (Hamburg: Rowohlt, 1963). See also Boss, *Existential Foundations of Medicine and Psychology*, p. 40. —TRANSLATORS

†V. von Weizsäcker, *Der Gestaltkreis: Theorie der Einheit von Wahrnehmen und Bewegen* (Stuttgart, 1947).—TRANSLATORS

together. It is not the case that piecing separate things together could ever result in a synthesis. Such piecing together without having a unity in view beforehand could only always result in a summation. One will never be able to see a unity by simply seeing pieces together.

For instance, it is exactly like making the distinction between red and green. I cannot distinguish red from green if I do not see color. If I were to distinguish red from heavy, nothing reasonable would result. *Soma* and *psyche* are related to being human not like red and green are related to color because psyche and soma are not two different kinds of the one [generic] universal "human being." Red and green are variations of color, but psyche and soma are not variations of the human being.

p. 250

When I speak of different manifestations regarding the use of the concepts of psyche and soma, I speak of them as if they were different things. Even then I still speak in the manner of things when I speak of psyche and soma as two different media by which being human is realized. Such a distinction is already ontologically false because psyche and soma are not two species of a genus.

For Aristotle, psyche is the entelechy of the body or of soma. In his *De Anima* (412.a) he says: The psyche is the way of being of something living.

The entelechy of the human being is the *logos* [language].

In Christian understanding* the body is the evil and the sensual, and the soul must be saved. Instead of being [understood as] a way of being for something living, psyche is then objectified into something—into a soul-substance. This became necessary when the idea of the eternity of the "spark of the soul" [*Seelenfünklein*]† came about.

The whole terminology with which physicians speak about natural scientific matters is taken from a domain determined neither electrically nor chemically (e.g., language, writing letters, words, information, etc.).

What one means by language is certainly not obtained from chemical processes. All that is ascertainable is what natural scientists are able to demonstrate from the chemical-physical processes in the brain. There is nothing to object to. Nevertheless, one must not forget that all these

---

*Heidegger is referring to the "popular" view of the body in Christian thinking, which was influenced by Platonism, Neoplatonism, and partially by Augustine.—TRANSLATORS

†The young Heidegger was influenced by the medieval theologian and mystic Meister Eckehart (ca. 1260–ca. 1327), who believed that a "divine spark" is contained in the depth of every human soul, which can mystically be united with God. See J. Caputo, *The Mystical Element in Heidegger's Thought* (Athens: Ohio University Press, 1948); T. Kisiel, *The Genesis of Heidegger's* Being and Time, p. 81 ff.—TRANSLATORS

results are only probable and hypothetical for counterevidence could appear at any time.

However, with all these statements, the phenomena of memory and recalling are not touched on. All these [chemical-physical] things are merely *conditions* for the emergence of the phenomenon. They are not *causes*, and surely not memory itself.

p. 251   [Remarks on Professor Akeret's Report about Memory at Burghölzli, July 10, 1965]

Memory has a double meaning:* memory as equivalent to recalling something [*Andenken*] and as retaining [*Behalten*]. Retaining is interpreted as storage [*Speicherung*], as entirely thinglike.

Memory is a retaining of something-which-has-been [*Gewesenes*] in the world in the standing-open of human existence. If I put a small purse into the closet, this is not a retaining and also not a memory process. Insofar as the human being is bodying forth, it cannot be denied that something happens in the brain thereby which is observable in the physical body [*Leibkörper*].

The phenomenon of remembering cannot be grasped by the methods of natural science. Only the bodily-corporeal [*leib-körperlich*] conditions of its performance can be ascertained. These are two entirely different matters.

One cannot measure the act of measuring something. Thinking in terms of calculability must be abandoned. Otherwise one cannot see the phenomena.

Each variation of the conditions results in a change of what is conditioned.

[Heidegger's Discussions of "Affects" in His *Nietzsche* Book]

"Disposition" [*Zustand*] refers to being-in-the-world as being one's Self.

When I am in a mood of sadness, then things address me quite differently or not at all. Here we do not mean feeling in the subjective

---

*See *ZS* 213 f., 215–16. See also "What Calls for Thinking?" *Basic Writings*, 1st ed., p. 352.—TRANSLATORS sense that I have a feeling for something. Feeling [as existential mood] concerns my whole being-in-the-world as my being a Self. Attunement [*Gestimmtheit*] is not something standing for itself but belongs to being-in-the-world as being addressed by things. Attunement and being related [*Bezogensein*] are one and the same. Each new attunement is always only a reattunement [*Umstimmung*] of the attunement always already unfolding in each comportment.

One must see that even when I am neither in a joyful, nor in a sad   p. 252
mood, nor in some other dominant mood, even then an attunement is prevailing. A purely theoretical comportment, such as making observations during laboratory research, is also an attunement in a specific way. This attunement is then not indifference but a kind of [undisturbed] equanimity [*Gleichmütigkeit*]* in which nothing else is able to address me but the matter being researched.

("Adjustment" [*Einstellung*], as in the adjustment of a telescope, is too mechanistic a title.)

November 28, 1965, Zollikon   p. 253

The following has to be said as a critique of Häfner's book about psychopaths. When Häfner maintains that psychiatric Daseinanalysis takes its method from Heidegger he maintains an impossibility, because Heidegger's fundamental ontology is an ontological method, but psychiatric Daseinanalysis is not an ontology.

Continuity, materiality, and consistency are not determinations of an [ontological] world-projection [*Weltentwurf*], but these matters can only show themselves in different ways in beings which are disclosed within this world projection. Here Binswanger is referring to beings [in an ontic sense] which through the world-projection are accessible and which appear in this or that way. Binswanger confuses the ontological world-projection with the beings disclosed in the world-projection which are able to appear in this or that way, that is, he confounds the *ontological* with the *ontic*. World-projection has a double meaning: to project [a] world, and that which appears on the basis of this projecting. One can call this [i.e., what appears] that which is projected. Binswanger erroneously calls that which is projected the world-projection [itself].

---

*See Heidegger, *Being and Time*, p. 172 f.—TRANSLATORS

November 29, 1965, Zollikon

Remarks concerning W. Blankenburg's Critique[1]

The clearing of being [*Lichtung des Seins*] is not given at all in the immediate, ontic things of everyday [experience], but we see it only in [reflective] thinking [*Denken*].

By "mediation" [*Vermittlung*] Blankenburg means the transition from the ontological to the ontic. There is no transition possible at all, and therefore there is also no mediation. Blankenburg believes that what appears in the clearing has to be mediated. Yet it is just this clearing of being which makes the appearance of beings possible. Therefore, there is no place for mediation.

When Blankenburg uses the words "point of departure" [*Ausgangspunkt*] and "starting point" [*Ansatz*], he takes the ontological determination of the *clearing of being* for a concrete being, for something ontic, existing on its own, with which one must then mediate empirically appearing things. Yet, the meaning of the clearing is to make possible the appearance of what is given ontically. There is no place for mediation at all.

In contrast to Binswanger, Blankenburg indeed sees the ontological difference, but he misinterprets it because he also takes being [*Sein*] as *a* being [*Seiendes*] which must then be mediated with the other. Binswanger's statement about the "way between the analytic of Dasein and the particular subject areas of psychiatry" can itself only stem from a wrong conception. It stems from a conception according to which ontology is [positioned] above like the sun and the concrete object domains are below it. Then he constantly wants to run back and forth between the above and the below, between the two domains. However, in reality there is no upward and downward at all because they are not separated [from each other]. For the ontological difference [between being and beings] is surely not a separation. It is exactly the opposite.[*]

Furthermore, when Blankenburg speaks of "initiating principles" [*Anstösse*], then the same misunderstanding occurs as in the "initiating-point of thinking" [*Denkansatz*], that is, [the misunderstanding] that the ontological is a matter for itself.

When Blankenburg further states that there is "an extremely tense relationship [*Spannungsverhältnis*] between science and ontological reflection," then such an extremely tense relationship is actually also out of

---

[*] See *Identity and Difference*, pp. 27 ff., 64 ff., 90 ff. —TRANSLATORS

the question. For any ontological reflection refers to something belonging to science inherently, that is, to what is indispensable [*unumgänglich*] for science. When I say it is inaccessible [*unzugänglich*] to science, it still remains indispensable for science. Therefore, a tense relationship is out of the question here.

Therefore, *existentialia* are not initiating principles for the Daseinanalytic way of seeing in psychiatry. Rather, they are exactly the *content* [of the analytic of Dasein]. They exactly co-determine the concrete description of a state of anxiety in a particular human being. For instance, *anxiety* is not an initiating principle, but I recognize anxiety beforehand in a way in which the *existentiale* attunement characterizes it as a distinctive way of being attuned.

What kind of scientific structure does the field of psychiatry have? Binswanger has not said anything about the scientific structure of his Daseinsanalysis anywhere.

When Blankenburg speaks of a "preservation of the principal boundary between science and ontology," he means that the ontological is not accessible to an ontic-scientific approach. It is exactly this boundary that Binswanger did not preserve; instead, he misinterpreted the ontological as something ontic.

This matter can be made clearer: Science on its own has the possibility of glancing at ontological structures but not of comprehending and reflecting on them as such. But if this happens—that is, the actual thematization [of ontological structures] for an ontological reflection— it does not mean that it [the ontological structure] would be isolated as a special realm so that a gap would arise between it and the so-called factical. Nevertheless, the ontological would thereby remain the determining factor of the factical itself. This [the factical] is properly seen in the first instance precisely through the ontological reflection as such.

p. 256

Regarding Binswanger's article about a "heel phobia"[2] [*Absatz-Phobie*] —why does Binswanger get to "continuity" at all? In reality, this category is a way of [Da-sein's] "falling" [*verfallen*] and of that which has "fallen." Falling is always a falling toward those beings which are not Da-sein. It is possible to observe something like continuity in those things which are not of the kind of Da-sein. Thus, it would be a [categorical] objectification of "falling."

The girl's anxiety regarding the break in "continuity" means that the girl is already living [the mode of] falling toward things and that she experiences the things in their character of connectedness and stability. It is a question of [being] an uninterrupted self, of being gathered unto herself. Anxiety is connected with being secure with one's mother. This is a particular kind of being-with [*Mitsein*] and not a formal [continuous] unity.

One must explore how the sick person's relationship to the world is disturbed by the interruption of the interconnection between usable things [things ready-to-hand in the environment]. Ready-to-handedness is encroached upon. Dasein is absorbed in a particular, everyday world. In no way is this a projection of a world toward a [formal-ontical] "continuity" [of things present-at-hand].*

p. 257

The fixation on the shoe is a separate question. For instance, the girl does not have anxiety in the case of breaking the leg of a chair. The chair does not have the same closeness to the girl's body as does the heel of the shoe, all of which belong to bodying forth in almost the same way as a button on a piece of clothing. Thus, one must carefully explore how these particular things like a heel, the leg of a chair, a button, or spittle are making a claim [*Anspruch*] on the girl. To speak about a break in continuity here, or to characterize the [existential] projection of the world by the category of continuity, as Binswanger does, is a formalization of [Da-sein's] existing emptying it of any factical [existential] content.

p. 258

November 29, 1965, Zollikon

Remarks on Boss's Planned Lectures in Argentina in 1966

Standing-open is attuned [*gestimmt*]. It is always a standing-open to a specific environment. *Clearing* is not an *existentiale*. The standing-open of Dasein stands out into the clearing.

All existing, our comportment, is necessarily a bodily comportment, but not only [bodily comportment]. It is bodily [*leiblich*] in itself. However, existing must be determined beforehand as relationship to the world.

---

* See Heidegger, *Being and Time*, p. 475 f., concerning the derivative mode of the "continuity" of something present-at-hand, originally based on the "ecstatical stretching-along" of Da-sein's temporality. Binswanger misinterprets the temporal-ecstatic projection of the world ("Being-in-the-world") with the category of "continuity" of things present-at-hand (e.g., the girl's loss of the heel of her shoe in the skating rink as a break in "continuity," causing the phobia in the form of a fainting spell). Whereas psychoanalysis explains the phobia as an unconscious "pre-oedipal" fear of separation from the mother, Binswanger explains it as a sudden interruption of "a world-design exclusively based on connectedness, cohesiveness, continuity" (Binswanger, "Über die daseinsanalytische Forschungsrichtung in der Psychiatrie," p. 204). According to Heidegger, Binswanger misinterprets things "ready-to-hand" for Da-sein's being-in-the-world as things "present-at-hand" in their spatial-temporal continuity.—TRANSLATORS

To speak of bodiliness *as* a "condition" is not a phenomenological interpretation, but rather is said from the outside. If I speak of condition, I objectify both bodiliness and existing. If I speak of condition, I am already outside, actually separated from existing.

November 30, 1965, Zollikon

p. 259

Consciousness always presupposes Da-sein, not conversely. Knowledge and consciousness are always already moving in the *openness of the Da*. Without this, they would not be possible at all.

In its basic character, Binswanger's "Daseinanalysis" is an ontic interpretation, that is, an *existentiell* interpretation of the particular, factical Dasein.

When understood historically, the relationship between ontic interpretation and ontology is always a correlative relationship insofar as new *existentialia* are discovered from ontic experience.[*]

It follows from this interpretation that Daseinanalysis as ontic science would be an entirely new science. Science means the systematic ordering of interpreted experience. Each science is rigorously bound to its subject domain, but everything rigorous does not involve exactitude [*Exaktheit*] in a [natural science's] calculative sense.

The unifying pole in psychotherapeutical science is the existing human being.

1965, Zollikon

p. 260

Freud's metapsychology is the application of Neo-Kantian philosophy to the human being. On the one hand, he has the natural sciences, and on the other hand, the Kantian theory of objectivity.

For conscious, human phenomena, he also postulates an unbroken [chain] of explanation, that is, the continuity of causal connections.[†] Since there is no such thing "within consciousness," he has to invent

---

[*]See Heidegger, *Being and Time*, p. 32 f., concerning the fundamental relationship between ontic-ontological, existenti*ell* and existent*ial*.—TRANSLATORS

[†]See Richardson, "Heidegger among the Doctors," pp. 49–63, for J. Lacan's interpretation of the Freudian "unconscious" as a symbolic language rather than as a chain of psychic-mechanical causality (J. Lacan, *Ecrits* [Paris: Seuil, 1966]). See *ZS* 348, 350. See also

"the unconscious" in which there must be an unbroken [chain of] causal connections. The postulate is the complete explanation of psychical life whereby explanation [*Erklären*] and understanding [*Verstehen*] are identified. This postulate is not derived from the psychical phenomena themselves but is a *postulate* of modern natural science.

What for Kant transcends [conscious] perception, for instance, the fact that the stone becomes warm *because* the sun is shining, is for Freud "the unconscious."

I speak of thinking and experience and not of knowledge, since knowledge means knowledge in the sense of indubitable certainty.

My thesis is that the unfolding essence of the human being is the understanding of being [*Seinsverständnis*]. I can experience the unfolding essence of the human being from the understanding of being. This experience becomes a hypothesis only at the moment when I set myself the task of apprehending and observing the human being in a particular [scientific] way.

p. 261 # March 6–9, 1966, Zollikon

In his *Logical Investigations** of 1900–1901, Husserl speaks about meaning bestowing acts [*Bedeutung verleihende Akte*]. According to Husserl, the constitution of an object of consciousness occurs in such a way that the hyletic data, pure sensations, are given as primary and then receive a meaning as *noemata* [intentional objects of consciousness]. In other words, a meaning [*noema*] is ascribed to the [sensory] stimulus by a psychical [noetic] act. Nevertheless, the whole is a pure construct.

In genuine boredom, one is not only bored because of a definite thing, but one is bored in general. That means that nothing whatsoever is of interest to oneself. Time plays a role in boredom [*Langeweile*], as the German word suggests.† There is no longer a sense of future, past,

---

E. Craig, "An Encounter with Medard Boss," Special Issue: "Psychotherapy for Freedom: The Daseinanalytic Way in Psychology and Psychoanalysis," ed. E. Craig, *Humanist Psychologist* 16 (1988): 34.—TRANSLATORS

*E. Husserl, *Logical Investigations*, trans. J. N. Findlay, rev. ed., 2 vols. (London: Routledge, 1970).—TRANSLATORS

†In German *Langeweile* means "lengthening of the while," i.e., time becomes long. See Heidegger, "What Is Metaphysics?" in *Basic Writings*, p. 101. Also see Heidegger, *Fundamental Concepts of Metaphysics*, p. 152.—TRANSLATORS

or present. The unnoticed claim of being [*Anspruch des Seins*] occurs in boredom.

Concerning perception, see Kant, "Anticipation of Perception" (*Critique of Pure Reason* A.166 ff., B.207 ff.).

When I inadvertently touch a hot plate and immediately pull back before I have perceived anything, then this, in fact, is nothing more than a purely meaningless, blunt stimulus [*Reiz*]. It is merely intensity without quality; an intensive quantity. This reduction of being-in-the-world to the intensity of a stimulus does exist and, for instance, plays a great role in pain.

When the burdening [*Belastung*] ceases, [what remains] is not just being-unburdened, [*Nicht-Belastung*], not simply the negation of being burdened. For how can something purely negative be able to burden? The burdening [still] remaining in being unburdened is rather the fact that being addressed constantly [by the burden] has ceased. The character of being-in-the-world [*Welthafte*] [of being burdened] has withdrawn, and I have lost my hold on it. I have no hold [*ratlos*]. Having a hold [*Rat*] is something I can rely on. So one speaks about having something to hold on to [*Vorrat*] which is at a person's disposal beforehand. In being unburdened [*Entlastung*] the basic character of being addressed [by the burden] is threatened. We are dealing with the privation of being addressed [by the burden]. In boredom a removal [*Sich-entziehen*] of beings as a whole occurs, but [it is] not a total slipping away [*Verschwinden*] [of beings], as in anxiety.* p. 262

The *hermeneutical circle* is not a lack but what is genuinely positive in the human being's Da-sein. *Motive:* "Movement"—what addresses me [but] does not cause [something in me].

Regarding the painter Cézanne, one could have said that he pursued his motive. The mountain he paints is not the cause of his picture. Rather, what he saw determined the way and manner of his action and of his procedure in painting. The mountain he saw in this or that way is the determining ground [motive]—that by which the painter's comportment is determined in this way or that.

Object—science—concepts—universally valid calculability: The comportment toward the world as setting-upon [*Stellen*], as challenging [*Herausfoderung*],† is what is grounding all this. Causality plays a role in calculating the lawlike sequence of one state after another. Since one

---

*See Heidegger, *Basic Writings*, pp. 101, 103.—TRANSLATORS

†Heidegger is referring to the essence of modern technology, which in itself is nothing "technological" and which he called "Enframing" [*Ge-stell*]. See "Question

does no calculation whatsoever in the phenomenological way of seeing, causality has no meaning here as well. The manipulation of nature and the manipulative comportment toward it are only different names for the same matter, that is, setting upon [and challenging] nature.

When one is about to take an examination, the exam brings forth, causes, tension and burden. When the *cause* ceases, the *effect* ends. One also says that the exam is the *motive* for the burden, but here motive is [erroneously] equated with cause.

If one talks this way, burdening and unburdening simply become processes and sequences. Thereby, my being-involved [*Dabei-sein*] is no longer taken into account at all. The phenomena of burdening and unburdening are simply objectified and are no longer seen as belonging to being human. This is not appropriate because my way of being involved is no longer taken into consideration. I am surely not a sequence of processes. That is not human.

p. 263

For example, that an exam takes place is not simply a process as, for instance, as when it is raining, but it is something historical, [occurring] in a human situation and within the history of a human life.

Instead of always only speaking of the so called I-Thou relationship, one should speak of a Thou-Thou relationship instead. The reason for this is that an I-Thou is always only spoken of from my point of view, whereas in reality we have a mutual relationship here.

If *occasion* [*Anlass*]* is equivalent to release [*Auslösen*], does this mean that an [efficient] cause begins to work? For instance, when I give quinine to someone suffering from malaria, I am merely the occasion for the quinine killing the amoebas. The patient's body [as cause] then heals him. If the physician understands his role as merely being-the-occasion [*Anlass-sein*], then it is indeed still possible that the being-with [the

---

concerning Technology," in *The Question concerning Technology,* pp. 3–35. See also Inwood, *A Heidegger Dictionary,* pp. 209–12 (s.v. technology, machination, and enframing).—TRANSLATORS

*Anlass [occasion, Latin: *ob-*, toward, *cadere-*, to fall] is one of many words from the root *lassen* [to let] which Heidegger frequently employs, for instance, in *sich einlassen* [to engage in, to enter into], *veranlassen* [to occasion, to induce], etc. Here Heidegger uses *Anlass* [occasion] like *Auslösen* [releasing] in a deeper existential sense of letting something come into presence, bringing something forth out of concealment into unconcealment, i.e., what the Greeks thought as bringing-forth in *physis* (nature) and *poiesis* (arts, crafts). The "occasioning," which is ontologically prior to "causality," is the doctor's existential "being-with" [*Mitsein*] the patient, in contrast to treating him as an "object" of medical expertise. Concerning the difference between Heidegger's distinctions between "cause," "occasion," and "occasioning," see *Basic Writings,* p. 292 f.—TRANSLATORS

patient] can continue. But if the physician were to understand himself in such a way that he has brought about [caused] the healing of the patient as an "object," then the being human and the being-with are lost.

As a physician one must, as it were, stand back and let the other human being be. These [dealings with the patient as "being-with" or as an "object"] are entirely different modes of comportment, which cannot be distinguished from outside at all. Herein lies the existential difference between a family doctor and a specialist in a clinic. It is characteristic that family doctors are a dying breed.

Attunement is not only related to mood, to being able to be attuned in this or that way. Rather, this attunement, in the sense of moods, at the same time contains the relationship toward the way and the manner of being able to be addressed and of the claim of being. Each ontological disposition [*Befindlichkeit*] is an [existential] understanding [*Verstehen*], and each understanding is ontologically disposed. Thus, ontological disposition and understanding are equiprimordial. In the third place, discourse [*Rede*] is equiprimordial [with disposition and understanding]. Ontologically disposed understanding in itself is a "saying" [discourse], a showing of something.*

Hegel's "mediation": Mediation of the representational mode of understanding [*Vorstellen*] with the ego.†

Each physical experiment is related back to the realm of the sensory p. 264 because it must start with it and return to it. Therefore, atomic physics also remains dependent upon the corporeal, notwithstanding the transformability of particles into energy.

July 7, 1966, Zollikon p. 265

Phenomenology is more of a science than natural science is. This is especially true if one understands science in the sense of primordial

---

*See Heidegger, *Being and Time*, secs. 29, 31, 32, 33, 34, concerning the equiprimordiality of ontological disposition, understanding, and discourse.—TRANSLATORS

†Heidegger critiqued dialectical thinking in Kant, Fichte, Schelling, and Hegel as the high points in Western, metaphysical thinking. Heidegger wrote: "The method of dialectical mediation misses the phenomenon . . . by itself keen wit cannot get to what still withdraws from our thinking . . . dialectic is dictatorship over the unquestioned; and in its net every question is choked off (stifled, smothered) and suffocates" (M. Heidegger, *Aus der Erfahrung des Denkens* [1954] *GA*, 13:13). See also M. Heidegger, *Hegels Phänomenologie des Geistes, 1930–31*, ed. I. Görland (Frankfurt am Main: Klostermann, 1980).—TRANSLATORS

knowledge [wisdom] as expressed by the Sanskrit word *wit,* meaning "to see." When natural science insists on its scientific character, then this decisive event already lies a few centuries behind it. The decisive event already occurred with Galileo. Today's natural scientists are really no more than latter-day workers in a domain already disclosed to them long ago. Whereas Galileo in his time created a [new] projection of nature according to which nature was [understood] as the unbroken connection of moving points of mass, today [the task] is to bring about the outline of the projection [*Aufwurf des Erwurfes*] of being-in-the-world. But this is infinitely more difficult than Galileo's projection of nature because now it is no longer merely a matter of inanimate nature, but rather we are dealing with *the human being.* This [conception of the human being] must prevail over the traditional, anthropological rep-resentation of [the human being as subject], which itself is given only in a hazy way.

The decisive point for the projection of nature by Galileo was calcu-lability. For the analytic of Da-sein, the decisive point is the questionable-ness [*Fragwürdigkeit*] of the human being and of his being able to exist in today's world. Seen from the perspective of Da-sein, what one calls "strivings" [*Strebungen*] in psychology take place in the domain of care [*Sorge*], ontically in the domain of working [*Arbeiten*]—of "working" in its broadest sense.

p. 266 # November 13, 1966, Zollikon[1]

It looks as if the demonstration of the processes by which a condition orig-inated (e.g., a condition of illness) is the only possible way of determining what the condition [*Zustand*] is.

The meaning of, let alone the necessity for, the *genetic viewpoint* seems to be evident to everyone. It is considered as self-evident. Yet it suffers from a defect which one overlooks all too easily and which, therefore, is mostly overlooked.

In order to be able to give a genetic explanation of how a condition of illness originated, a clarification, of course, is needed beforehand regarding what this condition of illness is in itself. As long as this remains unclarified, any wish to explain the matter genetically has no thematic view at all for *what* has to be explained. An explanation presupposes the clarification of the essence [*Wesen*] of what should be explained.

The insight into this matter already upsets the [self-evident] role which the genetic viewpoint takes for granted. But the matter does not end here. Indeed, it could be that an objective clarification of the essence of a condition of illness could lead [to the insight] that its essence rules out the possibility for the desired, causal-genetic explanation.

Whoever insists on a genetic explanation without *clarifying the essence* of what needs to be explained beforehand is like a man who wishes to reach a goal without having previously brought the goal itself into view. All explanation extends only so far—if it is appropriate to the subject matter—as far as that which has to be explained is clarified in its own essence beforehand.

What good is all explaining if what has to be explained remains unclear? Or does one indeed hold the mistaken view that what is unclarified in *itself* could ever by clarified by a [genetic] explanation?

July 6, 1967, Zollikon   p. 267

If we human beings speak about something, we make a general presupposition which we do not think about much at all because it is so simple, that is, that something endures as the same thing—that something remains the same. This is the "principle of identity" [*Satz der Identität*] which we presuppose. Science has the ambition of proving its subject matters. But then it must know what it means to demonstrate something. What does it mean to prove? What does it mean to prove a proposition? To prove means "to provide a ground" [*begründen*]. All sciences presuppose the principle of reason [*Der Satz vom Grunde*]. Nothing is without ground [reason]. Up till now, this principle of reason has not been discussed sufficiently. Science presupposes nature as a definite domain of beings which can be measured. Its presupposition is measurability, and the presupposition of measurability is the homogeneity of space and time.

One can still have an intuition of Newtonian space, that is, to have it [space] immediately present [to the mind]. In contrast, in most recent times something fundamental has occurred in nuclear physics. The experimenter himself and his machinery participate in the very experiment so that the result is influenced by the experiment itself—so that the object itself is no longer accessible intuitively. How do they still want to experiment under these [new] conditions?

A model gives some help here, for instance, the atomic model of Niels Bohr. The model becomes necessary here. Bohr's model is taken from the planetary system. This model gives directions on how to ask questions. Even now this [model] is already outdated. There are other models: the atomic nucleus surrounded by waves. According to one model, one can calculate location [of particles]; according to another model [one can calculate] velocity. Where objects have become inaccessible to intuition, and where, nevertheless, the necessity for calculability is maintained, the model comes into play. When the experimental machinery necessarily

p. 268

changes the objects, then one still has only the change in hand and no longer the object. Has the object become inaccessible to intuition? Only in physics is the concept of a model meaningful. Where a model appears, the projection [of nature] still has a merely instrumental character, but no longer an ontological character.[*]

All of this is said only as an example of what a *presupposition* is.

As distinguished from nuclear physics, a conversation [*Gespräch*] with other human beings is what we are ourselves. It is something which can be experienced immediately and constantly, but it is not something like an object. Yet [the fact that] human conversation cannot be objectified is something entirely different from the projection of nuclear physics, which [also] can no longer be objectified. One presupposition for conversation is language.

With reference to Johann Gottfried von Herder, Arnold Gehlen orients the human being in relation to animals. Compared to animals, man is a defective being [*Mangelwesen*]. Man lacks the security of the animal's adjustment to the environment. Gehlen called this "world-openness," which has nothing to do with what we called openness in the sense of our clearing [*Lichtung*].

There is a process under way to the effect that the representation of language is no longer determined from its own being, that is, from talking with one another, but from the way and manner in which a computer "speaks" and "calculates." [This is] the assimilation of language to the computer. The fate of physics, which has now reached nuclear physics, worries the more reflective physicists insofar as they can see that the human being, put into this world as constructed and projected by nuclear physics, no longer has access to the [human] world. What is accessible is still only what can be calculated and its effect. In this

---

[*] Agreeing with Heidegger, Boss is also critical of the idea of a "model." "Models are superfluous and senseless to an understanding of human nature, anyway, because human beings are self-conscious beings capable of expressing themselves through language. The model-building of psychology and psychopathology misses and misconstructs the decisive character of human nature in visualizing human nature as an object that, like other objects in the world, is occupying at any one time only a single place in a given space. Once human nature has been thus misrepresented, the most any therapy can hope to do is make a better object, not a healthier person" (Boss, *Existential Foundations*, p. 63).—TRANSLATORS

situation, one tries to help oneself [in the same way] as Heisenberg did, for instance, when he held a lecture about Goethe and modern, natural science. There, he tried to do something completely untenable: to show that the aim of physics—namely, a [universal] world-formula, a reduction to a simple proposition—corresponds to Goethe's "primordial phenomenon" [*Urphänomen*] or to the Platonic "Forms." Heisenberg simply overlooked the fact that a mathematical formula, even if it is ever so simple, is fundamentally different from Goethe's "primordial phenomenon." But Heisenberg's dilemma is even greater. He is unable to bring his physics into a living relationship to human beings. Other physicists link science with faith.   p. 269

To speak means to say, which means to show and to let [something] be seen. It means to communicate and, correspondingly, to listen, to submit oneself to a claim addressed to oneself and to comply and respond to it.

July 8, 1967, Zollikon   p. 270

"Proof" means to draw conclusions from presupposed axioms or facts, for example, from a basic assumption [*Grundannahme*] about the constitution of the human being. But a basic assumption cannot be proved. There are hypothetical, basic assumptions, evident in themselves.

From the fact that a basic assumption cannot be proved, one can conclude that all such presupposed, basic assumptions are of the same value.

Nowadays, human beings reject the importance of things experienced directly. They do not count. Meanwhile, most proofs rest on mere hypotheses.

One cannot prove that one exists.

One can only ascertain scientifically something like metabolism if one has already presupposed that the matter to be ascertained exists, that is, both the existing human being and his metabolism. One discovers it [metabolism], and yet its existence cannot be proved.

If Dr. M. asserts that psychotherapy can be done only if one objectifies the human being beforehand, then what is decisive thereby is psychotherapy and not the existence of the human being. Since one can [supposedly] only do therapy, which is a concerned handling of objects, and thus something purely technical, then the outcome of such psychotherapy cannot result in a healthier human being. In such a therapy, the human being is finally eliminated. At best, such a therapy could [only] result in a more polished object.

Is [existential] being-with-one-another an encounter or does the potentiality-for-encounter presuppose being-with-one-another? The latter is the case.

p. 271
November 22, 1967, Zollikon

Psychological theories arise under the pressure of tradition because tradition does not know anything else than the character of being as substantiality, objectification, and reification. This must not always be as crude as in Scholasticism with its positing of an eternal soul-substance.

Psyche and psychology are attempts to objectify the human being.

Something noncorporeal is acknowledged, but it is determined simultaneously according to the method of corporeal [physical] objectification. The method of its determination is not derived from the "psychical," from the noncorporeal itself, but occurs without [further] determination [from] within the horizon of scientific research, which alone counts as scientific. The justification of psychology lies in the fact that it acknowledged something noncorporeal, and its limitation lies in the fact that it wanted to determine it [noncorporeal reality] with the method of physical research—[with the method] of natural science.

The justification of psychology consists only in its point of departure and in its taking the noncorporeal seriously. But then its justification already ends because it researches this noncorporeal with inappropriate methods. It is a justification turned into something unjustified.

p. 272
March 8–16, 1968, Lenzerheide

The standing-open [*Offenständigkeit*] as which the human being exists must not be misunderstood as something present-at-hand, as a kind of empty, mental sack into which something could fall on occasion. Rather, the human being as this standing-open is a [existential] being-open [*Offenständigsein*] for the receiving-perceiving of presence [being] and of what is present [beings]. It is an openness for the thingness of things [*Dingheit*].* Without such standing-open, nothing could appear by

---

*See Heidegger, *An Introduction to Metaphysics*, pp. 79–164; *Early Greek Thinking*, trans. D. F. Krell and F. A. Capuzzi (New York: Harper and Row, 1975); and "The Thing," in *Poetry, Language, Thought*, pp. 213–29.—TRANSLATORS

itself, not even the table here. The openness, as which the human being exists, is always openness for being claimed [*Anspruch*] by the presence of something.

Determinism denies freedom, and yet by denying it, it already must *presuppose* a certain idea of freedom. Freedom as represented in the natural sciences has always been understood as noncausal, as an a-causal occurrence. Therefore, determinism [as causal determination] remains outside of freedom from the start. Freedom has nothing to do with causality. Freedom is to be free and open for being claimed by something.* This claim is then the ground of action, the motive. It has nothing whatsoever to do with *causal* chains. What claims [the human being] is the motive for human response. Being open for a claim [*Offensein für einen Anspruch*] lies outside the dimension of causality. Thus, determinism does not even come close to the realm of freedom in the first place. It cannot say anything about freedom at all. Therefore, as far as freedom is concerned, it does not matter at all whether we know all the causes, or none of the causes, or how many causes a thing has.

It is a basic determination of Da-sein to be open for being claimed by the presence [being] of something. A plant is related to light as well, but it is not open to light *as* light. For it, the sun or the light is not present as sun or light.

Verbal articulation [*Verlautbarung*] is given by the fact that existing is bodily existing.

The presence of the table is something addressing me, even if under certain circumstances it [addresses me] merely unthematically. But without this being addressed, the table could never show itself as something present. I cannot exist at all without constantly responding to this or that address in a thematic or unthematic way; otherwise, I could not take so much as a single step, nor cast a glance at something.

p. 273

In this domain, one cannot prove anything. One must abandon the belief that only what can be proved is true. There are matters like presence [of being] or freedom refusing any claim of measurability. We are not dealing with a theory here, but with the insight into what we ourselves always already are.

In contrast, a theory is a supposition making possible the calculation of a thing. To stand under the claim of presence is the greatest claim made upon the human being. It is "ethics" [in the original sense].†

---

*See Heidegger, *Basic Writings*, 1st ed., pp. 114–41, esp. p. 126 ff. ("The Essence of Freedom"). —TRANSLATORS

†Heidegger critiqued Western metaphysics' concept of ethics. He related ethics to the original Greek, pre-Socratic experience of *ethos:* "The saying of Heraclitus (frag.

To furnish a room is something entirely different from when a human being moves into a room (*sich einräumen*). As in the beginning of part 2 of *The Foundations*,[1] a preliminary remark must be made: that the "philosophizing" occurring now has to be kept in view constantly in order to understand the later chapters on pathology and therapy. Therefore, what follows is far from being just superfluous philosophizing for doctors. Man sojourns with what concerns him. He is in relationship to things and to other human beings. Since ancient times, inanimate things have been represented as being in space and time. But the human being exists in an entirely different way in space and time than things insofar as he, as a human being, is spatial and temporal *himself*. When I translate "ek-sists" as "standing out into," I say this in opposition to Descartes and against his idea of a *res cogitans* in the sense of immanence. Yet, in opposing Descartes, I am still going along with his position. "To exist" might be more adequately translated as "sustaining a realm of openness" [*Ausstehen eines Offenheitsbereiches*].*

p. 274

Each willing is a striving, but not every striving is a willing. Willing belongs to freedom, to being-free for a claim to which I respond. Then

---

119) goes *ethos anthropoi daimon*. This is usually translated, 'A man's character is his daimon.' This translation thinks in a modern way, not a Greek one. *Ethos* means abode, dwelling place. The word names the open region in which man dwells. The open region of his abode allows what pertains to man's essence, and what in thus arriving resides in nearness to him, to appear. The abode of man contains and preserves the advent of what belongs to man in his essence. According to Heraclitus's phrase this is *daimon,* the god. The fragment says: man dwells, insofar as he is man, in the nearness of god. . . . If the name 'ethics,' in keeping with the basic meaning of the word *ethos,* should now say that 'ethics' ponders the abode of man, then that thinking which thinks the truth of Being as the primordial element of man, as one who eksists, is in itself the original ethics. However, this thinking is not ethics in the first instance, because it is ontology. For ontology always thinks solely the being . . . in its Being. But as long as the truth of Being is not thought all ontology remains without its foundation. Therefore the thinking which in *Being and Time* tries to advance thought in a preliminary way into the truth of Being characterizes itself as 'fundamental ontology.' [Cf. *Being and Time,* secs. 3 and 4, above.] It strives to reach back into the essential ground from which thought concerning the truth of Being emerges. By initiating another inquiry this thinking is already removed from the 'ontology' of metaphysics (even that of Kant)" (Heidegger, "Letter on Humanism," in *Basic Writings,* 1st ed., pp. 233, 234–35.—TRANSLATORS

*The German *ausstehen* is translated here as "to sustain," following Heidegger's own usage: "Because man as the one who ek-sists comes to stand in this relation that Being destines for itself, in that he ecstatically sustains it, that is, in care takes it upon himself, he at first fails to recognize the nearest [being] and attaches himself to the next nearest [beings]" (Heidegger, "Letter on Humanism," in *Basic Writings,* p. 211 f.).—TRANSLATORS

claim is the motive for willing. I only will [something] when I am engaged in [*einlassen*] a motive, when I appropriate it as such, when I accept it. In Latin: *Nemo vult nisi videns* [No one wills except when he "sees"].

One can only will what one can carry out and realize by oneself. Therefore, one cannot will it to snow. One can will the impossible too, but only if one considers the impossible to be possible.

Propensity [*Neigung*] and resistance [*Abwehr*] are also modes of relationship to what is present. Psychical capacities are to be understood as modes of being addressed [*Angesprochensein*] and of responding [*Entsprechen*].

In wishing, one does not carry out anything. Yet it is not a matter of indifference to wish either that someone might get well or that they go to the devil.

A responding can only exist when one is able to say yes or no. If one speaks of a responding, even then, when it involves being urged [*Gedrängtsein*], responding is devalued to a mere [external] relation. In the case of an urge to stab [someone], one must say: To be delivered over to, or to have lapsed into what addresses itself in this way or that. In an urge [*Drang*], the experience of something *as* something is not explicit.

The more exclusively the patient[2] is absorbed in the love for her child and the closer she is to him in this exclusionary love, the more this closeness takes on the characteristics of narrowness [*Enge*] and choking [*Erwürgen*]. In order to save herself from this entanglement [*Verstrickung*] and narrowness, the child must be removed and strangled. The mood of choking does not disappear even when she bathes her child because the child's closeness as her child lends a distinctive character to this general atmosphere of entanglement and narrowing down. Then [the child] is absorbed into what narrows down and [even] becomes what narrows down. What chokes overcomes the patient completely. Precisely what was close [the child], so to say, now acquires the distinction of being the means by which choking can be interrupted [by strangling the child].

p. 275

Regarding the titles, I would propose: "Some basic characteristics of a trouble-free, human Da-sein." In the preliminary remarks to this chapter, it should be noted that these are only a few basic characteristics, and, furthermore, they were selected regarding the theme of medicine.

Regarding the chapter on *memory*, it should be noted that memory is not only a retaining. For instance, when we write a dedication in memory of . . ., then what is called memory here is not characterized by retaining. It is also not true when I arrange a celebration in memory of someone. It is not only a question of not forgetting the one to whom the celebration was dedicated, but rather [of being aware] that he remains constantly present as the one who co-determines my Da-sein, even when he is no longer living. This is not a mere retaining. This refers to the deep affectedness [*Betroffen-sein*]* by the whole tradition in which Da-sein stands. For example, medical doctors should remember that there was a Newton and that he is still present in the whole application of physics. They [the doctors] are simply living from day to day. The difference between what is "past" [ontic time] and "what has been" [ontological temporality] emerges here. The memory of what has been as what is still present and still determining the present and the future—this is not a mere retaining. Retaining [*Behalten*] is too primitive [a notion]. Mere retaining is not sufficient [for articulating] that I stay within a tradition and that any so-called progress is a confrontation [*Auseinandersetzung*] with tradition. In this way man is a historical being, whether human beings reflect upon it or not. Everything is a confrontation with history, with "what has been." The present confronts what has been in

p. 276 relation to what is coming [*das Künftige*]. The psychological theory of memory only refers to what one does not have present right now, [i.e.] to what is not present at a particular moment. The idea of memory as a container is [the notion] of a completely a-historical and a-temporal apparatus.†

In the chapter on *consciousness*, the difference between the relationship between ec-static Da-sein and consciousness and the relationship between *psyche* and consciousness must be highlighted more distinctly.

p. 277 # May 14, 1968, Zollikon

Language is identical with the understanding of being, and without this one could not experience death as death, that is, as the uttermost possibility approaching Da-sein.‡

---

*See Heidegger, *Being and Time*, p. 436 f., concerning Heidegger's distinction between individual fate [*Schicksal*] and communal destiny [*Geschick*] in the historical tradition.—TRANSLATORS

†See Boss, *Existential Foundations*, pp. 114–19 ("human memory and the historicity of human existence").—TRANSLATORS

‡See Heidegger, *Being and Time*, secs. 48–53, concerning the existential analysis of death ("Being-towards-death"), and *Contributions to Philosophy*, pp. 198–201. See also Boss, *Existential Foundations*, pp. 119–22.—TRANSLATORS

The essential determination of any matter is composed of three elements.

The first subdetermination that is necessary is the determination of what something is as something. In relation to human Da-sein, the answer is: as being-in-the-world, as comportment to what is present. The description has these titles so that one knows what the matter is about in the first place.

The second subdetermination [*Unterbestimmung*] refers to the condition for the possibility of being this way. Applied to Da-sein, this condition for the possibility to exist as Da-sein is the understanding of being.

The third subdetermination refers to where this condition for the possibility itself regarding human Da-sein is grounded: in the destiny of being [*Seinsgeschick*].* If being were not sent to Da-sein, there could be no understanding of being. Sartre's primary error consists in the fact that he sees being as something posited [*Gesetztes*] by the human being's subjective projection.

MEDARD BOSS:

1. From the perspective of the analytic of Da-sein, how can one understand that any stimulation of a nerve, somewhere in its course, is always sensed at the nerve endings?

2. Phantom limb pains

3. The insensitivity to pain [provided] by an intense distraction of attention

MARTIN HEIDEGGER:

Problem 1. The perception of pain is by no means localized at the nerve ending, but rather it is the relationship toward being struck or being stimulated.

Problem 2. As for phantom limb pains, one must say that they are precisely the testimony for ecstatic bodiliness [*Leiblichkeit*]. My relationship to my toes is a bodily one [*leiben*] and not a corporeal [*körperlich*] one. The feeling of something through my toes was earlier understood as the mere being present-at-hand of the toe. Yet this understanding does not reach far enough. Sensitivity to pain goes beyond the toes.

p. 278

Problem 3. As for insensitivity to pain, one must first ask: What does attention [*Aufmerksamkeit*] really mean? If one imagines it as

---

*"This simultaneous juxtaposing of the destining [destiny] of being and the doing of man is absolutely fundamental for Heidegger's thinking" (W. Lovitt, introduction to Heidegger, *The Question concerning Technology*, p. xxviii). —TRANSLATORS

a searchlight, then noticing and seeing the light is based upon the understanding of being.

p. 279   # September 27, 1968, Lenzerheide[1]

If one understands "phenomenology" and "phenomenological" as titles for a philosophical method, and if one takes as its fundamental task the projection of beings [*Entwurf des Seienden*] as such toward being [*auf das Sein*], that is, *ontology*, then the comparison of the two titles "The Basic Character of the Scientific Research Method" (pp. 8–20) and "The Basic Character of the Phenomenological Method of Research" (pp. 259–69) is wrong and misleading from the start.[2] In both cases we are dealing with a procedure of medicine as a science of a being, that is, of the human being. This research method, which is "entirely different" from that of natural science, is not a philosophical-ontological one. In the same way as the method of natural science, it refers to existing man in his various conditions (see p. 205): "The immense manifoldness of the ways of comportment. . . ." The title "phenomenological" is then used in an ontic sense. Similarly, the title "phenomenon" refers to that particular being showing itself in this or that way. Medicine deals with and investigates *this* phenomenon. But the decisive question is: In light of what kind of being is this being (the human being) experienced? The title on page 249 speaks of an "anthropology appropriate to Da-sein."

Now, is medicine an anthropology, or does it necessarily rest on one? If the latter is the case, then what does "appropriate to Da-sein" mean? After what has been said, this can only mean that medicine, as an ontic science of this or that human being [as an object], experiences it in the light of being human, whose basic character is ontologically determined as Da-sein.

p. 280   But thus the title "appropriate to Da-sein" is still not yet sufficiently clarified. "Appropriate to Da-sein" could mean that all assertions about being human as such must refer to the character of Da-sein in the sense of "the basic characteristics of the trouble-free Da-sein" (p. 269 ff.). These basic characteristics determine human being as Da-sein, as being. Therefore, they are ontological assertions. But "appropriate to Da-sein" can also mean that the human being in the sense of being (Da-sein), whether healthy or sick, is experienced, viewed, and treated in each particular case in the light of the projection of the human being as Da-sein. To let this being exist as Dasein in this or that condition is only possible if we abandon the projection [*Entwurf*] of the human being as a "rational animal," as a subject in the subject-object relationship, and as a self-producing animal (Marx). Only if the projection of human being as Da-sein is enacted and constantly sustained beforehand—only in the light of this projection can this being (the human being) be investigated [in a way that is] appropriate to Da-sein.

Just this most difficult task is demanded of the investigator, that is, to make the transition from the projection of the human being as a rational animal to [the projection of] the human being as Da-sein. Therefore, it is not the case at all that the theme the doctor investigates could be "an extremely simple one" (p. 250). The letting-be of this being (the human being) in light of Da-sein is extremely difficult, unfamiliar, and must always be examined anew by contemporary scientists, but also by the one who has already gained familiarity with the projection of Da-sein. The "letting be," that is, accepting a being as it shows itself, becomes an appropriate letting-be only when this being, the Da-sein, stands constantly in view beforehand. [This can only happen] when the investigator has experienced and continues to experience himself as Da-sein, as ek-sisting, and when all human reality is determined *from there*. The elimination and avoidance of inappropriate representations about this being, the human being, is only possible when the practice of experiencing being human as Da-sein has been successful and when it is illuminating any investigation p. 281 of the healthy or sick human being in advance.

The immediate letting-be [*Seinlassen*] of beings is possible only then, and as long as, it is mediated each time beforehand, that is, made possible and granted by the enactment and the reenactment of the projection of being human in the sense of Da-sein. But how difficult this is has been demonstrated by decades of misinterpreting being-in-the-world as an [ontic] occurrence of the human being in the midst of other beings as a whole, of the "world."

The appearances, which showed themselves in the previously mentioned letting-be, are those of the human being in this or that condition, but they are not "phenomena" in the sense of phenomenology as ontology. These "phenomena" (cf. *Foundations*) provide the light by which we can glimpse the existing human being as Da-sein in the first place, and then guided by this glimpse we can describe the respective appearances. The method of investigation "appropriate to Da-sein" is not phenomenological in itself but is dependent upon and guided by phenomenology in the sense of the hermeneutics [interpretation] of Dasein [*Hermeneutik des Daseins*].*

---

*See Heidegger, *Being and Time*, p. 62.—TRANSLATORS

Engaging oneself [*Sicheinlassen*] with the letting-be of the existing human being in the sense of Da-sein already presupposes the acceptance [*Hinnehmen*] of the *being* as Da-sein, which was unveiled in the ontological-phenomenological projection.

The ontological (genuine) phenomena cannot be "seen" immediately in the same way as ontic appearances can. These too—color, weight, and so forth—are ontologically determined beforehand as "property." Color is a quality. Yet, this is neither colored, nor heavy, nor thick, nor long. It [quality] is not an ontic determination, but an ontological one.

The letting-*be* [*Sein-lassen*] of beings in their particular being so and so [*So-und-So-Sein*] is fundamentally different from letting-be, that is, from allowing being as such [*Sein als solches*], letting it be shown from a line of sight [*Blickrichtung*] in which the particular being shows itself unthematically as being granted in its being from what is explicitly seen ontologically.

p. 282   The table's *being-what* [*Wassein;* Latin: *essentia*] is an ontological determination in the same sense as its existence [*existentia*]. Of course, the relationship between both [being-what and existence] and their origin has not been clarified for the last two and a half millennia because they have never been asked about sufficiently [*erfragen*].*

Freud's basic approach [genetic-causal explanation] is far from [providing] a phenomenological direction. It specifically neglects to determine the human being's character of being [*Seinscharakter*], [the character] of the human being, who radically articulates his being human with language.

Were there even a trace of a phenomenological-ontological determination present in Freud's basic approach, then it would have prevented him from the aberration of his "theory."†

---

* Concerning the traditional metaphysical distinction between essence (being-what) and existence (being present-at-hand), see Heidegger, *Being and Time,* pp. 67–68. See also Heidegger, *Basic Problems of Phenomenology,* pp. 77 ff., 99 ff., and *Contributions to Philosophy,* pp. 191–92.—TRANSLATORS

† See Boss, *Existential Foundations,* p. 196: "The phenomenon itself should take precedence over any investigation into origins. This holds not only in the particular area of psychoanalytic theory but in all medical thinking. It is the particular duty of the phenomenological orientation to clarify the essential meanings inherent in the object of investigation itself."—TRANSLATORS

March 18, 1969, Zollikon

p. 283

The basic character of being is presence [*Anwesenheit*]. The traditional meaning of presence is insufficient for a determination of the human being. A book lies beside the glass. How are two people, standing next to each other, related to each other? Why can the glass not have a relationship to the book and to the table beneath it? Because it cannot receive-perceive the table and the book *as* table and *as* book.

"To be-in-the-open" [*im Offenen sein*], as the glass is in the open, is absolutely different from my being-open [*Offen-sein*] to the glass, from the way and manner in which the glass is manifest [*offenbar*] to me. The glass is open to me in such a way that it is in space for being grasped by my action. Is the human being in space the same way as the glass?

In *Being and Time*, being-*open* (*Da*-sein) means *being*-open (Da-*sein*).* The "Da" [of Da-sein] is determined here as "the open." This openness has the character of space. Spatiality belongs to the clearing. It belongs to the open in which we sojourn as existing [human] beings and in such a manner that we are not expressly related to space as space at all.

Space and time belong together, but one does not know how. Spatiality and temporality both belong to the clearing [*Lichtung*]. Now, how is it with consciousness? To stand in the clearing, yet not standing like a pole, but rather to sojourn in the clearing and to be occupied with things.

The decisive question is the following: What is the relationship between this sojourning in the clearing of being (in which being is not noticed thematically) and what we understand as consciousness? Taken in a pure linguistic sense, the word "consciousness" speaks of knowledge, and knowledge means to have seen something, to have manifest something as something. *Bewissen* [con-sciousness] means someone is conscious, and this means that someone finds his way [*sich zurechtfinden*]. The term is as old as the word Da-sein and has been in use only since the eighteenth century. The difficulty in experiencing consciousness lies in the meaning this word received at the time of its origin. When does "consciousness" begin in philosophy? With Descartes. Each consciousness of something is simultaneously self-consciousness, whereby the self, which is conscious of an object, is not necessarily conscious of itself. The question is whether

p. 284

---

*See Lovitt, introduction to Heidegger, *The Question concerning Technology*, p. xxxv, n. 2. See also M. Inwood, *A Heidegger Dictionary*, pp. 42–44.—TRANSLATORS

this "finding one's way" amidst things present-at-hand, whether this consciousness is the presupposition for Da-sein, or whether Da-sein, that is, the sojourning in the open, provides the possibility for comportment in the first place, in the sense of "finding one's way," thus, of consciousness. Obviously, the second is the case. Let us return once more to the word *bewisst*. It means to find one's way, but where? In an environment, amidst things. At the same time, it means that finding one's way is relatedness to what is given as objects. Then in the eighteenth century, the words "conscious" and "consciousness" acquired the theoretical meaning of the relationship to objects, which can be experienced. For Kant: [Relationship] to nature as the realm, which can be experienced by the senses. Then it went still one step further. Natural science took this so-called empirical consciousness, this finding one's way, as the possibility for the calculability of physical processes.

Kant also speaks of pure consciousness. This is the kind of knowledge no longer referring to sensory, perceptible, empirical objects, but to what makes possible the experience of objects, that is, their objectivity. The objectivity of the objects—the being of beings—is oriented toward consciousness. This is called Idealism. It lasted up to, and includes, Husserl. Modern philosophy is Idealism.

Thus, the title "consciousness" has become a basic conception of modern philosophy. Husserl's phenomenology belongs to it too. It is a description of consciousness. *Intentionality* is the only new thing Husserl contributed. And in a sense, Husserl's teacher Brentano had seen intentionality.

p. 285 Intentionality means: Each consciousness is consciousness of something. It is directed toward something. One does not have representations, but one represents. To represent means to make present. "Re" means back upon me. *Repraesentatio* is what I present back to me, for me, whereby I do not expressly represent myself [as an object]. Therein lies the possibility that this "re" (i.e., to present back toward me) becomes explicitly thematic. [It is] the relationship to myself, who is then determined as the one who represents [*Vorstellender*]. Then every consciousness is self-consciousness. There is no consciousness without self-consciousness whereby the self does not have to become explicitly thematic. This is the general structure of representation, or in Husserl's sense, the consciousness of something. Even if I *imagine* a golden mountain, not existing at all, I still must do this "imagining" myself. I can encounter the glass in front of me [in its immediacy].

July 14, 1969, Zollikon

p. 286

If Binswanger believes that what he calls the "cancer of psychiatry," by which he means the subject-object split, can be overcome by his idea of letting subjectivity "transcend" from out of itself to the things of the external world, then, first of all, he has not read my essay *The Essence of Reasons* or he has entirely misunderstood the *transcendence* mentioned there. Second, he does not tell how such a transcending in the above-mentioned sense could occur, that is, how a subjectivity, primarily represented as immanence, could ever get even the faintest idea of an external world. For being-in-the-world is never a property of a subjectivity no matter how it is represented, but from the beginning it is the human being's way of existing.*

Binswanger shows this complete misunderstanding of my thinking in the most striking way in his huge book *Grundformen und Erkentnis menschlichen Daseins* [Fundamental forms and knowledge of human Dasein]. In it, he believes it is necessary to supplement *Being and Time*'s care [*Sorge*] and solicitude [*Fürsorge*] with a "dual mode of being" and with "being-beyond-the-world." With this, he merely shows that he misunderstands the fundamental *existentiale* called "care" as an ontic [psychological] way of behaving in the sense of a particular human being's melancholy or concernful-solicitous behavior. Yet as a basic, existential constitution of the Da-sein of the human being in the sense of *Being and Time, care* is nothing more and nothing less than the name for the whole, unfolding essence of Da-sein, insofar as Da-sein is always already dependent on something showing itself to it [being] and insofar as it is always absorbed from the start in whatever specific relationship to it [to what shows itself].†
Therefore, all the ontic ways of comportment of those who love, of those

---

* A similar gap between a "subject" (with its "ideas": Descartes, Locke) and an external world of "objects" is widely presupposed in contemporary analytic Philosophy of Mind. Only a phenomenology of the mind, in the sense of human Da-sein as the original being-in-the-world, overcomes this pseudo-problem. G. McCulloch, *The Mind and Its World* (London: Routledge, 1995), p. 149, in quoting Heidegger in this context, states the following: "As soon as the subject turns to the phenomenology of the mind, contemporary analytical philosophers are apt to become reticent. Some will affect not to know what the issue is. Many will only talk here, if at all, about bangs and flashes, 'qualia,' 'raw feels,' sensations. This goes along with the unquestioned assumption that the phenomenology of the mind has to do with how (if at all) my mind appears to me, your mind appears to you and so on. The roots of this tendency, of course, are deep in the Cartesian tradition."—TRANSLATORS

† See Heidegger, *Being and Time*, sec. 39.—TRANSLATORS

who hate, and of the objectively oriented natural scientist as well are grounded equiprimordially in *being-in-the-world* as *care*. If one does not confuse ontological insights with ontic matters as Binswanger did, then there is likewise no need to speak about a "being-beyond-the-world." In the sense of the analytic of Dasein in *Being and Time*, "world" even permits within its domain what lies beyond Binswanger's world to also become manifest. Thus, the *holding sway of the world* [*Welten*], [when] understood correctly in connection with human existing as described, for instance, in *The Essence of Reasons*, not only does not require "being-beyond-the-world" but does not allow such a thing to become possible at all.

p. 287

p. 288 March 2, 1972, Freiburg-Zähringen[1]

When one wakes up, one cannot say that he then finds himself in the same world [as in dreaming], but rather the other way around: Waking up consists precisely in [the fact] that one encounters the world as the same one he is accustomed to in being awake. The waking world is characterized by the identical enduring [*identisch Sich-durchhalten*] of things, of other human beings, and of how they move about in it. Awakening means nothing else than *waking up into* the same world. In this, it is essential that the sameness [*Selbigkeit*] stays the same through our everyday being accustomed [to this world].

While dreaming, one does not encounter the same [*dasselbe*], but in the best case—in the so-called stereotypical dreams—[one encounters] what is alike [*das Gleiche*].*

In waking, it is the moment of coming back [to the same world]. In a stereotypical dream, one comes back to particular situations. It is a repetition of what is [always] alike, but not the same [which unfolds in Da-sein's existence].

Awakening is coming back into the same world, the sameness of which is determined by the everyday historicity of Da-sein [*Geschichtlichkeit*]. In

---

*Here "the same" (*dasselbe, das Selbe*), sometimes translated as "the self-same" (see Heidegger, *Being and Time*, p. 150), refers to the historical being-in-the-world and to the existential temporalizing of Dasein's ek-sisting, self-subsisting "Self" (*Being and Time*, p. 351). In contrast, "the alike" (*das Gleiche*) refers to the repetitive, stereotypical identity of the dreamworld. See *ZS* 10, 30, concerning the later Heidegger's understanding of the belonging-together of identity and difference. See also Boss, *Existential Foundations*, pp. 45–46, and "*Es träumte mir vergangene Nacht . . . ,*" *Auflage: Mit einem Vorwort von Marianne Boss* (Bern: Verlag Huber, 1991), pp. 201–44; ZS 308.—TRANSLATORS

any case, it does not belong to the essence of dreaming "to dream" in the same world as it belongs to the essence of waking up, to wake up into the same world.

There are dreams of things, houses, and regions one knows only from dreaming and in which the "aha-experience" of encountering them again is experienced explicitly. One can also dream that one awakens in one's own bed and gets up as one usually does after awakening.

A comparison between waking and dreaming is basically not possible as a comparison between objects because the same person awakens from dreaming and then endures as the same. Of course, one can notice differences between waking and dreaming. The sameness is based in being awake because having-dreamt is a matter of being awake. If philosophers say that one awakens to what is alike [*Gleiche*], then this is limited to the content [of the dream]. It is important that it is also always *my* dreaming. The different way of being in dreaming and in waking belongs to the continuity of the historicity of the particular human being. It is *not* possible to compare the state of dreaming and the state of being awake as, for instance, one can compare a fox with an eagle. Waking and dreaming are not different objective realms, the difference between which could be recorded by the characteristics of their content [*inhaltliche Merkmale*]. This is precisely because the basis, what endures, the historicity, or better yet, everyday historicity is the dimension in which the difference between a dreaming being-in-the-world and a waking being-in-the-world usually occurs. The dream world cannot be separated as an object domain unto itself, but rather the dream world belongs in a certain way to the continuity of being-in-the-world. It is likewise a being-in-the-world. p. 289

The moment of recognition belongs to awakening, even if it is not an explicit act of recognition but a simple coming back. Precisely because stereotypical dreams recur only as long as the problem contained in them is not resolved and is not completely worked out in the waking state, these dreams are not a return to the same [*das Selbe*], not a taking up anew, and not a continuing on as in the waking state, but a return to the alike [*das Gleiche*].

If it were the same, then this matter, for instance, my *Abitur* examination, would be further unfolded in the dream. While dreaming, the matter would unfold forward or backward in some way or come to a close. But in stereotypical dreaming, this matter is not further unfolded but merely dreamt again. If it were the same, a difference [*Verschiedenheit*] would have to occur in which the matter is unfolding.

For instance—as in your patient's dream—if a woman, dressed in red, is at first dead and then finally in later dreams is dancing, then this development does not occur within dreaming itself. It does not belong p. 290

to the content of the dreamworld itself that this story develops in such and such a way, so that the earlier stages are remembered or their further development is expected in dreaming itself. This proves that in every case of re-dreaming a dream there is no return to the same world as there is in waking.

Each dream is a being-in-the-world and can have a particular history in itself (as for instance, in the mountain-climber dream), but the dreamer, as it were, is not in control of the possibility of returning to the same matter in his dream world. This means that he is indeed dreaming what is alike [*das Gleiche*], but he does not develop it any further.

In order to see the specific [historical] continuity of dreams, in spite of all their likeness, the continuity of waking being-in-the-world is required. In spite of all the dream's alikeness [*Gleichheit*], it is never the dreaming of this particular, like dream, which would have a historical continuity in itself.

That questions regarding a criterion are asked insufficiently is a consequence of failing to take into consideration the fact that one cannot demarcate the realms of waking and dreaming as one can demarcate objects. Rather, the dreamworlds *belong to waking life.*

The difference between waking up from a dream state and from a non-dream state: If one did not have [an innate] tendency to find one's way back to the waking world, then there would be no problems in not finding one's way back from a dream to the waking world.

The decisive point is that one continues and develops the earlier dream in a later dream by *remembering,* that one resumes the earlier one, that one does not only actually repeat the same activity, and that a dreaming history does not exist in addition to the waking, historical unfolding of Da-sein.

p. 291   In conclusion, the question of the method of comparison: If things stand this way with the criterion of comparison, on what basis does one then speak about dreams at all? That one always only speaks about them [dreams] in waking and does not speak about waking in dreams indicates that *dreaming* belongs to waking. Nevertheless, this is only possible because of the continuity of the waking Da-sein. Indeed, otherwise I could not compare dreams with each other. Therefore, one may not take waking as self-evident but must take waking as the essential presupposition for being able to talk about dreams at all and to interpret them. In being able to look at dreams, a very specific relationship between dreaming and waking is already implied. Corresponding to the characterization of the particular way of being-awake, the possibilities for characterizing dreams themselves within the waking world are modified. In dreams there is no communication about dreams among dreamers.

Dear Dr. Boss, please permit me to make a great leap away from dreaming since night is already approaching. I would like to bequeath you a question which concerns me very much. How does the thing [*Ding*] belong to the disclosive appropriating Event [*Ereignis*] if the thing as such is seen in its new determination? The question is meant as a lure for you. I will probably not finish it anymore.

March 3, 1972, Freiburg-Zähringen   p. 292

MEDARD BOSS: The earlier seminars of 1965 about the *body* and the *psyche* were rather unsatisfactory for the participants. They want to be better oriented about where their limitation lies if they are always to understand the relationship between the bodily and the psychic only as simultaneous. Otherwise, it is clear to everyone that there cannot be any talk of causality. No one believes any longer that psychological perception—for instance, [perceiving] a butterfly in its significance as a butterfly—can be positively determined by the electric nerve impulses in the back of the head. Other [people] took up the reproach of Jean-Paul Sartre, who wondered why you only wrote six lines about the body in the whole of *Being and Time*.

MARTIN HEIDEGGER: I can only counter Sartre's reproach by stating that the bodily [*das Leibliche*] is the most difficult [to understand] and that I was unable to say more at that time.

Nevertheless, from the Da-seinanalytic perspective, it remains decisive that in all experience of the bodily one must always start with the basic constitution of human existing, that is, from being-human as Da-sein—as existing, in the transitive sense, of a domain of standing-open-toward-the-world; therefore, from this standing-open, in the light of this standing-open, the significant features of what is encountered address the human being. Because of the human being's basic constitution, Dasein is always already related to something unveiling itself to him. In his essential receptive-perceptive relatedness to what addresses him from his world-openness, the human being is also already called upon to respond to it by his comportment. This means that he must respond in such a way that he takes what he encounters into his care and that he aids it in unfolding its own essence as far as possible.

Yet, the human being would not be able [to do this] if he consisted only of a "spiritual" receiving-perceiving [*geistiges Vernehmen*] and if he did not also have a bodily nature. How else could it be pos-   p. 293

sible to grasp, to form, and to transform other animate or inanimate "material" things which are encountered?

Then everything we call our bodiliness, down to the last muscle fiber and down to the most hidden molecule of hormones, belongs essentially to existing. Thus, it is basically *not* inanimate matter but a domain of that nonobjectifiable, optically invisible capacity to receive-perceive the significance of what it encounters, which constitutes the whole Da-sein. This bodily [nature] develops in such a way that it can be used in dealing with the inanimate and animate "material things" which are encountered. Yet, in contrast to a tool, the bodily spheres of existing are not set free [*entlassen*] from being-human. They cannot be cared for in a toolbox. Rather, they remain in the sway of being human, held in it, and belonging to it so long as the human being lives. Of course, in dying this bodily domain changes its way of being into that of an inanimate thing, into the substance of a corpse, which drops out [*herausfallen*] from existence.

Of course, during its lifetime the bodily [nature] of Da-sein already admits to being seen as a material, inanimate object and as a kind of complicated machine. Of course, for someone who sees it this way, the essential, unfolding character of bodily [nature] has already disappeared from view forever. Perplexed helplessness [*Ratlosigkeit*] regarding all essential phenomena of the bodily [nature] is the result of such an inadequate view.

Therefore, regarding the whole bodiliness, we must repeat what we have mentioned before about seeing and our bodily eyes: We are not able to "see" because we have eyes; rather, we can only have eyes because, according to our basic nature, we are beings who can see. Thus, we would not be bodily [*leiblich*] in the way we are unless our *being-in-the-world* always already fundamentally consisted of a receptive/perceptive relatedness to something which addresses us from out of the openness of our world, from out of that openness as which we exist. Thereby, in this address, we are always already directed toward things disclosing themselves to us. It is only because of our Da-sein's essential *direction* [*Ausrichtung*]* that we are able to distinguish between in front of and behind, above and below, left and right. It is due to the same directedness [*Ausgerichtetsein*] toward something addressing us that we can have a body at all, better: To be of a bodily nature. We are not first of a bodily nature and then from it have what is in front and behind, and so forth. Only one must not confuse our existentiell bodily being [*existenzielles Leiblichsein*] with

p. 294

---

*See Heidegger, *Being and Time*, pp. 135, 143.—TRANSLATORS

the corporeality [*Körperhaftigkeit*] of an inanimate, merely present-at-hand object.

MB: I am afraid that my scientifically trained colleagues will only laugh at such a view. After all, such [a view] presupposes that something invisible, a "pure" spiritual reality which can be neither weighed nor measured—as is the case with human potentialities for comportment as such—could transform itself into something material which could be grasped and measured as bodily organs are.

MH: Is it not precisely the natural scientist who should no longer be unfamiliar with how a nonmaterial, optically invisible potentiality of comportment can be transformed into a "bodily-material" [*Leiblich-Materielles*] reality? In the meantime, did you not learn from Einstein that *energy* and *matter* can be completely transformed into each other, that is, that therefore they are of the same nature? Yet Einstein could not teach us what energy and matter essentially are in themselves because these questions concerning something's essence are philosophical ones.

MB: Thus, no physicist can say what energy really is. Nowadays the term is simply applied anywhere where something changes, where something appears or disappears.

MH: A whole book could be written about the etymological development that this word, namely, ἐνεργεια, has undergone from antiquity until the present. Furthermore, this comparison with Einstein's formula $E = mc^2$ is a lame one. Neither Einstein's "mass" nor "the velocity of light" possesses a potentiality for seeing and receiving-perceiving characterizing the basic constitution of human Da-sein. In any case, one must by no means expect an understanding of the human being and his world from modern *systems theories* [*Systemtheorien*]. In their essence, they all remain bound to the principle of causality, and thus they go along with the objectification of everything that is. In this way they have already blocked forever the view of the human being's proper being-in-the-world.

p. 295

MB: By way of illustration, is it permissible to compare the "bodily" and "spiritual" spheres of human Da-sein with different physical states of one and the same kind of thing, for instance, [to compare] invisible vapor with visible, fluid water and with ice, which are all H_2O?

MH: Of course one could [do this], but one must not. Thereby, one would make the impermissible mistake of objectifying human Da-sein and of taking it as a mere thing and object present-at-hand. All possibilities for comparison stop here exactly because being-in-the-world, as which the human being exists, has a unique nature which cannot be derived from anything else.

MB: Apropos causality. Did I already tell you that I also heard about an Ajati doctrine in India? For over a few thousand years it has taught that the concept of causality has no value. For if there were really something like causality, then either the effect would already be contained in the cause, or one would have to be able to say when, where, and how occurs the transformation of the cause into the effect. Yet no one has succeeded in doing this.

p. 296 MH: No, I do not know anything about this Ajati doctrine yet. But the decisive point in our context is our insight into the immediate emergence of all of our so-called material, bodily nature from the physically intangible capacities for receiving-perceiving and for comporting oneself, in which our Da-sein in its unfolding essence consists. This insight allows us to grasp easily how immediately and how limitlessly all bodily nature belongs to the [human] way of existing and how it is, and remains, in this mode of *being* [*Seinsart*]. Therefore, this insight may also be called the fundamental philosophy of all psychosomatic medicine.

MB: Therefore, much could be gained for psychosomatic medicine if doctors learned to appropriate the experience that all bodily nature, down to the last nerve fiber, originates from, develops from, and remains contained in that unique characteristic, which cannot be derived from something else and which one must call the determination of the unfolding essence of human Da-sein. But this is precisely the totality of the nonmaterial, non-energylike capacities of understanding and comportment extending wide into the world and which fundamentally constitute Da-sein.

MH: Yes, I would also say it in precisely these words.

PART III

FROM THE LETTERS
TO MEDARD BOSS,
1947 – 1971

Martin Heidegger's Answer to Medard Boss regarding His Request for Assistance in Philosophical Reflection

Todtnauberg, August 3, 1947

Esteemed Dr. Boss:

I thank you for your friendly letter. Slow readers are more reliable than those who understand everything all at once.

The subjects touched upon in the article also exceed my capacity and force [my] thinking into ever new attempts to say what is essential [*das Wesentliche*] in a simple way for once. You know that the problems of psychopathology and psychotherapy regarding their principles interest me very much, although I lack the technical knowledge and command of the actual research. For this reason, I am very excited about your *habilitation* thesis.

. . .

If it were possible on some occasion to support my capacity for work with a *little* package of chocolate, I would be very grateful.

With friendly greetings,

Yours respectfully,
M. Heidegger

September 1, 1947, from Todtnauberg

Esteemed Colleague:

. . .

Whenever I receive something from you, my desire grows to get to know you in person and to discuss scientific-philosophical problems with you. Perhaps the occasion will arise for you to come to Freiburg for a lecture, where the medical society at the university has just now reestablished its lecture activities. . . .

Perhaps you know that [Professor] von Gebsattel, with whom I recently discussed many questions concerning the philosophical foundation of psychotherapy and anthropology, is director of a sanatorium in Badenweiler and at the same time is commissioned with lectures at the Beringer Clinic which have been very well received.

In many respects, it would be fruitful for all participants if the close vicinity to Switzerland could soon be expanded and opened up for an intellectual colloquium so that not only accidental and limited encounters are all there is.

. . .

December 15, 1947, from Freiburg im Breisgau

Esteemed Mr. Boss:

In the meantime your book has arrived. I think that I will be able to work through it to a certain extent before your next visit, which I am very much looking forward to. I will give a copy to Professor von Gebsattel. You know how difficult it is to get books. Therefore, with your permission, I would like to give the second copy as a gift to a physician acquaintance of mine who is interested in anthropological questions.

. . .

March 20, 1948, from Freiburg im Breisgau

Sometime I would also be pleased to hear how you have arranged your lecture courses. In view of your research, very much depends on whether and how the teacher establishes a dialogue with the students. Only in this way can one clearly verify whether and how each one of them can intuitively make-present [*Vergegenwärtigung*] and [directly] demonstrate [*Ausweisung*] to himself what he has heard.

p. 301

It is especially the case in psychiatry that the continuous encounter between the thinking of the natural scientist and that of the philosopher is very productive and exciting.

. . .

Since the import of books into the French zone is forbidden, the two copies of your books were returned to you again from the customs office here.

June 14, 1948, from Todtnauberg

. . .

Since I very definitely sense from the hints in your letters how resolutely you are advancing toward the core of my own attempted ways of thinking, I wish for the opportunity for a dialogue with ever increasing enthusiasm. Such a dialogue still continues to be the right way to follow the paths of thought in their most subtle distinctions and thereby to examine each other's view and thus to learn in a mutual way. Lectures can surely provide the impetus, perhaps even make one sense the atmosphere of thinking, but they very easily run into the danger of remaining a matter of mere display, especially in today's hustle and bustle [*Betrieb*]* in this field.

Real thinking cannot be learned from books. It also cannot be taught unless the teacher remains a learner well into old age.

Therefore, let us hope for a dialogue.

With cordial greetings,

Yours,
Martin Heidegger

December 22, 1948, from Freiburg im Breisgau

. . . I hope that a lecture can also be arranged for you here next year. Only now have the various scientific associations been reassembled so p. 302 that lectures can be conducted again. We have a well-informed circle of younger people here who are very interested in anthropological problems and in the position of anthropology in the whole of the sciences.

. . .

August 2, 1949, from Todtnauberg

Dear Mr. Boss:

. . . We think fondly again and again of the friendly and very auspicious visit from you. . . .

---

* *Betrieb* is usually translated as "ongoing activity" when it refers to science and research: see Heidegger, *The Question concerning Technology*, p. 124. We translate *Betrieb* in a broader context of busyness as "hustle and bustle."—TRANSLATORS

I wish very much that an occasion for a conversation will come again soon. In this way, we will be able to approach the subject matters more directly.

December 30, 1949, from Freiburg im Breisgau

Dear Mr. Boss:

I thank you very much for your letter and, at the same time, on behalf of my wife, for the nice invitation to your little house in the mountains. But meanwhile there is still the border. Yet we hope very much that in the coming year such a beautiful encounter may happen again either here or there, as was the first one, which unfortunately was only too short. . . .

. . .

In cordial friendship,

Yours,
Martin Heidegger

p. 303 ## November 25, 1950, from Freiburg im Breisgau[1]

. . . In addition to the pure medical decision, the question of communication (the way and manner, the right moment, the hearer and the reader) is of the greatest importance here and in all essential matters. [It is] something which all of us people of today still reflect upon too little and, therefore, do not have an adequate view [*übersehen*] of in all respects.

Socrates knew about that better than anyone else up to the present. But we hardly know anything of what he knew. And that is no accident. For the question of communication cannot be solved and organized in a schematic way. . . . I also believe that a philosophical discussion with Mitscherlich* would be totally fruitless. He did not understand anything about my summary at all. One can notice the aim of the whole report and get upset, if that were worthwhile. Since the publication of

---

*W. Mitscherlich was a famous German sociologist. —TRANSLATORS

Being and Time [in] 1927, I have had to endure so much foolishness and superficiality that I am hardened in this respect. Nevertheless, occasionally we can again learn for ourselves how difficult it has become to say something in public today.

. . .

During our time together viewing the Rhine River, I had to think time and again about Hölderlin's hymn "The Rhine," which I tried to interpret in 1934–35 in a long lecture series. Read this powerful poetry sometime in a quiet hour.*

A mysterious repose radiates from it, a destiny, a stillness, which we must reach in order to endure.

. . .

My "exercises in reading" are still very preliminary. My most p. 304 important observation is that the young people apparently lack any sense and any preparation for this methodical way of thinking. Opinions, incidental bits of information, and arbitrary ideas are expressed and played off against each other. Perhaps there will be an occasion someday for you to participate in such an hour. . . .

December 15, 1950, from Freiburg im Breisgau

. . .

Today I come with a request for advice. A few days ago I received an invitation from the students of the University of Zurich to give a lecture there in February. I am inclined to do it, but I am completely in the dark about what I should speak about. The question of communication appears again. I have an even less sufficient idea about the students' condition there than about the ones here. I have no desire to hold a lecture just for display and only for publicity.

On the other hand, there is the possibility of initiating something here or there, if only indirectly. For just this reason a suitable theme must be chosen.

---

*See Heidegger, *The Question concerning Technology*, p. 16, concerning the difference between the present Rhine River, which is dammed by a hydroelectric power plant, and the "Rhine" and its old wooden bridge, which was described in Hölderlin's hymn. Also see M. Heidegger, *Hölderlin's Hymnen "Germanien" und "Der Rhein"* (Winter Semester 1934–35), ed. Susanne Ziegler, vol. 39 of *GA* (Frankfurt am Main: Klostermann, 1980).—TRANSLATORS

Perhaps you could offer a suggestion and could give me a hint in a few words.

. . .

March 7, 1951, from Freiburg im Breisgau

If you want to invite friends sometime, I would be delighted to talk with them. On the whole, [I] would prefer to be there privately and incognito, as far as that is still possible at all for someone like me with a public voracious for news.

. . .

Today I received a very interesting letter from Professor Staiger[*] from New York, where he is giving lectures.

p. 305   Schultz-Henke[†] attended some of my lectures during my first semesters as a *dozent* [assistant professor] in Freiburg when the question of being had already been posed but the analytic of Da-sein was still in its infancy.

. . .

January 26, 1952, from Freiburg im Breisgau

I still owe you my heartfelt thanks for your friendly New Year's letter; these lines should express them. Even if we were not sharing the same hours for our lectures, I would still think of you often, of your work, and of your nice family, and together with my wife would be thankful for your friendship. Hopefully, you were in a state of creative alertness for the "dreams" during the vacations. I always think that the work could be of great and fundamental importance and could turn all therapy away from "psychology." I am anxious to hear about the progress of your work, but also about the study group with the younger doctors.

. . .

---

[*] E. Staiger, German professor of Literature. See the exchange of letters between Heidegger and Staiger in M. Heidegger, *Aus der Erfahrung des Denkens (1910–1976)*, vol. 13 of *GA* (1983), pp. 93–109.—TRANSLATORS

[†] Schultz-Henke was a famous German psychiatrist.—TRANSLATORS

My lecture "What Is Called Thinking?"[*] is increasing in attendance. I decided to continue it in the summer semester and to prepare it for print during the summer vacations. Therefore, I am already taking great pains to make the procedure clear and to pay attention to its precise formulation. The simpler things are, the more trouble it causes. In view of these plans for summer, I would like to entirely concentrate on this task from the middle of April on. Therefore, I also will not hold any seminars during the summer semester.

How does it stand now with the Italian journey and the dates? Would the second half of March still be too early? And what do you think about the route? My wife and I do not know anything about Florence and Tuscany yet. To travel about *too much* is also not relaxing. . . .

. . .

March 15, 1952, from Freiburg im Breisgau   p. 306

. . . The question of "behavior" is very far-reaching. I have examined the manuscripts several times regarding that point and discovered that I really should examine the entire work once again.

But that would require renewed reflections on your part, which would finally end up with the difficult question of "Animal and Man." Once again, the task of this work is not to clarify this question. After long consideration, I found a way out which is not an escape but rather corresponds only to what is worth questioning in a sufficiently adequate determination of the unfolding essence of the human being, animal, plant, and rock. We must still consider whether my remarks, which I try to sketch in the following, ought to be added in the text in an appropriate place as a footnote or in the introduction. At the moment, I can hardly decide this matter because the whole work regarding the subject matter and the linguistic usage of "behavior" is not sufficiently clear in my mind. Roughly speaking, it concerns the following point: The inquiry speaks about the behavior of both the human being and animals without specifically accentuating or even attempting to grasp sufficiently the essential differences existing here.

In order to refute the theory of projection, among other things, as not corresponding to the phenomenological data, it is already

---

[*] See M. Heidegger, *Was heisst Denken?* [*What Is Called Thinking?* trans. J. T. Wilde and W. Kluback (New Haven, Conn.: College and University Press, 1968)].—TRANSLATORS

sufficient to notice that an animal merely *is* insofar as it moves within an environment [*Umwelt*] open to it in some way and is guided by this environment which itself remains circumscribed by the nature of the animal. The animal's relationship to this environment, which is never addressed [by the animal itself], shows a certain correspondence to the human being's ek-sistent relationship toward the world. Thus, in a certain way the human being in his ek-sistent Da-sein can immediately participate in and live-with the animal's environmental relationship without ever coming to a congruence [*decken*] between the human being's being-with and the animal, let alone the other way around. Linguistic usage, according to which one speaks of human and animal "behavior" indiscriminately, does not take into account the unfathomable, essential difference between the relationship to a "world" [*Weltbezug*] and to an "environment" [*Umgebungsbezug*]. According to its own proper and essential relationship to the environment, the animal's situation makes it possible for us to enter into this relationship, to go along with it, and, as it were, to tarry with it. But it is not enough to consider only that. It remains far more essential to see that an animal (as opposed to a rock) shows itself to us only then *as* an animal insofar we humans as ek-sistent have *engaged in advance in* [*eingelassen*] the relationship to the environment proper to the animal. It does not matter thereby that the immediate apprehension of the environment proper to the animal and, thus, also the genuine apprehension of the animal's relationship to the environment remain inaccessible to our knowledge. The strangeness of the unfolding essence of animals is concealed in this inaccessibility (or something like that).*

p. 307

April 14, 1952, from Freiburg im Breisgau

. . .

On Monday before noon after our return, Mr. Beaufret was already here from Paris. This [circumstance] and the mail and preparation for the semester have delayed my greeting to you. . . .

Thanks to your concern for us, our Italian journey was so beautiful, harmonious, and pleasing for us that it will bear only the best fruit and will still be felt long afterward.

---

*See Heidegger, *Fundamental Concepts of Metaphysics*, secs. 45–63. —TRANSLATORS

August 2, 1952, from Todtnauberg

. . .

The move here delayed my answer to your warm and friendly letter. The added section is clear and correct (introduction to the book by Medard Boss, *Der Traum und seine Auslegung* [1953]).* In p. 308 the final paragraph, an addendum would be suitable. It would simply sharpen what you already state and what pervades the whole work: not to give a causal explanation and derivation of the dreams, but to let the dreams themselves tell their own stories by what they say and reveal in their orientation toward the world. Dreams are not symptoms and consequences of something lying hidden behind [them], but they themselves are in what they show and *only* this. Only with *this* does their emerging essence [*Wesen*] become worthy of questioning.

My lecture came to a good close. I still have to add a very difficult passage which I omitted. Then I will proceed with the other thing. Hopefully, the start will be successful. Last night the examination dream [*Abituriententraum*] promptly reappeared.[2]

February 10, 1953, from Freiburg im Breisgau

. . .

Ruffin arrived a while ago, and with a look of desperation he asked me to be sure to visit him while Binswanger is there. The latter was armed with a gigantic manuscript about "eccentricity" [*Verschrobenheit*].

This thing, the treatise about "eccentricity" has been cooked up jointly (with Szilasi) in Brissago. Then, when I stated my critique and clearly said, among other things, that the analysis strikes me as very eccentric, Szilasi agreed with me. Binswanger became embarrassed because he had to recognize that what I objected to stems from Szilasi himself.

I avoided all sharp critique because it was not worthwhile to touch p. 309 upon the more essential points.

---

*Translated by A. J. Pomerans as *The Analysis of Dreams* (New York: Philosophical Press, 1958). The second edition of *Der Traum und seine Auslegung* (Munich: Kindler Verlag, 1974) [trans. S. Conway (New York: Gardner Press, 1977)] was published under the new title: *"Es träumte mir vergangene Nacht, . . ." Sehübungen im Bereiche des Träumens und Beispiele für die praktische Anwendung eines neuen Traumverständnisses*, with a foreword by Marianne Boss (Bern: H. Huber, 1991).—TRANSLATORS

That this reciprocal flattery belongs to this business may explain a few things to you about why Szilasi is regarded as an important philosopher. But it is not worthwhile to occupy oneself with this busybodyness too long.

. . .

September 30, 1953, from Freiburg im Breisgau

Dear Friend:

I am thinking about your first letter, which already sealed our friendship from afar and from the unknown. And since then, it has been good to come closer and to have mutual encouragement get under way. Questions too, even stubborn ones, are encouraging.

Thus, my heartfelt wishes for your fiftieth birthday come from a joyful, thankful sentiment, animated with the hope that your chosen path will lead to penetrating questions and fruitful perspectives in your science.

. . .

My wife and I have been up at the hut until the day before yesterday. I could concentrate very well, and the problems of technology and causality became clearer during the transcription of a larger manuscript, which still lacks final form. . . .

. . .

Your answer to Szilasi is to the point. This sensitivity goes a little too far. If I had to answer each critical remark that way, I could fill a day's work with it.

. . .

In cordial friendship,

Yours,
Martin Heidegger

p. 310 ## October 28, 195[3], from Messkirch

. . .

You guessed correctly that I am kept very busy by the lecture in Munich ("The Question about Technology") and with an interrelated correspondence with Heisenberg. At the hut I wrote a wide-reaching sketch and thereby got deeply into the question of causality. But now the main burden is to stick to a simple line for a two-hour lecture which at the same time looks at our relationship to both nature and art and which, most of all, is not too difficult, too Heideggerian! As is always the case with such digging, many other lucrative things [come up], but do not belong to the theme. . . .

In January, the second half, I will give talks in Bern and Lucerne. Then we could stop over in Zurich for a few days, in case you want us there. I would also like to see the Marburg theologian Bultmann, who gives lectures in Zurich during the winter semester. We had a wonderful study group during our time together in Marburg. You will like him too.

Then I could speak about technology [*Technik*] in a small group with you in Zollikon. Perhaps it would be possible to invite a few younger people as well.

I often discover that only now have I come so far as to *begin* to think in the right way to a certain degree.

I greet you cordially dear friend and your dear wife,

Yours,
Martin Heidegger

December 19, 1953, from Freiburg im Breisgau

. . .

In the event that the lecture in Zurich does take place, this will not preclude our arranging a small gathering at your house. The living word and the discussions cannot be replaced by anything—except that as an individual one can scarcely satisfy all demands if some time is still to remain for concentrated work.

. . .

p. 311

Enclosure with the Letter of December 19, 1953, from Freiburg im Breisgau

Goethe: "The greatest would be: to comprehend that *all* facts are *already* theory." (*Maxims and Reflections*, no. 993)[3]

January 2, 1954, from Freiburg im Breisgau

. . .

So we have free time available from January 30 until February 2 for a discussion in your house, where I would like to read the section about causality.

. . . perhaps it would be better, . . . if you would invite some of the younger people to your house when the discussion takes place. . . .

The lecture does not exist yet, as little as does the contribution to the commemorative publication of the Konstanz Gymnasium—about *Heraclitus*, which should be submitted in February. So hardly any time remains for "concentrated work," as you call it, and for essential things during the next months. And finally, I will be sixty-five this year, and some day there will be an end to this so-called creativity, and yet I still have something to bring into language and into form.

. . .

Merely to serve as the editor of my own posthumous works is less stimulating. I am also too little bent on literary publicity and on the edition of *Collected Works* as to be able to consider such work already today as the last possibility [for me].

. . .

p. 312 February 11, 1954, from Freiburg im Breisgau

The preface[4] is correct as it is. . . . I believe it is worthwhile for you to put some effort into working out the fundamental issues for the lecture in Munich. Besides—one himself learns the most that way.

. . .

I am glad that the young generation can take something away from the evening gathering at your house. Such gatherings can never be replaced by mere writing and "reading" . . .

Beaufret wrote all of a sudden—he has not been well—presumably "emotionally." He is coming next Sunday for a few days. . . .

July 7, 1954, from Freiburg im Breisgau

. . .

I find the final lecture to be very good, not to mention dramatic. The concluding section, which brings up the "The Turning" [*Die Kehre*],[*] you must read very slowly and emphatically.

On the whole, it would still be good to cut the more run-on sentences and to keep them simpler. Hopefully, you will find time to write down

---

[*]See Heidegger, *Question concerning Technology*, pp. 36–49 ["The Turning"].
—TRANSLATORS

the whole once more. I have allowed myself to make a few external linguistic changes.

Binswanger was at my Konstanz lecture. . . . I believe something dawned on him during the lecture "What Is Called Thinking?" [*Was heisst Denken?*], which fascinated him.

. . .

September 10, 1954, from Todtnauberg

. . . Even though we just wished a journey for my brother, *we* would now like to delay it until next spring for a time when my wife can also see the p. 313 Alpine meadows in bloom for once.

We will certainly find occasions for a discussion about "thinking" in the coming months.

. . .

October 13, 1954, from Freiburg im Breisgau

. . . Your beautiful gift with the printed and handwritten dedication remains a great honor and joy to me.[5] And when I study it, it will become clear again how far thinking is still lagging behind its most urgent tasks. But everyone goes as far as he can, according to the best of his abilities.

Your sentiment of friendship is thereby a greater help than you think. Therefore, your and your family's birthday wishes have been a special joy to me. And I would like to especially thank you for following them up with an invigorating gift of chocolate.

January 3, 1955, from Freiburg im Breisgau

. . . , that I gladly accept your invitation to the Lenzerheide for the end of February/beginning of March. I have the feeling I am about to enter into a productive phase, different from the previous one, which will last longer. For this reason, I especially welcome the opportunity to work close to you at the Lenzerheide. . . . That will not exclude our conversations. . . .

Allemann sent me his essay, which I find excellent. In addition, he writes that he will soon turn again to Hölderlin entirely. . . . I have p. 314

now worked through his dissertation once more, and I admire this accomplishment more and more. . . .

The "Celebration of Peace" [*Friedensfeier*] is superhuman in purpose, but in the same year of its origin, Hölderlin also gave up the idea of reconciliation in order to find his way into the "Turn-about to the Fatherland" [*Vaterländische Umkehr*]. Father-land is land of the father, of the god of gods. Allemann was the first to see this turnabout clearly and already outlined it in its decisive characteristics. The newly found hymn is a surprising confirmation of his discovery, which gives an entirely new basis to my own partially erroneous attempts [at interpretation].*

. . .

February 8, 1955, from Freiburg im Breisgau

The book (*On the Sense of the Senses* [Vom Sinn der Sinne]) by E. Straus with its critique of Descartes, mentioned by Bally, is such an obvious imitation of *Being and Time* that Binswanger cannot get around it as well in his review of it (*Schweizer Archiv für Neuro-Psychologie*, vol. 38 [1936], p. 1). How little Bally reflects upon [Viktor von] Weizsäcker's position is shown in the fact that Bally does not see that Weizsäcker's agreement with Sartre is already sufficient to prove that Weizsäcker did not get beyond subjectivity. . . .

Here at home the slogan is now "Anti-Heidegger," which is the most fashionable thing on all sides. The "young generation," which probably cannot read a single chapter of Aristotle, let alone think it through, is now writing about the "nonsense [*Unfug*] of being."

p. 315 ## June 30, 1955, from Messkirch

Dear Friend:

During the past weeks I have been entirely buried in work. Renewed thoughtful attention to language and to the questions posed once more about the "In-itself" [*An-sich*] of objectivity and science have brought me

---

* M. Heidegger, *Erläuterungen zu Hölderlins Dichtung*, vol. 4 of *GA*, ed. F. W. von Herrmann (1982), "Hölderlin and the Essence of Poetry," trans. D. Scott, *Existence and Being*, ed. W. Brock (Chicago: H. Regnery, 1949), pp. 270–91.—TRANSLATORS

back in their own way to the question of "grounding" [*Begründung*] and of the "ground" [*Grund*], in which the problem of causality also has its root. The manuscripts I have here came to my aid in this. Some things in them proved to be outdated; but otherwise there is a mountain [of manuscripts] here, which surely must remain "posthumous works." . . .

I have often thought of you and your family over there. But your fear that our friendship could be spoiled somehow by the "travel problem" in spring is completely unfounded. If such a thing could happen, our friendship would not have grown in the right soil from the beginning.

It was a sincere joy to me that your presentations in Paris were a genuine hit. . . . But prior to your journey to India, we must by all means still have ample time to see and to talk to each other.

We will be at the hut from the middle of July until the end of August. Then I have to go to France, namely, to Cerisy, a castle in Normandy where the meetings in Pontigny, founded before the First World War, will be reestablished. My wife and I have been invited there for a week, and *before* that we would like to be in Paris and its surroundings at the end of August. I imagined that the whole thing would be very "private"—but now the whole of France already seems to know about it. They are already reporting the plan to Germany so that our people from Freiburg and from other places also want to be present in France with us. To be someone with a famous name is a gruesome thing. Even the Foreign Institute in Stuttgart has sought me out *here* and has sent a Japanese person, who invited me to Japan for several months during next year.

When I am by myself daily or with my brother, who is not in great p. 316 shape—he is *too* isolated here and too overworked by the bank to initiate something on his own—when we were walking along the country road or through the woods, the business of the world seemed like an insane asylum.[*] My plans are still uncertain for fall. Much depends on how I get the discussion about language on the right track. The issue becomes darker by the day, and at the same time, more exciting. Today I am amazed that years ago I dared to give the lecture on language. The greatest omission belongs to the fact that the possibility for a *sufficient* discussion about the East Asian languages is *lacking*. . . .

I greet you in cordial friendship,

Yours,
Martin Heidegger

---

[*]Heidegger's brother Fritz Heidegger was an employee of the Volksbank in Heidegger's native Messkirch.—TRANSLATORS

November 17, 1955, from Freiburg im Breisgau

By no means should it happen that you travel to India without our having seen and talked to each other once again. . . . Therefore, I suggest that you already come to the lecture next Friday on November 25.

I am still waiting for important protocols of some sessions from the tardy French. I have the impression that the thinking over there is still very far removed from my paths [of thinking]. But at least they have finally become aware of it.

July 16, 1956, from Messkirch

Dear Friend:

I thank you for your letter reporting your auspicious return home [from India]. For the past three weeks I have been buried in work here—essentially reaping the fruit from the winter lectures about the principle of reason [*Der Satz vom Grund*]. Of course, I will not be finished with it. But now I see a few things more clearly; and I reviewed the notes from the Lenzerheide on this occasion. This preface about me should merely indicate that in the meantime I can listen more attentively to what you will be able to say about [your] great experiences [in the Far East]. For that, the right peace [and quiet] would be necessary. . . .

. . .

p. 317

September 29, 1956, from Todtnauberg ("The Hut")

My wife and I would still like to see the Cézanne exhibit in Zurich; on the other hand, I would still like to take advantage of the working days up here. Now Dr. Petzet* believes that the last day, Sunday, October 7, is very unsuitable and that we should be in Zurich Saturday before noon at the latest, which is somewhat unsuitable for us. My wife comes back on

---

*See H. W. Petzet, *Encounters and Dialogues with Martin Heidegger, 1929–1996*, trans. P. Emad and K. Maly (Chicago: University of Chicago Press, 1993), p. 140 f.
—TRANSLATORS

the same day of the visit to the exhibit; then we plan [to take] the trip to Hermann in Bonn. I myself would very much like to stay one more day with you in Zollikon.

With the most cordial greetings, so long,

Yours,
Martin Heidegger

April 24, 1957, from Freiburg im Breisgau

. . .
. . . My lectures for the summer semester worry me quite a bit; the simpler things become, the more difficult they are to say.
. . .

October 19, 1959, from Todtnauberg

p. 318

. . .
. . . My plans are now firm that I will come to Zurich for a few days on November 2 and that we will continue our discussion at Burghölzli at the same time. I also thank you for the contribution to the commemorative publication [Festschrift], which I read first. It seems to me that it must make one especially pensive because it interweaves [your] personal way [of thinking] and thoughtful attention to objective matters.

On the whole, I hope to receive much stimulation and inspiration from the commemorative publication for the now approaching tranquil time for the completion [of my life's work], inasmuch as such a word is ever permitted for my being "on the way" [*unterwegs*].
. . .

November 9, 1959, from Freiburg im Breisgau

Dear Friend:

I thank you . . . for the beautiful hospitality in your house.
In retrospect, I think that both evenings indeed could have kindled

a small spark of light here and there. At the same time, the talk about India showed me that my attempts do not remain totally isolated.

. . .

March 7, 1960, from Freiburg im Breisgau

. . .

Sometimes I consider how the young doctors could be freed from their extreme involvement with their expertise and pure practice. But, of course, this case is not unique; the difficulty appears everywhere. It will continue to increase in the future with the overpowering predominance of the technical.

. . .

If you could—but only at your leisure—find out and share with me the Indian words for "ontological difference," that is, for "being" and "beings," for "unconcealedness" [*Unverborgenheit*] and "forgetfulness" [*Vergessenheit*], I would be very grateful.

. . .

p. 319

March 26, 1960, from Messkirch

. . .

You have not written when and where the Congress of Psychology will be. The theme is rather humorous, but perhaps it would be good if you gave the lecture. If the congress is only in summer or fall, we could best discuss it *verbally*. Or you might send me a *preliminary sketch*, and I could offer my comments on it.

First, it is not clear to me what "human motivations" means. Does it mean the human being as Ego, the *motivating* one, or the Ego within the human being otherwise still *motivated*? Are "human motivations" a medley of influences? Are causation and motivation distinguished from each other? Or is the fatal distinction between the conscious and the unconscious hidden behind this whole [excuse me] hodgepodge?

An excellent work by Heinrich Ott has been published by the Evangelical Publishing House in Zollikon: *Thinking and Being: The Path of Martin Heidegger and the Path of Theology* [*Denken und Sein: Der Weg Martin Heideggers und der Weg der Theologie*].

. . .

April 19, 1960, from Freiburg im Breisgau

In the meantime, the crocuses [at the Lenzerheide] will have been covered by snow once again. Yet, by the time of our arrival there, spring will certainly have gotten the upper hand.

. . .

August 10, 1960, from Freiburg im Breisgau

I thank you for your detailed letter with the description of the plan to work with you in Washington for three weeks. All this sounds tempting. p. 320 On the whole, I am inclined to take a chance on it.

One major difficulty is my very poor command of *English*. I cannot speak the language at all and can barely understand spoken English.

Through translation everything gets changed and becomes wearisome. My way of thinking and the phenomenological approach will probably still be strange over there.

. . .

August 16, 1960 (Without Indication of Place)

Dear Friend:

I am still stuck in the "abyss" of Nietzsche. I will write more in detail as soon as I have some more spare time.

. . .

December 18, 1960, from Freiburg im Breisgau

Dear Friend:

Once again I have to apologize from my heart that I canceled my planned trip to Washington, and with such late notice, that is, only after you went through all the trouble of preparation.

Of course, I knew that "Nietzsche" would keep me very busy until next year, but I did not think that I would have much additional work to do. I would not have been able to prepare for the trip sufficiently.

Furthermore, in the end the looming specter of American publicity deterred me.

As soon as I can catch my breath, that is, when I have the galley proofs behind me, I will inform you about Burghölzli. But I must ask you to tell me again about the present state of the discussions there.

p. 321   I would still regard it as the most fruitful [if I were] to *read* the appropriate text in your circle sometime. Open discussions become scattered too easily.

. . .

February 1, 1961, from Freiburg im Breisgau

This day an inquiry came from Professor Ebeling (Systematic Theology) as to whether at some point I would like to participate in his four-hour seminar dealing with my "philosophy" which will have 78 participants. . . . Ebeling would lead the first session and would deal with Luther's *Disputatio "de Homine."* I would lead the seminar the next day.

I would accept this offer only if I could combine it with your seminar and with the discussions with you. Perhaps it would also be instructive for you to participate in the theological seminar.

. . .

February 14, 1961, from Freiburg im Breisgau

. . .

Between the Burghölzi seminar and the one with Ebeling, I would like to have Thursday, March 2, as a free day, since indeed quite a readjustment has to be made. . . .

I have already put your name down for the theological seminar with my colleague Ebeling. The subject matter might come to be of interest to you. . . .

. . .

March 14, 1961, from Freiburg im Breisgau

. . . This time both meetings with your seminar turned out especially well. It seems to me that the participants woke up and that they now see

the other way more clearly. Of course, this will all need more practice. p. 322
Perhaps a description of an especially instructive case of hallucination
could be prepared for the next time.

. . .

September 9, 1961, from Freiburg im Breisgau

. . .

I read your "Remarks on Freud" during my trip home. I find them
excellent.

In this restless time, we all wish that a remnant of peace might still
remain.

. . .

November 15, 1961, from Freiburg im Breisgau

. . .

I have not commented on your congress lecture any further since I
found it excellent in its present form.

I also find your young colleague's presentation about hallucinatory
perception *very remarkable,* and I consider it as a good common basis for
the discussions. It would be fruitful, of course, if a *second* case could be
presented, since a comparison is always very instructive.

. . .

March 15, 1962, from Freiburg im Breisgau

. . .

On the same day you returned from America, I returned from Berlin
again. I was invited there for a commemoration of Max Kommerell in
the Academy of Arts. Max Kommerell died of cancer in 1944, at the age
of forty-two, and he would have been sixty years old now. He was—and
still is—the most important literary historian and poet—but [has been]
completely ignored and that means exploited. Following the celebration,
there were still two days of sessions in the academy; everything was rather
strenuous because people rush at me. Finally, I caught the flu there and p. 323
stayed in bed here for a whole week . . . therefore, in all respects the best
thing is to postpone the seminar until May.

. . .

I thank you for the short, but important, notes about the discussion.

. . .

January 28, 1963, from Freiburg im Breisgau

. . .

Thank you for you informative letter and for the book [textbook on psychiatry by Bleuler].

. . .

The chaos generated by conceptual confusion is indeed great. A basic flaw already appears externally: The description of a well-functioning memory scarcely comprises two pages, while disorders are dealt with in six pages.

I do not yet see how one can cope with this "science," which comes up with [such] erudite titles. The whole thing proceeds from purely mechanistic, causal, calculative representations.

A few hints about thinking, thanking, and memory can be found in *What Is Called Thinking?* [*Was heisst Denken?*] (pp. 5 ff., 91 ff.).

The oldest, detailed discussion of *memoria* can be found in Augustine's *Confessions* X.8 ff.

. . .

February 2, 1963, from Freiburg im Breisgau

. . .

Now that we have received a supply of heating oil, your visit on the 16th would be possible indeed. I would prefer that to a written presentation of the questions, where I would not be sure if it addressed your concerns. Everything remains more open in the give-and-take of a dialogue.

p. 324 The domination of technical-calculative thinking depends so much on the effect and on the fascination with progress that it can hardly be shaken off nowadays. But for that reason, the simple "seeing" of phenomena must not be abandoned, if only because technical thinking is also necessarily, and therefore everywhere, grounded on a minimum of phenomena, seen immediately. The main difficulty is that one does not see the forest through the trees of technical successes, that is, [one cannot see] simple Da-sein. In the meantime, even Da-sein is increasingly exposed to the corrosive effect of technology.

. . .

March 3, 1963, from Freiburg im Breisgau

Dear Friend:

Heartfelt thanks for your letter. Your visit was very invigorating. It made me confident that you will successfully fulfill the task before you at Harvard in the right way.[6] . . . I wish very much . . . that you could take up your work at the Lenzerheide and get ahead in the essentials so that the structure's outline and the kind of procedure are clearly delineated. You can arrange the "materials," "cases," and "examples" quite easily. The more often I think about your project, the more the *didactic element* seems to me to be decisive in the *arrangement* of the *whole*. You must succeed in obtaining a transformation in the listeners' way of seeing and in awakening the sense in which the questions must be asked. The paragraphs about Da-sein's spatiality would be a suitable test [*Prüfstein*] and an imperative to practice the other way of seeing, as contrasted to positivistic, causal thinking and the exclusive calculation of effect. The step to seeing the "clearing" and to seeing the ecstatic dimension of time within it can also succeed as fast as possible by way of spatiality. And you must always try to draw the attention of your listeners, that is, of the ones who catch on sooner, to the fact *that,* and *how,* an understanding of being is *already* at work in their *everyday* behavior and thought in a *non*thematic way, above all, in the manner they come to you asking questions. If you discuss all this without haste, but unremittingly by means of *one* phenomenon, more is gained than by a critical discussion of theories, where, for the most part, the critique's position, horizon, and viewpoint come to light only insufficiently, that is, only indirectly.

p. 325

For that purpose you yourself are required, for instance, to have an easy command of seeing Da-sein's spatiality in order to immediately notice where and how the questions under consideration go astray.

In case you are interested in having the seminar's protocol at your disposal for working through *Time and Being,** I will try to get a copy to you.

---

* "Time and Being" is the substitute for the unpublished third division of the first part of *Being and Time,* which signaled the later Heidegger's "Turning" [*Kehre*] from "Being and Time" to "Time and Being." See M. Heidegger, *On Time and Being,* trans. Joan Stambaugh (New York: Harper and Row, 1972).—TRANSLATORS

With the most heartfelt greetings and wishes for your work and for your well-being,

Yours,
Martin Heidegger

P.S. We have big plans for complete relaxation and rejuvenation. We would like to fly to Taormina in Sicily for fourteen days, from the end of April to the beginning of May, leaving from Zurich. Would you like to go [too]?

March 8, 1963, from Freiburg im Breisgau

. . .

If you could come with us [on the vacation trip to Taormina], it would be a great joy for us and a deep comfort for both of us to have along our doctor-friend who from long experience is familiar with Italy, knows the language, and the circumstances of air travel. Regarding the time (after Easter week), we would leave it entirely up to you.

p. 326

We would be especially thankful to you for this kind of assistance. Although one should not be so calculating among friends, in view of the quite unexpected new possibility of making the trip, nevertheless I would like to tell you that it would be a pleasure for me, and at the same time a wholesome self-examination, to do a phenomenological exercise based on *Being and Time.* . . .

With most cordial greetings to both of you and your sons from both of us,

Yours,
Martin Heidegger

March 20, 1963, from Freiburg im Breisgau

. . .

It is beautiful and invigorating to think about our impending trip to Sicily. Your perplexity will surely be overcome. Let us put aside the English translation of *Being and Time,* against which frequent objections are raised, in order to first clearly show the subject matters so that then the proper word will emerge automatically. That is why I regard space and spatiality as very important—because from here the phenomenon of the world can be elucidated in connection with openness [*Offenheit*] and clearing [*Lichtung*] as soon as possible. The whole procedure, *the* method, which is not a technique, but belongs to the subject matter itself, is determined from here. For that, it would be good if you could explain the current ideas (psychological and anthropological in the United States) in even more detail while we are in Sicily. . . .

April 1, 1963, from Freiburg im Breisgau   p. 327

. . .

At any rate, I wanted to write to you now regarding two fundamentally different things.

While reflecting on our forthcoming discussions, it became clear to me that we must not limit them to spatiality, although just this phenomenon is important for explaining what the word "world" refers to. Since I would like to conduct the discussion by means of *texts* from my writings, I ask you to let me know with which themes you would like me to deal. Then I could tear out the respective page from my works. After all, we cannot transport a whole library to Sicily. On the whole, we will indeed go over your whole lecture (at Harvard) one way or another. But, nevertheless, the seminars which you planned (in Zollikon) have a special character and require special preparation.

Now to the totally different "cares." Since I have never stayed in such a hotel, and since I am not familiar with the customs as far as my "suit" is concerned, I must indeed go along with how "they" [the people] do it there. Therefore, I request some *very brief* instruction from you. I thought this: a suit for travel, a lighter one for the stay, and a "black" one for evenings. Surely, one does not have to drag an uncomfortable hat along. The Basque beret is enough, . . .

I already live entirely in the Greek world. It will be beautiful to think toward Greece from Sicily and to discover that both are the same.

. . .

April 11, 1963, from Freiburg im Breisgau

It becomes clearer from the survey how the weights are balanced—in accordance with the predominant technical-practical interest. Nevertheless, the *Foundations'* theme serves as an occasion to discuss   p. 328

the phenomena and to show how this procedure is unavoidable. The texts from Goethe are a good aid for that. I will still bring two more separate prints of the lecture *Wissenschaft und Besinnung** [Science and reflection] with me. It is a tactical question whether [or not] you first *start* with the *example* (woman on the street by the train station)—to discuss it in the *Foundations'* direction for a while, and only then go over to numbers 1–5, and subsequently come back again to the example in a more fundamental way. You will have to ask the listeners from where they know that the foundations of anthropology are "mystical" and what they mean by "mystical." All this [needs to be done] without giving the impression that the listeners should do "philosophy" first—it is enough to lead them to the insight they themselves (they, who demand *facts* and proofs) insist on *un*proven and *un*demonstrated presuppositions.

. . .

P.S. What the Greek thinkers already knew, Goethe once expressed in a sentence: "The greatest would be: to comprehend that all facts are already theory."[7]

That means: There are never bare and pure "facts." If we consider that the "notion about something" [*Ansicht*] refers to "the way it looks" [*Aussehen*], the εἶδος, the ἰδέα, then Goethe's sentence becomes understandable: "When notions disappear from the world, things themselves are often lost. Indeed, in a deeper sense one could say that the notion is the thing."[8]

p. 329

May 6, 1963, from Freiburg im Breisgau

Dear Friend:

These lines are meant to be a token of my appreciation for your ever-friendly assistance which made the journey to Sicily and the stay there so beautiful and so full of diversity for my wife and me. . . .

Each day in Taormina had its character: the regular hours for discussion before noon, which, of course, were not sufficient for clarifying all important questions; the restful walks through the garden

---

*See M. Heidegger, "Wissenschaft und Besinnung," in *Vorträge und Aufsätze* (Pfullingen: G. Neske, 1967), pt. 1 ["Science and Reflection," in *The Question concerning Technology,* pp. 155–82]. —TRANSLATORS

of San Domenico; strolling through the place's alleyways; and finally the excursions into the interior of the island.

After an unusually beautiful flight back to Zurich, my wife and I arrived in Freiburg at exactly eight o'clock in the evening, . . . Here the apple and pear trees are in full bloom everywhere. Our native land appears new again in contrast to the sea and the island and its people, which we saw.

. . . You yourself still ought to find hours for concentration in order to be well prepared for carrying out your task. As a result of this, if a light goes on, remains, and shines on for just a few listeners, then this is already enough.

The enclosed little text merely sketches the stations on the way to, and through, phenomenology, the enactment of which becomes more difficult for the people of today the more exclusively they fall prey to calculative thinking, which is superior to the unconcealed, immediate glimpse at the unfolding essence only in appearance. Everything depends on practicing the same, simple looking at what essentially addresses us in a tacit, but ever-present, way. *Practice:* To stay with the same, to awaken sensibility for the simple—not the hurried running from one project of progress to the next and the boasting about useful results.

After the journey, I again sense the old freshness for working in the workshop [of thinking]. p. 330

. . .

July 1, 1963, from Freiburg im Breisgau

. . .

I am still thinking quite a bit about our conversations. When I have your text, perhaps I can still make a few addenda. During the past days I received an invitation to the International Philosophy Congress in Mexico, from September 7 to September 14. Travel and expense free. But I will decline because the whole thing is too strenuous and "useless"—most of all, because I do not think much of congresses, especially philosophical ones.

I would like to know how far your preparation for Harvard has progressed. . . .

. . .

I feel very fresh and good at my work. U. Sonnemann's book is less pleasant.

. . .

June 19, 1963, from Freiburg im Breisgau

I immediately read your notes of our conversation in Taormina. I found them excellent, and I thank you very much for them and for the letter.

Expansions of the text could be made everywhere, but that would, indeed, again dissolve the concentration of the whole. I will merely mark down a few grammatical oversights. . . . On page 7, at the end of (a), there should be added: "Even the largest accumulation and intensity of stimuli [*Gereiztsein*] never creates the 'is.' This already remains presupposed in each [act of] *being* stimulated."

p. 331 ## August 31, 1963, from Freiburg im Breisgau

. . . Now everything seems to have succeeded in the best way—up until the annoying professors of philosophy and their questions. I rejoice with you about your success. The real effect and its duration and importance can never be assessed in such cases. It takes its own path.

I will fulfill your wish with pleasure. . . . also, I would not like to interrupt my own work too much, which is "proceeding" much better than before my illness. . . .

. . .

P.S. My liver seems to be quite all right. I do not notice the least bit of trouble with it.

October 2, 1963, from Todtnauberg

Dear Friend:

On your sixtieth birthday I greet you very cordially in the name of my wife. Our wishes for this day are simple: a peacefully preserved life . . . , the strength for fruitful work in the helping profession; the gift of thoughtful reflection, from which will grow the planned work of a "psychology" by which a turn in thinking will be suggested to the physicians, which would bring them to an undisguised relationship to the human being and to his contemporary world. Such a work requires long preparation. May years free from trouble and misfortune be granted to you.[9]

A small gift will come for the festive day. It is the written text of the preface to a reading of Hölderlin's poems, which will be published as a recording. Your relatives, your friends, and all of those whom you helped (either the sick or the physicians who received guidance and training from you) will take care that your birthday will be well celebrated. p. 332

. . .

Enclosure with the Letter of October 2, 1963, from Todtnauberg

For Medard Boss on his sixtieth birthday,

In cordial friendship,

Martin Heidegger

A Word on Hölderlin's Poetry

[I wonder] whether we will recognize it once more?
Hölderlin's poetry* is a destiny for us. It is waiting for the moment when the mortals will respond to it.
What does Hölderlin's poetry say? Its [crucial] word is: the Holy.
This word speaks about the flight of the gods.† It says that the gods, who have fled, are saving us‡ until we are inclined and able to dwell near them. This site is the proper place of being at home. Therefore, it

---

*Heidegger believed that Hölderlin's unique poetry overcame metaphysics and pointed to a new advent of the divine in history and a new revelation of being. Heidegger, therefore, understood Hölderlin's poetry as a "destiny" for Western man. See Heidegger's lectures on Hölderlin's poetry (hymns): Heidegger, *Hölderlins Hymnen "Germanien" und "Der Rhein"* (Winter Semester 1934–35), vol. 39 of *GA*; *Hölderlins Hymne "Andenken"* (Winter Semester 1941–42), vol. 52 of *GA*; *Hölderlins Hymne "Der Ister"* (Spring Semester 1942), vol. 53 of *GA*; *Erläuterungen zu Hölderlins Dichtung* (Frankfurt am Main: Klostermann, 1953). See also Brock, ed., *Existence and Being*, pp. 270–91, and Heidegger, *Contributions to Philosophy*, pp. 297–341.—TRANSLATORS

†Heidegger speaks about the modern age as the completion of Metaphysics, i.e., as "the time of the gods that have fled *and* of the god that is coming" ("Remembrance of the Poet," trans. D. Scott, in *Existence and Being*, p. 288). See also Heidegger, "The Turning," in *The Question concerning Technology*, pp. 36–49, and *Contributions to Philosophy*, pp. 277–93.—TRANSLATORS

‡See the beginning of Hölderlin's hymn "Patmos" in which the poet says: "But where danger is, grows / The saving power also" (Heidegger, "The Turning," in *The Question concerning Technology*, p. 42).—TRANSLATORS

remains necessary to prepare for the sojourn in this nearness. Thus, we take the first step on the path which leads us there, where we respond properly to the destiny, which is Hölderlin's poetry. In this way, we arrive only at the place of the [poetic] word [*Wortort*] in which "the god of gods" perhaps appears.

For by itself and on its own, no human calculation and *design* [*Machen*] can bring forth a turning [*Wende*] in the world's present condition. Especially not, because human design is already formed by this very condition of the world and has fallen prey to it. How then could it [human design] still gain control over it [the world's condition]?

Hölderlin's poetry holds a destiny for us. It is waiting for the moment when we mortals will respond to it. The response leads the way toward a coming near the place of the gods, who have fled; that means into the place of the flight, which saves us.

Yet, how should we recognize and remember all this? By listening to Hölderlin's poetry.

p. 333 Meanwhile, only a few poems can be recited here. And from these few a limited selection has been made. It remains subject to the appearance of arbitrariness. This appearance is eased the more often we listen and the more often we willingly follow the guiding words, which are taken from Hölderlin's poetry.

The first guiding word reads:

"Everything is intimately interrelated [*innig*]."

This means: One is intimately appropriated [*vereignet*] to the other, but in such a way that thereby [each] remains in its own proper domain: Gods and men, earth and heaven. Intimate interrelatedness [*Innigkeit*] does not mean a merging and effacing of differences. Intimate interrelatedness means the belonging together of the unfamiliar, the sway of strangeness, and the claim of reserve [*Scheu*].

The second guiding word is a question:

"How do I render thanks?"

Thanking is the awe-inspiring, reverential, accepting remembrance [*Andenken*] of what was granted, and it is only a sign pointing toward the vicinity of the fleeing gods, who are saving us.

The third guiding word is:

"It can be perceived by a deep testing."

The testing must have been performed "on one's knees." Willfulness has to humble itself and disappear. Only one thing is incumbent on thought and meditation: to think ahead of poetry in order then to give way to it. By listening repeatedly, we become better at listening. But we become more attentive as well to how the saying of the poet might be brought into words. For more difficult than the selection of the poems is to find the right tone. It [the right tone] may come about by a stroke of luck in the moment when it [the poem] is recited in technically correct manner, but it may miscarry just as easily.

The poet himself knows it, and he knows it as no one else that the right tone is often lost.

It is said in the verses of the later poems:

> Troubled by little things,
> Out of tune as if from snow,
> The bell was ringing
> For the evening meal.

p. 344

The uncommon, the great, is named with these words through little common things. "The evening meal" is the evening of time, when the turning happens. The "snow" is the winter:

> Woe is me! When it is winter,
> From where do I take the flowers,
> And from where the sunshine,
> And the shadow of the earth?

But "the bell"—its toll—is the song of the poet. He calls into the turning of the time [*Wende der Zeit*].

December 18, 1963, from Freiburg im Breisgau

. . .

Yes—the young people! You cannot talk about colors to the blind. But perhaps one can open their eyes. The precondition for this is that these people glance out beyond their profession and practice and that for once they open themselves and let themselves into something entirely different.

Therefore, I propose that we read my little treatise on Kant's *Thesis about Being* together, i.e., *some passages* of it. . . . It does not do any harm for physicians to have something about Kant in their libraries too. In Kant's philosophy Western thinking since Descartes has intersected, [at least] in its beginnings, with the thought of the past one-and-one-half centuries. Therefore, there should be a seminar where there is no talk about psychology and psychoanalysis—ways of representational thinking that are especially prone to becoming bungled [*verhockt*] because the whole world can be explained by reducing it to unclarified subjectivity. One cannot get at this pigheadedness by discussing particular questions.

. . .

p. 335 ## February 10, 1964, from Freiburg im Breisgau

. . .

. . . I am glad that "it [the last seminar] has been a hit." But now we need to practice this seeing and to methodically exclude scientific preconceptions. It must not become a matter of writing down certain sentences and then keeping them in mind.

. . .

April 30, 1964, from Messkirch

. . .

First I wanted to ask you to consider a few question for our meeting again on May 8, which should be discussed in the next seminar. Perhaps in the meantime some of the participants have also thought of some of these questions. I would like to be informed in order to think this over in Ägina. At the same time, I will write down something there which is very important to me and for which I need the atmosphere of Greece. I recently completed a text for UNESCO's Kierkegaard meeting in Paris, which Beaufret read. Theme: "The End of Philosophy and the Task of Thinking."[*] But of course they failed to understand what is essential.

June 5, 1964, from Messkirch

. . .

I have reviewed your aide-mémoire. The only difficulty is in the distinction between the two kinds of evidence. This difference can be discussed only if an initial clarification of ontic and ontological evidence is obtained prior to it. I have purposely postponed the question about this distinction.

. . .

---

[*] The essay first appeared in a French translation by J. Beaufret and F. Fedier in *Kierkegaard vivant: Colloque organisé par l'Unesco à Paris du 21 au 23 avril 1964*, Collection idées, vol. 106 (Paris: Gallimard, 1966). The German text appeared in M. Heidegger, *Zur Sache des Denkens* (Tübingen: M. Niemeyer Verlag, 1969), pp. 61–80. The English translation appeared in Heidegger, *Basic Writings*, pp. 373–92.—TRANSLATORS

October 1, 1964, from Freiburg im Breisgau

p. 336

Dear Friend:

On your birthday I would like to tell you that your birthday letter, which I accept thankfully, was the most beautiful gift. But my wish for you is a corresponding one: that you may be successful in realizing your task. For this "psychology" is the most necessary thing for medical science. Viewed from the outside, it might appear almost hopeless to stand up against the reckless power of natural scientific thinking. Nevertheless, there are some signs that the thoughtful reflection on the inherent limitation of the fundamental science, that is, of nuclear physics, and thus of physics as such, is beginning. Dr. [Friedrich] von Weizsäcker* was in Todtnauberg for two days around September 20. I will have to say something about this at the next seminar.

We spent the late summer days at the hut. Against all my opposition, the rush of congratulating guests has been great. . . . In the midst of all this kindness, I had to think about the task still ahead of me, which has matured but awaits the proper moment.

Today Larese† will pick me up for Amriswill, where tomorrow I will read the lecture "Sprache und Heimat" [Language and homeland] (an interpretation of the poem "Der Sommerabend" [The summer evening] by Johann Peter Hebel) . . . ,‡ which has already been printed.

October 19, 1964 (Without Indication of Place)

. . .

Of course, it is necessary to coordinate the questions with a few concrete phenomena because spatiality and temporality are gigantic themes. The participants must first be trained methodically and must not expect solutions to all the world's problems. Perhaps you could explore once again in what direction the main difficulties are located. . . .

p. 337

. . .

---

*The German philosopher and physicist Friedrich von Weizsäcker was a former student of Heisenberg and a good friend of Heidegger.—TRANSLATORS

†Franz Larese was the director of the Erker Gallery in St. Gallen, Switzerland. —TRANSLATORS

‡Johann Peter Hebel was a German Romantic poet, whose *Allemannische Gedichte* (1803) initiated "dialect" poetry in Germany. See M. Heidegger, *Hebel: Der Hausfreund* (Pfullingen: Neske, 1958).—TRANSLATORS

January 11, 1965, from Freiburg im Breisau

. . .

Because of the excellent protocol from the last two evening seminars, the participants themselves might come up with *questions*. It would be nice to have those beforehand so that the next steps do not become too difficult, but pay attention indirectly to the experiential horizon of the physicians. The purely philosophical theme of space and time and of time and space leads to an ocean [of difficulties].*

. . .

February 4, 1965, from Freiburg im Breisgau

. . .

I started immediately with the review of the protocol sketch and have more corrections this time around. Above all, I have included supplementary notes so that we might have a text which is coherent in content and language. After a preliminary and cursory reading of the sketch, the gaps and inaccuracies were not immediately noticeable. Consequently, in the future I consider it more important to review the protocol calmly only after the two sessions, when I have had a chance to recover from the evenings. I would, therefore, like to arrange the time of my stay with you in a different way. I will come only *one* day before the first seminar and remain longer after the second one. Thus, we can have a better opportunity to discuss the progress of these matters.

. . .

March 5, 1965, from Freiburg im Breisgau

Cordial thanks for the protocols, which turned out nicely. A few minor mistakes must still be corrected. . . .

p. 338 ## May 3, 1965, from Freiburg im Breisgau

I am not sure whether the misinterpretation of "making-present" [*Vergegenwärtigung*] has been removed already, but we can immediately start clarifying the meaning of "having" without discussing the "having" of time in more detail. There is still a long way to go.

---

*See Heidegger, *Contributions to Philosophy*, pp. 257–71.

From "having," we can turn to "having-a-body," or rather "being a body"—in order to remove a great obstacle in this way. . . .

Of course, at the same time one must enter into a discussion of what cybernetics is and wherein its foundation lies as a phase of development of the beginning of modern physics.

I understand very well that your colleagues have become impatient and that they have the impression the I am taking a circuitous route by which they can encounter nothing tangible.

Perhaps the way we must now pursue is also fruitful, insofar as the seminar participants notice that we are led back to where we stand now.

. . .

June 10, 1965, from Freiburg im Breisgau

What you write about East Berlin will also be true before long in regard to the West—in a disguised form first. And East Asia? What is happening there? The Americans are still on their high horse. Your Indian friends will sadly resign.

. . .

July 14, 1965, from Freiburg im Breisgau

. . .

Since the last seminar, it has become still clearer to me how necessary the reflection on method and the characterization of phenomenology will be.

The discussion of the *Intuitus* in Descartes cannot be done without p. 339 going into Husserl's *Cartesian Meditations*. It will be a good transition to "phenomenology" in the next seminar.

May I expect the protocols soon?

. . .

August 17, 1965, from Freiburg im Breisgau

. . .

So far I have only been able to glance over your important excerpts from Uexküll (his book on psychosomatics) because I am still totally involved in my work, which I cannot interrupt. This is also the reason why I would like to postpone the next seminar until the beginning of the upcoming winter semester. This time I need more leeway to prepare for it because the correct introduction to the methodological problem creates considerably more difficulties than everything else to date. As I already told you, it became quite plain to me during the last seminar that the methodological question regarding its various possibilities can no longer be avoided. If the book by Uexküll is valued so highly, I probably have to read it all in order to ultimately see its main thought [*Duktus*] in context. Even earlier, inspired by Grassi, he took up philosophical questions as well.

. . . [Friedrich von] Weizsäcker traditionally arrives with questions for two days in the last part of September. I hope to be able to discuss methodological questions about nuclear physics with him on this occasion.

. . . As for the French authors, I am always disturbed by [their] misinterpretation of being-in-the-world; it is conceived either as being present-at-hand or as the intentionality of subjective consciousness . . .

With regard to my own work, I must more and more resolutely renounce reading current "literature." I limit myself to texts belonging immediately within the scope of my work.

. . .

p. 340

September 12, 1965, from Freiburg im Breisgau

. . .

. . . Presumably, you completed the outline of your planned book at the same time. Day by day, the overpowering force of calculative thinking strikes back more decisively at the human being himself as an object. [Therefore,] thoughtful thinking [*besinnliches Denken*] must realize that it will remain isolated in the future and will address only a few.

I am anxious [to hear] about your experiences in South America when you return.

. . . I would like it very much if you could indicate possible dates for the seminar at the beginning of the semester after your return.

I am still not quite clear about how to proceed with the reflection about *method*.

The great burden on the colleagues and participants makes it almost impossible to expect that they deal carefully with the philosophical texts. Nevertheless, in accord with my teaching experience of many years, this dealing with philosophical texts is still the best way to proceed in order to provide a proper foothold for continuing thoughtful reflection [*Besinnung*].

. . .

September 20, 1965, from Freiburg im Breisgau

. . .

Greece is on the horizon again, and because the islands and the sea belong to it, we planned the cruise, which we checked off—above all, because we plan on visiting the magnificent temple of Bassai on this tour. It would be beautiful if you could come . . . with us. . . .

September 26, 1965, from Todtnauberg p. 341

. . . We are especially joyful that you are willing to undertake the journey to Greece.

The date for the next seminar, the week of November 21–28, suits me very well. The questions you posed are important—I will discuss them within the appropriate *context*. They simply cannot be dealt with piecemeal. The most important thing remains that the participants get a more secure grasp of the way and manner of seeing, which, of course, becomes more and more difficult because of the scientific and technical way of thinking, which is thoroughly and increasingly consolidating itself. I am very curious to hear how far your own work has progressed. Yesterday Dr. Friedrich von Weizsäcker was here for a day. It was a very stimulating discussion, that is, as soon as one got the scientist into [reflective] thinking, question after question would arise. Being reproached of "hostility against science" is superficial and dumb and is based upon a groundless absolutization of "the" science.

November 10, 1965, from Messkirch

. . .

. . . On October 30 I spoke at the Binswanger celebration in Amriswill. I had declined at first, but Larese had already taken it upon himself to notify Binswanger that I would give a talk. Thus, I was obliged. I will bring the text with me and will read it aloud at the seminar.

. . .

December 16, 1965, from Freiburg im Breisgau

. . .

This very day I am mailing the corrected protocol and hope that it will still reach you before the trip to the Lenzerheide.

p. 342   It turned out to be a little long, but some repetitions in it are perhaps quite useful.

. . .

Of course, it is a great self-deception to believe that the concrete descriptions, separated from "philosophical" reflection, could be sufficiently enacted [*nachvollziehen*]. I am very skeptical in this regard.

In truth, what is "philosophical" is concrete, and the descriptions are abstract, that is, removed from the ontological meaning which sustains them.

In order to be able to give a sufficiently clear interpretation of the relationship between the psychiatrist and the patient for this exploration, some medical experience, which I lack, is necessary as well. Here, as elsewhere, I am dependent on the cooperation of the seminar participants.

It is fine with me if you inform Dr. Blankenburg about my critical remarks regarding his writings.

. . .

January 18, 1966, from Freiburg im Breisgau

. . .

Today, with cordial thanks, I certify the arrival of your letter with the protocol and the very enlightening separate copy of the questionnaire about the concept of stress. This title conceals an inferno of confusion and thoughtlessness. I find the contribution by Plügge to be very thoughtful. Your contribution ought to be titled: "Answer to an unsuccessful inquiry by questionnaire." For those for whom these texts do not serve as an eye-opener about the dictatorship of scientific thinking any attempt at thoughtful thinking is in vain. Of course, the question becomes more urgent: How, and in what place in today's existence, is it still possible during the [present] age to preserve a tradition which may have to survive underground for a long time?

p. 343   Perhaps the questionnaire's text about "stress" would be very suitable as a basis for the next seminar. It could certainly be made available to the participants. Then it could be shown what kind of concoction of unreflected philosophy is necessarily hidden away in these "concrete" research programs.

I have long suspected that the seminar has been abused. Surely, B. could state his opinion about my antiquated notion of method in the natural sciences instead of entertaining an audience that is not informed about the procedure and aims of the seminars.

. . .

P.S. . . . Dr. Blankenburg asked by letter for a talk. He writes that you have informed him about my objections with a series of points. I do not recall his text very well anymore. He thinks the text is kept general on purpose in view of the "archive."[*]

February 3, 1966, from Freiburg im Breisgau

. . .

I will come then on Sunday, February 27, on the usual train. The theme remains "stress." But in one way or another, a difficulty remains with the seminar, which has its basis in the [present] state of "science" and "philosophy." Either the discussion turns out to be too "abstract" for the participants, or else—when it becomes "concrete" for them—I, for one, talk about things about which, professionally speaking, I understand nothing.

. . .

Then I would like to draw your attention to a book that was already published in 1964 but that strangely enough has escaped my notice until now. I received it at the beginning of January as a present from Pastor Hassler in Basel. I did not recognize the name of the author, who is now a full professor in Bonn: Wagner, Friedrich, *Die Wissenschaft und die gefährdete Welt: Eine Wissenschaftssoziologie der Atomphysik* [Science and the endangered world: A sociology of the science of atomic physics] (Munich: C. H. Beck Verlag). p. 344

An *exciting* book, still to be thought out more radically in its foundation; a "concrete" confirmation of *technological enframing* [*Gestell*].[†] Each seminar participant ought to read it. Perhaps then they may finally see the light.

In regard to Plügge, you are correct of course—the "situation" [with the children] comes out of the blue.

In regard to Blankenburg: A "scientific" discussion of "clearing" [*Licht*ung] makes less sense than a differential equation for Cézanne's Mont Ste. Victoire.

. . .

---

[*]See *ZS* 254.—TRANSLATORS

[†]*Ge-stell* [enframing: frame, framework; literally, com-positing), must not be understood ontically as a framework for something but rather ontologically as a calling-forth and as a challenging claim by being itself (in its withdrawal) in the age of technology in which the human being objectifies everything as a standing-reserve [*Bestand*] for interminable use and control. See Heidegger, *The Question concerning Technology*, pp. 3–35.—TRANSLATORS

March 27, 1966, from Freiburg im Breisgau

. . .

I do believe indeed that the seminar participants were "unanimously filled with enthusiasm" by that last seminar. That kind of discussion is in many ways closer to them. Yet it loses its unified, concise focus through its "liveliness." Hence, the natural connection between the steps is concealed to further reflection. Therefore, Frau Dr. B.'s protocol is "incomplete." Moreover, nothing can be seen of the *way* of the discussion anymore. I tried hard to remedy this shortcoming somewhat.

. . .

If one gives full reign to discussion, notes of the seminars can be rendered only by complete shorthand, or else [the notes] can be recorded by a *free* reproduction of the main content, which then amounts to an independent treatise. . . .

During a seminar evening, once a theme is advanced and something is achieved, there is little time left to check to see whether the participants are really getting acquainted with "seeing" the phenomena or whether, in their opinion, they believe they have "understood" something useful. I have repeatedly observed that if they are asked, they have "forgotten" what we had spoken about earlier. Yet if one has once *seen* the phenomenon in question, one cannot "forget" it any longer.

p. 345

It seems that an even slower proceeding is necessary. A further difficulty remains in the transition from usual, scientific terminology to the language which describes the phenomena. . . . How far we are from the illuminating [*lichtend*] (liberating)* power of the Greek light!

June 2, 1966, from Freiburg im Breisgau

. . .

. . . I can stay with you then until July 11 and discuss the *Foundations*[10] with you. We must still talk about how we want to handle the protocols from the next seminars, which are very important.

. . .

---

*See *ZS* 16 concerning the double meaning of *lichten* ("lighten up" and "alleviate" = liberate). —TRANSLATORS

June 10, 1966, from Freiburg im Breisgau

. . .

I am sending back the galley proofs I reviewed by return post. I allowed myself four linguistic corrections.

The matter cannot be made clearer unless one takes pains to think through the distinction between ontic-ontological.

. . .

June 15, 1966, from Freiburg im Breisgau

. . .

My dental problem has lasted longer and is more annoying than I thought. Most of all the prosthesis of the lower jaw presents difficulties to eating and speaking. The one demands soft food; the other, practice in speaking, which I do by reading Goethe's *Italian Journey* aloud.

p. 346

. . .

So we have to postpone the seminar until fall. The same had to be done with the *Der Spiegel* interview. But in spite of that, I could come to see you very privately to talk over the *Foundations* with you. Now the question is whether you can take enough time from July 4 to July 11 so that we perhaps can talk exclusively about the *Foundations*, possibly at the Lenzerheide. . . .

. . .

August 15, 1966, from Freiburg im Breisgau

. . .

In the meantime, a month has passed since you, from your seclusion, sent me the article about molecular biology by Schwyzer.

Through its sovereign, clear presentation, it is indeed exemplary for its strange identification of purely chemical processes with events of linguistic communication. The definitive identification [between chemical processes and communication] is put forth as the processing of information. Measured against it, the disclosing communication of saying [*Sagen*] is reduced to a mere series of reciprocal releasing mechanisms. Measured against it, the course of chemical processes is simultaneously elevated to linguistic communications. Both that reduction and that elevation presuppose that the specific and objective character of the two domains (material-energy process and language event) is disregarded. And this is due to the exclusive focus on information. This information is distinguished by the relationship of reciprocal steering mechanism [*wechselseitige Regelungen*]. In this [scientific] projection, everything is focused on these [steering mechanisms] in order to guarantee an all-pervasive capacity for steering everything. This steering capacity [*Steuerbarkeit*] is considered the leading characteristic of all events because by this standard a uniform, universal procedure is secured for all areas of science. Only then is the absolute "victory of [scientific] method" over science made possible.

p. 347

But then any clear insight into these matters and into their consequences—not to mention the question of their origin—is lacking in the sciences. Nevertheless, the customary habituation to calculative thinking, ruled by technical efficiency, is so decisive that it means nothing to the sciences anymore if they disregard the subject matter of the subject areas in favor of the unconditional possibility for rule by method so that these [subject matters and areas] can no longer address one. Therefore, the uncanniness of this destiny is no longer experienced. The justification for research is furthering progress in order to be able to dominate the "world."

I hope that you have put a few things behind you in the last weeks and that you are satisfied. At the moment, I am once again about to measure my thinking against that of the early Greeks in order to appraise proximity and distance at the same time. This kind of self-critique is more wholesome than having to deal with contemporary objections, which lag behind the subject matter.

. . .

August 24, 1966, from Freiburg im Breisgau

. . .

Cordial thanks for your letter. I am glad that your work is progressing. The seminar protocols are here so that they can be *utilized* and have a further effect on science, which someone like myself cannot really bring about. I do not think that there are any problems with using them here, especially when you are scientifically qualified through your own works.

. . .

"Symposia" on Heidegger are now on the rise in the United States. Your initiative there was indeed important.

. . .

October 16, 1966, from Messkirch

p. 348

. . .

So on November 10 I could come to see you for a few days, but only to discuss your book and questions relating to it. A seminar with our colleagues could then be arranged for the first weeks of the new year.

. . .

December 4, 1966, from Freiburg im Breisgau

. . .

I very much wish that you will be successful with the condensed presentation of the *Foundations,* which should lead to a basic clarification of the main concepts and demonstrate the correct method for self-reflection in medicine.

Surely, you have also received the thick book by Lacan (*Ecrits*).[*] For the moment I have not gotten around to reading this obviously baroque text. From what I hear, it is causing the same sensation in Paris as Sartre's *Being and Nothingness* once did.

Completely apart from the *Heraclitus Seminar,* I am daily more pre-occupied with a renewed reflection on the relationship to today's thinking and its task with respect to its authoritative beginning with the Greeks.

. . .

January 15, 1967, from Freiburg im Breisgau

. . .

I think the theme "motivation and causality" could indeed become important for the seminar participants. So that I do not "slip over" into the area of principles and "pure philosophy" too much, it would be good if at least some specific questions from the previously mentioned domain of themes could be formulated and brought to my attention in time—after inquiry among the participants.

p. 349

. . .

I am very focused on the Greeks, far beyond the framework of the Heraclitus Seminar. They are the only great teachers of thinking.

---

[*]J. Lacan, *Ecrits: A Selection,* trans. A. Sheridan (New York: Norton, 1977). Also see *ZS* 260.—TRANSLATORS

In the meantime, "science" continues on its questionable, victorious course. I am referring to the last issue of *Der Spiegel* (no. 530 [1966], on "futurology"). To recapitulate the seminar on time, we could reflect on a few things to clarify that peculiar science, especially where the questions on causality and the sequence of time must be readdressed.

. . .

February 17, 1967, from Freiburg im Breisgau

. . .

But it also seems important to make clear to the seminar participants what fundamental opposition lies behind the properly made distinction between causality and motivation.

It must become clear that it is not only concerned with a methodical (technical-practical) distinction, but with a fundamentally different way of determining being human and determining the human being's position in contemporary world civilization. Only by reflecting on this does the full importance of the distinction come to light.

. . .

March 5, 1967, from Freiburg im Breisgau

. . .

Considering the long interval, it would be good if I were to give a review during the first hour and a preview of the theme at the same time. In this way we can hardly avoid pointing to the broader horizon within which the distinction between causality and motivation is located.

p. 350 Of course, now as before, it remains difficult to connect the fundamentals with a fruitful discussion of concrete questions. But in the meanwhile, I have also learned something from the previous seminars.

I am especially delighted with the way that the new, younger participants are coming along.

. . .

April 24, 1967, from Freiburg im Breisgau

. . .

I returned home fine yesterday and I am already fresh at work today. The mail is tolerable, and I am enclosing a letter from Lacan. It seems to me that the psychiatrist needs a psychiatrist. Perhaps you can write a few short notes for me when you send it back. The thesis is a copy of a doctoral dissertation.

In retrospect, both seminars seem to have had good results—in part because of the participants' familiarity with the subject matter; in part because a few of them may be feeling that philosophy cannot answer all their questions. The theme "Hermeneutics of Exploration" (in our version) is promising insofar as it moves in the *sphere between* [too little and too much philosophy] and does not run the risk of becoming too philosophical.

. . .

August 14, 1967, from Freiburg im Breisgau

. . .

"Immanence" is a fixed term for the "immanence of consciousness."

It is difficult to find an immediately understandable phrase for the "worldlessness of things merely present-at-hand" [*Weltlosigkeit bloss vorhandener Dinge*]. This state of affairs is foreign to science. It does not see "world" and "world-liness" [*Welthafte*] at all.* It takes things as objects of scientific thematization and does not know anything else. It overlooks   p. 351 the referential assignment things truly have on their own toward the region in which human Da-sein immediately exists on an everyday basis. To someone for whom the "true world" remains reduced to scientific objects, a thing such as "worldlessness" [*Weltlosigkeit*] can be shown as little as color [can be shown] to the color-blind.

. . .

September 24, 1967, from Messkirch

. . .

As for the "anticipated flashes of insight," little can be communicated in a few sentences, least of all in pure propositions, because that is a matter of change in experiencing and seeing.

The openness of Da-sein "is" the enduring [*Ausstehen*] of the clearing. Clearing and Da-sein belong together beforehand, and the

---

*See Heidegger, *Being and Time*, pp. 51–52; *Fundamental Concepts of Metaphysics*, p. 176 f.—TRANSLATORS

unity determining this togetherness is the "appropriating Event" [*Ereignis*].* The fastest way for you to arrive in the dimension of this region is to think through my lecture on *Identity and Difference* once again and to use the brochure on *The Question of Being*† as an aid.

I would like to postpone the question about "consciousness" and "consciousness and Da-sein" until the seminar.

. . .

October 1, 1967, from Messkirch

. . .

I am very sad that I cannot write you the right thing from "flashes of insight" because the themes you put forward cannot be settled with a few suggestions.

. . .

I greet you cordially in true friendship,

Yours,
Martin Heidegger

December 29, 1967, from Freiburg im Breisgau

p. 352

. . .

I believe that I cannot go wrong when I suggest you put off the publication of the "Foundation Book." It should become the legacy of all of the practical and theoretical work that you have done in your life. This task will wait until tomorrow; it still needs more decisive clarification and organization of the basics.

You may be assured of my help. The questions raised in the last seminar will gain increasing importance in the future. Cybernetics and its possibilities are viewed more and more positively within "science." Within "philosophy," logical positivism, with its theory of language,

---

*The singular *Ereignis*, which takes place within being itself and which brings being and human beings into their own [*eigen*]. See Heidegger, *Time and Being*, p. 23 f.; *The Question concerning Technology*, pp. 36–49.—TRANSLATORS

†Heidegger, *Zur Seinsfrage* (1956) [*The Question of Being*, trans. W. Kluback and J. T. Wilde (New Haven, Conn.: College and University Press, 1958)].—TRANSLATORS

is pushing its way to the forefront ever more clearly. This must all be met by way of reflection on the principles—even though there seems to be no chance for immediate success. "Cells" of resistance will be formed everywhere against technology's unchecked power. They will keep reflection alive inconspicuously and will prepare the reversal, for which "one" will clamor when the general desolation becomes unbearable.

From all corners of the world, I now hear voices calling for such a reflection and for ways to find it—voices that are renouncing the easily attainable effects of technology's power.

Postponing the publication of *Foundations* is but only one way to proceed. It seems to me that the other way must be to put forward the rich "materials" of your medical experience—and that should be done in a form pointing tacitly to the necessity for the *Foundations* and awakening the need for it. Then you yourself create the advantage by *referring* to [your] rich experience in the *Foundations,* and thus you are able to give more substance to considerations of principles.

Now the question arises regarding our further work. I am stuck for the time being and have been suddenly pressed into a revision of my lecture "Time and Being" and the manuscripts connected with it from five years ago. At the same time, I am occupied with a new reflection on "the ontological difference," and finally I am rethinking enframing [*Ge-stell*] in relation to its "subject": industrial society. I would not like to interrupt this work now, especially because I am in good shape to work. Therefore, I propose postponing the seminar in which the above-mentioned questions would have been discussed.

p. 353

But before that, I would like to support your further work, and I dare to propose that we work together for about a week at the Lenzerheide in the early course of next year at the beginning of March and thereby prepare the seminar for the beginning of the summer semester.

. . .

January 10, 1968, from Freiburg im Breisgau

. . .

Many thanks for your letter. It made it clear to me that we cannot delay your publication (*Foundations* book) too much longer.

Therefore, I will arrange my work so that we have enough time at the Lenzerheide in March for thoroughly discussing the most important questions.

. . .

March 19, 1968, from Freiburg im Breisgau

. . .

I think we have now arrived at the point with your book that it can *stand* on its own and that the unavoidable detail work can take its secure course.

I will review the text of the "introduction" and the first chapter on "the natural-scientific foundation" as soon as I am finished with the mail.

. . .

p. 354 ## April 2, 1968, from Badenweiler

. . .

The theme of the [next] seminar is difficult to formulate in detail. We will not get away from the question we discussed concerning the relationship between "consciousness and Da-sein" because "consciousness" plays a fundamental role for Marx—originating with Hegel—but is essentially different from the psychological concept. . . .

. . .

August 22, 1968, from Freiburg im Breisgau

. . .

I will be back from Provence on September 10 and would like to come see you as soon as possible to talk about the book exclusively. I do not want to have too much of an interval between my return here (on October 10) and the trip to Zollikon in order to have sufficient and uninterrupted time for the work ahead of me after my stay with you. But, of course, I will leave it up to you. . . .

. . .

December 7, 1968, from Freiburg im Breisgau

. . .

The question of the seminar can only be answered thematically by discussing the fundamentals one day and, thus prepared, dealing with a concrete theme the next day. I have not decided about the content yet. Here, I will also gladly defer to the wishes of the participants. I do not like traveling in January and February. So March would be suitable.

I am asking to abstain from an interview. I am too awkward in these matters, especially when it concerns my family; and besides, Ernst Jünger's statement is true in this case: "Whoever interprets himself is not up to his own standard."

January 5, 1969, from Freiburg im Breisgau

p. 355

. . . I have thought through the arrangement of the (*Foundations*) book again. Nothing more should be changed. Only the organization of chapter 3, part 2, "Fundamental Characteristics of Human Beings," must be reviewed. It should make decisive points without claiming to present a complete "anthropology."

. . .

January 27, 1969, from Freiburg im Breisgau

. . . I am glad about, and eagerly anticipate, the March seminar and the conversation about "the book" in which nothing more should be changed.

. . .

July 7, 1969, from Freiburg im Breisgau

I have postponed my arrival until July 14 so that we can finally prepare the manuscript (*Foundations of Medicine*) for printing with new vigor. . . .

Enclosure with the Letter of July 7, 1969

From Heidegger's Assistance with the Introduction to the *Foundations* Book

. . .

Thereby, we experience the extent to which the research method of the natural sciences is very soon confronted with a domain which is inaccessible to it [by its methods]. Of course, this presupposes an acknowledgment that the theme of medicine involves the human being in his entire, everyday lived reality. For this very reality differs essentially from any other reality known to us. This difference may be indicated in advance and may be terminologically determined.

p. 356   We say that only the human being exists. The basic characteristic of his existence is Da-sein. But in saying this, it is in no way asserted that material nature and organisms (plants, animals) are not real [because they do not exist as Da-sein], are not beings, but are mere appearance. It is merely said that the reality of the aforementioned nonhuman domains is other than that of existence. But insofar as this [human existence] remains distinguished by Da-sein, the term "Da-sein" too must already be understood differently from the usual meaning of the word "Dasein." This may be indicated by spelling this word in a different way. The usual meaning of "Dasein" is being present—thus, for instance, in the discussion about the proofs of God's existence. Nevertheless, the human being *is* not already human by being something present and by being something identifiable as such. Insofar as he ek-sists as Da-sein [in a transitive sense] by enduring it, insofar as he takes it upon himself to preserve the Da-, that is, the manifestness of beings, by complying with it [*sich fügen*] and by shaping it, the human being *is*.

As just presented, the characterization of Da-sein and existence is not meant to serve as a definition. It contains only an indication of a way of seeing from where distinct phenomena of Da-sein should subsequently come into view and be elucidated.

The talk about the foundations of medicine as appropriate to Da-sein always merely points to a task to be carried out: Bringing into view the distinctiveness of being human as enduring Da-sein beforehand, continuously, and always more resolutely must be done in order to keep this [distinctiveness] in view for the future.

In contrast to all former views of nature, modern natural science has not only led to new results. Above all, "new" is its sustaining, basic relationship to nature, expressed in a new conception of nature. The more resolutely this conception itself enters common awareness through the distinction between classical and nuclear physics, the more the

p. 357   insight asserts itself that natural science is subject to historical change, especially in its foundations. Therefore, reflection on the basic character of the scientific method of research finds itself referring to the historical tradition of natural science. Questioning this history belongs to basic research [*Grundlagenforschung*] itself, aware of its own task, and does not merely serve as a secondary, antiquated [*antiquarisch*] interest in the history of science.[*]

---

[*] See C. Chevalley, "Heidegger and the Physical Sciences," *Martin Heidegger. Critical Assessments,* 4:342–64.—TRANSLATORS

August 2, 1969, from Freiburg im Breisgau

. . .

Here comes the desired proposal to simplify your somewhat complicated text on repression. It always concerns the same basic phenomenon: to see and to describe ecstatic-intentional relations to the world instead of a psychical mechanics or dynamics.

. . .

Enclosure to the Letter of August 2, 1969

Then repression [*Verdrängen*] shows itself as one of the possible modes of human comportment, which is characterized by not admitting things which address and afflict the human being. Repression is a looking away from . . . , a fleeing from . . . , and thus it is not a mechanistically represented pushing away, so to speak, of psychical states, a letting disappear of psychical materials. In repression, what concerns the human being is to avoid so little that instead it affects the one who tries to repress it in an even more obstinate way. In the will to repress being afflicted [*Andrang*] by what must be repressed, it is intensified even more. The phenomenon of repression can only be seen in its uniqueness if it is brought into view in advance as an ecstatic-intentional relationship to the world of things, living beings, and fellow human beings.[*]

November 20, 1969, from Messkirch
p. 358

. . .

Thanks for your letter and for the provisions. At the time of my birthday, untouched by all the goings-on outside but burdened by them, I was especially concentrated on what *is*, and I have been asking and pondering how it must be *said*. I sense quite clearly that the appropriate word is as yet to be found. Thinking is merely continuing to manage with preliminary words [*Vor-wörter*]. At the same time, idle talk becomes more powerful, and the wear and tear of language seems to be irresistible.

. . .

---

[*] See Boss, *Existential Foundations*, pp. 244–47 ("Psychic Repression").—TRANSLATORS

December 8, 1969, from Freiburg im Breisgau

. . .

Your friendly greeting in the *tabula gratulatoria,* on television and in the article in the *Neue Zürcher Zeitung,* is a one of a kind thank-you which I perhaps really do not deserve. For measured by what is given as a task of thinking, I could and can set only little things in motion. Here I am not speaking with false modesty but only with a daring look ahead to the determined destiny of thinking.

The confrontation [of my thinking] with the uncanny power of "science" is still only in its inadequate beginnings. Perhaps even a retreat in thinking is necessary to dare the attack, which does not have a warlike character but that of a quiet deprivation of *"science's"* power. I sense that an almost uncanny favor of destiny and the much undeserved help of relatives and friends hold sway over my path of thinking.

Thus, it is almost temerity for me to keep looking forward to a time which will grant me undisturbed concentration until the end, so that I can bring what must be thought—as far as I can see it—into the form I imagine and which, crudely put, lies between scientific statement and the poetic word.[*]

p. 359 I thank you for your friendship, and I ask you to greet not only your family for me but also the ones who follow, the young physicians for whom it will always be more difficult to withstand the power of "science."

In good remembrance, I greet you cordially,

Yours,
Martin Heidegger

February 20, 1970, from Freiburg im Breisgau

. . .

. . . I am slowly returning again to my own thinking, which was interrupted by my birthday. I hope that I can still successfully formulate what I have in mind.

---

[*]Heidegger, *On the Way to Language* and *Poetry, Language, Thought.* —TRANSLATORS

With good wishes for you and your work,

In old friendship,

Yours,
Martin Heidegger

P.S. I am very glad that you found the appropriate teaching position at the university.

August 16, 1970, from Freiburg im Breisgau

. . .

Now I do not know *where* to find you and to find out how you are. My wish and thought is that you are convalescing well. I am including a little volume in which the lecture by the Japanese is very instructive.

The *Foundations* is now, perhaps, showing another face, although the accelerated frenzy of technology and science, the "information" science, remains what it is.

Taking the necessary precautions, I am well. My wife and I swim in our swimming pool almost daily, but I avoid people and extended conversations if possible.

. . .

September 8, 1970, from Freiburg im Breisgau   p. 360

. . .

. . . Are you giving lectures again during winter semester?

I have limited the real work of thinking and am busy ordering the manuscripts. An assistant of Professor Fink will help me in the following months. In addition, I will reduce the size of my library substantially. I had an invitation to Provence again, but I declined it. But thinking continues, that is, it remains the *same*, although the power of technological enframing is increasing daily in all domains of life. There is also the possibility of mankind's death. Reasons cannot be given why the people now populating the planet and destroying it in every possible way should continue to exist without end.

Der Spiegel is presently running a series of articles on Brazil and South America. If this subcontinent explodes and others with it, then Karl Marx will have achieved his "change of consciousness" in classical form.

But there are still invisible islands and words [i.e., language] defying all information science and not needing any "society," that is, not needing any confirmation by it.

. . .

February 21, 1971, from Freiburg im Breisgau

. . .

Colleagues and friends are equally co-honored by the high, rare honor* awarded to you, and it will stimulate all of them to renewed cooperation in the newly founded association.[11] To give advice about reading my writings is difficult because the preparation of the older and recently added participants (of the seminars) will be different, just as the direction of interests is.

p. 361

As a first reading, I would like to propose the lecture *What Is Called Thinking?* in which the discussion of Greek texts can be omitted. Following then: *Der Satz vom Grund,*[†] because a contrast could be drawn with causality as thus represented in the natural sciences. A contrast could also be drawn with the currently emerging "science of information"—the science of the construction and operation of computers. Finally, the book *Gelassenheit*[‡] could be contrasted with the *Feldweggerspräch.*[§] The lectures on Nietzsche are important as an introduction into the modern awareness of Da-sein. The *Wegmarken*[¶] could open up a perspective. But this should happen later on. I would like to dissuade you from the literature *on* Heidegger.

. . .

With the wish that the beginning of the society's work may be successful and make firm progress, I greet you and the participants. . . .

---

* "The honor" refers to [being] awarded the Great Therapists Prize by the American Psychological Association. The "newly founded association" refers to the Swiss society for Daseinanalyse.—TRANSLATORS

† M. Heidegger, *Der Satz vom Grund* (Pfullingen: Neske, 1957) [*The Principle of Reason*, trans. R. Lilly (Bloomington: Indiana University Press, 1991)].—TRANSLATORS

‡ M. Heidegger, *Gelassenheit* (Pfullingen: Neske, 1959) [*Discourse on Thinking*, trans. J. M. Anderson and E. H. Freund (New York: Harper and Row, 1966)].—TRANSLATORS

§ M. Heidegger, *Der Feldweg* (Frankfurt: Klostermann, 1953). "The Pathway" is translated by T. Sheehan in *Heidegger: The Man and the Thinker* (Chicago: Precedent, 1981), pp. 69–71).—TRANSLATORS

¶ M. Heidegger, *Wegmarken* (Frankfurt: Klostermann, 1978) [*Pathmarks*, ed. W. McNeill (Cambridge: Cambridge University Press, 1998)].—TRANSLATORS

March 14, 1971, from Freiburg im Breisgau

. . .

. . . Now all that matters is that the right people can be found for the "internal" establishment of the "Association" and that the new flood of structuralism and of the positivism of "Critical Theory" does not indeed inundate everything. Even the rare phenomenology has stiffened into dogmatism.

. . .

In autumn a lecture of mine will be published at Niemeyer, but I have exempted myself from the edition's work.

For the many new things which are still going on anywhere else, I am too old.

p. 362

With good wishes for your recovery,

Yours, Martin Heidegger

May 2, 1971, from Freiburg im Breisgau

. . .

I am well. Thanks for the friendly inquiry from America. But of course I have to avoid all stress now and limit visits and letters. We hope to be able to move into our small "old-age home" in the summer. A young couple from the circle of our friends will move into our big house. Then, if necessary, they can also assist us old folks.

With cordial greeting and special wishes for your health and for your work,

Always yours,
Martin Heidegger

Afterword

Medard Boss

Nothing is better suited as an afterword for this book than the "Letter of a p. 363 Friend," which the editor wrote for Martin Heidegger's eightieth birthday and which was published in the *Neue Zürcher Zeitung* on October 5, 1969 (no. 606, p. 5). Its appropriateness as an afterword is due to the fact that it was not merely a birthday letter and a letter of thanks but in a certain sense already a farewell letter too. For quite a few signs—especially the content of virtually all the letters which Heidegger wrote to me after 1969—indicated that my friend had begun to retire more and more into himself and to prepare for dying. My letter read:

> When I am among those finding themselves somewhat pushed into the limelight during the celebration of your birthday, then I am grateful merely for the fact that for a quarter of a century I had the privilege of being united in friendship with you.
>
> It is true that at first there appeared to be no common ground where something could take root between us. Seen from the outside, everything seemed strongly against it. It was only when I could encounter you in person for the first time up at your Black Forest hut that I was most deeply moved. This was not because of your exterior appearance, although it too could have caused astonishment. I was used to meeting such folk among the winegrowers of Southern France, but not among Germans. Yet all of this receded into the background in comparison to your eyes and your high forehead. A power of thinking radiated from there which was extremely p. 364 passionate and sober at the same time and which seemed to penetrate all boundaries of a human intellect. Secretly and softly woven into it was a stunning tenderness and sensitivity of heart. Only twice in my life had I encountered eyes which could look at you in a similar way. The first time was nearly twenty years earlier when I stood face to face with Sigmund Freud at the Bergstrasse in Vienna. A good ten years after my first visit with

you it happened again in the hermit's cell of probably the greatest sage of present-day India.

Since I was definitely more versed in the ways of the world, I immediately considered it my duty to break through the complete seclusion from people in which I found you. I interpreted our first journey abroad in the early 1950s to Perugia and Assisi as a first, small success. Never before had I seen you as joyful as then, when you spent time in the midst of the land and among the people of Italy.

For a long time I had been searching for a sound, scientific foundation for my whole medical practice. I could no longer consider as valid the absolute claim made for science and for its finding of truth which the scientific method of research had imposed ever more authoritatively, even in relation to sick people. It [the scientific method] did not know any other way to justify it [absolute claim] than through its certainly admirable, practical success in dealing with the human body.

Yet even such an astonishing capacity to manipulate things does not in itself guarantee an appropriate insight into the essence and meaning of what is to be manipulated. During my years of study, Eugen Bleuler, the esteemed teacher and great psychiatrist, had already opened my eyes to the fact that modern, scientific investigations cannot find any access to

p. 365

what is properly human in our patients. The suppositions of their own thinking prevent them fundamentally, and hence forever, from gaining this access. This was a devastating insight for a novice doctor. Then how could this science ever show him the correct guidelines and the meaning of his medical art?

In this distress, afflicting so many of my colleagues and myself, you came to our aid. Thanks to your untiring effort, my originally faint notion of the fundamental importance of your thinking for the realm of medicine too has changed in the course of the years into an increasingly more secure knowledge. In the basic structures of the way of human existing which you elaborated, I recognized the most reliable outline of an art of healing, which I had glimpsed till then during my wanderings through the history of philosophy and medicine and during my expeditions to the Far East and the Far West. Since that time, you have also become the most genuine representative of basic research in medicine for me. It is only with the background of your thinking that the results of modern biology, anatomy, physiology, psychology, and pathology can be understood in their essential significance.

The joint idea of the Zollikon Seminars originated in your wish to grant the aid of your philosophical thinking to as many suffering people as possible and in my need for a solid support for my medical science. It has already been over ten years since these meetings had their beginning.

You never shirked the heavy burden of being my guest one, two, three times per semester in order to bring the best of my students and co-workers closer to a fundamental thinking over which they as one-sided, scientifically educated psychiatrists had so little command. Today dozens of young Swiss doctors and former seminar participants from abroad are deeply grateful to you for the patience with which you always grappled again and again with the clumsiness of our one-track vision. With these seminars you created numerous and indissoluble bonds connecting you with my hometown and my country. It is quite clear how your decisive and enduring way of teaching the circle of novice psychiatrists and psychotherapists in Zurich influenced the style and form of their medical practices and made them more human in character. Yet, what unending effort you had to expend until you brought these young people to the insight that for them as doctors—and especially for those who are involved with living, human beings—a philosophical reflection on the foundations of their science is a necessary presupposition for the true, scientific character of the healing art and is not merely a playful, spare-time activity.

p. 366

Later on, we understood that and [also understood] why man's constitution and the meaning of his existence cannot be comprehended as long as one takes being-human [*Mensch sein*] itself as the starting point and the goal of the investigation in the manner of the traditional, psychological anthropologies. You demanded from us that we turn to the fundamental question of philosophy, which wants to know what it really means that something can be, and "is" at all, rather than that simply nothing is. Thus, you were teaching us to marvel at the greatest wonder: That something "is"; that there is "being." The question of being as such has kept you occupied ever since your original studies of Brentano and Aristotle. Your life is consumed by it. What being human is can be revealed in its most proper way only in light of this question. In view of this [question of being], being-human shows itself as something that is claimed by something much higher than itself. Being-human fundamentally means to be needed [*gebraucht*] as a domain of a capacity, open-to-the-world to receive-perceive [*Vernehmenen-Können*], so that the given things, making up the world by their significance and referential relationships, can emerge in it, can manifest themselves, and can come to their presencing and to their being. If there were not something like open-standing being human, then how, and into what, should something come into presence at all, manifest itself, that is, come into being? With these discoveries of your thinking, you let us doctors know the true dignity of man.

p. 367

Yet, in demonstrating that this dignity of man is not something made by man himself, a third source, namely, the basic source of our friendship, came to light. We were both inspired by the knowledge, coming from afar, that man is claimed and needed by something far surpassing him. Although my devotion to such a mandate was rather dim in nature before you opened my eyes, and will always remain in varying degrees of strength because of the distance between a genius and a common man, my similarly directed effort seemed to be worth the attention of your friendship.

Thus, the common ground already uniting us is the fact that, in your view, the "machination" of man as a subject, as claimed by the now prevailing spirit of technology, is losing its claim to predominance. The boasting of the modern homo faber about the human being's subjectivity appears groundless to someone considering himself a shepherd and guardian of something higher. Although it is unnameable and wants to remain hidden, many names have already been given to what is higher than man, to what releases him into his own existence, to what also sends things, capable of being received-perceived and to be guarded by man, into their being present-at-hand. It could be that the sheer, unlimited openness of your thinking for the advent of this absolute has its ground in its inexhaustible power for attracting the watchful people of our godforsaken times. Without describing it with words, which would not shelter, but bury it, your statements tacitly refer to what cannot be said.

Numerous, of course, are the cynics who consider the "later" Heidegger to be a mere poet or mystic who long ago abandoned the foundation of "scientific philosophy." Nevertheless, such superficial minds overlook, first, that the "later" Heidegger in no way separated himself from the "early" Heidegger, no matter what one might think of the "turning." Heidegger's thinking is always still to think the same about the same, [a practice] for which a Sophist once mocked Socrates, not noticing that it is precisely this which is the most difficult and important task. Second, your critics fail to compare the rigorous appropriateness and "objectivity" (in the best sense of the word) of what was said in your early and later thinking with the luxuriant, black magic holding sway over so many concepts of modern science.

Since most people are somewhat out-of-date by the time they are eighty, you too will hear with increasing frequency that your philosophy has now finally become outdated and untimely. No one who speaks in such a way has even come close to understanding it. How else could one account for the fact that your thinking is just now experiencing such a great breakthrough in Japan and America? Obviously, the ablest technicians of our world just now are noticing that you are something more than merely an old-fashioned critic of our technical age. On the contrary, they sense that you have been able to think through the proper, unfolding essence of technology as no one before. This spirit [essence] of technology is not something technical in itself. Therefore, it cannot be apprehended in a scientific-technical way, but

p. 368

can only be apprehended philosophically through thinking. Yet you were capable of doing it in such a way that you could lead us from a demonic state of being spellbound by technology to a free comportment toward it. You are teaching us to comprehend the technical comportment to the world in which we people of today must exist as a destiny of [the whole of] human history. With this you let us become aware of its unavoidable character as a mandate, yet at the same time you are removing the fateful character [*Verhängnishafte*] of something absolute and ultimate which has finally befallen us.

With such a determination of [the relationship between] "technology-nature," you returned again to the domain of the doctor—if one only conceives of the healing art broadly enough. By having clarified the spirit of technology, you have also become the founder of an effective, preventive medicine. The vast majority of all modern ailments already belong to the illnesses of man which are called by the unfortunate term "psychosomatic." They all finally have their origin in the sick person's comportment to the modern industrial society of our time, with which he could not cope in a way worthy of a human being. The first supposition for a preventive correction of such pathogenic, social behavior is clear insight into the proper, emerging essence of technology, which determines this society.

Yours,
Medard Boss

TRANSLATORS' AFTERWORDS

Heidegger's Philosophy and Its Implications for Psychology, Freud, and Existential Psychoanalysis

Richard Askay

I. The Significance of Heidegger's Philosophy for Psychology

The existential-phenomenological approach to psychology has come to play an increasingly significant role in the evolutionary development of American psychology during the past few decades. This is evidenced by a number of developments. To begin with, work involving this orientation has substantially increased in the American Psychological Association conferences and journals. Moreover, well-established journals focusing on this approach have emerged—for example, the *Review of Existential Psychology and Psychiatry* and the *Journal of Phenomenological Psychology*. Further, this approach has been typically introduced in most standard textbooks across the spectrum of relevant topics within the discipline of psychology. Some psychology departments across the country have chosen this orientation as their primary focus (or at least one of them). Finally, significant anthologies and histories on the existential-phenomenological impact on psychology have appeared—for example, *Existential-Phenomenological Alternatives for Psychology, Phenomenology in Psychology and Psychiatry, A History of Humanistic and Existential Psychologies, Existential-Phenomenological Perspectives in Psychology,* and *Psychoanalysis and Existential Philosophy.* Numerous texts on existential and/or phenomenological psychology have also appeared. It was Heidegger's hermeneutical phenomenological ontology that served as one of the primary historical impetuses for these extensive developments and advances.

With the publication of Heidegger's *Zollikoner Seminare: Protokolle-Gespräche-Briefe Herausgegeben Von Medard Boss,*[1] the question of the relationship and significance of Heidegger's philosophy to psychology has, in the words of a recent commentator, been "placed high on the intellectual agenda."[2] Indeed, commentaries on the seminars have started to appear in various contexts,[3] and references to it are abundant throughout the literature. With this English translation of the *Zollikoner Seminare,* this discussion will no doubt increase.

The *Zollikon Seminars* is a text which includes several unique features within the corpus of Heidegger's works. For the first time, we see Heidegger directly, concretely, and extensively engage the discipline of psychology. In doing so, Heidegger exhibits his pedagogical skills while entering into a dialogue with psychiatrists and psychotherapists who had been primarily trained in the natural sciences. Heidegger is seen trying to make his ontological insights immediately accessible to persons outside of the context of professional philosophy. Also, we witness an immediate and concrete confrontation between Heidegger's phenomenological approach and the scientific method. Throughout the seminars, Heidegger constantly invokes the methods of phenomenological inquiry to enable the psychiatrists to overcome scientistic prejudices. Furthermore, in these seminars, conversations, and correspondence with Dr. Medard Boss, Heidegger systematically addresses various crucial questions for the first time: What is the nature of the relationship between psychology and philosophy, generally speaking? What is the relationship between psychology and technology, and what does it portend for the future? Are Freudian psychoanalysis (with its sweeping influence) and Heideggerean hermeneutical phenomenological ontology compatible? Why or why not? What is the nature of the relationship between Heidegger's analytic of Dasein and that of Binswanger and Boss? What is the relationship between the analysis of the lived body as so powerfully conducted by French philosophers/psychologists and Heidegger's analysis of Dasein? Is our being-in-the-world more primordial than our bodily being? Or is it the other way around? Are the two possibly equiprimordial? Heidegger also addresses other issues throughout the text such as relativity theory, cybernetics, and oriental philosophy. Clearly, these seminars are indispensable for anyone interested in the above fundamental questions.

II. The Historical Context of the Zollikon Seminars

To appreciate the philosophical significance of the Zollikon Seminars, it is important to have a sense of the complex historical context from which they emerged. It was from within this historical flow that Heidegger was seeking to transform and overcome the traditional Western metaphysical

perspective. The flow itself was constituted by the powerful predominance of Cartesian ontological and epistemological developments and
the eventual turn to, and focus upon, transcendental subjectivity in the
Kantian revolution. It was Franz Brentano's initial investigation into the
"intentionality" (i.e., the directedness of consciousness, consciousness
constant consciousness of something) and his acceptance of the equation
of consciousness with the psyche that performed a pivotal historical role
in the major divergence which was about to occur. Sigmund Freud and
Edmund Husserl had both been students of Brentano, yet each reacted
to the philosophical vantage point he represented in vastly different ways.
For Freud, who had been primarily influenced by Kant, Schopenhauer,
Nietzsche, and Hartmann, the equation of the psyche with consciousness
was a philosophical prejudice to be overcome. Much more was to be
gained by hypothesizing the existence of an unconscious dimension of
the psyche. Hence, Freud developed psychoanalysis with a focus upon
the Unconscious (while very little attention was given to consciousness).
Husserl, on the other hand, believed that the best way to make philosophy
into a "rigorous science" was to focus on conducting a descriptive analysis
of the universal and necessary structures/acts of consciousness (with
little or no interest in an Unconscious)—hence, the development of
phenomenology. Against this direction, Heidegger insisted that the focus
of philosophical inquiry should be on the question of the meaning of
Being. Thus Heidegger developed his phenomenological ontology that
he described as "hermeneutical."

The historical context of the emergence of Daseinanalysis was equally
complex. In fact, it was more than fitting that Heidegger conducted
his first session of the Zollikon Seminars in 1947 in the Burghölzli,
the psychiatric clinic of the University of Zurich. Sixty years earlier, it
had been one of the first mental hospitals to conduct a serious study
of hypnosis. It was there that Eugen Bleuler had turned the course of
Swiss psychiatry away from the anatomical dissection of brains to explore
the role of personality in directing the course of diseases. Later, Carl
Jung, a collaborator of Bleuler's and one of Freud's students, became
its chief physician and began to reassess Freudian psychoanalysis from
a less reductionistic and more individualistically oriented direction. The
Swiss Daseinanalysts, Ludwig Binswanger and Medard Boss, had both
worked under Bleuler, and had been students and collaborators of Jung's.
In addition, Binswanger had developed a lifelong friendship (1907–
38) with Freud, and Boss had been Freud's analysand (1925). Each
had experienced the strengths of psychoanalysis, yet each came to hold
some grave doubts about Freud's theory and to believe that it lacked

an adequate philosophical grounding. Binswanger and Boss agreed that it was Heidegger's hermeneutical ontology that could most adequately provide such a grounding.

III. Heidegger's Relationship to the Original Daseinanalysts

With the publication of *Being and Time*[4] in 1927, Binswanger suggested that it was Heidegger's ontology from which existential analysis received its primary impetus, its philosophical foundation and justification, and its methodological guidelines. Hence, Binswanger clearly supported the "ontological turn" of phenomenology. He proceeded to develop a "phenomenological anthropology" (i.e., one which focused on Dasein's immediate everyday experience) which would serve as the foundation for psychiatry as a science. However, Binswanger began raising certain objections to what he understood to be Heidegger's philosophy. It was in his book *Grundformen und Erkenntnis menschlichen Daseins* [Basic forms and knowledge of human Dasein][5] that Binswanger argued that Heidegger's analysis was inadequate. Binswanger's goal was to offer a "phenomenological anthropology" of fundamental forms of human existence which he believed went beyond, and improved upon, Heidegger's analysis of Dasein. Binswanger contended that Heidegger simply failed to offer a sufficient account of the primordial social dimension of love in human existence, that he neglected a special kind of "knowledge of Dasein" (expressed in "imagination of love"). According to Binswanger, Dasein's love disclosed the irreducible dual mode of human existence ("we-hood") as more fundamental than Heidegger's notion of *Mitsein* (being-with) that was part of the care structure and grounded in temporality. As Binswanger put it, Heidegger left love to freeze outside the doors of his projection of being. Binswanger described this "we-hood" ("we of love" as "being of loving encounter") as an original structure (*Urform*) of Dasein's existence. According to Binswanger, Heidegger's conception of care was not entirely open to the unity of being but only to itself in the world as *mine*. It was love, he believed, that disclosed an openness toward being which could most accurately be described as *ours*. "Love" was understood by Binswanger as the ontological possibility of "we-hood." In loving coexistence, we are fully engaged in an interdependent presence with the other which is rooted in our very being, yet through it we "leap beyond" our own singular Dasein. In love, then, we go "beyond" the cares of everyday being-in-the-world and participate in an "eternal now." For Binswanger, then, not only is Dasein being-in-the-world as care,

Dasein is being-beyond-the-world in love. That is, humans are being-in-the-world-beyond-the-world [*In-der-Welt-uber-die-Welt-hinaus-sein*]. Hence, Binswanger believed that the opposition between love and care could be reconciled in a new anthropological form of being.

Heidegger's response to Binswanger was direct and blunt: Binswanger had simply failed to grasp the true significance of the fundamental ontology developed in the analytic of Dasein in *Being and Time*. For Heidegger, this led to a plethora of errors and disastrous results. First, according to Heidegger, Binswanger had fundamentally misinterpreted *Being and Time* as solipsistic and subjectivistic. Misinterpreting care as function on the ontic level (as an ontic comportment, e.g., melancholy [*ZS* 286]), Binswanger simply failed to grasp its ontological sense, for example, Dasein's openness to being as necessarily shared with other Daseins and Being-with as intrinsic to the structure of being-in-the-world (*ZS* 151). Since Binswanger understood Dasein as an isolated subject, he found it necessary to supplement care with love, with the dual mode of we-hood as "being beyond the world," so that Dasein could "get over to" other subjects. Care, however, when correctly understood (i.e., from a fundamental ontological perspective) is never in opposition to love; rather, love is founded in the structure of care as the understanding of being (*ZS* 242). Heidegger concluded that not only was Binswanger's supplement not necessary, it was not even possible (*ZS* 286).

Second, although Binswanger correctly considered being-in-the-world, Heidegger pointed out that he utterly failed to grasp its primary ontological meaning: the understanding of being. He neglected to realize that the fundamental meaning of *Being and Time* was the posing of the question of being. Binswanger overlooked Dasein as a clearing within being toward which Dasein is open in such a way that it has an original understanding of being. As a result, he generated a wrong-headed interpretation of being-in-the-world and transcendence. Due to his uncritical allegiance to his philosophical heritage (i.e., Descartes, Kant, Husserl, etc.), Binswanger's analysis remained immured in the realm of subjectivity (*ZS* 152, 236–40). And, of course, Binswanger never explained how it is possible that subjectivity transcends to an external world (*ZS* 259).

Third, according to Heidegger, Binswanger conflated the ontological with the ontic level of analysis. Heidegger believed that this happened in a number of ways. For instance, in the *Zollikon Seminars* (*ZS* 163–64), Heidegger carefully drew the following distinctions:

1. Analytic of Dasein: the analysis of the ontological structure (existentialia) of Dasein (as conducted in *Being and Time*)

2. Daseinanalysis: actual concrete illustrations of this ontological structure
3. Daseinanalyse: a description of concrete existential experiences on the level of an ontic anthropology
   a. Normal anthropology
   b. Daseinanalytic pathology
4. Concrete Daseinanalyse: a description of specific examples of actual individuals in their various modifications of being-in-the-world, care, and temporality.
   a. Normal
   b. Pathological

Heidegger argued that Binswanger proceeded to conflate levels 1 and 2 with levels 3 and 4. However, the former were demarcated by the fundamental task of posing the question of being, that is, of uncovering the unity of the ontological conditions for Dasein's existence in its relation to being, whereas the point of the latter was to espouse an empirical anthropology.

Fourth, Heidegger charged that Binswanger conflated the ontological and ontic levels of analysis through his notion of world-projection. Heidegger suggested that Binswanger conflated the ontological projection of the world itself with the beings which become accessible through this world-projection (i.e., what appears because of this projection) (ZS 253, 286).

Fifth, for Heidegger, Binswanger failed to appreciate sufficiently "the ontological difference" (between being and beings). This difference involved no division between fundamental ontology and specific disciplines as Binswanger seemed to think. Fundamental ontology is not above/below in any foundational way (ZS 255, 238). Binswanger sought to eliminate fundamental ontology from his Daseinanalysis, but this was impossible since the former moved within and was indissolubly involved with the foundation of each discipline. Heidegger ultimately denied that his own analytic of Dasein was complete enough to serve as the basis of a philosophical anthropology (ZS 163).

Obviously, Heidegger had no qualms about the development of a properly oriented psychiatric Daseinanalysis (ZS 163–64).Otherwise, he would not have proofread Boss's books which had this as their aim. What he did vociferously object to was that someone (e.g., Binswanger) develop a Daseinanalysis that was grounded in what Heidegger regarded as a fundamentally misguided interpretation of his ontological project. Such an endeavor did more harm than good, in Heidegger's eyes.

Interestingly enough, Binswanger himself later conceded the validity of some of Heidegger's criticisms. He characterized his own endeavors as being *not* an "analytic of Dasein," but a phenomenological-anthropological analysis of love. He acknowledged that Heidegger's interest was "entirely different" from his own, and he finally admitted in the preface to the fourth edition of the *Grundformen* that the aim of the *Grundformen* had made no pretense at being "a rejoinder to *Being and Time* but was rather a phenomenology of love." He went on to acknowledge that his "productive misunderstanding" consisted of his understanding "the existentialia not as such, not as ontological, but merely in the sense of offering some most fruitful, categorical guidelines/clues to our inquiry." Binswanger admitted that he should have paid more attention to the fact that Heidegger clearly distinguished his existential analytic from anthropology, psychology, and biology which led to his own anthropological misunderstanding of fundamental ontology.

By contrast, Heidegger felt very differently about Medard Boss and his formulation of Daseinanalysis. Heidegger highly appreciated Professor Boss as a respected friend and colleague. The first book by Boss which reflected Heidegger's influence was the *Meaning and Content of Sexual Perversions: A Daseinanalytic Contribution to the Psychopathology of the Phenomenon of Love,* published in 1947. Next came *The Meaning of Dreams and Investigations into Psychosomatic Medicine* in 1954. They were quickly followed by *Psychoanalysis and Daseinanalysis* in 1957. And finally, Boss's magnum opus appeared in 1975: *Existential Foundations of Medicine and Psychology.* The last was a result of over three decades of Boss's evolutionary development working in collaboration with Heidegger and was a concrete application of what he had gleaned from the Zollikon Seminars. In it, Boss sought to humanize medicine and psychology by showing the limitations of the model of natural science and by disclosing how medicine and psychology were best grounded existentially in Heidegger's hermeneutical phenomenological ontology.

As opposed to Binswanger, Medard Boss had the open support of Heidegger in the development of his form of Daseinanalysis. Heidegger worked closely with Boss on the *Existential Foundations of Medicine and Psychology,*[6] which is evident from their conversations and correspondence (also see the edited galley proofs by Heidegger). The primary reason for this was that what distinguished Boss's approach from Binswanger's was his emphasis upon human "perceptive world openness"—namely, Heidegger's description of human existence as a clearing or illumination of being. Following Heidegger, Boss acknowledged that humans exist only insofar as they relate to (i.e., disclose and perceive) others, self, and the world. People are world-disclosing in their very being; humans and world require each other for their very being. Hence, each individual's "world-relations" are one's own ways of being human, of openness to the world as such which includes an immediate and direct understanding of others.

Agreeing with Binswanger, Boss thought that neurotic and psychotic patients suffered from a constriction, or "blockage," of their world openness. Occasionally, for example, an individual refused a "world-relation" through a "bodily-jamming." Once again, in accord with Heidegger, Boss agreed that the body was "one of the media through which the world-disclosing relationships which constitute existence are carried out."[7] Boss's Daseinanalysis attempted to determine what specific modifications of normal being-in-the-world accounted for the occurrence of such experiences. The aim of Boss's Daseinanalysis, then, was to make the individual human being transparent in his/her own structure, to adhere to the immediately given objects and phenomena of the world of human beings.

IV. Heidegger's Critique of Freudian Psychoanalysis

We now turn to the relationship between Heidegger's philosophy and Freud's psychoanalysis.[8] Freud and Heidegger did not have any direct contact with one another. As mentioned, it was Binswanger and Boss who served as catalysts for the historic meeting of Heidegger's hermeneutical phenomenological ontological approach and Freudian psychoanalysis. Binswanger had developed a lifelong friendship (1907–38) with Freud, and Boss had been Freud's analysand (1925). It was Boss who formed an extended friendship with Heidegger (1947–76), and Binswanger who had been Heidegger's intermittent acquaintance.

On the one hand, it is clear that Freud had at least some acquaintance with Heidegger's philosophy via his friendship with Binswanger. In 1936, Binswanger sent Freud a copy of his lecture "Freud's Conception of Man in Light of Anthropology." In it Binswanger argued, among other things, that "man is not only mechanical necessity and organization, not merely world or in-the-world. His existence is understandable only as being-in-the-world, as the projection and disclosure of world—as Heidegger has so powerfully demonstrated."[9] Freud's response to it was characteristically pointed: "In it I rejoiced over your beautiful prose, your erudition, the scope of your horizon, your tact in disagreement. . . . But, of course, I don't believe a word of what you say."[10] Freud's reaction was hardly surprising given his well-known ambivalence to philosophy and his clear commitment to the scientific *Weltanschauungen*.[11]

On the other hand, Heidegger's familiarity with and reaction to Freud's work was considerably more complicated. Medard Boss had been an analysand of Freud's over dozens of sessions in 1925, and it was he, as a trained psychoanalyst, who introduced Heidegger to Freud's metapsychology:

> Even before our first encounter, I had heard of Heidegger's abysmal aversion to all modern scientific psychology. To me, too, he made no secret of his opposition to it. His repugnance mounted considerably after I had induced him with much guile and cunning to delve directly for the first time into Freud's own writings. During his perusal of the theoretical, "metapsychological" works, Heidegger never ceased shaking his head. He simply did not want to have to accept that such a highly intelligent and gifted man as Freud could produce such artificial, inhuman, indeed absurd and purely fictitious constructions about homo sapiens. This reading made him literally feel ill. Freud's "Papers on Technique," in which he gives advice on the practical conduct of the therapeutic analysis of the neurotic patient, made Heidegger more conciliatory. He immediately discovered the crass mutual contradiction of these writings: namely, the unbridgeable gulf between the absolute, natural scientific determinism of his theories and the repeated emphasis of the freeing of the patient through psychoanalytic practice.[12]

In his book *Psychoanalysis and Daseinsanalysis,* Boss extended this point by arguing that the entire system of philosophical presuppositions underlying Freud's "metapsychology" and his "therapeutic techniques" were fundamentally diverse, and the latter were at least compatible with Heidegger's hermeneutical ontology.[13]

To understand the reason for Heidegger's dual reaction to Freud, one need only consider the following pronouncements by the latter: "[Psychoanalysis] must accept the scientific Weltanschauung . . . the intellect and the mind are objects for scientific research in exactly the same way as non-human things. . . . Our best hope for the future is that intellect—the scientific spirit, reason—may in process of time establish a dictatorship in the mental life of man."[14] Science was the only source of genuine knowledge for Freud the theorist. Such remarks could have only caused the greatest ontological dyspepsia in Heidegger. On the other hand, for Heidegger more palatable remarks were strewn throughout Freud's papers on technique. Freud often alluded to the human capacity for free choice, the truth-disclosing and truth-fleeing tendencies of human beings, the capacity for being absorbed into an anonymous group mentality, thereby forfeiting individual distinctiveness, freedom, concomitant responsibility, and so forth. Indeed, in stark contrast to the quote above, in his essay "The Ways of Psycho-analytic Therapy" Freud stressed that "we cannot accept . . . that psycho-analysis should place itself in the service of a particular philosophical outlook on the world and should urge this upon the patient in order to ennoble him. I would say that after all this is only tyranny."[15] Of particular interest to Heidegger here would have been Freud's observations that the individual often permits oneself to be absorbed in an anonymous group mentality.

As a result, Freud's metapsychology was one of the primary targets of Heidegger's critique in the *Zollikon Seminars*. One of Heidegger's explicit goals in the *Zollikon Seminars* and elsewhere was to break the hold of "the dictatorship of scientific thinking" (ZS 342) that Freud had advocated. Heidegger made it clear that he saw psychoanalysis as a major threat: "the view that psychology—which long ago turned into psychoanalysis—is taken in Switzerland and elsewhere as a substitute for philosophy (if not for religion)."[16] Heidegger was concerned that psychoanalysis, and scientism, were becoming quickly the dominating theoretical influences in Europe.

According to Heidegger, Freud epitomized a contemporary scientific mind who had uncritically adopted, and subsequently become entrapped by, the tacit ontological commitments of his philosophical heritage. Freud's tacit ontology had its genesis in Cartesian philosophy, with its quest for the development of a unified, comprehensive, scientific philosophy; and then in Galilean-Newtonian physics, which became absorbed into Kantian philosophy; and finally in the Helmholtz school of Neo-Kantianism. Heidegger was explicit: "Freud's metapsychology is the application of Neo-Kantian philosophy to the human being" (ZS 260). Everything had its basis in physiology.

Heidegger sought to break the hold of the dictatorship of scientific thinking by conducting a critical reflection upon some of the most basic philosophical presuppositions of Freud's metapsychological theory. In order for the reader to gain a better understanding of Heidegger's critique, a summary of Freud's most fundamental assumptions are provided.

Freud's Cartesian presuppositions included the following:

1. The subject/object dichotomy is intrinsic to our mental operations.[17]
2. Only objective "beings" or "things" exist.
3. Two forms of objective reality exist: the psychical and the material.[18]

Freud then went on to hypothesize:

1. Psychical reality is composed of conscious and unconscious processes.[19]
2. Psychical reality is powered by an energy analogous to and reciprocally transformable with physical energy.[20]
3. Psychical energy is ultimately derivable from bodily/organic processes.[21]
4. Mind and body are connected via the instincts.

5. The instincts are responsible for the development of mental processes and images.[22]
6. The instincts, Eros and Thanatos, are the ultimate causes of all activity, and hence free will is an illusion.[23]

Freud's Kantian-like assumptions included:

1. Cathexis via the psychical reservoir continually modify internal and external reality—the Ego knows only a "phenomenal" world.[24]
2. The real natures of the independently existing world and the underlying psychical processes are ultimately unknowable.[25]
3. Space and time are "forms of thought."[26]

In light of the above presuppositions, Heidegger argued that Freud made other assumptions with regard to the nature and function of physical and psychical processes. First, he assumed that both domains operated in the same mechanical way (ZS 24), and that everything was ultimately grounded in somatic processes (forces) (ZS 233). As a result, he argued that both the physical and psychical were considered to be involved in a continuous nexus of causal relations (ZS 7–8). Hence, everything is necessarily subjectable to reductionistic scientistic analysis (ZS 148, 104), and everything that exists is measurable (ZS 7–8). Thus, Freud postulated the complete explainability of psychical life (ZS 260) in causal terms (ZS 148). However, since no "uninterrupted explainability" appeared in consciousness, Freud found it necessary to (a) "invent 'the unconscious'" (ZS 260), thereby introducing the "fatal distinction" between the conscious and unconscious (ZS 319); (b) resort to the hypothesis of "unconscious purposes" as explanations (ZS 214); and (c) mistakenly construct the idea of "unconscious motivation" (ZS 233), and conflate "cause" and "motive" (ZS 25 f.).

According to Heidegger, Freud's "erroneous theory" (ZS 282) failed for two primary kinds of reasons. The first, and less important, one for Heidegger was that it failed on scientific grounds, that is, it neglected to satisfy its own methodological criteria. For example, Freud resorted to unverifiable presuppositions and nonempirical concepts (e.g., "the unconscious," "the instincts," etc.) (ZS 218–19). Moreover, he, like any natural scientist, failed to give an adequate account of the connection between the mind and body and the transformation of the nonmaterial into the "bodily-material" (ZS 294).

Far more significantly for Heidegger was the fact that Freud simply failed to see the "clearing" (ZS 228) and neglected to ascertain the ontological characteristics of the being of man (ZS 282). Yet these were what made Freud's theoretical account possible in the first place, according to Heidegger. For example, Heidegger pointed out that Freud's libido theory eliminated the person in that humans get reduced to a configuration of wish impulses, urges, instincts, and so forth. Freud's theory becomes even more intractable when one realizes that it is not possible to construct the significance/meaningfulness of being-in-the-world from such psychical acts as wishing, urging, and propensities. Rather, it is Dasein's being-in-the-world which is always already presupposed (ZS 217–19). Similarly, Freud's conceptions of "introjection," "projection," "empathy," and "transference" turn out to be contrived constructions predicated upon a subject/object model which is oblivious to the primordiality of being-in-the-world (ZS 208, 228). In addition, such Freudian conceptions presuppose, yet abstract from, the being-with dimension of Dasein which is intrinsic to the unity of being-in-the-world (ZS 207–10).

V. What Heidegger's Philosophy Offers Psychology

Finally, it might be asked what Heidegger's philosophy specifically has to offer the discipline of psychology. Its importance for psychology (and its subdisciplines such as psychoanalysis, psychotherapy, etc.) can be most easily seen by focusing upon the word "analysis" and some of its implications. First, as Heidegger himself noted in the *Zollikon Seminars* (ZS 148), one of its meanings in Greek was "to loosen, for instance, to release a chained person from his chains, to liberate someone from captivity." Heidegger believed that by reclaiming the Greek sense of the word "analysis," psychology (et al.) would become free to engage in the "freeing activity" of analysis.

Heidegger's "freeing activity" occurred on a multiplicity of different levels. Heidegger employed negative and positive notions of freedom in his analysis. First, psychologists (et al.), clients, and other individuals are "freed from" their uncritically held ontological precommitments. Second, all are then "freed to" be open to the presencing of being as it is disclosed by Dasein (i.e., to obtain the "transformation in the listener's way of seeing and in awakening the sense in which the questions must be asked") (ZS 324). Dasein can only be free in the sense of "freedom of choice" because it is primordially exposed to the free and open dimension (i.e., the clearing) of being in the first place.

Heidegger wanted to free psychology (and its relevant subdisciplines) from its uncritical adherence to Cartesian "thing" ontology and its concomitant trappings. "Science is, to an almost incredible degree, dogmatic everywhere, that is, it operates with preconceptions and prejudices which have not been reflected on. There is the highest need for doctors who *think* and do not wish to leave the field entirely to the scientific technicians" (*ZS* 134). It is due to science's failure to reflect on its preconception and prejudices which prevents it from giving "an unequivocal and ontologically adequate answer to the question about the kind of Being which belongs to those entities which we ourselves are."[27] Once the ontologically adequate answer Heidegger provided is secured, psychology would then be freed to pursue its inquiry with genuine openness and understanding of what it means to be. Psychology would be in a position to "let beings be," free from any preconceived "dogmatic constructions." Similarly, psychologists would be freed from their propensity to cling so tightly and uncritically to the "scientistic" Weltanschauung. In this way, the "scientific" character of psychology would gain a new opportunity for critical reflection upon itself.

Next, on the level of psychotherapy (psychoanalysis, etc.), the therapeutic relationship would be freed of the danger of the uncritical imposition of theoretical frameworks by therapists on clients. The latter is what Heidegger described as the kind of concernful being that "leaps in" for the Other. "In such solicitude the Other can become one who is dominated and dependent, even if this domination is a tacit one and remains hidden from him."[28] The less subtle intervention of giving advice or making decisions for the client by the therapist would thereby automatically be precluded as well. The therapist then would be freed to be open to the very presencing of being through the client.

Finally, Heidegger's philosophy offers individuals some resources for gaining a more authentic self-knowledge:

> The kind of knowing-oneself which is essential and closest, demands that one become acquainted with oneself. And when, indeed, one's knowing-oneself gets lost in such ways as aloofness, hiding oneself away, or putting on a disguise, Being-with-one-another must follow special routes of its own in order to come close to Others, or even to "see through them."[29]
>
> Dasein's resoluteness toward itself is what first makes it possible to let the Others who are with it "be" in their own-most potentiality-for-Being, and to co-disclose this potentiality in the solicitude which leaps forth and liberates. When Dasein is resolute, it can become the "conscience" of Others. Only by authentically Being-their-selves in resoluteness can people authentically be with one another.[30]

By authentically knowing oneself, the client is "free from" uncritically adopting various ontological frameworks and "free to" be open to whatever comes to presence from oneself or through others.

Notes

1. M. Heidegger, *Zollikoner Seminare: Protokolle-Gespräche-Briefe Herausgegeben Von Medard Boss,* ed. M. Boss (Frankfurt am Main: Klostermann, 1987).

2. F. Dallmayr, *Between Freiburg and Frankfurt: Toward a Critical Ontology* (Amherst: University of Massachusetts Press, 1991), p. 210.

3. See, e.g., ibid., pp. 210–37; C. Guignon, "Authenticity, Moral Values, and Psychotherapy," in *The Cambridge Companion to Heidegger,* ed. C. Guignon (Cambridge: Cambridge University Press, 1993), pp. 215–39; K. Hoeller, ed., *Heidegger and Psychology* (Seattle: Review of Existential Psychology and Psychiatry, 1988); W. Richardson, "Heidegger among the Doctors," in *Reading Heidegger: Commemorations* (Bloomington: Indiana University Press, 1993), pp. 49–63.

4. M. Heidegger, *Being and Time,* trans. John Macquarrie and Edward Robinson (New York: Harper and Row, 1962).

5. L. Binswanger, *Grundformen und Erkenntnis menschlichen Daseins,* 4th ed. (Zurich: Niehans, 1964).

6. M. Boss, *Existential Foundations of Medicine and Psychology,* trans. Stephen Conway and Anne Cleaves (New York: Aronson, 1979).

7. M. Boss, *Psychoanalysis and Daseinanalysis,* trans. L. Lefebre (New York: Da Capo, 1963), p. 40.

8. For a more comprehensive exposition, see R. Askay, "A Philosophical Dialogue between Heidegger and Freud," in *Journal of Philosophical Research* 24 (1999), pp. 415–43.

9. L. Binswanger, *Being-in-the-World: Selected Papers of Ludwig Binswanger,* trans. Jacob Needleman (New York: Harper and Row, 1967), p. 169.

10. Ibid., pp. 3–4.

11. S. Freud, *Standard Edition of the Complete Psychological Works of Sigmund Freud* [*SE*], trans. J. Strachey (London: Hogarth Press, 1964), 22:160 f.

12. Hoeller, *Heidegger and Psychology,* pp. 9–10.

13. Boss, *Psychoanalysis and Daseinanalysis,* pp. 61–74. We should note, however, that Freud would have rejected the above distinction. For him, psychoanalysis as a whole was a unified science—a research procedure, therapeutic method, and collection of psychological information, all of which were interrelated and grounded in his metapsychological theory (*SE* 22:138, 153, 156; 18:235). The psychoanalytic doctrine was merely a superstructure which, through scientific progress, would be shown to have its ultimate foundation in an organic substructure. Mental life would then be shown to be ultimately rooted in physical processes, which of course was the goal of his metapsychological theory (*SE* 14:78). Hence, any talk of fundamental philosophical differences between his theoretical and therapeutic approaches would have been utterly unacceptable to him.

14. *SE* 22:171.

15. S. Freud, *Collected Papers,* trans. Joan Riviere (New York: Basic, 1959), 2:399.

16. H. Petzet, *Encounters and Dialogues with Martin Heidegger—1929–1976* (Chicago: University of Chicago Press, 1993), p. 49.

17. *SE* 14:134.

18. Ibid., 1:103–13; 20:247; 23:144–45, 151, 158.

19. Ibid., 5:612–14; 6:178; 12:257, 260; 14:167–70; 19:12–13; 20:31, 194.

20. Ibid., 1:295.

21. Ibid., 23:151, 158.

22. Ibid., 14:121–22.

23. Ibid., 18:38–41, 46–51; 19:40–47.

24. Ibid., 14:171.

25. Ibid., 23:196; 6:229.

26. Ibid., 22:74, 76; 18:28.

27. Heidegger, *Being and Time*, p. 75.

28. Ibid., p. 158.

29. Ibid., p. 161.

30. Ibid., p. 344.

The Question of Being, Language, and Translation

Franz Mayr

I. Translating German into English

Difficulties in the translation of Heidegger's works are legendary, and the translation of the *Zollikon Seminars* was no exception. Most difficulties have usually been attributed to Heidegger's penchant for creating neologisms in order to overcome a one-sided objectified understanding of "being" and a one-sided representational view of human language, which has characterized all Western metaphysics since Plato and Aristotle. Some translators have suggested that these difficulties are a result of Heidegger's own idiosyncratic translations of the ancient Greek language and its etymological derivations or of his predilection for the poetic use of language. Since *Being and Time* (*BT*), Heidegger himself considered the basic difficulty of all translation to be the fact that every language has its own historical context and is embedded in its own cultural matrix, which in itself is an essential, constitutive moment of man's primordial understanding of being (*Verstehen*, *ZS* 236). The later Heidegger maintained that prior to any instrumental or computerized use, prior to any objectification as a sign-system, and even prior to any logical formalization, language is the historical address of being to the human being. Being appropriates Da-sein for its self-revelation in language. The primordial Event of the self-manifestation of being happens as sounding and re-sounding (*Hallen*) and as tone in the ontological sense, not the phonetic sense (*ZS* 226, 232). To use Heidegger's cryptic phrase: "Language is the house of being" (*ZS* 226). Yet being simultaneously reveals and conceals itself in language, in every historical language, and especially in the words of poets.

In order to understand the special difficulties of any translation of Heidegger's thinking and writings into English, one must take into account matters which are very familiar to linguists and historians, but not equally well known to philosophers.[1] Both the English and German languages belong to the Indo-European language family, but despite their original closeness, the two languages diverged in their linguistic structure and historical development. German, like ancient Greek, remained a highly inflectional language with word endings on nouns, verbs, and adjectives and with nouns indicating the morphological and logical function of the word within the sentence. In large measure, English lost its word endings and became a more isolating-analytical, noninflectional language. The tendency of English to pronounce nonstressed vowels indistinctly—for example, the weak *e* in "solves," wolves"—and to finally omit them entirely led to an emphasis on monosyllables. Without word endings, the precise position of the single, "isolated" word and the accent within the English sentence became very important. This loss of word endings also led to a greater use of pronouns and propositions, to a preference for simple rather than compound sentences, and to a greater emphasis on word order, preferably subject-verb-object. English completely abandoned German's logical superordination and subordination of words and acquired an abundance of idiomatic phrases and fixed word combinations as a substitute for the inflectional-logical function of word endings. With its open, flexible, more "univocal" vocabulary, English assimilated many foreign words and linguistic roots. Rather than remaining with the synthetic and holistic, mostly "analogical," way of thinking which characterizes the German language, English gradually became more analytical, which in turn proved to be an excellent medium for science, international communication, and trade.[2]

Thomas Hobbes, one of the original formulators of English philosophical language, noted the connection between the language of Rome and the English language during the age of late medieval nominalism and early capitalism. At that time, human reason increasingly came to be identified with "computation" and "reckoning" and with "addition" and "subtraction."[3] During the Age of Enlightenment, calculative reason became the paradigm for reason in general. In his *Leviathan*, Hobbes states: "The Latins called account of money 'rationes' and accounting 'ratiocinatio' "; and that which we call items in bills or books, they call "nomina," that is, names; and they then seemed to proceed to extend the word "ratio" to the faculty of reckoning in all other things.[4] In contrast to the background of our older humanist and "rhetorical tradition" (as in Vico [1668–1744]), English gradually became the chosen language of the Enlightenment, of modern political democracy, of economic liberalism, and of individual rights. At the same time, it became the most appropriate language for the development of British empiricism and the analytical philosophical tradition,[5] and the most adequate instrument for international discourse in the natural sciences.[6]

The individualism of the Renaissance, of Protestantism, and of Puritanism brought many words expressing Ego and Self to the foreground in both the German and English languages. Descartes's philosophical elaboration of "consciousness" and of the "human subject" encountering a world of "objects" (ZS 142, 283–84), as well as a religious community emphasizing the sinful self, responsibility, and self-discipline (ZS 228), helped to develop words like self-reliance, self-knowledge, self-confidence, self-control, self-respect, self-restraint, self-conceit, self-fulfillment, and so on. Although the English-speaking world held strong ideas about "fair play," "contract," and "society" (in contrast to "community"), the tacit assumptions of the English worldview have stressed individualism ever since the seventeenth century. Part of Heidegger's critical stance toward the English and French languages, influenced by the Latin, may have its roots in this linguistic phenomenon (ZS 156–57, 320), which tended to understand man as a "self-enclosed subject" rather than as an ek-sisting "being-in-the-world" (ZS 339).

Furthermore, the English and German languages differ in their worldviews because of their respective rootedness in, or uprootedness from, their historical word families. German is rooted in its own historical word-family and, until recently, has been subject to very limited foreign influences. As a result, the German language is forced to construct new words from a minimal root system, which often gives new words an archaic sound. In contrast, the English language has a very large vocabulary with words drawn from many different language families. To a great extent, these words have been dissociated from their original, historical language families. English is replete with synonyms, for instance: hearty-cordial, ask-demand, wish-desire, avoid-eschew, foreword-preface, kingly-royal-regal. So many synonyms attest to the versatility of English, which is unconcerned with historical and linguistic roots and pragmatically gathers its words from any linguistic tradition that serves its purpose.

While the German language is more holistic, historically oriented, synoptic, and interconnective, the English language is given to pluralism, favors the concrete, the empirical, the particular, and "the given." It takes a nominalistic approach to reality. The term "reality" is from the Latin *res* (thing). In German, it is *Wirklichkeit*, from *wirken* [to be active or effective]. This term implies action, activity, and an orientation to the future. Yet Heidegger reminds us that even the German *Wirklichkeit*, which is a translation of the Latin a*ctualitas*, is already a distortion of the original Greek word ενεργεια [*energy*, being at work] (ZS 117).

For the German language, the historically rooted meaning of words has remained very important. In order to form new words, the German language, like the Greek, the mother language of Western philosophy (*ZS* 117), is forced to go back to the "origin" (*Ursprung*), to the "ground" (*Grund*), and to the "beginning" (*Anfang*) of words, things, and events. Etymology, which implies a historically founded and oriented ontology and a holistic view of being, is a Germanic passion that Heidegger shared in his "quest for being."

In its thought and speech patterns, German is more contextual than English and more synthetic than analytical. When Wilhelm von Humboldt said that language is not a finished work (*ergon*) but the ongoing activity (*energeia*) of the speaker and the historical speech community, he was stressing the historically rooted nature of the German language. In contrast, a native English speaker is less interested in the history of words or etymology and is much more concerned with the present meaning of words in their ordinary and technical use. German is diachronic; it is concerned with an extended, historical time line, from past to future. English is more synchronic; it focuses on the simultaneity and co-existence of present events (*ZS* 56–61, 73–86). Like the ancient Greek language, German is prone to classify, to categorize, and to generalize. In a kind of "linguistic Platonism," German sometimes comes dangerously close to hypostasizing "words" into thinglike "entities." Adjectives turn easily into nouns. English has no such tendency. It is antisystematic and opposed to excessive, logical categorization. In German understanding, language is primarily "expressive," concerned with the internal unity of meaning, feeling, and contextual reference. Germans believe that creative poets and thinkers are the guardians of language and being (*ZS* 223) and that the whole language community finds its deepest expression in the sayings of its great poets and thinkers. For the English speaker, language is predominantly an instrument based on the conventional, "representative" sign character of the language which is similar to the Latin relationship between *res* and *signum*. It is interesting to note that a similar nominalistic understanding of language underlies much of the philosophy of language in the English-speaking world. German philosophers of language tend to support the "expressive" view of language, unless, like Kant and Husserl, they have drifted closer to the analytical and "calculative" style of English because of their original "analytical" education in mathematics or the natural sciences (e.g., E. Mach, G. Frege, the early L. Wittgenstein; the Vienna Circle: M. Schlick, R. Carnap, H. Reichenbach; see also *ZS* 248–49, 324, 340).

The German language fosters for the most part a synthetic sentence structure, which is "hypotactic," that is, prone to syntactic subordination, organic-integrative, and systematic with logical supraordination and subordination. English prefers an analytic structure. It is more "paratactic," placing words and phrases one after another without subordinating connectives. It has an associative-additive sentence formation. German has a predilection for the generic-collective meaning of words and a tendency to espouse "general" principles and as yet unrealized "possibilities." Heidegger spoke from within his own Germanic context when he described the human being as a "potentiality-for-being" (*Sein-können*, ZS 209) rather than as a "rational animal" (Aristotle), "thinking subject" (Descartes, Hegel), or "producing subject" (Marx: ZS 280, 354). He spoke from his own Germanic background when he described time as ecstatic temporality (ZS 41 ff.) rather than as a sequence of neutral "nows" as in Aristotle, Augustine, Bergson, and Husserl (ZS 43–48). In similar manner, he rejected the metaphysical concept of being as a static presence and permanence but interpreted it as a unique happening and event which grounded the whole history of Western thought [*Ereignis*, disclosive appropriating Event; *Seinsgeschick*, destiny of being] (ZS 242). The same is true for ecstatic "being-in-the-world," "being-with-one-another" (ZS 145) especially in the relationship between mother and child (ZS 208, 261). Heidegger's understanding of "being-in-the-world" as relational is also the basis for his critique of the Freudian models of projection, introjection, and transference between "subjects." The same critique also applies to Norbert Wiener's cybernetic model of human language (ZS 119–20) and to modern brain research (ZS 123).

The English language has an atomistic view of being, which tends to reduce being to discrete entities and objects. This view underlies modern logic, mathematics, and science. Ever since the German logician and mathematician Frege and the English philosopher Russell laid the foundation for "logical atomism" in modern, analytic philosophy, it has been argued that there are three meanings of Being: "the 'is' of existence," "the 'is' of predication," and "the 'is' of identity."[7] This atomistic view is especially contrary to Heidegger's understanding of the unified meaning of being (BT 202; ZS 155). Heidegger argued that this atomistic view reduced the primordial multidimensional meaning of being to these three theoretical categories, in spite of the fact that they are always already based upon an implicit *preunderstanding* of being (ZS 20, 96, 155, 236, 325) by human Da-sein in its contextual, practical being-in-the-world [*Zuhandenheit*, ready-to-hand]. By treating the "is" of existence, which Heidegger called the presence-at-hand of things [*Vorhandenheit*], as a mere propositional function ("there is at least one value of x for which the propositional function is true"), Frege and Russell tried to eliminate the whole "question of being" from philosophy altogether. Via the existential quantifier ($\exists x$) "being" was reduced to the meaning of "a" being, that is, an entity. The "ontological difference" between being and beings (entities) (*ZS* 20–21) was overlooked or forgotten as was the "analogical" character of the concept of being as understood in ancient and medieval ontology (*analogia entis*).[8] Modern science too had come to deal only with "objects" (*ZS* 136–44). Yet being can never be totally made an object of reflection because of Dasein's finitude and being's historical self-concealment (see *BT,* sec. 71–76; *Contributions to Philosophy,* 75–87, 312–54).

Heidegger renewed the whole question of being in *Being and Time* and continued his effort in the Zollikon Seminars. Working with the seminar participants, who had been educated in science and medicine, Heidegger faced great frustration in trying to get the participants to "see" the original, but "covered up," phenomenon of being:

> The last seminar was rather a failure. However, the difficulty lies in the subject matter itself. As Kant says: The point is to catch a glimpse of being. We tried to do this with the example of the table [in the previous seminar of July 6, 1964]. Nevertheless, the difficulty lies in the subject matter, which is *being* itself. For science the domain of objects is already pregiven. Research goes forward in the same direction in which the respective areas have already been talked about prescientifically. . . . However, it is not the same with being. Of course, being is also illuminated in advance, but it is not explicitly noticed or reflected upon. Since being is not the same as beings, *the difference between beings and being* is the most *fundamental and difficult* [problem]. It is all the more difficult if thinking is determined by science, which deals only with beings. The prevailing opinion nowadays is [that it is] as if science alone could provide objective truth. Science *is* the new religion. Compared to it, any attempt to think of being appears arbitrary and "mystical." Being cannot be glimpsed by science. Being demands a unique demonstration, which does not lie in the human being's discretion and which cannot be undertaken by science. As human beings we can only exist on the basis of this difference [between being and beings]. The only thing that helps us catch a glimpse of being is a unique readiness for receiving-perceiving [*Vernehmen: ZS* 3]. To let oneself into this receiving-perceiving is a distinctive act of the human being. It means a transformation of existence. There is no abandonment of science, but on the contrary, it means arriving at a thoughtful, knowing relationship to science and truly thinking through its limitations. [*ZS* 20–21]

The human being's prior temporal understanding of being (*ZS* 44) and its difference from "beings" and the metaphysical concept of "being-ness" [*Sein* as οὐσία, *Seiendheit*] exerts itself repeatedly in the very wording of the propositional function itself: "something that *is* so and so"; *X,* such that *X is* . . ."; "there *is* at least one value of *X.* . . ." The theory of the three meanings of beings (existence, predication, identity) is originally rooted in Da-sein's pretheoretical, temporal understanding of being (*ZS* 207, 230).[9]

In a manner similar to its "atomistic" understanding of being, English also prefers contingent "external relations" between beings (entities), which can be formalized logically (XRY; xRy; see analytic philosophy since Russell). In contrast, the German language has a preference for understanding and expressing "internal relations," that is, the immanent interconnection of things with things and the relations of part to whole or of whole to part. German vocabulary is embedded in historical context, social interrelationship, and interaction, that is, the internal constitutive relationship which constitutes the nature of things, persons, and events (cf. Hegel's dialectic; Marx's relational ontology; Heidegger's "hermeneutical circle" of understanding [*ZS* 46]; cf. also Heidegger's existential relations within Da-sein's ontological "clearing" of being [*Lichtung*; *ZS* 16, 204, 223, 228, 232, 239, 242, 283]. Many German words have the prefix "*Ge-*" [together, "gathered"] indicating a completed action as in *Geschenk* [gift] and *Gestalt* [completed figure] or community and interrelationship, as in *Gemeinschaft* [community], *Gesellschaft* [society], *Gebirge* [mountains: *ZS* 118], *Geschick* [destiny: *ZS* 277], *Gebärde* [to bear, to bring forth: *ZS* 115], *Geschlecht* [gender, sex: *ZS* 212; see Heidegger's interpretation of Trakl's poems], *Geviert* [the fourfold: *ZS* 333]. Heidegger used the old German word *Gestell* [technological enframing; *ZS* 224, 262] to describe the whole "collective," man-and power-centered nature of technology in modern, industrial society (*ZS* 353). In contrast to the "modern, mathematical meaning of [external] relation" (*ZS* 232), Heidegger adopted the relational sense of German words and phrases when he provided the phenomenological description of human Da-sein's ontological relatedness to a meaningful and significant "world" as "being-in-the-world" [*In-der-Welt-Sein*] and as ec-static transcendence toward being (*ZS* 240–42). In his Nietzsche book (I, 226) Heidegger called man's being "outside himself" *eros*. This relatedness is more important and fundamental than both these entities, the human being as "subject" and the world of "objects" which appear in it. The semicircles Heidegger drew on the blackboard at the first seminar symbolize Da-sein's openness to world and being. In his *Hölderlin-Interpretations* and in his reflections on the *Origins of the Work of Art* as an event of truth, the later Heidegger made the "earth" in its primordial relation to the "world," the creative strife between them, a new theme of his relational thinking. Environmentalists have popularized and distorted this idea into an ontic-cosmological concept. H. G. Gadamer points to the earth as an *ontological* dimension: As a counterconcept to "world," "earth was not simply the referential field related solely to human beings. It was a bold stroke to claim that only in the interplay between earth and world, in the shifting relationship between the sheltering, concealing earth and the arising world, could the philosophical concept of 'Da' and truth be gained. This opened a new way of thinking."[10] For Heidegger, the same relational and dynamic character characterizes the phenomena of language in general (*ZS* 232) and of ontological truth as unconcealedness [*Aletheia; BT,* sec. 44). To him, truth is not primarily a logical correspondence of thought to things (Aristotle, Aquinas: *ZS* 130), but rather the original and unique ontological event where being simultaneously discloses [*Aletheia*] and conceals [*Lethe*] itself from the human being (*ZS* 216). Concealment and self-withdrawing of being is the positive "overflow" [*Übermass*], the gift [*Geschenk*] to Da-sein and beings (*Contributions to Philosophy,* p. 176). Heidegger repeatedly uses the term "being-together-ness" [*Zusammengehörigkeit*] or "belongingness" [*Zugehörigkeit, ZS* 223], which is derived from *hören* [to hear, to listen] and *zusammen* [together]. In contrast to logical identity [tautology: *ZS* 30], this ontological togetherness, that is, identity and difference in their temporal-historical "one-folded" belonging, marks being itself in its strifeful "ontological difference" to beings. Heidegger often refers to the famous Heraclitus-Fragment (53): "War is father of all, yet king of all, and it showed some as gods, others as men, made some slaves, others free." The later Heidegger especially stressed interconnection and interrelatedness when he spoke of humans who dwell (sojourn, *Aufenthalt: ZS* 204–5) on earth under the "fourfold" configuration of Earth-Sky-Mortals-Divinities (*ZS* 207, 332–33)[11] and when he spoke of the destiny of being [*Seinsgeschick*] holding sway over human historicity and history (*ZS* 230). Even Heidegger's fundamental word *Da-sein,* which literally means "to be there"—that is, within a worldly environment—describes human existence as "openness" where beings can present themselves for the human Da-sein and the human Da-sein for himself (*ZS* 157). Human Da-sein is a way of existence (ek-sistence) rather than a "thing," "substance," "subject," or "entity" (*ZS* 3, 272). The term Da-sein incorporates interconnection and interrelatedness, as well as the German sense of the dynamic and the historical (*ZS* 145). In sharp contrast to the modern, analytical distinction between the "is" of existence, predication, and identity, Heidegger saw the primordial, temporal, and unified meaning of being in the same experience of the mutually inclusive unity-in-difference within being itself ("ontological difference," later "the disclosive appropriating Event" [*Eräugnis*], "dif-ference" [*Unterschied*], "issue" [*Austrag:* as the resolution of the difference of being and beings] [*ZS* 240–41], and "fissure" [*Zerklüftung*] of being [*Contributions to Philosophy,* 196 f.]).

It is noteworthy that in many respects the German language has its roots in medieval, communitarian feudalism and in late medieval and early modern mysticism as exemplified by Meister Johannes Eckehart (ca. 1260–ca. 1327) and Jakob Böhme (1575–1624). These movements and those of the heretic "Free Spirit" in the later Middle Ages greatly influenced Luther's Reformation, his translation of the Bible, as well as subsequent German philosophy as exemplified by Leibniz, Christian Wolff, Kant, Johann Georg Hamann, Herder,[12] Fichte, Schelling, Hegel, Marx, and the Romantic movement (F. Schleiermacher).[13] It is also significant that historical philology and linguistics became the dominant subject at German universities. Nietzsche became the first philologist-philosopher to espouse this German, historical approach to language. In 1761 the first philological seminar in Göttingen provided the end to the classical era of a-historical, Cartesian linguistics and its concern with "General Grammar." Of course, Heidegger was also critical of the Enlightenment's a-historical view of language and of Romanticism's subjectivist historical view. He considered both to have descended from Greek metaphysics. His view implied a critique of "modernity" (ZS 135 ff.), especially of rationalism and of empiricism, but also of Wilhelm von Humboldt's "expressive" theory of language.

Given this perspective, it is understandable that Heidegger preferred the poetry of the German poet Hölderlin rather than classical German literature. Heidegger maintained that classical German literature had inherited a Latinized metaphysical and "humanistic" interpretation of Greek culture. Although Heidegger often quoted Goethe, he nonetheless believed that Goethe, Schiller, and other classical Germans viewed Greek antiquity through Roman eyes. According to him, it was only Hölderlin who experienced and expressed the original but forgotten legacy of Greece in his lyrics, odes, and hymns. In reopening a nonmetaphysical interpretation of the Greek world, Heidegger believed that Hölderlin's poetry marked a "turning" (*Kehre*) in the destiny of Western man. Having overcome metaphysics, Hölderlin's poetry, and the later Heidegger's thinking as well, announced "another beginning" and a possible new disclosure and advent of being itself (ZS 332–34; see also *Contributions to Philosophy*, 297–98). In a letter on the occasion of Dr. Boss's sixtieth birthday, Heidegger wrote: "Hölderlin's poetry holds a destiny for us. It is waiting for the moment when we mortals will respond to it. The response leads the way toward a coming near the place of the gods, who have fled. That means into the place of the flight, which saves us" (ZS 332). According to Heidegger, Hölderlin's use of the German language is similar to the ancient Greek language because it stands in close proximity to, and affinity with, the primordial yet forgotten experiences of being

(*Basic Writings,* 241 f.). Therefore, Heidegger considered his own thought as lying "between scientific statement and poetic word" (*ZS* 358).[14] Otto Pöggeler has reminded us of the other side of Hölderlin, which Heidegger did not acknowledge: "Heidegger tried to remove Athens from its contiguity with Jerusalem, Carthage and Rome; thus he had to overlook how Hölderlin in the final phase of his creativity relativized the relation of German to Greek and the hope for an immediate return of the divine."[15]

II. Heidegger and Philosophy of Language

Heidegger did not subscribe to the traditional, metaphysical philosophy of language which interpreted language as vocal or written utterance of inner thoughts and ideas in the human mind. (See Heidegger, *"Letter on Humanism"*: *Basic Writings,* p. 221 f., and *Contributions to Philosophy,* 350–54.) Based on the Aristotelian definition of man as *animal rationale,* this traditional view splits language into a bodily, sensible part (sound-word) and a nonbodily, suprasensible part (meaning-idea). The human body and vocal utterance as well are considered corporeal things and, therefore, belong to the realm of sensible, physical, and physiological reality. The mind and its meanings and ideas belong to the realm of suprasensible, spiritual reality. This traditional, metaphysical understanding of language, which appears in two versions, the "representational" view and the "expressive" view, is permeated by a metaphysical dualism between mind and body, between *psyche* and *soma,* and a worldless "subject" (Internalism) and a separate world of "objects" (Externalism). In *Being and Time* Heidegger attempted to show the limitations of this prelinguistic, mentalistic, and visual-eidetic view of reality, which has occurred throughout Western philosophical tradition from Descartes to Husserl. He tried to overcome this dualistic, metaphysical understanding of thought and language (*ZS* 232). He introduced the hermeneutical phenomenology of human Da-sein and being-in-the-world, which also included a new holistic, existential view of language. The insight into the phenomena of receiving-perceiving (*Vernehmen*) and making-present (*Vergegenwärtigung*) undercut the subject-object split (*ZS* 3) and the "representational" and "expressive" view of language (*ZS* 87 ff., 240, 243). The later Heidegger deepened his view by seeing language as the "house of being" and as the "saying" power of poets and thinkers. In the *Zollikon Seminars,* Heidegger provides a synthesis of his earlier and later thought about language.[16]

Some of the unusual difficulties in the translation of the *Zollikon Seminars* can be best understood from the background of these two different traditional views of language, as well as from the background of Heidegger's own thoughts on language and translation in the Zollikon Seminars. The first view of language, usually called the "representational" view, has been the dominant theory of language in the English-speaking world ever since the seventeenth century and the age of Descartes, Hobbes, Locke, and Hume. It also includes Frege's view of "meaning" and "reference," as well as Husserl's view of "signification" and "expression." Here, language is interpreted as a-historical "representation," that is, the naming or designation of ideas, representing, resembling, or mirroring things in the external world. It is concerned with the analysis of the invariant, a-historical structure of language, the formalization of natural languages, and a behavioristic or cognitive model of language. The second view of language, usually called the "expressive" view, originated in German Idealism and Romanticism as exemplified by Hamann, Herder, Goethe, W. von Humboldt, Hegel, and Nietzsche. The "expressive" view considers language to be the historical matrix of a worldview. It is the human subject's self-"expression" from within a holistic, social, cultural, and historical setting (*ZS* 116–18). According to this theory of language, language is understood as historically contextual, relational, and "hermeneutical," that is, as expressing a historical interpretation of a total "worldview." It is these two very different views of language which provide the background for Heidegger's new thinking about language.

Heidegger opposed both the "representational" and the "expressive" view of language because they partially misunderstand the ontological nature of language (*ZS* 19, 183) and because both are rooted in the human "subject" or "mind." According to Heidegger, the autonomous, epistemological, mirrorlike "subject," described by Descartes and other thinkers of the Enlightenment, as well as the culture-bound, acting, and historical "subject," described by German Idealism and Romanticism, are symptoms of an anthropocentric, metaphysical "humanism." As J. C. Edwards notes:

> As is clear from the references in his essays, the later Heidegger is most specifically concerned to oppose the second account, especially as it was developed by Humboldt; but this opposition to language-as-expression is in no way an attempt to rehabilitate language-as-representation. Both accounts are equally bad, he thinks, and for the same reason. . . . Although the representational account of language came to full bloom only with Locke and Descartes, its roots reach at least to Aristotle's *De Interpretatione*.[17]

In the Analytic of Dasein in *Being and Time*, especially in the context of the "hermeneutics of Dasein" (*BT* 37 f., 236; see also *ZS* 46, hermeneutical circle of question and answer; *ZS* 103, 157, 163, 232, 350, 281), Heidegger was concerned with language as existential "discourse" or as original Logos [*Rede*], which, as articulation of intelligibility, is equiprimordial with existential "understanding" [*Verstehen*] and "onto-logical disposition" [*Befindlichkeit*] of Da-sein as praxis-oriented "being-in-the-world." Language [*Sprache*] is subordinate to existential discourse and is its expression. Primordial "understanding" as the prepredicative disclosure of Da-sein and the "thrown projection" (*BT* 183, 185) of its possibilities unfolds temporally into "interpretation" [*Auslegung*], "asser-tion" [*Aussage*], and "communication" [*Mitteilung*]. According to Hei-degger, assertion as "apophantic" (to "show" something as something) and "propositional" Logos, which had been the model for language in general since Aristotle, is a derivative and deficient mode of the original "hermeneutical" Logos of discourse and interpretation (*BT*, sec. 34). Heidegger's early acquaintance with theological hermeneutics as the art of the interpretation of Holy Scripture led him to the philosophical problem of the general relationship between being and language. In 1954 Heidegger remarked in *On the Way to Language:*

> At that time, I was particularly agitated over the question of the relation between the world of Holy Scripture and theological-speculative thinking. This relation, between language and Being, was the same one, if you will, only it was veiled and inaccessible to me, so that through many deviations and false starts I sought in vain for a guiding thread.[18]

In spite of the new "hermeneutical" understanding, *Being and Time* still harbored a hidden metaphysical dualism between prelinguistic "mean-ings" [*Bedeutungen*] and independent "words" [*Worte*] (*BT* 161; *ZS* 19, 126, 248–49). According to Heidegger, the question of "meaning" (*BT* 191) is rooted in Da-sein's existential understanding and interpreta-tion of its being-in-the-world. The relational network of being-in-the-world makes up the "significance" [*Bedeutsamkeit*] by which Da-sein always already understands and interprets its own potentiality-for-being [*Sein-kömen*] in the world. Thus "meanings" are derivative from "significance": "Hence only Dasein can be meaningful or meaningless" (*BT* 193).

As a contrast to a pure scientific, genetic, physiological, and psy-chological explanation of psychosomatic data, Heidegger applied and illustrated his own "hermeneutical phenomenology" with regard to bod-iliness [*Leiblichkeit*] and "bodying-forth" [*Leiben*] (*ZS* 112, 126, 200, 244, 251, 292, 296), with regard to the phenomenon of dreaming (*ZS* 288 f., 308), with regard to the interpretation of the case history of a young schizophrenic (*ZS* 66–70), with regard to a mentally ill person's relation-ship to existential temporality (*ZS* 55), to the phenomenon of hallucination (*ZS* 199), to modern "stress" (*ZS* 149 f.) and the psycho-somatic (*ZS* 100 ff.).

On a later and more originary path of thinking after the 1930s [*Kehre:* turning, reversal], Heidegger deepened his view of language through a renewed meditation on the sayings of the earliest Greek thinkers Anaximander, Parmenides, and Heraclitus. In a different view from *Being and Time,* where language was derivative from existential discourse and an action of man, the later Heidegger saw man as under the address and claim of language. Language is the revealing-concealing advent of Being itself (*Letter on Humanism, Contributions to Philosophy*). By the 1940s Heidegger had become concerned with the sayings of the German poet Hölderlin, and by the 1950s with the poet Stefan George. The later Heidegger made a new experience of language, namely, a patient "listening" and "responding" to language as exemplified by poets and thinkers in their creative, that is, receptive, hours of inspiration. In the original sense of poetic language, language "names" or calls things forth from their encompassing "world," from the "fourfold" regions of the world (Heaven, Earth, Mortals, Divinities) into the nearness of man.[19] More and more Heidegger emphasized the analogy of "hearing" and "listening-in" to language (*ZS* 126) as the site of the historically unfolding and withholding mystery of being. Being became the "disclosive appropriating Event" [*Ereignis: ZS* 223, 241, 291, 351] from which world, earth, gods, and men emerge. The crossing out of being (S̶e̶i̶n̶: *ZS* 240) also indicates the "fourfold" and their gathering in the intersection. In this event [*singulare tantum*] language and man, world and thing, being and beings are "appropriated" to each other [*vereignet*].[20] Language as poetic saying is ultimately rooted in silence, the "soundless voice" of being.[21] It is being's primordial gift to mortal and finite man. Man did not invent language, least of all the language of being. He is rather handed over [*übereignet*] to being and *its* language. He only discovers things and himself in and with language. Heidegger called this new attitude toward language and being "releasement," "letting things be" [*Gelassenheit*]. In contrast to Heidegger's ontological *Gelassenheit,* the Middle High German *sich lazsen* referred, as in Meister Eckhart, to the mystic's self-abandonment of his sinful self and to "taking leave" of his will in obedience to the divine will. The ontological-existential releasement is very difficult for modern man and especially for modern scientists (*ZS* 280–81).

In the *Zollikon Seminars,* Heidegger spoke about the contemporary, one-sided assimilation of natural language to computer language, which deals with language and words as "things" present-at-hand [*vorhanden*] (*ZS* 268). In itself, this may be the sign of the forgetfulness of being and of originary language in our age of technology. He pointed out how "showing" and "saying," seeing and hearing, belong together in all natural languages within man's being-in-the-world (*ZS* 232). This happens prior to any formalization or computerization of language: "To speak means to say, which means to show and to let [something] be seen. It means to communicate and, correspondingly, to listen, to submit oneself to a claim, addressed to oneself, and to comply and respond to it" (*ZS* 269; see also *ZS* 182–83).

In a thought-provoking yet easily misunderstood way, the later Heidegger viewed the speaking human being as under the sway of the historically unfolding "destiny" [*Geschick*] of Being and Language (*ZS* 230). In different "epochs" [gr. *epoche*, restraint, withdrawal], this destiny has simultaneously revealed and concealed itself in the history of Western metaphysics. Heidegger also described language as the ultimate self-revelation and self-concealment of the Logos of being, which must be understood as ontologically prior to all human languages. Man does not speak only on his own, but language speaks through him [*Die Sprache spricht*].[22] Language conceals and reveals man's finitude; so does death. Both death and language are fundamental characteristics of the simultaneous disclosure and concealment of being to mortal man. "Language is identical with the understanding of being, and without this one could not experience death as death, that is, as the uttermost possibility approaching Da-sein" (*ZS* 277; see also *ZS* 230: ontological difference, "Nothing," and death). The poet and the thinker, each in their own way of "distress" [*Not*], keep open Da-sein's finite and death-bound way toward the "holy" (*ZS* 332) and toward "being" (*ZS* 157–59, 332 f.). The poets and thinkers are the hermeneuts, the original interpreters and translators of being. With their words, they make present the "soundless voice" of being.

Guided by a line in Stefan George's poem "The Word"—"Where the word is wanting, no thing may be"—Heidegger glimpsed the original power and gift of language as letting beings come forth in their being (see also *ZS* 280 f., regarding the "letting-be of beings"). Often quoting a passage from Hölderlin, "But what endures, the poets establish," Heidegger pointed out the need for a new experience of language, which in our age of science and technology can be found primarily by listening to the poets. According to Heidegger, such a "listening to the poets" demands a transformation in man's relationship to language and to being. Heidegger talked about a future "turning" (*ZS* 332–34) away from the forgetfulness and abandonment of being and of language, which had taken place during the ages of Western metaphysics and modern science and technology (*ZS* 32–34, 136–44, 224, 262). According to Heidegger, Western "nihilism" (first noticed by Nietzsche), the meaning of which is not yet comprehended, is the consequence of this abandonment by being (see *Contributions to Philosophy*, 80, 96). He called for "another beginning" and for the dawn of a new "destiny" [*Geschick*] of being.[23] "In his later years, Heidegger's thinking revolved almost exclusively around the power of technology and the destruction of language: a third theme was always contained in these: the disintegration of Europe"[24] (*ZS* 133; see also *ZS* 324, 329).

III. Heidegger and Translation

For Heidegger, the word "translation" [*übersetzen*] has two meanings: (1) the ordinary translation or transfer of terms, phrases, and sentences between two languages, and (2) the original translation of one's own language as the unfolding and interpretation of its historical spirit. When the stress is on the suffix *setzen* of the word *übersetzen* (to translate), Heidegger said that reference is made to the ordinary translation of terms, phrases, sentences, and passages between two languages. Here, language is understood as a system of conventional signs, "representations," or "expressions" of ideas in the human mind or, in a more contemporary way, as a system of meanings which can be computerized as in information theory, computer languages, and cybernetics (*ZS* 96, 268). When the stress is on the prefix *über* in *übersetzen*, then translation is the crossing over to "another shore" in one's own mother tongue. This crossing and recrossing is founded in Da-sein's own circular ("hermeneutical") understanding of being and itself. It refers to unfolding, that is, to reappropriating and transmitting the forgotten or covered-up depth of the whole history of one's own, native language [*Überlieferung: ZS* 275].[25] In Heidegger's sense, this "original" translation, which reaches its height in poetic language, is the movement from the untranslatable to the translatable, and conversely, from the unthought to the thought within one's own historical mother tongue. This is what Plato called the "dialogue of the soul with itself." "We [usually] believe that translation is the transfer of a foreign language into another tongue or, conversely, transfer of a mother tongue into another language. However, we fail to see that we constantly translate our own language, the mother tongue, into its own words."[26]

Words are not merely translated grammatically but are transported [*über-setzt*] from one historical and linguistic context to another. This includes the encounter with a strange and unfamiliar world, first and foremost in one's own mother tongue. Thus, all translation is always a dangerous venture toward the limits of human language. Translation reveals and conceals because being shows itself by withdrawing and withholding its own mystery (*ZS* 229). In one of the best-known fragments of Heraclitus, about which Heidegger often commented, we read: Φύσις κρυπτεσθαι φιλει [Being (as *Physis*) likes to conceal itself]. As the concealment and unconcealment of being belong together, so do hearing and speaking, silence and word, in language (*ZS* 19, 126, 232, 268–69). Because of the way being shows itself and how it is experienced in different epochs, translation is ambiguous and open to failure and misunderstanding (*ZS* 129, 153). For example, this happened when Greek words were "translated" into the Roman world. According to Heidegger, this happened "behind the back of the translators," who unknowingly were under the sway of the destiny of being, concealing itself in the course of Western metaphysics. Being, which lets things be present, and ontological truth, as unconcealing and manifesting being, appeared differently in Greece than in Rome, as well as in medieval and modern philosophy (*ZS* 152–55). Thus, translation is unavoidably always an interpretation and reinterpretation of what was said. What is said is already surrounded by the unsaid. Therefore, all translation occurs by retrieving the translatable from the abyss of the untranslatable, first in one's own language, and then in the foreign language.

The usual problems of translation were heightened in the translation of the *Zollikon Seminars*. Since Heidegger was addressing physicians, psychotherapists, and psychoanalysts with little or no philosophical training, he attempted to aid their understanding by using a blend of common, everyday language and a highly technical, philosophical German as grounded in its historical context. In order to teach the seminar participants "to see" and to apprehend phenomena (*ZS* 6 ff., 75 f., 86 ff., 96, 97 f., 105 ff., 111, 132 f., 143 f., 155, etc.), Heidegger sometimes used archaic German words or words from his Swabian dialect, which "showed" the phenomena more powerfully. In spite of Heidegger's intentions, the seminar participants had difficulty stepping out of their scientific paradigm and "seeing" the phenomena anew. Heidegger complained that the "blindness to phenomena not only dominates the sciences, but non-scientific behavior as well" (*ZS* 97).

As the text shows, the dialogue between Heidegger and the seminar participants was very difficult in the beginning of the seminars. In addition, the seminars and conversations were transcribed after the fact from memory or from shorthand notes. As a result, there are numerous gaps, incomplete thoughts, and occasional sentence fragments throughout the text (see the discussion of the term "transcendence," *ZS* 239–42). Nevertheless, these features make the seminars come alive and illustrate Heidegger's superb ability to bring the seminars back on track. As Heidegger stated, he too always remained a learner. Although Heidegger often referred to his early masterpiece *Being and Time* and to many of his other works, he preserved the freshness of his original thinking in the

Zollikon Seminars. His habit of correcting himself, ever searching for better formulation for his insights, was a mark of Heidegger's style of thinking. David Krell offered the following anecdote in his article "Work Sessions with Martin Heidegger": "Occasionally I would bring [Heidegger] a text of his that simply would not reveal its meaning; he would read it over several times, grimace, shake his head slightly and say, 'Das ist aber schlecht!' (That is really bad!). He would reconstruct the German text and say: 'Do it that way.' "[27]

Heidegger's position on the possibilities of translation was somewhat negative. Referring to his "very poor command of English" and to the chances for adequately rendering his new, phenomenological approach into English, he wrote: "Through translation everything gets changed and wearisome" (*ZS* 320). Heidegger's interview with the magazine *Der Spiegel* echoed his pessimistic attitude toward translation: "Thinking can be translated as little as poetry can. At best it can be paraphrased. As soon as a literal translation is attempted, everything is transformed. . . . What a momentous transformation Greek thinking suffered when it was translated into Roman Latin, an event that still bars our way today to sufficient reflection on the fundamental words of Greek thinking."[28] Heidegger suggested: "But every translation is already an interpretation. Every interpretation must first of all have entered into what is said, into the subject matter it expresses. . . . To enter into what is said in the phrase "being-is" remains uncommonly difficult and troublesome for the reason that we are already with-in it."[29]

Notes

1. See the excellent introduction to this linguistic problem in M. Inwood, *A Hegel Dictionary* (Oxford: Blackwell, 1992), pp. 5–18; K.-O. Apel, *Die Idee der Sprache in der Tradition des Humanismus von Dante bis Vico,* Archiv. für Begriffsgeschichte, vol. 8 (Bonn, 1963); W. Luther, *Sprachphilosophie als Grundwissenschaft* (Heidelberg: Quelle and Meyer, 1970), esp. p. 155 ff. (a comparison of English and German); C. J. Berry, *Hume, Hegel and Human Nature* (The Hague: Nijhoff, 1982), p. 72; F. Mayr, "Philosophische Hermeneutik und Deutsche Sprache," *Tijdschrift voor Filosofie* 48 (1986): 237–79, 449–68; J. Macquarrie, "Heidegger's Language and the Problems of Translation," in *Martin Heidegger: Critical Assessments,* ed. C. Macann (London: Routledge, 1992), 3:50–57. See also M. Inwood, *A Heidegger Dictionary* (Oxford: Blackwell, 1999), pp. 1–11, 114–16.

2. M. Shell, *Money, Language, and Thought* (Berkeley and Los Angeles: University of California Press, 1982). See also D. Wood, "Reiterating the Temporal:

Toward a Rethinking of Heidegger on Time," in *Reading Heidegger: Commemorations,* ed. J. Sallis (Bloomington: Indiana University Press, 1993), pp. 136–59, esp. p. 147; K. Held, "Fundamental Moods and Heidegger's Critique of Contemporary Culture," trans. A. J. Steinbock, in *Reading Heidegger,* pp. 287–303. See M. Heidegger, *Contributions to Philosophy (From Enowning),* trans. R. Emad and K. Maly (Bloomington: Indiana University Press, 1999).

3. See T. Hobbes, *On Computation or Logic,* vol. 1 of *De corpore The English Works of Thomas Hobbes of Malmsburg,* ed. Sir William Molesworthy, 11 vols. (London: John Bohm, 1839–45).

4. See Hobbes, Thomas, *Leviathan,* ed. R. Tuck (Cambridge: Cambridge University Press, 1991), p. 39.

5. R. J. Howard, *Three Faces of Hermeneutics* (Berkeley: University of California Press, 1972), p. 86 f.; M. Murray, ed., *Heidegger and Modern Philosophy* (New Haven, Conn.: Yale University Press, 1978); S. Rosen, *The Limits of Analysis* (New York: Basic Books, 1980), pp. 89–148; J. Richardson, *Existential Phenomenology: A Heideggerian Critique of the Cartesian Project* (Oxford: Clarendon Press, 1986); C. Taylor, "Overcoming Epistemology," in *After Philosophy,* ed. K. Baynes, J. Bohman, and T. MacCarthy (Cambridge, Mass.: MIT Press, 1987); F. Olafson, *Heidegger and the Philosophy of Mind* (New Haven, Conn.: Yale University Press, 1987); O. Pöggeler, *Martin Heidegger's Path of Thinking* (Atlantic Highlands, N.J.: Humanities Press, 1987); J. C. Edwards, *The Authority of Language: Heidegger, Wittgenstein, and the Threat of Philosophical Nihilism* (Tampa: University of South Florida Press, 1990); R. Rorty, *Essays on Heidegger and Others* (Cambridge: Cambridge University Press, 1990), pp. 21–22; G. Steiner, *Martin Heidegger* (Chicago: University of Chicago Press, 1991); H. L. Dreyfus, *Being-in-the-World: A Commentary on Heidegger's Being and Time, Division I* (Cambridge, Mass.: MIT Press, 1991); B. Preston, "Heidegger and Artificial Intelligence," *Philosophy and Phenomenological Research* 53, no. 1 (March 1993); Th. Kisiel and J. van Buren, *Reading Heidegger from the Start* (Albany: State University of New York Press, 1994).

6. O. Jespersen, *Growth and Structure of the English Language* (Garden City, N.J.: Doubleday, 1955); M. Pei, *The Story of the English Language* (New York, 1967); W. F. Bolton, *A Living Language: The History and Structure of English* (New York: Random House, 1982); T. McAruther, ed., *The Oxford Companion to the English Language* (Oxford: Oxford University Press, 1992).

7. B. Russell, "The Philosophy of Logical Atomism," in *Logic and Knowledge,* ed. R. C. Marsch (London: George Allen and Unwin), p. 245; G. Frege, *Funktion, Begriff, Bedeutung,* ed. G. Patzig (Göttingen: Vanderhoeck) p. 36 n., 68, 77. See also A. Kenny, *Frege* (New York: Penguin, 1995).

8. Regarding the importance of the Analogy of Being (*analogia entis*) for the early Heidegger, see H.-G. Gadamer, *Heidegger's Ways,* trans. J. W. Stanley (New York: State University of New York Press, 1994), pp. 70, 87, 165, 168, 184. See also M. Heidegger, "The Origin of the Work of Art," in *Basic Writings,* pp. 149–87.

9. J. Watanabe, "Categorial Intuition and the Understanding of Being in Husserl and Heidegger," in *Reading Heidegger,* pp. 109–17; T. Kisiel, "The Language

of the Event: The Event of Language," in *Martin Heidegger: Critical Assessments,* pp. 151–67, esp. p. 160 f.; H.-G. Gadamer, "Heidegger's Later Philosophy," in *Philosophical Hermeneutics,* trans. D. E. Linge (Berkeley: University of California Press, 1977), pp. 213–28.

10. Gadamer, *Heidegger's Ways,* p. 190.

11. M. Heidegger, *Poetry, Language, Thought,* trans. Albert Hofstadter (New York: Harper and Row, 1971), p. 150.

12. I. Berlin, *Vico and Herder: Two Studies in the History of Ideas* (New York: Random House, 1977).

13. Inwood, *A Hegel Dictionary,* pp. 9–12.

14. See M. Heidegger, *Erläuterungen zu Hölderlin's Dichtung* (Frankfurt am Main: Klostermann, 1951); see also M. Heidegger, *Existence and Being,* with an introduction and analysis by W. Brock (Chicago: H. Regnery, 1970).

15. O. Pöggeler, "Does the Saving Power also Grow? Heidegger's Last Paths," in *Martin Heidegger: Critical Assessments,* pp. 407–27, esp. p. 421.

16. F. W. von Hermann, " The 'Flower of the Mouth': Hölderlin's Hint for Heidegger's Thinking of the Essence of Language," in *Martin Heidegger: Critical Assessments,* pp. 277–92; J. Sallis, "Language and Reversal," in *Martin Heidegger: Critical Assessments,* pp. 190–212; H.-G. Gadamer, "Heidegger and the Language of Metaphysics," in *Philosophical Hermeneutics,* pp. 229–40.

17. Edwards, *The Authority of Language,* p. 66; see also M. Heidegger, *On the Way to Language,* trans. P. D. Hertz and J. Stambaugh (New York: Harper and Row, 1966), p. 14.

18. Heidegger, *On the Way to Language,* trans. Peter Hertz (New York: Harper and Row, 1982), pp. 9–10.

19. Heidegger, *Poetry, Language, Thought,* p. 201.

20. W. Richardson, *From Phenomenology to Thought* (The Hague: Martinus Nijhoff, 1967); J. J. Kockelmans, *On the Truth of Being: Reflections on Heidegger's Later Philosophy* (Bloomington: Indiana University Press, 1984), p. 149; J. Derrida, "Heidegger's Ear. Philopolemology," trans. J. P. Leavy, in *Reading Heidegger,* pp. 163–219; R. Polt, *Heidegger. An Introduction* (New York: Cornell University Press, 1999).

21. M. Heidegger, "The End of Philosophy and the Task of Thinking," in *Basic Writings,* pp. 373–92; see also *Being and Time,* p. 206 f.

22. Heidegger, *Poetry, Language, Thought,* p. 198.

23. M. Heidegger, *Contributions to Philosophy,* pp. 5–74.

24. H. Petzet, *Encounters and Dialogues with Martin Heidegger, 1929–1976,* trans. P. Emad and K. Maly (Chicago: University of Chicago Press, 1993), p. 222. See also *ZS.*

25. P. Emad, "Thinking More Deeply into the Question of Translation: Essential Translation and the Unfolding of Language," in *Reading Heidegger,* pp. 323–40.

26. M. Heidegger, *Parmenides,* trans. A. Schuwer and R. Rojcewicz (Bloomington: Indiana University Press, 1992), p. 12.

27. D. Krell, "Work Sessions with Martin Heidegger," *Philosophy Today* 26 (1982): 138.

28. G. Neske, *Martin Heidegger and National Socialism: Questions and Answers* (New York: Paragon, 1990), p. 63.

29. M. Heidegger, *What Is Called Thinking?* trans. F. D. Wieck and J. G. Gray (New York: Harper and Row, 1968), p. 174.

Notes

PART I. ZOLLIKON SEMINARS, 1959–1969

September 8, 1959, in the Burghölzli Auditorium of the University of Zurich Psychiatric Clinic

1. A verbatim protocol of the entire seminar does not exist. The only record was the unique, graphic illustration of Da-sein, which Heidegger drew on the auditorium blackboard in chalk in his own hand as depicted. Heidegger's written note follows immediately after the illustration.

January 24 and 28, 1964, at Boss's Home

1. I. Kant, *Kritik der reinen Vernunft,* Philosophische Bibliothek Felix Meiner (Hamburg: H. R. Schmidt, 1956), A.598, B.626; [Kant, *Critique of Pure Reason,* trans. N. Smith (New York: St. Martin's Press, 1963), p. 504].
2. Aristotle, *Metaphysics* IV.4.1006a6 f.

November 2 and 5, 1964, at Boss's Home

1. I. Kant, *Prolegomena zu einer jeden künftigen Metaphysik, die als Wissenschaft wird auftreten können* (Hamburg: Felix Meiner, 1969), par. 14 [*Prolegomena to Any Future Metaphysics,* trans. Lewis White Beck, Library of Liberal Arts, vol. 27 (Indianapolis: Bobbs-Merrill, 1950), p. 42].
2. F. Nietzsche, *Nachgelassene Werke* (Unveroffentlichtes aus der Umwertungszeit), vol. 13 of *Nietzsches Werke* (Leipzig: C. G. Naumann, 1900–10), 2.S.79.

January 18 and 21, 1965, at Boss's Home

1. Compare Simplicius, *In Aristotelis Physicorum Libros Quattuor Priores Commentaria.* (Berlin: Hg. H. Diels, 1882), p. 695.
2. Saint Augustine, *Confessiones (Bekenntnisse),* trans. J. Bernhart (Munich: Kösel, 1960), p. 629, and *The Confessions of St. Augustine,* trans. R. Warner, with an introduction by V. J. Bourke (New York: New American Library, 1963), pp. 267, 274, 281.

3. Aristotle, *Physics* IV.14.223a16 f.

4. Compare ibid., IV.14.223.a21 ff.

May 11 and 14, 1965, at Boss's Home

1. R. Hegglin, "Was erwartet der Internist von der Psychosomatik?" [What does the Internist expect from psychosomatics?] *Praxis*, no. 30 (1964): 1017–20.

2. I. Kant, *Anthropologie in pragmatischer Hinsicht*, vol. 8, no. 1 of *Gesamte Schriften*, hrsg. von der Berliner Akademie der Wissenschaften (Berlin, 1900), p. 127.

3. N. Wiener, *Mensch und Menschmaschine. Kybernetik und Gesellschaft* (Frankfurt am Main, 1964), p. 94 [*The Human Use of Human Beings: Cybernetics and Society* (Boston: Houghton Mifflin, 1950)].

July 6 and 8, at Boss's Home

1. R. Descartes, *Regulae ad Directionem Ingenii*, ed. H. Springmeyer, L. Gäbe, and H. G. Zekl (Hamburg: F. Meiner, 1973), p. 22 [*The Philosophical Writings of Descartes*, trans. Elizabeth Haldane and G. R. T. Ross (Cambridge: Cambridge University Press, 1968), 1:9].

2. T. von Uexküll, *Grundfragen der psychosomatischen Medizin* [*Fundamental questions of psychosomatic medicine*] (Hamburg: Rowohlt, 1961).

3. R. Descartes, *Discours de la méthode*, trans. and ed. L. Gäbe (Hamburg: F. Meiner, 1960), p. 101 [*Philosophical Writings*, 1:119].

4. R. Descartes, *Meditationes de Prima Philosophia*, ed. E. C. Schröder (Hamburg: F. Meiner, 1956) [*Philosophical Writings*, 1:149].

5. I. Kant, *Kritik der reinen Vernunft*, A.158, B.197 [*Critique of Pure Reason*, p. 194].

November 23 and 26, at Boss's Home

1. F. Nietzsche, *Also sprach Zarathustra*, vol. 6 of *Nietzsche Werke* (Leipzig: C. G. Naumann, 1923), no. 2, p. 217 [*Complete Works: The First Complete and Authorized Translation*, ed. O. Levy (New York: Russell and Russell, 1964)].

2. E. Husserl, *Critique of Pure Logic*, vol. 1 of *Logical Investigations*, 3d ed. (Halle: M. Niemeyer, 1922), sec. 6.

3. J. W. von Goethe, *Maxims and Reflections*, trans. E. Stopp (London: Penguin, 1999).

4. Ibid. All references are according to the enumeration used in the edition of Günther Müller. No. 1236 is the standard enumeration.

March 1 and 3, 1966, at Boss's Home

1. W. Heisenberg, *Über den anschaulichen Inhalt der quantentheoretischen Kinematik und Mechanik* (1927). Reprinted in W. Heisenberg and N. Bohr, *Die Kopenhagener Deutung der Quantentheorie, Dokumente der Naturwissenschaft Abteilung Physik*, ed. A. Herann (Stuttgart, 1963), 4:34.

PART II. CONVERSATIONS WITH MEDARD BOSS, 1961–1972

April 24–May 4, 1963, during Their Vacation Together in Taormina, Sicily

1. M. Boss, *Grundriss der Medizin und der Psychologie* [*Existential Foundations*, pp. 3–17].

2. Fritz-Niggli, "Vom Gedächtnis" ["On Memory"]. First appeared in *Neue Zürcher Zeitung* 29, no. 1157 (1963): 5.

3. F. Nietzsche, *Morgenröte*, vol. 4 of *Nietzsche Werke* (Leipzig: C. G. Naumann, 1923), p. 126 [*Daybreak*, trans. R. J. Hollingdale (Cambridge: Cambridge University Press, 1982).

September 7, 1963, Zollikon

1. This refers to the passage in Freud's writings where he expresses the opinion that the word or language belong to consciousness. Yet at the same time he admits that it must not be said that little children, who cannot yet speak but nevertheless are able to play with toys, would still be without consciousness. Freud concludes the presentation of this matter with words of resignation—that everything is still in the dark here.

March 8, 1965, Zollikon

1. Heidegger's handwritten text.

2. Heidegger jotted down on little scraps of paper—for the most part in catchwords—the following critique of Binswanger's interpretation of *being-in-the-world* and *transcendence*.

November 29, 1965, Zollikon

1. Refers to W. Blankenburg's article, "Psychologie und Wesenserkenntnis. Zur daseinsanalytischen Kritik der Schule von Boss" [Psychology and essential knowledge. Regarding the daseinanalytic critique of the school of Boss], *Jahrbuch für Psychologie, Psychotherapie und medizinische Anthropologie* 12, no. 4 (19??): 300.

2. L. Binswanger, "Über die daseinsanalytische Forschungsrichtung in der Psychiatrie" [Regarding the daseinanalytic direction of research in psychiatry], *Schweizer Archiv für Neurologie und Psychiatrie* 57 (1946): 209–39. Reprinted in *Vorträge und Aufsätze*, pt. 1, pp. 190–217. Also see L. Binswanger, "The Existential Analysis School of Thought," in *Existence*, ed. R. May, E. Angel, and H. F. Ellenberger (New York, 1958), p. 203.

November 13, 1966, Zollikon

1. Heidegger's handwritten text.

March 8–16, 1968, Lenzerheide

1. M. Boss, *Grundriss der Medizin und der Psychologie* [*Foundations of Medicine and Psychology*]. The following titles refer to the manuscript of this book, which was being written then. See Boss, *Existential Foundations*, p. 85 ff.

2. Refers to symptoms of a patient mentioned in the book *Grundriss der Medizin und der Psychologie* [*Existential Foundations*, pp. 3–17]. See *ZS* 199.

September 27, 1968, Lenzerheide

1. Heidegger's handwritten text.

2. The headings and page numbers refer to Medard Boss's *Foundation* book, which was just in the process of being written (see n. 1, *ZS* 273).

March 2, 1972, Freiburg-Zähringen

1. The basis of the conversation is the preparation of the second dream book by the editor Medard Boss, *"Es träumte mir vergangene Nacht, . . ."*: *Sehübungen im Bereiche des Träumens und Beispiele für die praktische Anwendung eines neuen Traumverständnisses* (Bern: H. Huber, 1975).

PART III. FROM THE LETTERS TO MEDARD BOSS, 1947–1971

1. Following Heidegger's participation in a psychotherapeutic congress in which Boss discussed a castration [complex] therapy in a patient with a deep-seated fetish complex.

2. As Heidegger expressed it himself, it refers to the one dream, which he remembers and which has recurred continuously since his youth, although at increasingly greater intervals. In these dream states, he finds himself again and again in similar ways in high school [*Gymnasium*] and is examined by the same teachers who once gave him the final exam [*Abitur*] in his waking life. This stereotypical dream finally vanished when, in his waking life, he was able to perceive *being* in view of the *appropriating Event* [*Ereignis*], thus obtaining the "maturity" of his thought. See M. Heidegger, *The Question concerning Technology and Other Essays*, trans. and with an introduction by Q. W. Lovitt (New York: Harper and Row, 1977), pp. 36–49.

3. The standard enumeration is no. 575. See *ZS* 168. Heidegger's emphasis is in italics.

4. Refers to the introduction of the book by M. Boss, *Einführung in die psychosomatische Medizin* (Bern: H. Huber, 1954).

5. Refers to Boss, *Einführung in die psychosomatische Medizin*.

6. Refers to summer semester 1963, which the editor spent as a visiting faculty member at Harvard University.

7. Goethe, *Maximen und Reflexionen* [*Maxims and Reflections*]; no. 993 according to the enumeration of Günther Müller's edition and no. 575 according to the standard enumeration. See *ZS* 168.

8. Ibid., no. 1025 according to the enumeration of Günther Müller's edition and no. 1147 according to the standard enumeration.

9. Refers to the completion of the book by Boss, *Grundriss der Medizin und der Psychologie* [*Existential Foundations for Medicine and Psychology*]. See *ZS* 199.

10. Boss, *Grundriss der Medizin und der Psychologie.*

11. Refers to the newly founded Swiss Association for Daseinsanalyse and to the new training institute, the Dasein-analytic Institute for Psychotherapy— Medard Boss Foundation, in Zurich.

Index of German Terms

Name and Subject Index